The Illustrated History

SUPERHERO COMICS

OF THE GOLDEN AGE

• THE TAYLOR •

HISTORY

NUMBER 4

OF COMICS

The Illustrated History

SUPERHERO COMICS

OF THE GOLDEN AGE

M I K E   B E N T O N

Author of *The Comic Book in America*

TAYLOR PUBLISHING COMPANY
DALLAS, TEXAS

Published by
Taylor Publishing Company
1550 West Mockingbird Lane
Dallas, Texas 75235

Designed by David Timmons

**Library of Congress
Cataloging-in-Publication Data**

Benton, Mike
    Superhero comics of the golden age : the illustrat-
ed history / by Mike Benton.
        p.   cm.
    Includes index.
    ISBN 0-87833-808-X
    1. Comic books, strips, etc. — United States —
History and criticism. I Title.
    PN6725.B384   1992   92-13586
    741.5'0973'09034—dc20   CIP

Printed in the United States of America
10 9 8 7 6 5 4 3 2 1

Interior photography by Austin Prints For Publication
Jeff Rowe, photographer

The author gratefully acknowledges the work of the following comic book historians whose research has helped to create a better picture of the Golden Age of Superhero Comic Books: Tom Andrae, Jerry Bails, Jerry Defuccio, Ron Goulart, Howard Keltner, Lou Mougin, Robin Snyder, Jim Steranko, Roy Thomas, and Mike Tiefenbacher.

CONTENTS

Facing Page: *Atomic Thunderbolt #1* © 1946 Regor Company

The Story

Every civilization and its arts has a period in history of great accomplishments and flourishing activity. From the golden age of Ancient Greece to the golden age of silent movies, there is a time (often enhanced by nostalgia) which is judged to be the best of an era or the seminal period for an art form.

During twentieth-century America, there have been golden ages of radio (1930s), television (1940s–1950s), rock music (1960s), and even pro football (1950s). Comic books, and particularly superhero comic books, also enjoyed a golden age of unparalleled creativity, productivity, and popularity.

THE GOLDEN AGE OF COMIC BOOKS

The modern comic book, born in 1934 from the reprinted pages of Sunday newspaper comics, quickly grew from a newsstand novelty item to a thriving and beloved new entertainment medium.

From 1938 to 1945, the comic book industry went from a few shoestring publishers and printers to becoming the most popular producer of reading material in history for children and young adults.

Much of this growth was fueled by the new comic book heroes and costumed characters like Superman, Batman, Captain Marvel, Captain America, Wonder Woman, and the several hundred other superheroes who appeared in the years between a Great Depression and World War. Like the mythological heroes from the golden age of Greece, the comic book heroes of the early 1940s became part of our culture, our storytelling, our dreams. They soon appeared on the radio, in the movies, on notebook sketches by schoolchildren, and as mascot insignias for World War II bomber pilots.

The superheroes of the 1940s comic books were strikingly different from previous American fictional heroes and folklore characters. Dressed in eye-catching tights and capes, these new heroes possessed superhuman powers far beyond those of Paul Bunyan, Davy Crockett, or Tarzan. In the years before and during World War II, the costumed action characters were the perfect heroes for the vividly colored and highly exaggerated comic book medium.

Although the term "superhero" was used as early as 1917 to describe a public figure of great talents or accomplishments, the early comic book heroes of the 1940s were usually referred to by their creators as "costumed characters" or as "long-

Superman #14 © 1942 DC Comics, Inc.

underwear" or "union-suit heroes." The word "superhero" was generally not used in comic books until after the mid-1940s, and then, only infrequently. The costumed characters of the Golden Age of Comics, however, were indeed super, heroic, and immensely popular.

From the late 1930s to the end of the 1940s, there were over 25,000 comic book stories with hundreds of superheroes. The comic books were turned out quickly, often in assembly-line fashion, by artists and writers who labored in obscurity, yet produced prodigious amounts of entertainment material for millions of monthly readers.

Comic book writers and artists, driven by deadlines and numerous freelance opportunities in the thriving industry, worked frantically to keep their production rate high while learning their craft on the job. The young field attracted young people, many of them barely out of their teens, whose raw enthusiasm and crude energy made up for their inexperience. Boy editors worked with artists and writers in their early twenties to invent stories and heroes for a brand-new medium. There were no rules, save what the young creators made up as they went along.

Jerry Robinson, an artist who began his comic book career in 1939 at the age of seventeen by assisting Bob Kane on Batman, recalled that "every time we'd do something new, an innovation, it was the first, and it was exciting. We didn't have traditions or too many taboos . . . it didn't have any past. We were inventing the

Whiz Comics #112 © 1949 Fawcett Publications, Inc.

to the Golden Age of Comics can only be discerned by detective guesswork, publishing records, and the memories of the creators themselves. As Fawcett Comics writer and editor Rod Reed observed, "We who worked in the vineyards didn't know it was a Golden Age or we'd have made notes."

Still, the evidence of the legacy these men and women have left behind is immense. Without their contributions, there would be no Superman, Batman, Wonder Woman, Captain America, or the dozens of other comic book characters and heroes that have been a part of our culture for most of the twentieth century. Hundreds of millions of readers—more than at anytime in history—enjoyed, read, and were thrilled by heroes who were birthed in the comic books of the 1940s.

With hundreds of superheroes and an uncountable number of artists and writers, the Golden Age of Comics was a wildly rich and innovative time. In attempting any history of this period of the American comic book, the observation of 1940s comic book writer Otto Binder must surely apply:

"To attempt any sweeping, definitive picture is madness. Only in the tiny flashes of light given by individual anecdotes and recollections of those in the field at the time can come any rational picture of what to me is still an incomprehensible rise-and-fall of a great empire—the world of picture-story heroes whose peers will never again be seen."

language of the comics, the look and storytelling techniques, exploring its potential, experimenting and extending its parameters."

The excitement that the young comic book artists and writers felt in working in a new medium was often expressed in the superheroes they created. With dozens of new titles, publishers, and characters, there was unlimited opportunity for creative expression and experimentation. The Golden Age truly was, as comic book writer Otto Binder observed, "those days of yore when comics were in flower."

Although some comics creators of the 1940s signed their work, many either worked anonymously or appeared under house or studio names. Writers rarely received credits, and often the creation of a comic book story or superhero was the result of several people: editors, writers, and artists. As a result, the contributions of individuals

TAKE A MAN AND MAKE HIM SUPER

Two teenage boys, artist and writer, were bent over a kitchen table in a small apartment at the corner of Kimberly Avenue and East 106th Street in Cleveland, Ohio. It was 1931 and they were furiously dreaming about the future.

Superman #1 © 1939 DC Comics, Inc. Joe Shuster.

The writer said: "Two thousand years hence! Fantastic aircraft soar overhead! It is the year 3000 A.D.!"

The artist drew a rocketship, a propless plane, and two rows of towering skyscrapers and then leaned back from his "drawing board"—actually his mother's bread board borrowed from the kitchen.

The writer was just warming up: "With interplanetary travel came a new menace: space pirates! And in their wake—policemen of the skies!"

He paced about excitedly as the artist bent even closer to his paper and drew a space pirate blasting a rocketship with a raygun.

Jerry Siegel, the writer, and Joe Shuster, the artist, had just created their first comic strip: "The Interplanetary Police."

Siegel and Shuster met at Glenville High School in 1931 while working on the student newspaper *The Glenville Torch*. A lifelong friendship was formed when both boys discovered they shared a passionate interest in science fiction.

Siegel devoured the early issues of *Amazing Stories* and *Wonder Stories*, the first science fiction pulp magazines, and read the action-adventure novels of Edgar Rice Burroughs and the fantasy stories of A. Merritt. At the age of fourteen, he

even wrote his own amateur science fiction magazine, *Cosmic Stories*. Typed and duplicated on hectograph gelatin masters and sold by mail, the 1929 magazine (published by Siegel's grandiosely named Fantastic Fiction Publishing Company) was the first science fiction "fanzine."

Like Siegel, Joe Shuster also avidly read Burroughs, H. G. Wells, Jules Verne, and the other science fiction writers of the day. He especially liked the covers of *Amazing Stories* and *Wonder Stories* drawn by premier science fiction artist Frank R. Paul. Paul's illustrations inspired Shuster to draw spaceships, rocketships, and futuristic locomotives. When he was sixteen, Shuster used the back of a calendar as a drawing pad and drew tomorrow's metropolis, with darting space craft and a charging monorail. He titled his work "World in Future—1980" and wrote the date underneath: "May 2, 1931."

Before meeting Shuster, Siegel had attempted to collaborate with another artist by mail on a science fiction comic strip called "The Time Crusaders." Now that he knew a cartoonist twelve blocks from his home, Siegel decided to become a comic strip writer. Shuster would be the artist.

"When Joe and I met," Siegel recalled, "it was like the right chemicals coming together. I

Superman #1 © 1939 DC Comics, Inc. Joe Shuster.

The two sixteen-year-old boys were not giving up. They immediately set to work on a comic strip about a "scientific adventurer extraordinary" called "Steve Walsh." In his underground laboratory, Walsh "has invented along with other scientific miracles, the Pentascope, a machine which can peer through all material substance." With his invention, Walsh can make use of X-ray vision and super-hearing to detect criminal activity. The strip was submitted to several markets and was also rejected.

The two teenagers continued drawing comic strips that no one wanted to publish. Siegel was also collecting a wad of rejection letters from editors who didn't appreciate his early science fiction stories. Frustrated in their attempts to get published, the two boy journalists decided to start their own science fiction magazine by using the high school mimeograph machine.

The October 6, 1932, edition of *The Glenville Torch* announced the arrival of Siegel and Shuster's publication called *Science Fiction: The Advance Guard of Future Civilization*, which featured "action-adventure stories upon this and other worlds." It was one of the first times that the recently coined term "science fiction" appeared in a title of a publication. The newspaper article stated that its editor, J. Siegel, hoped to reach "in the vicinity of five million magazine readers" with ads in "practically every other pulp paper magazine on the newsstands."

The mimeographed magazine was actually mailed to only a few dozen readers of pulp magazines like *Amazing Stories* and *Weird Tales*, who were primarily young science fiction fans themselves. Still, Siegel and Shuster had finally found an audience for the products of their active imaginations. The third issue of *Science Fiction* in January 1933 featured a story called "The Reign of the Superman." Siegel wrote the story under the pen name of Herbert S. Fine and Shuster provided the illustrations.

"As a science fiction fan," Siegel recalled, "I knew of the various themes in the field. The Superman theme has been one of the themes ever since Samson and Hercules; and I just sat down and wrote a story of that type—only in this story the Superman is a villain."

Shuster's illustration for "The Reign of the Superman" showed a bald-headed megalomaniac hell-bent on conquering the universe—an evil

loved his artwork. Although he was only a beginner, I thought he had the flair of a Frank R. Paul, who was one of the best science fiction illustrators in the field."

Siegel submitted their first comic strip, "The Interplanetary Police," to United Feature Syndicate. After waiting "breathlessly" for weeks, they received a reply.

"My heart started pounding," Siegel recalled, "and I opened it. There was a real short letter, and the first line was 'Congratulations!' and I thought, 'Boy, we've made it.' The rest of the letter, however, was something like 'This is an interesting strip, but we can't use it.' Which was quite a letdown."

April	May
New York World's Fair Comics #1: The Sandman	*Detective Comics #27:* Batman

Superman who used his powers to wreak destruction and suffering.

Siegel and Shuster published two more issues of their amateur magazine and then turned their energies back to comic strips. After their science fiction strips failed to generate any excitement, they developed a caveman adventure strip that preceded V.T. Hamlin's *Alley Oop*. Fame and fortune, however, eluded them and they had nearly exhausted the possibilities offered by the newspaper syndicate market.

In 1933, however, Siegel noticed a different kind of magazine on the newsstand—a *comic* magazine. *Detective Dan, Secret Operative 48* featured a thirty-six-page, black-and-white comic strip story about an early Dick Tracy look-alike. At the time, there were no regular newsstand publications devoted to comics. *Detective Dan* was a novelty item from the Humor Publishing Company in Chicago. The only comic-related books were reprints of newspaper strips. *Detective Dan*, however, was an *original* comic publication featuring a *new* character.

Siegel realized that this 1933 magazine—this "comic book"—opened an entirely new market other than that offered by the newspaper syndicates that had rejected their comic strips. He was especially struck by the idea of having an entire publication devoted to a single comic character.

"When I saw *Detective Dan*, it occurred to me," Siegel recalled, "that we could get up an even more interesting comic book character." The rather crudely drawn detective hero by artist Norman Marsh inspired Siegel and Shuster to transform the villainous Superman character from their science fiction magazine into a comic strip hero. Siegel recalled that the decision to create a heroic Superman was also based on commercial considerations: "With the example before us of Tarzan and other action heroes of fiction who were very successful, mainly because people admired them and looked up to them, it seemed the sensible thing to do to make the Superman a hero."

After learning that the publisher of *Detective Dan* was coming to Cleveland on a business trip from Chicago, the two boys worked up a Superman story to show him. The first Superman story, according to Siegel, was "conceived as a comic book to fill up the entire publication."

Shuster drew the story and sketched a cover which showed a strongman character, dressed in a muscle shirt and trousers, holding a crook triumphantly over his head while blithely ignoring a stream of machine gun bullets:

A GENIUS IN INTELLECT—
A HERCULES IN STRENGTH—
A NEMESIS TO WRONG-DOERS—
THE SUPERMAN!

"It wasn't really Superman," Shuster recalled. "That was before he evolved into a costume character. He was more like a man of action. But we called him the Superman. That was

Superman #2 © 1939 DC Comics, Inc. Joe Shuster.

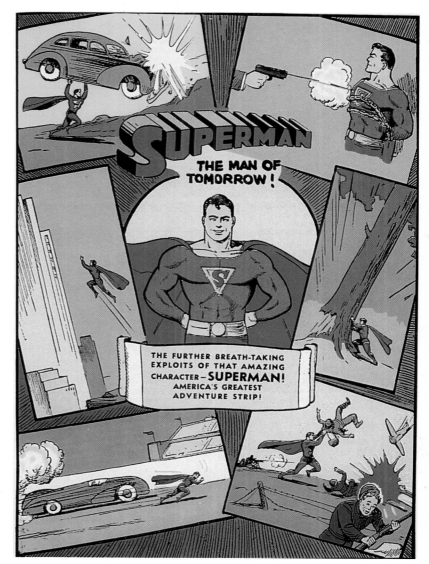

Above: *Superman #2* © 1939 DC Comics, Inc. Joe Shuster.

Right: *Action Comics #7* © 1938 DC Comics, Inc. Joe Shuster.

Joe Shuster

Joe Shuster loved adventure comics, swashbuckling movies, and science fiction. He drew his first comic strip for his school newspaper at Alexander Junior High in Cleveland, Ohio. Shuster's student strip, "Jerry the Journalist," prophetically appeared two years before he met Jerry Siegel, a high school journalist and aspiring science fiction comic strip writer.

Shuster had little formal art training, although he took some courses in illustration and anatomy. "What I considered the best inspiration," Shuster recalled, "was seeing the work of artists like Milton Caniff, Alex Raymond, and well-known science fiction artist Frank R. Paul. When I was very young, my favorite comic strip was "Little Nemo" by Windsor McCay." Shuster admits to being influenced by the *Tarzan* newspaper comics by Hal Foster and Burne Hogarth and also by Roy Crane's *Captain Easy*.

For Shuster, however, it was the movies that were the greatest influence on his artistic imagination—"especially the films of Douglas Fairbanks Senior." Films like Fairbanks's *Mark of Zorro* and *The Black Pirate* helped Shuster to visualize the Superman character: "Fairbanks may have

the second time we used the name, but the first time it was used for a character of goodwill."

The publisher was interested in the Superman story but later changed his mind. Upset, Shuster tore up the comic book except for the cover. "I'm a perfectionist and I think that the fact that the drawings had been turned down made me want to tear them up. I simply destroyed them. It was a very low period for us."

The Depression was in full force, jobs were scarce, and the two boys were graduating from high school. Odd jobs and delivery errands gave them enough postage money to submit their comic strips, but Shuster couldn't even afford drawing paper. "When I had no paper, some-

times I would use brown wrapping paper. I remember I once found several rolls of wallpaper. I was overjoyed. The back was white and I had enough drawing paper to supply me for a long time."

In 1934, Siegel and Shuster decided to use the Superman character again, but this time it would be rewritten and drawn as a newspaper comic strip. Siegel went home and started planning the third incarnation of their hero.

"I was up late one night," Siegel recalled, "and more and more ideas kept coming to me, and I kept writing out several weeks of syndicate scripts for the proposed newspaper strip. When morning came, I had written several weeks of

August

1939   *Mystery Men Comics* #1: The Blue Beetle

been an inspiration to us, even in his attitude. He had a stance which I often used in drawing Superman—his hands on his hips and his feet spread apart, laughing—taking nothing seriously."

For the new comic book medium, Shuster felt that he "was creating a movie and playing all the parts. I would become an actor . . . and director as well. I would follow Jerry's scripts and it seems Jerry was writing a scenario and that I was creating a movie."

For the early comic book work done for Major Malcolm Wheeler-Nicholson's *New Fun*, *More Fun*, and *Detective Comics*, Shuster developed a working style that allowed him to adjust to the demands of turning out complete comic book stories. "I did everything myself. After penciling, I would ink it and do all the lettering, borders, balloons—I just did it instinctively."

To meet deadlines, Shuster sometimes used both hands—one to draw and one to letter. "I draw with my left hand and I remember that when my left hand got tired, I would switch over and letter with my right. I taught myself to letter with both hands, although I could only draw with my left."

Shuster's early work was done in an

unheated apartment to save money. His partner, Jerry Siegel, recalled that "Joe would be working often wearing gloves, and several sweaters, and a jacket or two." On top of that, Shuster had vision problems that weren't corrected by his glasses. "I had to get down to about an inch above the paper in order to see the fine lines," Shuster recalled. As a result, Shuster felt that his close-range drawing became more "meticulous" and detailed.

In addition to "Superman," Shuster drew other 1930s comic features such as "Slam Bradley," "Federal Men," "Dr. Occult," and "Radio Squad" for the company that later became known as DC Comics. When "Superman" was sold as a newspaper strip to the McClure Syndicate in 1939, Shuster realized he had to hire assistants.

"We had to turn the stuff out like a factory," Shuster recalled. "I had to produce a complete page—or two or three—in one day." Shuster oversaw his small art studio in Cleveland and supervised the production of the newspaper strips as well as all the stories for *Action Comics* and *Superman Comics*.

"I was involved with the initial layouts, the penciling, and I did all the faces of Superman, every one of them. There was nobody else that could really catch the spirit—the feeling—of Superman."

material, and I dashed over to Joe's place and showed it to him."

Shuster sensed his sleepless friend's excitement about the new version of Superman and the two boys gathered around the kitchen table.

"That was one important day in our lives," Shuster recalled. "We just sat down, and I worked straight through. I think I had brought in some sandwiches to eat, and we worked all day long. I was caught up in Jerry's enthusiasm, and I started drawing as fast as I could use my pencil."

Siegel leaned over his friend's shoulder and watched him bring the new Superman to life. "When I saw the drawings that were emerging from his pencil, I almost flipped."

"My imagination just picked the concept right up from Jerry," Shuster said.

The concept was simple: An extraordinary hero with a most ordinary secret identity. Besides the all-powerful Superman, another equally important character was created that day: his meek and mild alter ego, reporter Clark Kent.

Like most adolescents, Siegel often daydreamed about being more powerful and more desirable. "As a high school student, I thought that some day I might become a reporter," Siegel recalled, "and I had crushes on several attractive girls who either didn't know I existed or didn't care I existed. . . . Superman could have a dual identity, and in one of his identities he could be

September

November

Amazing Man Comics #5: Amazing Man

Marvel Comics #1: The Human Torch, Sub-Mariner, and The Angel

Superman #4 © 1940 DC Comics, Inc. Joe Shuster.

cent and as a foppish member of British high society. Siegel himself had reviewed the book in the October 20, 1932, issue of his high school paper. *The Mark of Zorro*, one of Siegel and Shuster's favorite Saturday matinee movies, featured Douglas Fairbanks, Sr. as the son of a nineteenth-century aristocrat who masqueraded as an avenging swordsman against evil. Siegel himself exhibited his own fascination with alter egos and secret identities by writing his early pulp fiction efforts under pen names like Hugh Langley and Bernard J. Kenton.

Although super strongmen have been heroes since antiquity, Siegel and Shuster were directly influenced by three twentieth-century fictional characters in their creation of Superman. Philip Wylie's 1930 novel *Gladiator* featured a superhuman hero called Hugo Danner who could leap forty feet in the air, lift automobiles, and deflect bullets off his invulnerable skin. Siegel reviewed the book favorably in his mimeographed magazine *Science Fiction*.

Another favorite of both Siegel and Shuster was Edgar Rice Burroughs's jungle strongman, Tarzan of the Apes. Shuster collected and studied the *Tarzan* newspaper comic strips by Hal Foster. Siegel considered the ape-man to be "the greatest action hero of the time." He even created his own version of Tarzan in a parody he wrote for the May 7, 1931, issue of his high school paper. In a story called "Goober The Mighty," Siegel introduced his jungle hero (referred to as "Goober, Son of the Lion"), who swaggered around and made statements like: "By Jove, one year from now I'll be the strongest man on Earth!"

The third strongman who influenced Siegel and Shuster's Superman was an animated cartoon character—Popeye the Sailor. "We liked Popeye," Siegel recalled, "especially the animated cartoons which had a strong influence on me in writing—and Joe, too—because the super-strength and action in the animated cartoons were absolutely sensational. I thought: this is really great, but it's done strictly as comedy. What if it featured a straight adventure character? You could end up with a very dynamic adventure strip."

Besides a secret identity and super-strength, the third element which made the Superman character so memorable was his costume. Shuster recalled that he was inspired by the "costume pictures that Fairbanks did (*Mark of Zorro, Robin*

meek and mild, as I was, and wear glasses the way I do."

Shuster also shared his friend's wish-fulfillment fantasy of somehow being more powerful, stronger, and desirable. "I was mild-mannered, wore glasses, was very shy with women. I tried to build up my body. I was so skinny. I went in for weight-lifting. I used to get all the body-building magazines from the second-hand stores and read them."

The dual-identity hero was certainly not born with Superman. Baroness Orczy's novel *Child of the Revolution* featured the Scarlet Pimpernel, an adventurer of the French Revolution who led a double life as a costumed protector of the inno-

December	Winter
Feature Comics #27: Doll Man	*Blue Beetle #1*

1939

Hood, and *The Black Pirate*). Fairbanks would swing on ropes very much like Superman flying—or like Tarzan on a vine." Shuster designed the character with "a flowing cape" in order to give the static comic pictures a sense of "movement . . . the feeling of action as he was flying or jumping or leaping."

The costume also evolved out of the dress of classical heroes and strongmen. Shuster originally drew Superman with sandals laced halfway up the calf, and they were later covered over in red to look like boots when the comic was printed.

The final touch, the "S" insignia on Superman's chest, was added to make the costume uniquely distinctive. Shuster recalled that they wanted to put something on front of Superman as a trademark—like the first letter of the character's name. "We thought 'S' was perfect," Shuster recalled. "After we came up with it, we kiddingly said, 'Well, it is the first letter of Siegel and Shuster.'"

Superman, however, was more than a costumed strongman with a secret identity. He was also an alien from another planet—a science fiction character. Siegel acknowledged the influence of the Edgar Rice Burroughs *John Carter of Mars* series on Superman. "The John Carter stories did influence me. Carter was able to leap great distances because the planet Mars was smaller than the planet Earth, and he had great strength. I visualized Krypton as a huge planet, much larger than Earth; so whoever came to Earth from that planet would be able to leap great distances and lift great weights."

Although there were other comic strips with science fiction elements, notably "Buck Rogers" and the recently premiered "Flash Gordon," their heroes were ordinary people in either an extraordinary time (the twenty-fifth century) or an extraordinary place (Planet Mongo). Superman, on the other hand, was an extraordinary person in the most ordinary time and place: present-day America. The contrast was powerfully unsettling.

As Shuster pointed out, Siegel had "reversed the usual formula of the superhero who goes to another planet. He put the superhero in ordinary, familiar surroundings, instead of the other way around, as was done in most science fiction." Ironically, Siegel's innovation made the strip so unusual it would have a difficult time finding an open-minded editor or publisher.

Superman #1 © 1939 DC Comics, Inc. Joe Shuster. Lois Lane meets Superman.

After writing and drawing about two weeks' worth of the Superman comic strip, they again made the rounds of the newspaper syndicates. Siegel submitted Superman to United Feature Syndicate, which distributed the adventures of *Tarzan*, the most popular comic strip strongman. They rejected the boys' efforts as "a rather immature piece of work." Esquire Features returned the strip, labelling it too "crude and hurried." Bell Syndicate told Siegel and Shuster that it wanted only strips with "the most extraordinary appeal, and we do not feel Superman gets into that category."

Although Superman was meeting with no success, a minor bright spot occurred when Siegel and Shuster actually sold some comic strips to the *Cleveland Shopping News* for a 1934 Christmas tabloid giveaway produced for Taylor's department stores. One of these strips was a futuristic feature called "The Battle in the Stratosphere."

Seeing their work printed in color for the first time gave the boys an idea. Why not publish their own comic strips as a newspaper tabloid? There was already a precedent. *Comic Cuts*, a weekly twenty-four-page color comic strip tabloid which cost five cents, had appeared earlier

	January	February
1940	*Flash Comics* #1: The Flash and Hawkman *Pep Comics* #1: The Shield	*More Fun Comics* #52: The Spectre *Whiz Comics* #2: Captain Marvel and Spy Smasher

Superman #2 © 1939 DC Comics, Inc. Joe Shuster.

on the newsstands in the summer of 1934. Siegel and Shuster had even sent some of their strips to the publication, but without success. Now the time seemed right, as Siegel said, for a "nationally distributed monthly comics tabloid to get the country's mind off breadlines and overseas dictators."

They assembled a collection of twenty-five comic strip features, including efforts like "Goober The Mighty" (an adaptation of Siegel's high school Tarzan parody), "Bruce Verne, G-Man of the Future," and "Snoopy and Smiley" (a Laurel and Hardy–inspired strip), and put them together in a comic tabloid package they called *Popular Comics*. The boys convinced the *Cleveland Shopping News*, their first publisher, to print *Popular Comics*. A contract was signed in 1935, photostats were made of the artwork for printing, and it appeared that Siegel and Shuster were at last on their way. They began work on the second issue.

The publisher, however, backed out at the last minute. *Popular Comics* was canceled before the first issue was ever printed. "It was a low blow," Siegel recalled. "Things seemed awful blue

and depressing. The only thing that kept Joe and me from going bonkers was the delicious odor of corned beef wafting seductively from out of Solomon's Delicatessen on Cleveland's East 105th Street. Unfortunately, Joe and I could only inhale the mouth-watering fragrance. We were too broke to buy even one sandwich to wolf down between us."

Fortunately, help was on the way. The cavalry was coming—or at least a former officer in the U.S. Army cavalry. Major Malcolm Wheeler-Nicholson, an adventure pulp writer and would-be publishing mogul, set into motion a series of events in early 1935 that would change the lives of Siegel and Shuster forever.

The major had noted with interest the arrival of a new type of publication on the Manhattan newsstands in May 1934. *Famous Funnies*, a full-color, sixty-four-page comic magazine which sold for a dime, reprinted Sunday newspaper strips like "Mutt and Jeff," "Joe Palooka," and "Tailspin Tommy." Wheeler-Nicholson was struck by the fact that people would pay money to read comics which had already appeared in the newspapers. Surely, they would even be more eager to buy *new* comics, something that would give them *new* fun.

The major quickly assembled his meager resources, promised some cartoonists he would pay them $5 a page for their work, and then launched a comic magazine called *New Fun* (February 1935). The early comic, tabloid-size magazine featured both humor and adventure strips—all original material.

When *New Fun* first appeared on the Cleveland newsstands, Siegel and Shuster saw another opportunity to get their work published. Shuster recalled that "we submitted two strips to Major Wheeler-Nicholson, 'Henri Duval' and 'Dr. Occult.' One was done on brown paper, and one was on the back of wallpaper. When it was sold, they told us to redraw it and we went out and bought good paper."

The two strips appeared in the October 1935 issue of *New Fun*. "Henri Duval" was a costume swashbuckling strip, reflecting the boys' love of the Douglas Fairbanks movies, while "Dr. Occult" was a "ghost detective" along the line of "Jules DeGrandin," a popular occult detective series from the *Weird Tales* pulp magazine. Siegel and Shuster were euphoric. The American comic

March	April
Adventure Comics #48: Hourman	*Detective Comics* #38: Robin

1940

book had arrived on the scene and their prospects for more work looked good. Perhaps, they thought, there was now a market for their "Superman" strip.

"We saw the very early *Famous Funnies*," Siegel recalled, "and I submitted material to them. The rates they offered were extremely low, something like $5 a page. I remember they returned the package unopened, and among the stuff we submitted was 'Superman.'"

The major, however, continued using the comic strips that the two boys from Cleveland sent him. Their third feature, an action-packed strip called "Federal Men" starring G-Man Steve Carson, made its debut in the second issue of the major's second comic book, *New Comics* (January 1936)

Interestingly, the editorial in the first issue of *New Comics* promised readers that they would see "comic characters of every hue, knights and Vikings of ancient days, adventuring heroes, detectives, aviator daredevils of today and hero supermen of days to come!"

Siegel and Shuster's Superman, however, was still not among the "hero supermen of days to come" hinted at in the comic book. Reportedly, the major and his small staff got a big laugh out of the "Superman" strip when Siegel and Shuster dutifully submitted it for his consideration. The character was too outlandish—ridiculous looking. "Superman" was wrapped up and shipped back to Cleveland.

By early 1936, however, there were other comic books besides *Famous Funnies* and the major's comics. Appearing in February 1936, *Popular Comics* reprinted Sunday strips like "Dick Tracy," "Little Orphan Annie," and "Terry and the Pirates." The comic was put together by Max Gaines for Dell Publishing. Gaines, who had been instrumental in getting *Famous Funnies* developed and published, hired Sheldon Mayer, a teenage cartoonist, to help him put the new comic book together. No original comic strips appeared in the early issues of *Popular Comics*, but that did not deter Siegel and Shuster from submitting their "Superman" story for consideration. Max Gaines turned the strip down, but neither he nor his teenage editor forgot about it.

In July 1936, a fifty-two-page magazine-size comic book appeared called *Wow Comics* (or more precisely, *Wow What A Magazine!*). Since

the comic featured original material, Siegel submitted "Superman" for their consideration, along with a more conventional adventure story called "Spy." The principal packager of the comic book, nineteen-year-old Will Eisner, returned the features as not being professional enough. ("One of the great editorial judgments of my youth," Eisner wryly recalled fifty years later.)

Meanwhile, back at Major Malcom Wheeler-Nicholson's comic book company, Siegel and Shuster were asked to come up with an adventure strip for the first issue of a new comic book—*Detective Comics* (March 1937). "They wanted an

Superman #4 © 1940 DC Comics, Inc. Joe Shuster.

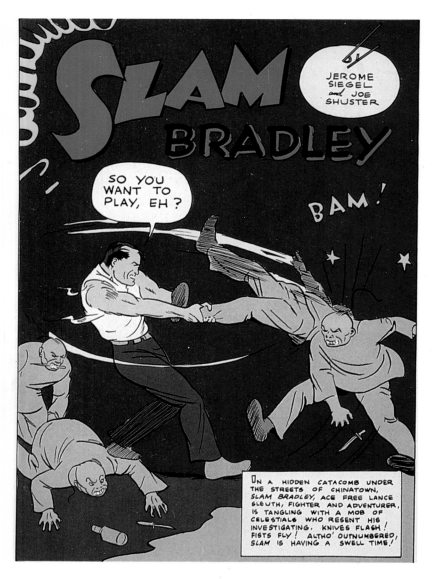

*Detective Comics #1 ©
1937 DC Comics, Inc.
Joe Shuster.*

Oyl, Olive Oyl's brother in the "Popeye" newspaper strip.

Shuster recalled that Slam Bradley was "a very important part of our lives, a very important part of our background." For the first time, the two young men were working on a monthly comic book story of significant length (twelve to thirteen pages). They used the opportunity to learn how to use the comic book medium to create a memorable character and story. "We turned it out with no restrictions, complete freedom to do as we wanted," Shuster remembered. "The only problem was we had a deadline. We had to work very fast."

To save time, Shuster broke away from the early comic book style of having at least eight panels (or pictures) per·page. Toward the end of the first Slam Bradley story, as they rushed to meet the deadline, Shuster dropped to seven, six, five, and finally only four panels per page. The result was a more open, active, and dynamic style of storytelling. Slam Bradley became a reader favorite and the first enduring character created for the comic books.

"Slam Bradley was a dry run for Superman," Siegel once explained. "Superman had already been created, and we didn't want to give away any of the Superman idea; but we just couldn't resist putting into Slam Bradley some of the slam-bang stuff which we knew would be in Superman if and when we got Superman launched."

As Shuster pointed out, Slam "couldn't fly, and he didn't have a costume."

There was another Siegel and Shuster comic book character at the time, however, who was flying about in a costume. Dr. Occult, their ghost detective from *New Fun Comics*, was appearing in the pages of the retitled *More Fun Comics*. Dressed in a red cape and blue trunks and sporting superpowers, Dr. Occult could have been the understudy for Superman. After appearing in costume for four issues of *More Fun* (October 1936 to January 1937), Dr. Occult became a plainclothes ghost detective again. Siegel and Shuster had hoped that this early attempt to sneak in a Superman prototype might open the way for their cherished creation. It did not.

The comic book field, however, was beginning to grow and open up other opportunities. For example, in late 1937, the McClure Syndicate

action strip," Shuster recalled, "and Jerry came up with the idea of a man of action with a sense of humor. The character had a devil-may-care attitude very much like that of Douglas Fairbanks's *Zorro*."

Slam Bradley, an "ace freelance sleuth, fighter, and adventurer," crashed and slugged his way through dens of thieves, kidnappers, and dope smugglers while making with the wisecracks. The strip had the raw energy of the early *Popeye* cartoons which Siegel and Shuster admired. Slam's sidekick, Shorty Morgan (a "would-be scientific detective") bore a likeable resemblance to Castor

June

1940

Blue Bolt #1: Blue Bolt
The Spirit: first appearance of weekly
newspaper section

July

All-American Comics #16: Green Lantern

was exploring the possibility of developing a weekly comic tabloid. They asked Max Gaines, their business partner and premier packager of comic books, for some possible comic features. Gaines and his editor at *Popular Comics,* Sheldon Mayer, recalled the "Superman" strip that Siegel and Shuster had sent them earlier. That December, Gaines wrote Siegel and asked him to submit Superman again for consideration.

The weekly comic tabloid, however, did not materialize, and once again, Superman lay unwanted on Max Gaines's desk. Sheldon Mayer noticed the strip and picked it up for a second look. Besides being Gaines's editor and sometimes unwilling office boy, Mayer was also a cartoonist and his work had appeared in some of the same comics with Siegel and Shuster's other comic strips.

"When the "Superman" strip first came in," Mayer recalled, "I immediately fell in love with it. The thing that fascinated me about Superman, the thing that really sold Superman in the first place, is the alter ego of the hero as contrasted to the crime fighter himself."

Action Comics #1 © 1938 DC Comics, Inc. Joe Shuster.

Mayer pressed Gaines to show "Superman" to Harry Donenfeld, the new owner of Major Wheeler-Nicholson's comic book company. Donenfeld, a pulp magazine publisher and distributor, had assumed control over the major's financially distressed company. Operating now as Detective Comics Inc., Donenfeld retained the services of cartoonists Whitney Ellsworth and Vince Sullivan as editors.

Sullivan's first project was to launch a new magazine called *Action Comics.* He needed something that would grab a kid's attention. Something like "Superman." Sullivan, along with Sheldon Mayer, saw a potential that others had missed in this fantastic character dreamed up by two Cleveland teenagers.

A deal was made. Detective Comics (later to be known more popularly as DC Comics) would buy a thirteen-page *Superman* story from Jerry Siegel and Joe Shuster for ten dollars per page. It would be published in the first issue of *Action Comics* (June 1938). And they wanted it immediately.

"Everything happened very fast," Shuster recalled when they finally heard someone wanted to publish *Superman* after all those years. "They were in a rush to meet the deadline on the first issue. They made the decision to publish it and said to us, 'Just go out and turn out thirteen pages based on your strip.' It was a rush job, and the only solution Jerry and I could come up with was to cut the strips into panels and paste the panels on a sheet the size of a page. If some panels were too long, we would shorten them—cut them off—if they were too short, we would extend them."

The cut-up and repasted Superman story was the lead feature in *Action Comics #1,* which also featured stories about cowboys (Chuck Dawson), magicians (Zatara), and do-gooder adventurers (Pep Morgan, Tex Thomson). The cover, based on a panel in the "Superman" strip, gave publisher Donenfeld some concern.

"He really got worried," Sheldon Mayer recalled. "He felt nobody would believe it; that it was ridiculous—crazy." Donenfeld was, of course, wrong. The kids believed in Superman and they began clamoring for his magazine. Sales of *Action Comics* quickly rose.

Within a year of his first appearance, Su-

Superman #3 © 1940 DC Comics, Inc.

September

October

Silver Streak Comics #6: Daredevil

All-American Comics #19: The Atom

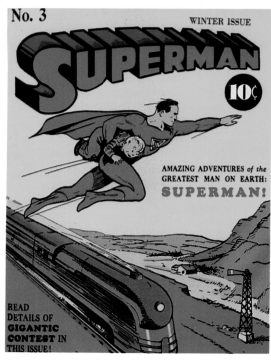

Superman #3 © 1940 DC Comics, Inc. Joe Shuster.

perman received a magazine of his own (Summer 1939). That same year, in what must have been sweet vindication for Siegel and Shuster, "Superman" also began as a newspaper comic strip under a contract with the McClure Syndicate, which had previously rejected the character more than once.

By 1940, there was a *Superman* radio show, and in 1941, a series of *Superman* cartoons by the Fleischer Studio, the producers of *Popeye* and *Betty Boop*. Superman was famous, but Siegel and Shuster were not rich. When they sold the first Superman story in 1938 to Detective Comics Inc. for 130 dollars, they also sold all their rights to the character. The publishers told Siegel and Shuster that this was the "customary" and "businesslike way of doing things." In the comic book industry at the time, the common practice was indeed to buy all rights along with the artwork.

Although they no longer owned Superman, Siegel and Shuster were now getting all the comic book work they could handle, thanks to the character's success. In 1938, they hired additional artists to help with the comic strip.

Siegel and Shuster set up a comic book

studio in a bedroom-size office in Cleveland. Shuster supervised art assistants Paul Cassidy, Leo Novak, and Wayne Boring. Siegel wrote scripts at a desk crammed into the entryway.

Boring recalled that "once some reporters came out to interview Jerry and Joe for the *Saturday Evening Post*. They had photographers and everything. So they were photographing Joe and talking to him and here I was working with my back to them. One of the reporters came over and said, 'Would you please leave because we need the room!'"

For a while Siegel and Shuster's tiny art studio at 10905 Amor Avenue was the only place in the world where stories about superheroes were dreamed, written, and drawn.

But not for long.

Superman #4 © 1940 DC Comics, Inc. Joe Shuster.

Fall

Winter

Human Torch #2: (#1)

All Star Comics #3: Justice Society of America

THE COMING OF THE HEROES

Cleveland may have been the birthplace of Superman, but Manhattan was the home of the comic book.

Wonder Comics #1 © 1939 Fox Features Syndicate. Will Eisner.

By 1936, there were six comic book publishers in the New York City area. Dell Publishing Company (*Popular Comics*, *The Funnies*), David McKay Company (*King Comics*), United Feature Syndicate (*Tip Tip Comics*), and Eastern Color (*Famous Funnies*) were operated by large firms which owned other newsstand publications. Their comic books consisted of reprinted Sunday newspaper comics. The other two companies were run by individual entrepreneurs who published comic books with original material. One was Major Malcolm Wheeler-Nicholson's company (better known later as DC Comics); the other was the Comics Magazine Company, which was started by two disgruntled business partners of the major's, John Mahon and William Cook.

The Comics Magazine Company used some of the major's cartoonists (including Jerry Siegel and Joe Shuster) who had worked on *New Fun* and *More Fun Comics* to produce the first issue of the *Comics Magazine* (May 1936). Mahon and Cook made plans to release three other comic books that year. One would be devoted to detectives (*Detective Picture Stories*), another to cowboys (*Western Picture Stories*), and the third to adventurers (*Funny Picture Stories*). All they needed was the artwork and stories.

The growing need for original comic book material by publishers like Mahon and Cook was shrewdly noted by Harry "A" Chesler. Chesler, described by one contemporary as the "living version of Daddy Warbucks from *Little Orphan Annie*," wore plaid suits and kept his business receipts inside his derby. He adopted "A" as his middle name because he felt it gave him an added air of distinction (It "didn't stand for *Anything*," as he was fond of noting).

Chesler opened the first comic book studio in the world in 1936 with the idea of putting together comic book stories and cartoon features to sell to publishers. Chesler would furnish them with written and drawn pages ready to print. He ran ads in the *New York Times* for cartoonists and picked from the flood of the often inexperienced and hungry applicants.

Ken Ernst, an eighteen-year-old from Chicago with a mail-order course in cartooning under his belt, was one of the first artists hired by Chesler to supply comic book stories for publishers like the Comics Magazine Company. Fred Guardineer, with a college degree in fine arts, was hired by Chesler in November 1936 for twenty dollars a week. He remembered drawing everything—"Indians, cowboys, gangsters, South Sea adventurers, and monsters from space"—to meet the growing demands of the new comic book industry.

Frank Gruber, one of the most successful detective and western pulp magazine writers of all time, wrote western comic scripts for Chesler at $1.50 per page ("racetrack money" his wife didn't need to know about). Gruber introduced Chesler to an artist he knew from his pulp magazine work, Jack Binder. Binder, who had not even heard of comic books at the time, later became Chesler's shop foreman and art director in 1937.

January-February	March
Captain Marvel Adventures #1	*Captain America Comics* #1: Captain America

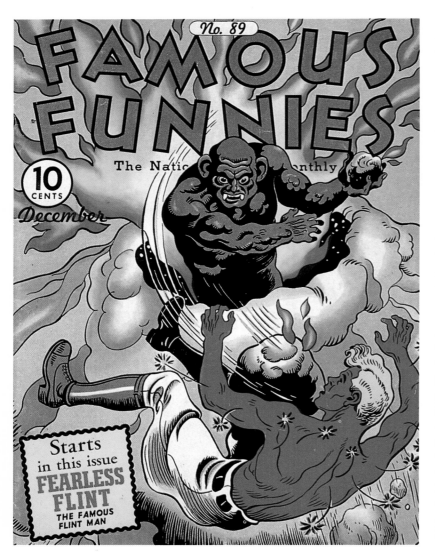

Famous Funnies #89
© *1941 Eastern Color Printing Co. H.G. Peter.*

later become one of the most prolific comic book writers of all time. "The comics bug had already bitten me as early as 1939," Binder recalled. "For one Harry Chesler, I was asked to write some *new* and *original* features—a really great innovation at that time."

Chesler's shop in 1936, when comic books were still novelty items, provided almost the only opportunity for artists and writers to learn about the new comic book medium. For thousands of other aspiring cartoonists in the middle of the Depression, jobs were incredibly scarce.

In 1936, Will Eisner, a soon-to-be high school graduate, wandered the streets of New York City trying to sell his cartoons. "When somebody asks me what got me into comics," Eisner recalled, "I can think of only one word: malnutrition."

Eisner heard about a new comic book called *Wow What A Magazine!* from Bob Kane, a fellow classmate at De Witt Clinton High School. Kane, who competed with Eisner for cartoon spots in their school newspaper, had sold a humorous feature called "Hiram Hick" to *Wow* and he suggested that Eisner show his cartoons to editor S.M. "Jerry" Iger. Iger, who had drawn humorous one-page strips featuring his kid characters Bobbie and PeeWee for *Famous Funnies*, liked Eisner's work and hired him to help put the magazine out. By the third issue of *Wow* (September 1936), Eisner was drawing three stories and the front cover. By the fourth issue, however, *Wow What A Magazine!* was out of business and Eisner and Iger were out of a job.

Eisner freelanced for the Comics Magazine Company and contributed to the first western comic book ever published, *Western Picture Stories* (February 1937), and also drew for *Detective Picture Stories* (March 1937). Meanwhile, Iger was making the rounds of New York City publishers and syndicates, looking for job leads. Neither was getting rich, but Eisner saw an opportunity in their freelance dealings with the early comic book publishers.

"Most of the publishers had no way of knowing whether or not they could even produce this material," Eisner recalled. Original comic book art was still in short supply. "They didn't even understand how to produce it. So there was this marvelous opportunity to take this and deliver an entire package ready for camera so the

As the comic book industry mushroomed during the next three years, the Chesler shop, under Binder's supervision, delivered work to nineteen publishers and provided opportunities for young artists like Jack Cole, Lou Fine, Charles Biro, Mac Raboy, and Paul Gustavson. Joe Kubert, a twelve-year-old who was already on his way to becoming a comic book artist, ran errands for Chesler's West 23rd Street shop. Carl Formes, an ex-opera baritone who left the stage to write comic books, was the resident elder creator at "sixty-something" years. Another comic book writer, Otto Binder (Jack's brother), got his start in the Chesler shop by writing science fiction comics at two dollars per page. Binder would

April	Spring
Adventure Comics #61: Starman Man	*Sub-Mariner* #1

Chesler was running ads, probably in the *New York Times*. I went in, told him I was doing Ripley (*Believe It or Not*) type pages and Hollywood profile stuff. Chesler said, "Let's see four sample fact pages." And I sat home for a week, did four pages, went in—I can remember standing in front of his desk and he looked at the pages and he says, "You got the job. You start Monday." I got so excited my nose started to bleed.
— *Gil Fox, comic book artist and editor*

printer could just run it off."

Following the lead of Harry "A" Chesler, Eisner decided to form his own comic book shop in late 1937 and package comic books for publishers. He asked his former editor, Jerry Iger, to be his partner. "We formed a shop called Eisner and Iger. I put up the money. The entire financing of that came to fifteen dollars, which I advanced, and that's how my name was first." Iger's job was to find publishers who needed original comic book material. Eisner's job was to locate and supervise the artists for the shop.

Eisner recalled that he and Iger eventually employed fifteen artists and writers at their comic book shop at 202 East 42nd Street. Comic book stories were turned out in an assembly-line fashion. "We ran it like a Ford Motor Company. We had to. We were selling pages at five and seven dollars each (with a net profit of $1.50), so we had to get large volume production. We worked buttock-to-buttock and communicated like cell-block inmates."

Some of Eisner's early "inmates" included artists Lou Fine, Alex Blum, Henry Fletcher, Henry Kiefer, Bob Powell, Mort Meskin, Chuck Mazoujian, Chuck Cuidera, Jack Kirby, and Nick Viscardi. Eisner also used Toni Blum, one of the first women to work in the comic book industry, as a staff writer.

Eisner recalled that the artists in his early studio "were there as a kind of stepping place—a first stop to either, hopefully, becoming a syndicated cartoonist for the newspapers, or going on into book illustration. Those who started never dreamed, including myself, that there was a future in that field, and they would grow up with their identity as a comic book artist."

Iger lined up their first job through Editors Press for comic strips which would be syndicated

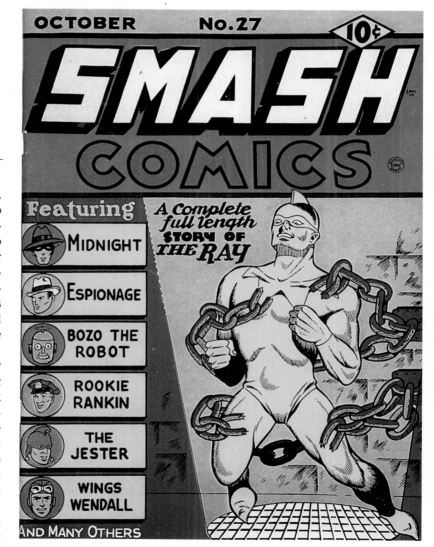

Smash Comics #27 © 1941 Comic Magazines, Inc. Gil Fox.

July

Daredevil #1

August

Police Comics #1: Plastic Man
Military Comics #1: Blackhawk

overseas in a publication called *Wags*. When Iger got Thurman T. Scott, the publisher of Fiction House pulp magazines, interested in publishing comic books, Eisner used the same comic strips and characters they created for *Wags* (including Sheena, Queen of the Jungle) for Scott's first issue of *Jumbo Comics* (September 1938).

The Eisner-Iger studio also supplied the first comic book to another new comic book publisher in 1938. For Monte Bourjally, a former editor of the United Feature Syndicate, they produced *Circus the Comic Riot* (June 1938), which

Blue Beetle #7 © 1941 Fox Features Syndicate

THE BLUE BEETLE strikes again at the underworld rackets!

Eisner remembered as "an ill-fated, classy comic book." In the early days, the studio also turned out syndicated comic strips for small weekly newspapers with a space at the end of the strip for local stores to drop in their ads ("a good idea," Eisner recalled, "but our salesmen were crooks").

The Eisner-Iger studio, along with Harry Chesler's shop, provided a wonderful opportunity for publishers and would-be publishers to enter the growing comic book business. As veteran comic book artist C.C. Beck once explained: "All the publisher had to do was to turn the finished pages of drawings over to his engraver and plate makers and then his printers."

The seemingly easy money to be made in comic books was well understood by Victor Fox. In late 1938, Fox was the accountant at DC Comics when the sales of *Superman* went up, up, and away. He knew about profit margins and printing costs. Almost before anyone else, he saw that *Superman* was on its way to making its publishers a tidy fortune. He wanted to be a comic book publisher. Jerry Iger said he could help.

"I want another Superman," Fox reputedly said. Iger agreed with his new customer and told Eisner. Eisner, following Fox's instructions, came up with a character called Wonder Man for the first issue of *Wonder Comics,* published by the newly formed Fox Features Syndicate. Eisner protested at the time that the hero, who had superpowers and a red costume with a big "W" on his chest, was too similar to Superman. Exactly, replied Iger; that's what Fox was paying for.

As soon as Wonder Man appeared on the newsstands in *Wonder Comics* (May 1939), Victor Fox and Fox Features Syndicate was slapped with a copyright infringement lawsuit by the publishers of *Superman.* Fox dropped Wonder Man after one issue but continued to fight the lawsuit. He also continued publishing *Wonder Comics* and using the services of the Eisner-Iger studio.

Fox was still convinced that costumed super characters like Superman were the wave of the future for comic books. He told Eisner and Iger that he wanted more characters like Superman—well, not exactly like Superman, but whatever the law would allow. Will Eisner got back to work.

For *Wonderworld Comics* #3 (July 1939; formerly *Wonder Comics*), Eisner and artist Lou Fine developed a costumed character called the Flame.

Fall

Green Lantern #1

November

More Fun Comics #73: Green Arrow and Aquaman

1941

For Fox's second comic book title, *Mystery Men Comics* (August 1939), the Eisner-Iger studio came up with two masked crime fighters: the Blue Beetle and the Green Mask.

To avoid another lawsuit, the similarities to Superman were played down. For the first few issues, the Flame had no well-defined super-powers. The Green Mask had neither a secret identity nor special powers, and the Blue Beetle didn't wear a costume in his first appearance.

The new Fox Features heroes had more in common with the Crimson Avenger from *Detective Comics* (October 1938) instead of Superman. The Crimson Avenger, like the Blue Beetle and the Green Mask, was a man of mystery who owed his origins to pulp fiction and radio heroes like the Shadow and the Green Hornet.

At the same time Fox was bringing out his heroes, Superman received his own comic book and was now starring in the monthly *Action Comics* and the quarterly *Superman Comics* (Summer 1939).

The publishers of *Action Comics*, like Fox, had also realized that Superman was worthy of imitation. The month that Fox brought out Wonder Man, *Superman*'s publishers premiered their second costume hero—the Batman—in *Detective Comics* (May 1939). Like Wonder Man, Batman was a calculated attempt to take advantage of the commercial success of Superman.

In late 1938 or early January 1939, as artist Bob Kane recalled, he was having a drink with Vincent Sullivan, the editor of *Action Comics*, and showing him some Flash Gordon drawings he had done. Kane, who had drawn humorous strips like "Peter Pupp" and "Van Bragger" for the Eisner-Iger shop, was now a freelance artist for DC Comics. Sullivan suggested to Kane, who was then drawing "Rusty and His Pals" (a "Terry and the Pirates" type feature) for *Adventure Comics*, that perhaps the artist should concentrate more on adventure strips. After all, Sullivan told him, "There's a character called Superman by Siegel and Shuster, and they are making $800 a week a piece."

Kane, who was making between thirty and fifty dollars a week, was suddenly very interested. "We're looking for another superhero," Sullivan continued. "Do you think you could come up with one?" Kane, noting that it was Friday, replied: "I'll have one for you Monday."

Mystery Men Comics #25
© 1941 Fox Features Syndicate

The twenty-two-year-old artist placed a sheet of tracing paper over his Flash Gordon sketches and tried several costume designs. He gave the character a set of bird wings to leap and soar about like Superman, similar to the Hawkmen characters from Alex Raymond's *Flash Gordon*. Then Kane recalled a sketch by Leonardo da Vinci of a human-powered flying machine. Da Vinci's invention was a glider-sled which was propelled by a man with a large pair of attached bat wings. Kane liked the way the black bat wings looked and he changed his bird-man character to a bat-man.

December

Whiz Comics #25: Captain Marvel, Jr.

Winter

All Star Comics #8: Wonder Woman

Batman #3 © 1940
DC Comics, Inc. Bob
Kane.

Detective Comics #32 © 1939 DC Comics, Inc. Bob Kane.

Detective Comics #27
© 1939 DC Comics, Inc.
Bob Kane.

Bob Kane

Bob Kane wanted to be a cartoonist even before his blackboard caricature of a music teacher landed him in the principal's office. Growing up in the Bronx during the Great Depression, Kane formed a neighborhood gang called the "Zorros," in admiration of Douglas Fairbanks's masked hero in *The Mark of Zorro*. Kane was named by the gang as the "Doodler" because of his chalk graffiti cartoons.

Kane's early favorite comic strips were Floyd Gottfredson's *Mickey Mouse* and Billy De Beck's *Barney Google*. He grew up with animated cartoons, like *Felix the Cat* and *Mickey Mouse,* which he rented for his home projector through the receipts of nickel tickets sold to neighborhood kids. Kane drew cartoons for his school paper and created comic advertisements for store merchants. The "Doodler" had become, in his words, a "neophyte cartoonist from the Bronx."

After a one-year art scholarship program at the Commercial Art Studio in New York City, Kane had to leave to take a job in his uncle's garment factory. He tried to further his career by visiting magazine publishers in Manhattan who bought cartoons. After selling a humorous comic strip to *Wow What A Magazine!* (September 1936) and a mystery comic story to *Detective Picture Stories* (April 1937), Kane quit

Also influenced by the Douglas Fairbanks, Sr., movie *The Mark of Zorro*, Kane hid his character's identity behind a domino mask. Like Fairbanks, Kane envisioned his bat-winged hero to be a daring athletic acrobat, leaping from ledges and swinging on a rope. To contrast with the black wings and mask, Kane dressed his "batman" in a bright red "union suit." Before he presented his new character to Sullivan, the young

artist wanted a second opinion. He called Bill Finger, who was his writer on "Rusty and His Pals," and asked him to take a look at his new hero.

Finger, along with Eisner and Kane, was also a graduate of De Witt Clinton High School. He met Kane at a party and the two continued their friendship with regular bull sessions about comic strips held in a park next to Edgar Allan

Summer	November
Wonder Woman #1	*Captain Marvel, Jr. #1*

1942

his job at the garment factory, determined to become a cartoonist.

In early 1938, Kane worked for the Eisner-Iger Studio and created humorous strips like "Peter Pupp" (*Jumbo Comics*) and the "Sidestreets of New York" (*Circus Comics*). That same year, Kane also began a freelance career with Major Malcolm Wheeler-Nicholson's comic book company (later known as DC Comics) with one-page and fill-in gag cartoons.

For the major, Kane specialized in funny features like "Ginger Snap," and "Jest A Second." In the period of a half year, Kane drew more than two hundred pages of humorous cartoons for the major, all on the promise of payment "next month." The major, who was always one foot beyond the brink of financial ruin, disappeared after the seventh "next month" and Kane lost his money.

After the major's company reorganized under its new and more financially stable owners, Kane returned with his first continuing adventure comic series called "Rusty and His Pals" for *Adventure Comics* (November 1938). Kane's first love was still the gag cartoons, but he realized that adventure strips were now more in demand. He had always admired Alex Raymond's illustrative approach in his work on *Flash Gordon* and *Secret Agent X-9*, and the influence of Milt Caniff on the "Rusty and His Pals" strip was also strikingly obvious.

When Kane sat down to create the Batman in early 1939, he also brought with him one other artistic influence. "I wanted my style a little cartoony—a cross between Dick Tracy and illustration." Kane borrowed elements from Chester Gould's detective strip, including the propensity for bizarre villains and exaggerated anatomy—even down to the same square jaw line shared by Tracy and Batman.

Kane recalled that he "always thought the square jaw connoted strength. Movie heroes like Tom Mix always had virile, strong jaws . . . like it was carved out of stone." Batman, like Dick Tracy, was almost a caricature of the slickly polished hero. "I never wanted to get into full illustration," Kane said regarding his Batman stories. "I wanted to retain the cartoon-comic quality that I admired early in my career."

As Batman grew in popularity, Kane hired assistants to help him on the art. George Roussos drew backgrounds, while Jerry Robinson did the lettering, inking, and some secondary characters. Eventually, Robinson and others would draw complete Batman stories. As Batman appeared in more titles and then in a newspaper comic strip, Kane turned the art over to assistants and "ghost" artists. Still, Kane drew the definitive Batman in 1939 and the early 1940s.

Jack Schiff, who later became the editor of the *Batman* comic books, recalled about Kane that "nobody who drew Batman could capture his inimitable style. He would inject the Batman with that dynamism and spirit that kids liked."

Poe's old cottage. A full-time shoe salesman and would-be pulp magazine writer, Finger began helping Kane more and more with his comic script continuities.

By late 1938, Finger was a part-time shoe salesman and part-time comic book writer. The rest of the time, he read pulp hero magazines like *Doc Savage* and the *Shadow*. At the time Kane called him about his new costumed hero, Finger was helping the artist launch a second adventure strip, "Clip Carson, Soldier of Fortune," for *Action Comics*.

Finger studied Kane's preliminary sketches of the bat-winged man and made suggestions. Replace his mask with a hooded cowl and pointed bat ears and make the eye slits tiny, more mysterious. Color the red suit blue-gray instead to make it more ominous, like a night creature.

December

Captain Marvel Adventures #18: Mary Marvel

Detective Comics #32 © 1939 DC Comics, Inc. Bob Kane.

Give him gauntlets. Change the bulky bat wings into a dramatic scalloped cape.

Kane made the changes and took the Bat-Man character to the offices of Detective Comics. Editor Vince Sullivan thought the new costumed character was great. Associate publisher Jack Leibowitz wasn't so sure. "It looks kind of mysterious and creepy," he said. "Do you think the public will like it?"

Kane recalled that he and Finger knew they had to come up with something different from Superman: "I didn't want a superhero with super-powers." Kane saw Batman as a masked vigi-

lante—not an all-powerful science fiction character. Finger also wanted a human hero who was vulnerable—one who survived and excelled by his own wits, advanced athletic powers, and acute observation.

Finger's script for the first Batman story built upon Kane's idea of a dual-identity hero. He came up with the alter ego of playboy Bruce Wayne (named after a Scottish patriot, Robert Bruce, and a colonial American hero, Mad Anthony Wayne) and created Gotham City and supporting characters like Police Commissioner Gordon. Patterning his writing after *Shadow* detective pulps and Warner Bros. gangster films, Finger wrote hard-hitting scripts that enhanced the mood of Kane's "mysterious and creepy" hero.

Kane and Finger's avenging Batman was in dark contrast to Siegel and Shuster's "gosh-wow" strongman. They had created a different kind of superhero—not an imitation of Superman but an innovation that other comic book artists and writers would follow. Bill Finger quit his job at the shoe store. Bob Kane began looking for assistants to help him produce more Batman stories. Superman was no longer a fluke; Batman proved that costumed characters were the way of the future—at least for Detective Comics (DC Comics).

By the spring of 1939, DC Comics, with Victor Fox nipping at its heels, had a temporary lock on comic book superheroes. Competition, however, would soon come from other publishers who saw opportunities in the developing comic book field.

By early 1938, the Comics Magazine Company had changed hands a couple of times and was now operated by Joseph Hardie as Centaur Publishing. At the time, Centaur was the only publisher besides Detective Comics, Inc. (Major Wheeler-Nicholson's company) to publish all-original comic books. Hardie himself wrote scripts for some stories and also ran a chatty reader column in his comics under the name of "Uncle Joe."

Hardie had plans to expand his lineup of comics beyond *Star Comics, Funny Pages, Funny Picture Stories,* and *Star Ranger Comics.* He hired Lloyd Jacquet to serve as editor for his growing line of all-original comic books. Jacquet, who had helped assemble the first issue of *New Fun Comics* for Major Malcolm Wheeler-Nicholson in

Summer

late 1934, was experienced in packaging new comic book material and knew how to work with freelance artists and writers. From 1938 to 1939, Hardie ("Uncle Joe") and Jacquet would launch more original heroes than any other comic book company.

Jacquet began gathering artists and writers for Centaur's new titles and features. From the Harry "A" Chesler shop, which had supplied comic stories for Centaur, Jacquet got the services of several artists, including Paul Gustavson and Carl Burgos. Bill Everett, an ex-art editor for a radio magazine, also joined Jacquet's group at Centaur.

For the cover of the first issue of Centaur's *Amazing Mystery Funnies* (August 1938), Everett created a costumed science fiction hero along the lines of Flash Gordon and Buck Rogers. Skyrocket Steele (from the Year X) became the star in this early science fiction and adventure anthology title.

The following month, Paul Gustavson drew the adventures of a second Centaur costumed hero called the Arrow for *Funny Pages* (September 1938). Cloaked in a totally concealing red costume, the faceless and nameless archer was a

Amazing Mystery Funnies #15 © 1939 Centaur Publications. Frank Thomas.

Marvel Comics #1 © 1939 Marvel Entertainment Group, Inc. Frank R. Paul.

mysterious vigilante in the tradition of pulp magazine heroes.

By 1939, the success of Superman was an industry fact and Centaur decided to bring out more costumed heroes. For *Amazing Mystery Funnies* (July 1939), Paul Gustavson created another masked man of mystery without an alter ego known only as The Fantom of the Fair. The Fantom was a scientific genius who wore a costume and ostensibly protected the 1939 World's Fair from saboteurs and racketeers from his un-

January

1945

More Fun Comics #101: Superboy

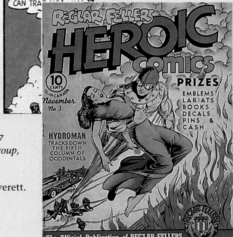

*Above: Marvel Mystery Comics #7
© 1940 Marvel Entertainment Group,
Inc. Bill Everett.
Right: Heroic Comics #3 © 1940
Eastern Color Printing Co. Bill Everett.*

Bill Everett

Bill Everett loved the sea. As a boy, he read about ships and sailing and eagerly followed the progress of Admiral Byrd's overseas expedition to the South Pole. At the age of fifteen, he joined the merchant marines for two years.

The boy also discovered he had an "inborn talent" for drawing. His father, unlike other parents during the uncertain days of the Depression, actually encouraged his son to become a cartoonist—a profession then as suspect as tap dancing or skywriting.

After his stint at sea, Everett pushed through his formal art courses at the Vesper George School of Art from 1934 to 1935. "I was credited with three years of training," Everett recalled, "but I went through those three years in about a year and a half. This was only due to the inborn talent and drive that I had to get somewhere fast."

Everett landed his first job with the Boston *Herald-Traveler* as an advertising artist "at an overwhelming salary of twelve dollars per week. I quit that job when they put me on the night shift, and went to work as a draftsman for civil engineers in Newton, Massachusetts. I got fired because I refused to chauffeur one of the partners,

derground hideout on the fairgrounds.

That same month, Ben Thompson drew the first adventure of the Masked Marvel for Centaur's *Keen Detective Funnies* (July 1939). Like other Centaur heroes, the Masked Marvel operated without benefit of a secret identity or any extraordinary super-powers. Like the Batman (who had made his debut three months earlier), the Masked Marvel was a self-trained sleuth who brought criminals to justice.

By summer 1939, Superman was appearing in two comic books, Wonder Man had come and gone as an obvious imitation, and now Batman was on his way to becoming a popular feature.

Centaur Publishing decided it was time to have a heroic "man" of its own.

Centaur's Amazing Man first appeared in his own comic book in September 1939 (*Amazing-Man Comics*). Created by Bill Everett, in association with Lloyd Jacquet, Amazing Man originally wore a double-breasted business suit instead of a colorful costume. Still, he did possess super-powers which came from his intensive training sessions with Tibetan monks.

Along with Amazing Man, three other superheroes made their debut in the first issue of *Amazing-Man Comics*. The Iron Skull, drawn by Carl Burgos, was an android hero with a nearly

whose rancid cigar smoke made me ill."

After looking, unsuccessfully, for work in Phoenix and Los Angeles, Everett returned to New York City to become an advertising artist for the New York *Herald Tribune*. From there, he got a job as assistant art editor for *Radio News* magazine in Chicago. Everett had a disagreement with his boss ("I was too big for my britches") and was fired again.

Back in New York, he collected unemployment in 1938 until he heard about a publisher who was doing comic books. Although Everett was a longtime fan of Milt Caniff's newspaper comic strips, he had never actually considered comic books. They were still a novelty item at the time, but as the hungry artist noted: "I was interested in *anything* at that point."

Everett's first comic book work appeared in *Amazing Mystery Funnies* (August 1938) from Centaur Publishing. Everett continued drawing science fiction characters and heroes like Skyrocket Steele, Dirk the Demon, and Amazing Man for Centaur's growing line of comic books. In 1939, the young man became the art director of Funnies, Incorporated, a comic book packaging studio begun by his former editor at Centaur, Lloyd Jacquet.

One of Everett's first creations for Funnies, Incorporated, was an expression of his boyhood love affair with the sea—the Sub-Mariner. Everett's aquatic superhero depended upon contact with water for his survival and unusual strength. The Sub-Mariner was partially inspired by the eleventh stanza of Samuel Taylor Coleridge's poem *The Rime of the Ancient Mariner* ("Out of the Sea came he; And he shone bright and on the right") and also from Everett's readings in mythology.

"I read a great deal when I was young," Everett recalled. "I read what was then considered the deeper novels, the high-class literature. I didn't go much for pulp material. I didn't even read the daily comics much. My background as far as education was kind of poor. I dropped out of high school and art school. I had to make up for this in reading. I wanted to be a writer and if I had any idol at all, it would be Jack London. I liked the way he told a story and I figured that rather than be the greatest novelist of all time I would attempt to tell a story in the simplest terms that I could summon."

Comic books provided Everett with his opportunity for simple storytelling. He both wrote and drew the early adventures of the Sub-Mariner, as well as other water-inspired comic book heroes like the Fin and Hydroman. "I think the best way to entertain someone is to put it in a way that he can readily and easily understand," he observed.

As a young talent in a young field, Bill Everett was one of the innovators. "I didn't want to swipe from anybody; it had to come from me. It wasn't the best, but it was all Everett. Storytelling was my strong point."

invulnerable, rock-hard body. Like Amazing Man, he had no distinctive costume. The two other characters, Mighty Man, a twelve-foot giant, and Minimidget, a hand-sized crime-fighter, covered the long and short ends of the superhero spectrum. Following the Centaur tradition, none of the heroes (except for Amazing Man) had a secret identity or alter ego.

During this flurry of creative activity at Centaur Publishing, editor Lloyd Jacquet decided to form his own comic company. Jacquet left Centaur and took some artists with him, including Bill Everett, Carl Burgos, Paul Gustavson, and Ben Thompson, as well as writers Ray Gill and John Compton. Together with John Mahon, a former publisher of the Comics Magazine Company, and Frank Torpey, a business manager and salesman, Jacquet formed Funnies Incorporated, a studio which operated from a two-room office on West 45th Street.

According to Everett, the original idea for Funnies Incorporated was to operate as a comic book publisher. Lack of money, however, forced Jacquet and his partners to become an art packaging studio, instead, for other comic book publishers. By late summer 1939, they were competing with the Chesler and Eisner studios for the four publishers who were regularly buying comic

Marvel Comics #1
© 1939 Marvel
Entertainment Group, Inc.
Paul Gustavson. First
appearance of the Angel
by artist/writer Paul
Gustavson.

book material. Funnies Incorporated needed a fresh client who was new to the comic book field. Frank Torpey, the shop's salesman, found him.

Martin Goodman, a publisher of pulp magazines since 1932, was always looking for the next trend in newsstand buying habits. He was one of the first publishers to cash in on the late 1930s boom in science fiction pulp magazines, launching *Marvel Science Stories* (August 1938). When Torpey spread out copies of *Superman*, *Amazing-Man Comics*, and *Amazing Mystery Funnies* and told Goodman the production price for a comic book page, the shrewd publisher saw possibilities. He ordered a package of stories to be delivered by Funnies Incorporated for a new comic book to be called *Marvel Comics*. He wanted a cast

of new and original heroes. Funnies Incorporated got to work.

Jacquet turned to the three artists who had drawn heroes for Centaur Publishing and asked them to each come up with a new character for *Marvel Comics*. Paul Gustavson, the artist on the Arrow and Fantom of the Fair, created another costumed "mystery man" hero called the Angel. Carl Burgos reused his idea of an android superhero from the Iron Skull and created a flaming artificial man called the Human Torch. Bill Everett (Amazing Man) contributed the Sub-Mariner, an underwater hero who wore only swimming trunks and had small wings on his feet. The three unlikely heroes premiered in the October 1939 issue of *Marvel Comics* (retitled *Marvel Mystery Comics* with the second issue).

Goodman ordered more stories from the Funnies Incorporated shop and made plans in late 1939 to launch his second comic book, *Daring Mystery Comics*. As Funnies Incorporated began to prosper, the shop employed other artists such as Ed Ashe, Sid Greene, George Mandel, Carl Pfeufer, Mike Roy, Harry Sahle, Bob Wood, Bob Davis, Sam Gillman, Irwin Hassen, and Dan Barry. Unlike the Chesler or Eisner-Iger shops, which kept the artists on-site and under a watchful eye, Funnies Incorporated often allowed its artists to work alone or at each other's apartments.

Mickey Spillane, a flamboyant young man, joined Funnies Incorporated as a staff writer before he embarked on his career as a best-selling mystery writer. Artist Dan Barry remembered that Spillane worked at a "smoking" typewriter in a corner of the bare floor office when he wasn't relaxing at a nearby bar on Times Square. "They paid him almost as much money as the artists," Barry recalled. "He wrote everything! He'd sit down and five pages would come out of the typewriter like that, in about an hour, and then he was out the door to go drinking. And womanizing."

The young comic book industry of the late 1930s provided new opportunities for young writers and artists and also for publishers, printers, and distributers. However, only a few people—

Feature Comics #48 © 1941 Comic Magazines, Inc.

Marvel Mystery Comics #19 © 1941 Marvel Entertainment Group, Inc. An early appearance of the Human Torch.

among them Everett M. Arnold, the future publisher of Quality Comics—realized that comic books were more than newsstand novelty items.

Arnold began preparing for his career as a comic book publisher during the 1920s when he sold color printing presses to newspaper syndicates to print their Sunday comics. He later became vice president of Greater Buffalo Press and oversaw the printing of Sunday comic sections for newspapers around the country during the early 1930s. He was known by friends and business associates as "Busy," a nickname he earned in school by his persistent talking.

In 1936, "Busy" Arnold arranged with John Mahon and William Cook to print the comic books for their new Comics Magazine Company. Ironically, the pair's early comic books, *Funny Pages* and *Funny Picture Stories*, were printed by

Smash Comics #26 © 1941 Comic Magazines, Inc. Lou Fine. The Quality Comics line featured several memorable superheroes from the Eisner studio, such as The Ray.

Arnold in Cleveland, Ohio, where other nascent comic book activity was taking place in the apartment of Joe Shuster. As Arnold searched for other customers in the emerging comic book market, he noticed the impressive sales figures of a comic book called *Famous Funnies*. Arnold got "busy" and formed a company (Comic Favorites, Inc.) to publish a comic book called *Feature Funnies* (October 1937).

Like *Famous Funnies*, Arnold's *Feature Funnies* reprinted popular newspaper comic strips. Among its lineup were *Joe Palooka*, *Mickey Finn*, *Dixie Dugan*, and a new strip by Rube Goldberg called *Lala Palooza*. Arnold also featured a smat-tering of original comic stories to fill out his sixty-four-page magazine. He got the new comic book features through William Cook, who put him in touch with freelance artists who had worked for his Comics Magazine Company. For the early issues of *Feature Funnies*, Arnold used such strips as George Brenner's early masked detective "The Clock" and Will Eisner's swashbuckling "Hawks of the Sea."

When Eisner's strip ran out, Arnold negoti-ated with the newly formed Eisner-Iger Studio for a new comic feature called "Espionage, Starring Black X" for *Feature Funnies* (October 1938). Black X, an American secret agent who affected a monocle, also appeared courtesy of the Eisner-Iger Studio in Arnold's second comic book title, *Smash Comics* (August 1939).

By the fall of 1939, Arnold was running more and more features created by the Harry Chesler and Eisner-Iger shops in *Smash Comics*, which featured all original material, as well as in *Feature Comics* (as *Feature Funnies* was now called). Eisner, who helped create a small line of cos-tumed heroes for Victor Fox's comics, presented Arnold with an idea for an original hero for *Feature Comics*. Doll Man, a costumed crime-fighter who could shrink to the size of a doll, first ap-peared in the December 1939 issue of *Feature Comics*.

By late 1939, the comic book industry was posed for an explosion of new titles and charac-ters. Seven new publishers had entered the field that year and Superman had been joined by more than a dozen costumed strongmen and masked crusaders. There were three major comic book shops and dozens of other freelance artists and small studios who were furnishing original comic book material and heroes to the new publishers.

Comic books—and comic book heroes—were about to become very serious business.

Costumed Characters and Secret Identities

Max C. Gaines knew the comic book business very well because he helped invent it. In 1933, he engineered the release of *Funnies On Parade*, the first modern comic book.

The next year, he helped with the premiere issue of *Famous Funnies*, the first regularly published newsstand comic book. By 1936, he was packaging and printing *Popular Comics*, the first reprint comic book to compete with *Famous Funnies*. In late 1937, he helped Superman find his way to *Action Comics*.

By late 1938, Gaines entered into a printing and distributing arrangement with publishers of *Superman* whereby he would produce a line of comic books under his company, All-American Comics. Gaines's new All-American comic books would be distributed along with DC Comics's *Action*, *Detective*, and *Adventure Comics*. For his editor, Gaines brought in Sheldon Mayer, the same teenager who helped him put together *Popular Comics*.

Gaines's lead title, *All-American Comics* (April 1939) was, like his earlier comic books, an anthology of mostly reprinted newspaper strips. For his next big title, Gaines turned again to the newspapers and brought out *Mutt and Jeff* (Summer 1939), the first newsstand comic book devoted to a single newspaper strip. The comic eventually proved to be Gaines's most popular title and occasionally outsold *Superman*.

While Superman and now Batman were performing well for his partners at DC Comics, Gaines still had doubts that the public would buy more "superman characters." According to several accounts, Gaines had strong ideas about what made for a successful comic book and he was not

an easy person to work for. "He was in a perpetual state of apoplexy," Mayer recalled. "He even whispered at the top of his voice." He wanted things done quickly. He was fond of yelling at his artists: "Don't give me Rembrandt, give me production!"

Mayer eventually talked Gaines into using more costumed heroes for his comic books and introduced a science fiction hero called Ultra-Man in the November 1939 issue of *All-American Comics*. Gaines was now ready to add a new title to his All-American line and gave Mayer the go-ahead for the first issue of *Flash Comics*. The comic book would contain original stories and feature the adventures of the fastest man alive—The Flash. To help create the costumed heroes and stories for *Flash Comics*, Mayer engaged the services of Gardner Fox, a young ex-lawyer and part-time comic book writer.

Fox, a law school graduate and former high school and college journalist, turned to writing comic books in 1938 when he discovered that "the law, back in those days, was not something at which to get rich." He recalled that he got into comic books when Vincent Sullivan, a boyhood friend who was now the editor of *Detective Comics*, "suggested I try my hand at writing comics— a completely new thing in those days." Using his law school background, Fox created a series called "Steve Mallone, District Attorney" for *Detective Comics* (August 1938).

By the time Mayer approached the young

All-American Comics #19
© *1940 DC Comics, Inc.*
Sheldon Moldoff.

Flash Comics #11 © 1940 DC Comics, Inc. Sheldon Moldoff.

part-time writer with the assignment for *Flash Comics*, Fox had written several Batman stories for *Detective Comics* and most of the Sandman adventures for *Adventure Comics*. Writing for costumed adventure characters came naturally to Fox, who had grown up reading the action fantasy stories of Edgar Rice Burroughs. For *Flash Comics* (January 1940), Fox created two heroes to headline the title. The Flash, a super-speedster in the tradition of the Greek god Mercury, gains his powers of acceleration through a science laboratory accident. Hawkman, a winged hero who uses ancient weapons to fight crime, is actually a reincarnated Egyptian prince.

With the addition of *Flash Comics*, Fox was now a full-time comic book writer for the DC Comics and All-American Comics line. He would eventually write more than 4,200 comic book stories for more than a hundred different characters for nine publishers. The hyperactive writer

was remembered by artist Creig Flessel as "the sweatiest man I'd ever met—even in December."

Much of Fox's prolific production was due in part to help from his editor Sheldon Mayer. "I used to go over to his house and collaborate on the stories," Mayer recalled. "Gardner would hand me a fencing foil and somehow ideas would come while I was walking around swinging the thing. He'd sit at the typewriter, throw out an idea, or catch one of mine, and we'd turn out enormous amounts of material that couldn't have been turned out any other way."

For *More Fun Comics* (May 1940), Fox created Dr. Fate, a magical superhero who hid his identity behind a golden mask. Three months earlier, for *More Fun Comics* (February 1940), Jerry Siegel had taken time off from *Superman* to create a back-from-the-dead costumed avenger known as the Spectre. With the addition of Hourman (a hero who was super for only an hour at a time) to *Adventure Comics* (March 1940), DC Comics, by early 1940, had a costumed hero on the cover of every one of its titles.

Gaines and Mayer were also eager to add more superheroes to the All-American line after the success of *Flash Comics*. For *All-American Comics* (July 1940), they introduced a superhero created by Martin Nodell called the Green Lantern, who operated with a magic ring and lamp. Later that year, a diminutive powerhouse called the Atom also took up residence in *All-American* (October 1940).

Under the imprint of DC Comics, the publishers of *Superman* and *Batman*, together with Gaines's All-American line of comics, were becoming the chief purveyors of superhero comic books in 1940. More than 90 percent of their comics featured a costumed hero as the main character. Barely two years had passed since Harry Donenfeld first published Superman in *Action Comics*. Now, the two young men who had created Superman were under a ten-year contract with Donenfeld. Siegel and Shuster received 500 dollars for each thirteen-page Superman story and a small percentage of the growing merchandising profits. In 1940, they made more than $60,000 from Superman—an amount that was dwarfed by the profits the publishers were now enjoying from the costumed comic book heroes.

The comic book profits, while still a very small portion of all newsstand publications sales, did attract the attention of other magazine publishers—in particular, they became a subject of intense discussion in the offices of Fawcett Publications.

Wilford "Billy" Fawcett, an ex-Army captain, built Fawcett Publications on a joke-and-cartoon magazine called *Captain Billy's Whiz-Bang*. Aimed at traveling salesmen and World War I veterans, the first issue of *Whiz-Bang* (named after a WWI artillery shell) appeared in September 1919 and was soon selling a half million copies a month.

Fawcett, along with his brother and sons, had an uncanny instinct for catering to the middlebrow set. By the late 1930s, Fawcett Publications had built an empire on such magazines as *Mechanix Illustrated*, *Motion Picture Magazine*, and *True Confessions*. Since a cartoon-and-joke magazine named *Whiz-Bang* began its fortunes, the Fawcett family was quick to notice the growing number of comic magazines and characters like Superman.

Ralph Daigh, the executive editor for Fawcett, looked for a person in September 1939 to head a new comic book line. Bill Parker, a recent college graduate and student of the classics, had been working with Fawcett for two years as a supervising editor on movie and detective magazines. His experience with Hollywood pictures and shoot-'em-up adventure stories made him an ideal candidate in Daigh's eyes for Fawcett's new "picture-story magazines." Besides that, he always wanted to be a writer and Daigh was going to give him his chance. Parker, in addition to editing the comic, was also to write the stories and create the heroes.

For the first issue of Fawcett's comic book, now tentatively titled *Flash Comics*, Parker presented Daigh with several ideas for traditional comic strip series: a magician (Ibis the Invincible), an aviator hero (Spy Smasher), a cowboy (Golden Arrow), and a sea-going adventurer (Lance O'Casey). For the lead feature, Parker boldly proposed that they have not *one*, but a *team* of heroes! Each hero would have a special superpower derived from a mythological god, like great strength or speed, and they would work together as a squadron under the command of Captain Thunder.

Parker's team of heroes, however, was vetoed as too cumbersome and lacking in opportunity for reader identification with a single character. Fawcett wanted another Superman—not a bunch of half-super heroes.

Parker decided to incorporate his squad of superheroes into Captain Thunder, the sole hero. He gave his hero, who appeared in a flash of thunderous lightning, the powers of six mythological and biblical heroes: Solomon, Hercules, Atlas, Zeus, Achilles, and Mercury. Parker noted that the first initial of the six heroes could be

*Whiz Comics #47 © 1943
Fawcett Publications, Inc.*

combined into a magical word: SHAZAM!

In a flash of brilliant inspiration, Parker made a young newspaper boy, Billy Batson, the alter ego for Captain Thunder. To accomplish the transformation from boy to superhero, Billy simply said, "SHAZAM!" and he magically appeared as Captain Thunder. Parker knew that a boy like Billy Batson would be an attractive fantasy figure for young comic book readers. With the arrival of Billy, kids could dream of turning into a superhero *now* instead of waiting to grow up to become one.

Captain Thunder was set to make his debut in the January 1940 issue of Fawcett's *Flash Comics*. Problems arose, however, when Max Gaines's claim to the title *Flash Comics* (January 1940) beat Fawcett's application to the copyright office by a few days. Not only was there a conflict with

Left: *Whiz Comics #2* © 1940 *Fawcett Publications, Inc.* C.C Beck.

Below: *Whiz Comics #2* © 1940 *Fawcett Publications, Inc.* C.C. Beck.

C.C. Beck

Charles Clarence Beck was born in 1910 in Zumbrota, Minnesota, to a Lutheran missionary minister and a rural school teacher. Beck had an early interest in writing, music, and art. He took a mail-order course in drawing, learned to play several musical instruments, and nurtured his artistic ambitions while attending high school in West Bend, Minnesota. After graduation, his parents sent him to the Chicago Academy of Fine Arts in 1928 during the height of the Roaring Twenties— a maturing experience for a small-town preacher's son.

Beck discovered he had a knack for cartooning and after a year at the Academy, he got a job drawing popular comic strip characters on lamp shades. He quit the last of a series of restaurant jobs and was soon making more money drawing cartoons than any of his "honest-working" West Bend classmates. Beck's commonsense upbringing and his early success in turning out production art turned him into what he proudly

the title, but Gaines's *Flash Comics* also had a character called Johnny Thunder. Fawcett had to change both the name of the magazine and its hero. Executive editor Ralph Daigh recalled that the hero's name was changed to Captain Marvel "as more befitting a hero of marvelous capabilities."

The comic was to have been retitled *Thrill Comics,* until Fawcett discovered Better Publications was releasing *Thrilling Comics*. After a slight delay, the comic book was renamed *Whiz Comics* (February 1940), in honor of Fawcett's original *Captain Billy's Whiz-Bang* joke magazine, and Captain Marvel made his first appearance in a story drawn by Charles Clarence Beck.

C.C. Beck had worked as a cartoonist for Fawcett since 1933 on humor magazines like *Hooey, Smokehouse,* and the venerable *Captain Billy's Whiz-Bang.* He was drawing for Bill Parker's movie magazines when he got the job as Fawcett's

first comic book artist. Based upon Parker's written instructions and Ralph Daigh's suggestions for the visual design of the character, Beck drew a likable superhero who bore an intentional resemblance to movie star Fred MacMurray.

Beck's simple and attractive cartoon style made Captain Marvel an instant favorite. As sales reports came in on the first three issues of *Whiz Comics,* Fawcett scheduled an entire comic book devoted to Captain Marvel called *Special Edition Comics* (August 1940). It also lined up other titles such as *Slam Bang Comics* (March 1940), *Master Comics* (March 1940), *Nickel Comics* (May 1940), and *Wow Comics* (Winter 1940). In addition to Captain Marvel, Fawcett now had Master Man, Bulletman, Mr. Scarlet, and several other costumed heroes on the newsstands.

Superman and Batman now had serious competition, and their publisher, DC Comics, took a close look at the Fawcett heroes as possible

called a "commercial artist."

With the stock market crash in 1929, Beck lost his lamp shade artist job and was soon living back with his parents, now in Minneapolis. For the next four years, Beck continued practicing his cartooning while looking for a job in the early days of the Depression. He recalled that he enjoyed reading and studying the popular newspaper comic strips of the early 1930s. Those that would be his greatest influence included Chester Gould's "Dick Tracy," Billy DeBeck's "Barney Google," and Harold Gray's "Little Orphan Annie." All three comic strip artists had a strong and simple line style that Beck grew to admire.

At the age of twenty-three, Beck landed a job as an illustrator for Fawcett Publications, a family-owned magazine publishing company in Minneapolis. He was paid a salary of fifty-five dollars every two weeks to do the jobs of two artists he replaced. The young artist was soon drawing cartoons as well as straight illustration for Fawcett's line of humor, movie, and detective magazines. When Fawcett moved its operations to New York in the late 1930s, Beck relocated to Long Island and became one of its most reliable "gag" cartoonists.

When Fawcett decided to enter the comic book business in 1939, it selected C.C. Beck to draw the lead feature for what eventually became Captain Marvel. Beck's simple, yet highly expressive, cartoony style made Captain Marvel an approachable and likeable hero. By 1941, the hero was so successful, Fawcett art director Al Allard set up a studio to help Beck keep up with the demand for new Captain Marvel stories which were now appearing in *Whiz Comics*, *America's Greatest Comics*, and *Captain Marvel Adventures*. At times, up to twenty assistants worked with Beck to deliver thousands of pages of Captain Marvel stories.

Beck continued his association with Captain Marvel until the end of the Fawcett comic book line in late 1953. His straightforward storytelling, clear and easy-to-read panels, and knack for depicting action and adventure in a crisp and wholesome style made Captain Marvel one of the most popular heroes in the history of comics. Beck, who became the most widely read artists of the Golden Age, faithfully followed his own advice to aspiring comic book artists: "Never put a single line in that isn't necessary. Don't try to show off."

> The earliest cartoons are in the days of the Egyptians and the cave painters in Spain.
> Ten thousand years ago. The stories were just a spin-off of the old myths. That's one reason Bill Parker's basing Captain Marvel on mythological characters was better than phony science fiction.
> —*C.C. Beck, artist for* Captain Marvel

infringements on their Superman character. Master Man ("the strongest man on Earth") was so similar in name and powers to Superman that DC Comics was able to have Fawcett drop the character after six appearances. Their earlier legal success against Victor Fox's Wonder Man was certainly a helpful precedent. As a result of that lawsuit, in which Will Eisner testified that Fox had instructed the Eisner-Iger shop to copy Superman, Fox dropped his contracts with Eisner and Iger and left owing them around $3,000 ("an absolute fortune at the time," recalled Eisner).

Fortunately, the Eisner-Iger shop had other clients. In early 1940, the studio was turning out comic book heroes with dizzying speed for "Busy" Arnold's line of Quality Comics. For *National Comics* (July 1940), Will Eisner created an early patriotic superhero called Uncle Sam, based on the character in James Montgomery Flagg's World War I recruiting poster ("I Want You"). That same month, Hercules, the Red Bee, and Neon the Unknown (created by Jerry Iger) appeared in Arnold's *Hit Comics* (July 1940). Doll Man, whose first appearance in *Feature Comics* was drawn by Will Eisner, was now enjoying the artwork of Lou Fine.

Fine, more than almost any other young comic book artist of the day, had a real feel for the heroic costumed genre. He had an uncanny eye for anatomy and delighted in showing off finely muscled characters in action. Fine drenched his stories with such detailed rendering, he often worked overtime and into the night to meet deadlines. For Quality's *Crack Comics* (May 1940), Fine drew the adventures of the Black Condor, a hero whose costume included wrist-to-waist glider wings. For *Smash Comics* (September 1940), Fine introduced the Ray, a yellow-sunburst superhero who harnessed magnetic and light rays to fight crime. Fine's work was the most impressive of the Eisner-Iger shop and he was eventually hired by Arnold to work directly for Quality Comics.

Arnold showed Fine's work, along with other features from his Quality Comics line, to several newspapers in hopes of interesting them in a Sunday comic book section that they could include with their weekly color funnies. Arnold's idea was to produce a "ready-print" comic book that newspapers could use as a circulation-builder during the highly competitive days of the syndicates. Reportedly, the newspapers liked the masked detective character from *Feature Comics* called The Clock, but not George Brenner's art. They did like Lou Fine's work and asked Arnold who the artist was and if he could do the lead feature for the proposed newspaper comic book. Knowing Fine's limitations as a writer and his reputation for late deadlines, Arnold knew he couldn't handle the job. Instead, he replied that the art came from Will Eisner (technically the truth, since it came from the Eisner-Iger studio) and that Eisner was quite capable of producing a weekly comic book tabloid for the newspapers. Arnold and the newspapers invited Eisner to

Left: *Wonderworld Comics #4 © 1939 Fox Features Syndicate.* Lou Fine.

Below: *Mystery Men Comics #8 © 1940 Fox Features Syndicate.* Lou Fine.

Lou Fine

Lou Fine's interest in art began as a teenager when he was stricken with polio. The disease, which shortened his left leg by two inches, left Fine with a lifelong limp which had made him the object of boyhood teasing. He became shy and retreated behind a pair of steel-rim glasses to draw and to create his own world. To compensate for his weakened leg, Fine worked with upper-body weights and built his forearms up to a sinewy musculature.

His illness forced him to spend more time reading and he soon became enthralled with the richly detailed pictures that illustrated the books and magazines of the early 1930s. In particular, the young Fine liked the finely rendered work of illustrators like Dean Cornwell, Heinrich Kley, Saul Tepper, and J.C. Leyendecker, who brought exotic scenes like African bazaars and medieval pageantry to life.

Fine attended the Grand Central Art School and Pratt Institute to study illustration, but by 1938, he found himself pursu-

meet with them about their project.

Drawing a feature for the newspapers was every comic book artist's dream at the time. As Eisner said, "The newspapers were the major leagues then, as far as cartoonists were concerned." After his meeting with the newspapers, Eisner entered into an agreement with "Busy" Arnold and the Register-Tribune Syndicate to produce a weekly comic book insert. Eisner would draw the lead feature and put together the rest of the tabloid's comic stories. Eisner recalled that the syndicate's only guideline was to produce "stuff that was in the genre of comic books."

Although the Eisner-Iger shop was financially successful, Eisner realized that he could no longer devote his full attention to both the shop and the newspaper comic tabloid. He sold his interest in the business to his partner Jerry Iger and set up his own shop ("a little studio in Tudor City"). By agreement, Eisner took five artists with him (Lou Fine, Bob Powell, Chuck Mazoujian, Chuck Cuidera, and Nick Vascardi) and Iger con-

> In 1940, comic book artists, if they were regarded at all, were not regarded. —*Will Eisner*

tinued to supply comic book publishers under the name of Iger Associates.

Eisner was now faced with an exciting challenge. He had the opportunity to create a hero for the Register-Tribune that could reach a wider newspaper audience than any other comic book character. Eisner recalled Arnold and the syndicate "wanted to have some kind of mysterioso character that emulated the so-called superheroes, so in my first discussions with "Busy" Arnold, his thinking centered around a superhero kind of character—a costumed character. We didn't use the word 'superhero' in those days."

ing engineering at the New York School of Technology. Running out of money, Fine used his drawing skills and joined the Eisner-Iger comic shop at a starting salary of ten dollars per week. He anticipated working there for only a few months—drawing comic books certainly didn't seem like a secure future. Fine's first comic book work, an adaptation of the *Count of Monte Cristo*, appeared in *Jumbo Comics* (December 1938). Fine picked up the series that was begun by Jack Kirby.

As was customary in the early days of comics, the artist also usually wrote the stories. Fine, while already an accomplished illustrator by the age of twenty-three, could not write a comic book story. Will Eisner pitched in with the writing, but soon decided to use Fine as a cover artist where no writing would be involved. Eisner also felt that Fine's "Herculean draftsmanship" would be better used on the front covers of the comics. After drawing covers for *Jumbo Comics* and Victor Fox's *Wonder Comics*, Fine began work on his first superhero series, the Flame, for *Wonderworld Comics* (July 1939).

By late 1939, the Eisner-Iger shop was also supplying "Busy" Arnold at Quality

Comics with new features. Fine took over Doll Man for *Feature Comics* and was soon involved with other heroes for Quality, including the Black Condor in *Crack Comics* (May 1940) and The Ray in *Smash Comics* (September 1940). Arnold was so impressed with his work, he hired Fine away from the Eisner-Iger shop at three times his current salary.

Fine's detailed and majestic heroes for Quality Comics earned him the reputation as the most classically "heroic" of all the 1940s comic book artists. His anatomy, figure work, and flair for portraying both action and expression influenced both his contemporaries and a future generation of comic book artists.

In 1942, Fine dropped his comic book work to take over the Spirit for the newspaper comic section after Will Eisner was drafted. Ironically, Fine had originally been the newspaper syndicate's first choice to draw the lead feature. Upon Eisner's return to the Spirit in 1946, Fine entered the world of commercial comic strip advertising art.

Will Eisner remembered Lou Fine as "a real solid draftsman, a great artist, one of the greatest in the business I think, and a very sensitive and intelligent man."

Left: *The Spirit © 1941 Will Eisner.* Will Eisner.

Below: *The Spirit #18 © 1949 Will Eisner.* Will Eisner.

Will Eisner

Will Eisner grew up around a world of theatrical make-believe. Born in 1917, Eisner recalled that "among my first memories is visiting the Second Avenue Jewish theaters where I would see the men working on the backdrops." Eisner, whose father built stage sets and scenery for New York plays, nursed an early ambition to become a stage designer. The boy's sensitivity to theatrical lighting, design, and architecture would ultimately serve him well in his eventual career as a comic book artist or, as Eisner prefers, "visual storyteller."

Eisner's path from would-be stage designer to visual storyteller came about through his own talent for cartooning and the unique opportunities offered by the new comic book medium. Eisner recalled that he considered himself very lucky. "I was born at a moment when the comic book medium was a-borning too, which gave me an opportunity to employ two skills which I

Eisner, who had his "bellyfull of creating costumed heroes" for Victor Fox and Arnold, argued that they should have a more urban kind of hero instead of another "freak" character. "I was aware I was about to write for a different audience than comic books. I wanted it to be varied and adult."

Working into the early-morning hours just days before the first issue of the comic tabloid was due, Eisner came up with an idea for "an outlaw hero who would be suitable for an adult audience." When Arnold called Eisner to check on his progress, Eisner told him about his idea. Arnold suggested that perhaps the character could be a ghost or metaphysical character to make him more mysterious. Eisner recalled that Arnold said: "'How about a thing called The Ghost?' and I said, 'Naw, that's not any good,' and he said, 'Well then call it The Spirit; there's nothing like that around—I just like the words The Spirit.' He was calling from a bar somewhere I think . . . "

Eisner started working on the Spirit on a

Thursday night. "By Saturday night and four phone calls to several bars, I got it in shape." *The Spirit Section*, as it was called, made its debut in the June 2, 1940, Sunday newspapers. Eisner's masked detective (who seemingly returned from the grave to continue his war against criminals) was soon appearing in the *Washington Star*, *Philadelphia Record*, and *Baltimore Sun*. The comic book had come to the newspapers.

Not only newspapers took note of the comic book's selling clout in 1940. Street and Smith, one of the oldest publishers of popular magazines in America, entered the comic book field with versions of its two best-selling pulp magazine heroes, *Shadow Comics* (March 1940) and *Doc Savage Comics* (May 1940).

MLJ Publications, which had entered the comic book field with *Blue-Ribbon Comics* (November 1939), began its line of superheroes by introducing the Wizard in *Top-Notch Comics* (December 1939), the Shield and the Comet in *Pep Comics* (January 1940), Steel Sterling in *Zip Comics* (February 1940), and the Black Hood in *Top-*

knew I had: the urge to tell stories, to write, and the ability to draw and to illustrate them—to visualize them."

As a youngster, Eisner developed his ability to draw stories by reading and imitating the popular newspaper comics of the early 1930s. One of his favorites was E.C. Segar's *Thimble Theater* strip starring Popeye. "I was terribly influenced by that," Eisner recalled. "Some stuff I did when I was fifteen or sixteen looks just like Popeye. I was also very fond of Alex Raymond's *Flash Gordon* and Caniff's *Terry and the Pirates*. George Herriman's *Krazy Kat* also influenced me tremendously. I still remember the impact his crazy backgrounds had on me."

Eisner also pursued his theatrical interests in high school while drawing cartoons for the school newspaper. Upon graduation, he studied drawing and anatomy at the New York Art Students' League for a year, which led to a job as an advertising artist for the *New York American* newspaper in 1935. To supplement his income, Eisner drew illustrations for western and detective pulp magazines.

In 1936, Eisner discovered the world of comic books and had his first story published in *Wow What A Magazine*! The following year, he sold freelance comic book stories to the Comics Magazine Company. In late 1937, Eisner formed one of the earliest comic book art studios with Jerry Iger, his former coworker from the *New York American* as well as ex-editor from *Wow What A Magazine*!

Although Eisner created dozens of comic book features and heroes from 1938 to 1940 for early publishers like Victor Fox, Fiction House Publishing, and "Busy" Arnold's Quality Comics, he is best remembered for the Spirit, a masked-detective hero who appeared in a weekly newspaper comic supplement from 1940 to 1952.

Eisner both wrote and drew the early Spirit stories and he discovered that the character was the perfect vehicle for his dramatic, visual storytelling. The *Spirit* comic strip grew from what Eisner called his "three major influences: the motion pictures I saw—and I saw a lot of them—short stories I read, which nurtured my own imagination, and my own life experience."

Notch Comics (October 1940). MLJ also starred two of its heroes together in one comic, *Shield-Wizard Comics* (Summer 1940).

Ace Magazines, which had published pulp and movie magazines, entered the superhero business with *Sure-Fire Comics* (June 1940), which featured Flash Lightning, and *Super Mystery Comics* (July 1940), with Magno the Magnetic Man. There were nearly a dozen other publishers which came out with their first superhero comics in 1940.

Eastern Color published *Heroic Comics* (August 1940), which featured Bill Everett's Hydroman from Funnies Incorporated. *Prize Comics* (March 1940) began the adventures of the Black Owl, while *Crash Comics* (May 1940) starred the Cat-Man. The *Green Hornet* (December 1940) was adapted from the popular radio show into a comic book by a closet-size studio run by Bert Whitman. Pelican Publications brought out the first and only issue of *Green Giant Comics*, based on a hero inspired by a supermarket food character.

For all the small publishers, offbeat characters, and would-be comic book entrepreneurs in 1940, there were also some major league players. Comic books achieved publishing respectability when Curtis Publishing Company, the company behind *Saturday Evening Post*, started its line of comics that year.

Under the name of Novelty Press, Curtis premiered *Target Comics* (February 1940) and *Blue Bolt Comics* (June 1940). Both comic books were packaged by the Funnies Incorporated studio, which had got Marvel Comics into the business a few months earlier. Carl Burgos, who created the Human Torch for Marvel Comics, reused his "android as superhero" theme for *Target Comics* with the White Streak, another super-powered, nonhuman hero. Joe Simon, whose first work for Funnies Incorporated in 1939 included creating a hero called the Fiery Mask for Marvel's *Daring Mystery Comics*, came up with a costumed character called Blue Bolt—the namesake of Novelty Press's second title.

Simon, who was twenty-four-years old

Lightning Comics Vol. 2 #4 © 1941 Ace Magazines, Inc.
Jim Mooney.

Green Giant Comics #1
© 1940 Pelican Publications. Harry Sahle.

together his own staff of artists and writers to produce a rapidly expanding line of comic books and second-rate newspaper strips. Besides the *Blue Beetle, Mystery Men, Wonderworld,* and *Fantastic Comics,* Fox was publishing (or planning to publish) *Science Comics* (February 1940), *Weird Comics* (April 1940), *The Flame* (Summer 1940), *The Green Mask* (Summer 1940), and *Samson* (Fall 1940).

Fox needed someone who could supervise the crew of recently recruited artists to make sure they turned out approximately three hundred to four hundred pages of art each month. He offered Simon the position of editor in chief of Fox Features Syndicate at eighty-five dollars per week.

Simon soon found himself redrawing and filling in for many of the inexperienced cartoonists. He was grateful, however, for the able help of two young Fox artists: Alfred Harvey, an Eagle Scout who had a feel for hand-lettering and cover design, and Jacob Kurtzberg, a twenty-two-year-old who was efficiently drawing the Blue Beetle daily newspaper strip while also batting out reams of production work. Kurtzberg, who also drew under pen names like Jack Curtiss, Curt Davis, and Lance Kirby, would soon adopt a new legal name as a comic book artist: Jack Kirby.

Kirby, who helped support his family in a lower-East Side tenement with his fifteen-dollar-a-week salary, recalled that in those early days of the comic book industry, artists were grateful for

when he broke into comic books with a western story sold through Funnies Incorporated, had previously drawn pen-and-ink illustrations for "true detective" magazines at Macfadden Publications. While continuing to freelance (at seven dollars per page) out of his room at a Columbia University boarding house, Simon looked for other chances to advance in the comics field. An ad in the *New York Times* caught his attention: "Artists and editor wanted for major comics company." Simon made an appointment and soon found himself in the huge office of Victor Fox, a man who described himself as "the king of the comics."

After losing the Superman-Wonder Man copyright suit, Fox had severed his connections with the Eisner-Iger studio. Now Fox was putting

Sparkler Comics #1 © 1941 United Features Syndicate

Although I had never read comics before (my interests were poetry and playwrighting and short stories), I answered an ad in the *New York Times*, and was immediately accepted by Victor Fox, president of Fox Publications. Well, not immediately. He asked me to make up a story as I was walking towards his football field-sized desk. All I could see of him was his bald head. I told the Bald Head that "A skeleton was driving an open convertible through Times Square, scattering terrified people in his wake! Not a *man* in a skeleton's costume! But a real *skeleton*!" When I was ten yards from his desk, Bald Head said: "I like a man who thinks on his feet. You're hired." — *Robert Kanigher, comic book writer and editor*

Fantastic Comics #13 © 1940
Fox Features Syndicate

Green Mask #2 © 1940 Fox Features
Syndicate

All Star Comics #1
© 1940 DC Comics, Inc.
The Spectre was Jerry
Siegel's second most-
popular superhero.

any job. "I was giving Fox his money's worth," Kirby recalled, "and everybody in that room was giving Fox his money's worth. And everybody was dead serious in doing the best they could."

Kirby's seriousness, technical skill, and steady speed impressed Simon. When he left Fox to resume a more profitable freelance career drawing the adventures of *Blue Bolt* for Funnies Incorporated (as well as packaging stories for Marvel Comics), Simon asked Kirby to work with him as a partner. Kirby still continued to hold down his "steady" job with Fox while moonlighting with Simon in a small, one-room office located just down the street from the Funnies Incorporated studio. By the time the two men had turned out a half dozen Blue Bolt adventures, Kirby decided to quit his staff job at Fox and become Simon's business partner in 1940.

The following year, comic books and superheroes would become even more popular and the team of Simon and Kirby would become one of the most recognized in comics.

SMACK IN THE FÜHRER'S FACE

Comic books, and especially superhero comic books, came into their own in 1941. Kids and adults were buying fifteen million comic books every month. Each week, more than a hundred titles competed for newsstand space. *Superman Comics* alone sold nearly ten million issues in 1941.

Thrilling Comics #17
© 1941 Better Publications, Inc.

DC Comics (including Max Gaines's All-American branch) grossed more than $44 million dollars that year on a product that sold for ten cents. Of the 102 comic books DC Comics published in 1941, 100 of them featured superheroes. During the year preceding World War II, the comic book industry and its legion of superheroes permanently encamped themselves in the popular culture of America.

DC Comics gave its popular heroes comic books of their own, such as *Green Lantern* (Fall 1941), *All-Flash Comics* (Summer 1941), and *World's Finest Comics* (Summer 1941) with Superman and Batman. It also introduced a secondary line of superheroes which included Starman in *Adventure Comics* (April 1941), Green Arrow and Aquaman in *More Fun Comics* (November 1941), and the Star Spangled Kid in *Star Spangled Comics* (October 1941). DC Comics also showcased minor heroes like the Crimson Avenger, Shining Knight, and Vigilante in *Leading Comics* (Winter 1941) as part of the Seven Soldiers of Victory. Most significantly, it introduced what was to become the most popular comic book superheroine of all time, Wonder Woman, in *All Star Comics* (December 1941).

Although DC Comics was the premier purveyor of superheroes in 1941, it had serious competition that year. Republic Pictures, bypassing DC Comics and Superman, negotiated instead with Fawcett Publishing to produce a Captain

Marvel movie serial. The first major movie adaptation of a comic book would star the hero from *Whiz Comics*. Superman had been upstaged.

In September 1941, DC Comics initiated the first of a series of lawsuits against Captain Marvel, claiming copyright infringement of its Superman character. Besides the movie serial, DC Comics had other good reasons to fear the success of Fawcett Publishing's Captain Marvel.

The "Big Red Cheese" (as the captain was disparagingly called by his archenemy Sivana) had grown beyond his berth in *Whiz Comics* and had his own magazine, *Captain Marvel Adventures* (January 1941), as well as a spot in Fawcett's new anthology title *America's Greatest Comics* (May 1941). Fawcett also had a growing line of titles like *Bulletman* (July 1941), *Minute Man* (July 1941), and *Spy Smasher* (Fall 1941). The proof positive, however, that Fawcett was nipping at DC Comics's heels was the appearance of Captain Marvel, Jr. (*Whiz Comics*, December 1941), a juvenile version of the captain which marked the beginning of the Marvel Family dynasty.

With such an explosion in titles and skyrocketing popularity of Captain Marvel, Fawcett Publishing required more artwork and stories than its staff artists and editors could supply. By 1941, Captain Marvel artist C.C. Beck was supervising a production studio of artists. Still, Fawcett had to contract with an outside art agency to fulfill their rapidly growing needs. The Jack Binder Stu-

Captain Marvel Adventures #11 © 1942 Fawcett Publications, Inc.

Publishing and other companies at a cost of about eight dollars per page.

Otto Binder, Jack's brother, wrote many of the stories which came out of the Binder Studio. Otto had already trained himself to be a fast and productive writer while knocking out science fiction pulp magazine stories in the 1930s. Binder wrote his first comic book stories for two dollars per page in 1939. By 1941, he was up to three dollars per page for the stories he was writing for Fawcett Publishing.

Binder recalled that "in March 1941 I first wrote for Fawcett with the Mr. Scarlet assignment. After Ed Herron, then chief editor, saw my stuff, he began grooming me for the big boy [Captain Marvel] by having me do Captain Venture, Spy Smasher, Minute Man, Bulletman, El Carim, Golden Arrow, Ibis, and Dr. Voodoo, all through 1941. My first Captain Marvel Comics script was written in December 1941 and appeared in the ninth issue, April 1942."

Binder quickly became the chief architect of the Captain Marvel legend and wrote more than half the stories ever published. "The end result of this some twelve years later in 1953," Binder recalled, "was a total of 529 stories about the Big Red Cheese alone. My home in Englewood, New Jersey, was dedicated at a Fawcett party as being 'The House that Captain Marvel Built.' Truer words were never spoken. He paid for it twice over."

Otto and Jack Binder had their hands in a lot of other superheroes in 1941 besides the Fawcett line. For Better Publications, the Binder brothers were producing the Fighting Yank for *Startling Comics*, the Black Owl for *Prize Comics*,

dio came to the rescue.

Jack Binder, who had served as art director for the Harry "A" Chesler shop since 1937, began his own comic book art studio in late 1940. He soon had six comic book companies for clients, including Fawcett Publishing, and a growing stable of artists, including Pete Riss, Ken Bald, and Bill Ward. By early 1941, Binder's studio was turning out 100 pages of comic book art every month. Each page was broken down into eight basic production steps: roughs, pencils (background, secondary figures, and main figures), inking (background, secondary figures, and main figures), and lettering. Each step was done by a different artist who was usually paid between 75 cents and $1.25 per page. In this manner, Binder was producing comic book pages for Fawcett

I can organize our armed forces within a week and clean up these warring nations. I shan't play any favorites. But I'll destroy anyone who interferes with the transportation of food or medical supply—no matter for whom they're intended!
— *Sub-Mariner* (Marvel Mystery Comics, *February 1940)*

and Doc Savage for Street and Smith Publishing. Jack Binder had expanded his comic book shop from a room in his Bronx apartment to the top half of a reconstructed barn in Englewood. Between twenty and thirty artists would work at tables on a wooden floor, turning out comic book pages in true production-line fashion. One artist recalled that whenever someone moved back from the table to take a break, the chair would squeak on the floor and Binder would rush over to see what the delay was all about. Another artist, who showed up for only one day's work, remembered a big dog chained to the studio door to keep the workers from taking an early baseball game break.

Besides Binder's studio, there were four other major art studios (as well as many two- and three-man shops) that supplied publishers with superhero comic book stories. Funnies Incorporated was furnishing Human Torch and Sub-Mariner stories for Marvel Comics and the Jerry Iger studio was handling much of the Fiction House comics. Harry "A" Chesler, the first comic book studio maven, was even publishing comics of his own with superheroes like Dynamic Man and Yankee Doodle Jones in *Dynamic Comics* (October 1941), *Yankee Comics* (September 1941), *Scoop Comics* (November 1941), and *Punch Comics* (December 1941).

Will Eisner's studio, which was producing the *Spirit* comic section for "Busy" Arnold was also turning out stories for other Quality comic books. For *Military Comics* (August 1941), the Eisner studio came up with the Blackhawks, a team of international war pilots who fought the Nazis wing tip-to-wing tip. That same month, another Nazi fighter, Uncle Sam from *National Comics*, also received his own Quality comic book.

Arnold, while using the talents of both the Eisner and Iger studios, also began assembling his own staff of artists and writers for Quality Comics. He hired Lou Fine from the Will Eisner studio and Reed Crandall from the Jerry Iger studio. Fine reveled in drawing heroic Olympian figures on the covers of *Hit Comics*, *Crack Comics*, and *Smash Comics*. Crandall drew the adventures of Hercules beginning in *Hit Comics* (May 1941) and Doll Man for *Feature Comics* (May 1941), two characters previously drawn by Fine. Crandall, with his eye for anatomy and perfectly balanced figures, also proved himself the equal of Lou Fine by taking over Fine's Ray in *Smash Comics* (June 1941). Together, Fine and Crandall earned Quality Comics its reputation for painstaking draftsmanship and slickly rendered stories. Fine recalled that he and Crandall often competed with

each other to produce the most lavish pages ("We were both a couple of prima donnas!").

Arnold completed his top triumvirate of Quality artists when he landed the talents of Jack Cole. Cole began at the Harry "A" Chesler studio in 1937 by drawing cartoon pages like "Insurance Ike" and "Joe Ticket." Cole had a talent for writing as well as drawing and, by 1939, was creating police and detective strips for *Blue Ribbon Comics*. He went on to draw the first adventures of the Comet for *Pep Comics* (January 1940) and was working as editor at *Silver Streak Comics* in the summer of 1940 as both writer and artist on the Daredevil strip. Arnold hired Cole to work on a new feature for *Smash Comics* (January 1941) that would be called Midnight. Similar to Eisner's Spirit, Midnight was also an urbane masked de-

Hit Comics #2 © 1940 Comic Magazines, Inc. Lou Fine.

Uncle Sam Quarterly #5 © 1942 Comic Magazines, Inc. Al Gabriele.

tective, "an eerie friend of the needy." Under Cole's fast-paced storytelling, Midnight became the star feature of *Smash Comics*.

Cole's biggest contribution to the comic book field came later that year. For the first issue of *Police Comics* (August 1941), Jack Cole wrote and drew a six-page story which began: "From time to time the comic world welcomes a new sensation! Such is Plastic Man!! The most fantastic man alive!"

Plastic Man, the pliable and sophisticated superhero, was written and drawn with delirious abandon and frantic pacing. Cole made his wise-cracking hero an animated delight who continually surprised the reader with his elastic, plastic feats of *s-t-r-e-t-c-h-i-n-g*.

While Quality Comics, DC Comics, and Fawcett Publishing were dominating the super-hero comic book marketplace in 1941, Marvel Comics was not far behind. Although the Human Torch and the Sub-Mariner had been successful enough to rate their own comic books, Marvel needed more heroes. Publisher Martin Goodman (whose company was now called Timely Publications) hired Joe Simon as editor and told him to come up with some new ideas.

Simon was working with his new partner, Jack Kirby, on *Blue Bolt* comics when he got Goodman's order to invent a new comic book character. Simon and Kirby had also worked together for Marvel Comics on the first and only issue of *Red Raven Comics* (August 1940). Since that time, however, changes were happening in the real world which were affecting the world of comics.

On September 7, 1940, the German bomb-

Left: Police Comics #1 © 1941 Comic Magazines, Inc. Jack Cole.

Below: Silver Streak Comics #6 © 1940 Lev Gleason Publications. Jack Cole.

Jack Cole

Jack Cole, born in 1914, was at the perfect age to read the early comic strips of E.C. Segar (*Thimble Theater*), Rudolph Dirks (*Captain and the Kids*), and George McManus (*Bringing Up Father*). As a boy, Cole loved the broad humor of these early cartoonists and marveled that anyone could make a living drawing such things. His future was determined the day he saw an advertisement for a mail-order cartoon course. He saved his lunch money by eating homemade sandwiches he smuggled from the kitchen inside a hollow book. By the age of fifteen, he had saved enough dimes to enroll in the Landon School of Cartooning.

The young Cole honed his art talents and was soon publishing his own cartoons and satire in a mimeographed magazine called *The Scoop*, a parody of his high school newspaper. Cole's cartoons, however, were not very flattering to the faculty at his New Castle High School in Pennsylvania and his journalism career came to an abrupt end when his father locked up the duplicating machine.

After a cross-country bicycle ride in 1933, Cole got a job at a canning factory

ing blitz against London inflicted heavy civilian damage. Nazi storm troopers were looting Paris and the war machine of the Third Reich had nearly flattened the last European resistance. Americans were chilled by daily newspaper reports of yet another German victory and outraged by movie newsreels which showed the Nazi atrocities.

Joe Simon, like most Americans in the prewar years, regarded Adolph Hitler as one of the worst villains of all time. While thinking about new comic book characters for Timely (or Marvel) Comics, Simon began to daydream. Wouldn't it be wonderful if there was an all-American hero who could stand up to a real-life villain like Hitler? It would take someone who was as brave and powerful as a superhero to beat the Nazis. Suddenly, Simon had his idea.

Simon showed Goodman his sketches for a proposed comic book hero who wore a red, white, and blue costume. Unlike Batman and Superman, who spent their time fighting crime and gangsters, Simon's flag-colored hero would fight Hitler and the Nazis. Goodman liked the idea so much, he decided to introduce the patriotic superhero in his own full-length comic book. Simon returned to his partner, Jack Kirby, and they got to work on the first issue of *Captain America Comics* (March 1941).

"The whole reason we put Captain America out was that America was in a patriotic frenzy," Simon recalled. An American hero fighting Hitler was an immensely popular idea, even if it was only in a comic book, and it appealed to a public which was being primed for the war by daily news accounts.

and started submitting his cartoons by mail. In 1935, he made his first professional sale to *Boy's Life Magazine.* He went to New York in 1936, determined to make his fortune as a cartoonist. Within months, he had spent his last nickel on a subway ride trying to collect payment for his one-panel cartoons.

Cole landed a job at the Harry "A" Chesler comic book studio in the summer of 1937. He was paid twenty dollars a week to draw one- and two-page humorous "filler" pages for early comics like *Funny Pages* (October 1937) and *Star Comics* (April 1938). On his own, Cole created a character called "Peewee Throttle" for another early comic book, *Circus the Comic Riot* (June 1938). He gradually realized that comic book artists who drew adventure strips were making more money than the cartoonists who drew the shorter funny features. He tried his hand at his first serious strip, a detective hotshot called Little Dynamite for *Keen Detective Funnies* (February 1939).

When the Chesler studio began supplying adventure strips to MLJ Publications, Cole drew the Comet (his first superhero) for *Pep Comics* (January 1940). He was soon drawing another adventure hero, "The Defender, the Man With a Thousand Faces," for *Rocket Comics* (April 1940). Cole's talents gained him recognition outside the Chesler studio and he began operating on his own

as writer, artist, and editor for *Silver Streak Comics.*

Cole's background in cartooning and humor served him well in his transition to adventure comics. His frantic pacing, exaggerated action, and animated caricatures were perfectly suited for comic book storytelling. Alex Kotzky, who worked with Cole in the 1940s, recalled that "Jack was a wild man, mentally. Anyone who knew him, knew he had one of the wildest imaginations."

After moving over to Quality Comics in 1941, Cole wrote and drew the adventures of Midnight for *Smash Comics,* "an enemy of crime" who wore a black-and-blue reversible suit and mask and was assisted in his crime-fighting adventures by Gabby, "his amazing talking monkey." His next creation for Quality's *Police Comics* was a stretchable hero named Plastic Man, a character so sophisticated and unusual, it outlasted hundreds of others.

Gill Fox, the editor of *Police Comics,* recalled his meetings with Cole: "The first time he brought in a page, it was a startling thing. You recognized you were seeing something different. I have run across very, very few guys with the kind of mentality Jack had. By that I mean, able to conceive something that's never been done before, entirely fresh. He had a wild mind."

Left: *Captain America #1* © 1941 Marvel Entertainment Group, Inc. Jack Kirby.

Below: *Blue Bolt #3* © 1940 Novelty Press. Joe Simon and Jack Kirby.

Jack Kirby

The son of an Austrian immigrant factory worker, Jack Kirby was born Jacob Kurtzberg in 1917 and raised on New York's Lower East Side during the Depression. "There were gangs all over the place," Kirby recalled. "Some of my friends became gangsters. You became a gangster depending on how fast you wanted a suit."

As a youngster, Kirby ran with a neighborhood gang and learned to fight on the streets. He also had another side, however, that loved the theater and the world of books. He read Edgar Rice Burroughs, H.G. Wells, *Robin Hood*, *The Three Musketeers*, as well as science fiction pulp magazines. Kirby recalled his first encounter with Hugo Gernsback's *Wonder Stories*: "I came out of school one day when I was about twelve. It had been raining. I spotted this magazine floating down the gutter and jumped for it. The cover was amazing! I'd never seen anything like it, space ships and fantastic cities. At that moment, something galvanized in my brain."

The boy's imagination, already fueled by such favorite Sunday comic strips as "Tailspin Tommy," "Moon Mullins," and "Barney Google," eagerly studied the science fiction illustrations. He decided he would become an illustrator, a cartoonist, a storyteller. He answered an advertisement for a correspondence course in cartooning. "Here I was twelve years old," Kirby recalled, "and counting the days until I had my own comic strip."

In 1932, he joined one of the first boys' clubs, the Boys' Brotherhood Republic. From 1933 to 1935, he drew a cartoon feature called "Kurtzberg's Konceptions" for the club's mimeographed newsletter. In late summer 1935, at the age of eighteen, he landed a job as an animator for the Max Fleischer Studio. He worked assembly-line fashion and drew the fill-in figures of Popeye for the cartoons. For nearly two years, the young artist drew thousands of animated cartoon figures over and over again in various frozen frames of motion.

In May 1937, Kirby left the deadening, piecemeal work of animation production to work as a staff cartoonist for Lincoln Features, a modest newspaper syndicate which supplied cartoons and articles to small-town weekly newspapers. His first works were one-panel cartoon fact features and editorial cartoons like "Laughs From Today's News" and "Your Health Comes First!!!" ("The emotion of anger causes indigestion! Avoid getting angry!"). He signed his early cartoons "Jack Curtiss." Working under the names of Curtiss, Bob Brown, Ted Grey, and Richard Lee, Jacob Kurtzberg created several weekly comic strips for Lincoln Features, including "Detective Riley," "The Black Buccaneer," "Abdul Jones," and a science fiction epic called "Cyclone Burke."

In late 1937, a boyhood dream came true when he got an assignment from Associated Features Syndicate to draw his first daily newspaper strip, a western hero called "The Lone Rider." He drew the strip under the name of Lance Kirby and it was later reprinted in *Famous Funnies* as "Lightnin' and the Lone Rider." In 1938, this time as Jack Curtiss, he drew an early science fiction strip called the "Solar Legion" for Whitman Publishing.

Kirby also worked briefly in the Eisner-Iger shop in 1938 for *Jumbo Comics* ("Wilton of the West," "Count of Monte Cristo") and then as a freelancer on comic book features like the Black Owl for *Prize Comics* (February 1940). Kirby began a staff job at Fox Features Syndicate in late 1939, where he did production work and also drew the Blue Beetle daily newspaper strip. While working for Fox (under the names of Floyd Kelly and Michael Griffith), he also drew comic book stories like "Wing Turner" for *Mystery Men Comics* (May 1940) and "Cosmic Carson" for *Science Comics* (May 1940).

Kirby met Joe Simon when Simon began working as an editor at Fox in early 1940. Simon took Kirby on as a partner later that year when he began freelancing for Novelty Publications (*Blue Bolt Comics*) and Marvel Comics (*Red Raven*). By now, Jacob Kurtzberg was legally Jack Kirby (a combi-

nation of two of his favorite pen names) and the duo of Simon and Kirby was on its way to becoming a well-known comic book creative team.

The two men drew the first issue of *Captain Marvel Adventures* (March 1941) and then went on to create one of the most exciting comic book series of the early 1940s, *Captain America* (March 1941). They moved over to DC Comics in 1942, where they drew such features as the Sandman, Manhunter, and Boy Commandos.

Kirby often relied on his familiarity with movies to tell his comic book stories. "I was a movie person. I think it was one of the reasons I drew comics. I saw myself as a camera; that's why I do a lot of foreshortening. I've developed a kind of three-dimensional style. You have to see a player from all angles, and having had animation experience helped a lot. I put a lot of movement into my characters."

Kirby quickly earned the reputation as a one-man comic book factory. He turned out prodigious amounts of work, rarely erasing. "I drew instinctively. My anatomy was self-taught. Mine was an instinctive style." Kirby recalled that "I had to work fast. I would draw three pages a day, maybe more. I would have to vary the panels, balance the page. I took care of everything on that page—the expressions of the characters, their motivation—it all ran through my mind."

It was while working on the *Captain America* comic book in 1941 that Kirby began developing a style that would serve him for a lifetime of drawing superhero comics, all the way into the Marvel Comics age of the 1960s and beyond.

"The pressure was tremendous," Kirby recalled of the days when he and Simon were turning out the Captain America stories. "I was penciling at a breakneck speed, as many as nine pages a day. I guess that was the reason my figures began to take on a distorted look; my instincts told me that a figure had to be extreme to have power. I feel that action and graceful movement symbolize beauty and life, and acrobatic characters are the perfect instrument to convey this. I always wanted to show mankind at its best."

Red Raven Comics #1 © 1940 Marvel Entertainment Group, Inc. Jack Kirby.

Captain America #7 © 1941 Marvel Entertainment Group, Inc. Jack Kirby.

Blue Ribbon Comics #19 © 1941 Archie Comics Publications, Inc.

Captain America was not the first costumed comic book hero to combine patriotism with crime fighting. The previous year had seen Joe Higgins, the son of a slain FBI agent, become the Shield. This super-powered "G-Man Extraordinary" was one of the first to wear a red, white, and blue uniform in *Pep Comics* (January 1940). The following month, in *Science Comics* (February 1940), Bill Powers donned a flag-colored costume and cape to become the Eagle. One month prior to Captain America's debut, Fawcett Comics premiered its patriotic superhero, Minute Man, in *Master Comics* (February 1941). The same month Marvel Comics's Captain America hit the newsstands also saw the appearance in *Feature Comics* (March 1941) of the comics' first female super-patriot, known simply as "USA" (or "the Spirit of Old Glory").

Captain America, if not the first, was the best-realized version of a patriotic crime fighter. The name, the costume, and the dynamic art by Simon and Kirby made the character one of the best-selling comic books of 1941.

Within six months of Captain America's debut, there were more than two dozen red, white, and blue imitators. Captain Courageous from *Banner Comics* and Captain Freedom from *Speed Comics* appeared the same month (May 1941) and were quickly followed by another nationalistic hero from *Marvel Mystery Comics* called The Patriot (July 1941).

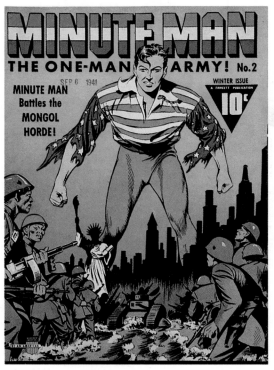

Minute Man #2 © 1941 Fawcett Publications, Inc.

By late summer, the floodgate opened for a wave of patriotic guys and gals, including Captain Victory (August 1941), Miss Victory (August 1941), Miss America (August 1941), U.S. Jones (August 1941), Yankee Eagle (August 1941), Yank and Doodle (August 1941), Pat Patriot (August 1941), Yankee Doodle Jones (September 1941), Fighting Yank (September 1941), Captain Flag (September 1941), The Flag (October 1941), Major Victory (October 1941), Super-American (October 1941), Star Spangled Kid and Stripesy (October 1941), Yankee Boy (November 1941), and Flag-Man (December 1941). All of these heroes were punching Nazis months before the United States entered World War II.

Bill Everett, who had the Sub-Mariner smashing Nazi submarines as early as February 1940 in *Marvel Mystery Comics*, recalled the mood at the time: "You could wave the flag like crazy. Most of us were flag-wavers, and I was one of the biggest." Many comic book artists at the time, like Everett, were young men of draft age who were highly patriotic.

Everett recalled that "I wanted to do some of that red-white-and-blue stuff as much as anyone else did—and this was a beautiful outlet and a change of scenery, a geographical cure, what have you. I was getting tired of dreaming up situations for the Sub-Mariner, and here was a built-in, ready-made situation; it was a patriotic thing, and it was the thing to do. So it was a natural."

The Nazis were natural enemies. If we couldn't fight them on the battlefield yet, we could salve our isolationist guilt by having our comic book heroes do our dirty work. Consequently, Captain America fought the Nazi mastermind known as the Red Skull, while Captain Marvel, Jr. squared off against Captain Nazi in *Master Comics*. The Shield and Dusty fought the Hun and the Son of the Hun (The Mad Nazi Rat!) in *Pep* and *Shield-Wizard Comics,* while the Hangman defended America's honor against Captain Swastika. Everyone from the Fighting Yank to the Black Cat was watching for Nazi saboteurs and spies on the home front.

By late 1941, our superheroes pretty much had the Nazis under control, but even they were unprepared for our first enemy of the war. On December 7, 1941, both the real world and the imaginary world of comic books changed forever. No longer would America's battles be fought by comic book characters and no longer were the Nazis our only concern. Pearl Harbor changed all of that.

America was at war.

A Good War Makes You Strong

The war years from 1942 to 1945 changed the comic book industry forever. Artists, writers, and editors were drafted into the service and paper shortages prevented new publishers from entering the field.

World's Finest Comics #7
© 1942 DC Comics, Inc.
Jack Burnley.

Yet at the same time, established comic book companies and their superhero characters enjoyed their greatest popularity ever. Sales of all comic books, and especially superhero comics, climbed steadily through the war years, thanks to an increased audience of children and servicemen.

The wartime shortage of adult labor led to three million schoolchildren between the ages of twelve and seventeen working by the summer of 1943. With the entry of more teenagers and children into the workplace to replace drafted adults, young readers had more money to spend on comic books and movies. By the early war years, 95 percent of all eight- to eleven-year-olds and eighty-four percent of all teenagers were regular comic book readers. More significantly, thirty-five percent of all young adults at the time (eighteen to thirty years old) also read comic books. Many of these readers came from the growing ranks of servicemen.

Of all the men in WWII training camps, forty-four percent read comics regularly and nearly two-thirds of them occasionally. At PXs, comic books outsold *Saturday Evening Post, Life*, and *Reader's Digest* combined by a ratio of ten to one. A special overseas edition of 35,000 copies of *Superman* went to the troops each month. By 1944, one out of every four magazines the government sent overseas was a comic book. The twelve million men and women in uniform, as well as those on the war's home front, were voracious readers, of comics and other books. Paperback sales went from sales of several hundred thousand in 1940 to forty million by the war's end. Bibles were rationed.

William Woolfolk, one of the most prolific comic book writers of the 1940s, recalled that right before the war ended, comic books were selling at an unheard of rate. "They were selling *102 percent*; that is, they were selling beyond the *spoilage* rate. If they had a magazine just lying around tattered, they would not turn it back because it would sell eventually."

Although sales were high, publishers could only print so many comic books because of wartime paper allotments. Paper, like all other commodities, was rationed and controlled by the government. Not only was the number of titles a publisher could print limited, but eventually even the page length of comic books had to be reduced. In a December 27, 1943, *Newsweek* article, "Escapist Paydirt: Comic Books Influence Friends and Make Plenty of Money Too," it was reported that comic book publishers would have to drop their page counts by four to eight pages to absorb a fifteen percent paper slash imposed by the government. "But the publishers," *Newsweek* noted, "expect no decrease in their output, now rollicking along at 25,000,000 copies monthly. Nor is the cut in size expected to affect mounting retail sales of the frankly escapist literature, which in 1943 added up close to $30,000,000."

Describing the booming prosperity of the war-years' comic book market, the article observed that "about 125 titles, the output of two dozen publishers, are currently on the newsstands. The average comic remains on the stands for a

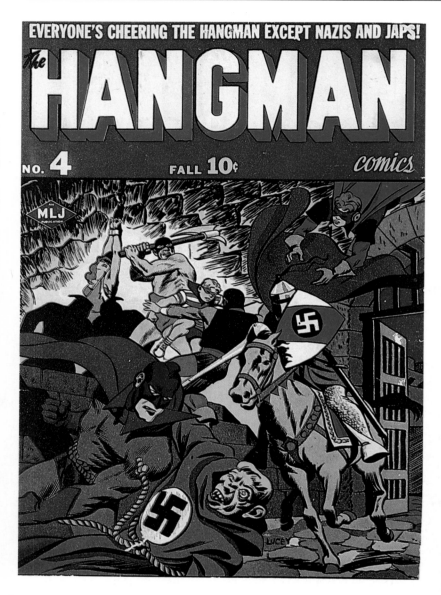

EVERYONE'S CHEERING THE HANGMAN EXCEPT NAZIS AND JAPS!

THE HANGMAN

NO. 4   FALL 10¢   comics

*Hangman Comics #4 © 1942
Archie Comic Publications,
Inc.* Harry Lucey.

they drew around the clock to stockpile stories for their publishers before they were shipped overseas. A few comic book studios, like those headed by Jack Binder and Jerry Iger, hired women as replacements. The artists left behind were either too old, too young, or too infirm for the military draft.

William Woolfolk, one of the first full-time comic book writers, recalled that "the war had broken out and writers were in very short supply. They were being drafted as prime cannon fodder." After three months in the service, Woolfolk received a medical discharge and promptly resumed his comic book writing career. With shortages in the industry, Woolfolk found himself being fought over by Fawcett Publishing and Quality Comics. He compromised by working for them both at the same time, as well as other companies.

"I always worked for four firms at once," Woolfolk recalled. "It was safer than working for only two or three companies." During the war years, Woolfolk established himself as the highest paid comic book writer in the 1940s. "I made $15,000 a year when people were making $1,000."

Woolfolk wrote the adventures of Captain Marvel, Plastic Man, Superman, the Spirit, Batman, Steel Sterling, the Shield, the Hangman, Doll Man, Blackhawk, Captain America, Human Torch, the Wizard, and a few dozen other heroes for Quality, Fawcett, DC, and Marvel comics. "Never along the way did I invent anything," Woolfolk admitted. "I was like an expert handyman. I sort of ran around doing any feature that was available. The editors were all delighted because it was smooth and they didn't have to edit it much. I handled anything that came along."

Another prolific writer during the war years and beyond was Otto Binder. He recalled launching new titles in those days with "machine gun rapidity." After writing comic scripts for three dollars a page before the war broke out, Binder recalled that the rates "kept shooting up through wartime to reach a standard rate of ten dollars per page. All of us writers at that time called it The Golden Rut, with a sneer, all the way to the bank."

The writers and artists on the home front kept the comic book industry rocketing along during its wartime growth. They also frankly poured their own pent-up patriotism into the superheroes and fought their own private wars across the comic pages. Comic book covers and stories exploded with images of costumed heroes beating the Axis powers.

An April 18, 1942, article in *Business Week*

month and normal returns range from 20 to 30 percent; right now, however, there are practically no returns at all."

With the growing success of comic books during the war years also came growing pains. The comic book business was still a young industry with mostly young workers. At the advent of war, most of the writers, artists, and editors were under twenty-five years of age—prime draft age. By early 1942, nearly every major comic book artist had either enlisted, been inducted, or was somehow involved with the military war effort.

Many tried to keep up with assignments while in training camps; Jerry Siegel continued writing *Superman* scripts while serving in the Army; artist Bill Ward sketched out stories on and off duty. After artists received draft notices,

noted that "one powerful ally, ignored by admirals and generals, is counted on by the kids of America to confound the enemy if the going gets really tough. It is Superman who, as every urchin knows, stops sixteen-inch shells with his bare hands, lifts automobiles with one finger, flies through concrete walls without the aid of dynamite. He could just as cheerfully kick in the hulls of the Jap battle fleet or knock down Nazi bombers with his knuckles because he's always in there punching on the side of virtue."

From 1942 through 1944, comic book covers became a wartime tableau of Nazi and Japanese villainy. German soldiers were pictured as depraved madmen, while the Japanese were shown as subhuman monsters. Alex Schomburg, who was one of the busiest comic book cover artists of the 1940s, recalled that during the war years the publishers told him to do "anything to make the Japs look ugly or the Nazis look like punks."

Superman was twisting tank turrets, Sub-Mariner was punching out submarines, and Captain America was sabotaging V-2 rockets. As Captain Marvel artist C.C. Beck recalled, "During the war, all the heroes had to be out there stopping bullets and tweaking Hitler's nose and punching Hirohito in the teeth and everything else. We had to do it for propaganda purposes."

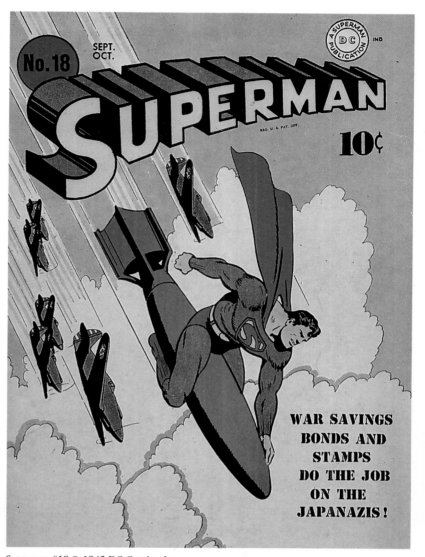

Superman #18 © 1942 DC Comics, Inc.

Sub-Mariner #10 © 1943 Marvel Entertainment Group, Inc.
Alex Schomburg.

Captain Marvel, in particular, did his part for the war effort by enlisting in *two* branches of the service: "Captain Marvel Joins the Army" (*Captain Marvel Adventures,* June 1942) and "Captain Marvel Joins the Navy" (*Captain Marvel Adventures,* September 1943). In the August 1942 issue, Captain Marvel "Swats the Japs" and a few months later "Smacks the Axis" (November 1942). Fawcett Publishing also had its most popular hero fighting Hitler with an "honesty ray" and lambasting a villain called Nippo the Nipponese in a story called the "Second Pearl Harbor."

Pearl Harbor was, of course, a recurrent theme in early 1942 comic books. The battle cry and most popular song of the time encouraged all Americans to "Remember Pearl Harbor!" The comic books were not going to let us forget either.

The Shield and the Hangman rang a huge Liberty Bell on the cover of *Pep Comics* (April

Captain Marvel Adventures #12 © 1942 Fawcett Publications, Inc.

All Star Comics # 14
© 1942 DC Comics, Inc.

Zip Comics #27 © 1942
Archie Comic Publications,
Inc. Charles Biro.

Exciting Comics #27 © 1943 Better Publications, Inc. Alex Schomburg.

1942) while urging its readers to "Remember Pearl Harbor!" That same month, *Captain America Comics* (April 1942) featured its "All-Out For America Issue!" with Captain America threatening a startled Japanese: "You started it—now we'll finish it! Remember Pearl Harbor!"

On the front cover of the May 1942 issue of *Daredevil Comics* was the blurb: "Daredevil goes to war and vows that one hundred Japs will fall for every drop of American blood spilled by their treachery! AMERICA WILL REMEMBER PEARL HARBOR!" Just in case readers missed the subtle pitch on the cover, there was also an advertisement which promised: "Extra! Play 'Slap the Jap' Exciting New Game Inside!"

In the June 1942 issue of *All Star Comics*, written a month after Pearl Harbor, writer Gardner Fox sent DC Comics's greatest heroes (Hawkman, Atom, Dr. Fate, Dr. Mid-Nite, The Spectre, Sandman, Johnny Thunder, and Wonder Woman) to battle in "The Justice Society Joins the War on Japan!" Later that year, in *All Star Comics* (December 1942), Fox moved the heroes behind the scenes to Occupied Europe in a humanitarian story entitled "Food for Starving Patriots."

Besides stories about superheroes battling Japanese and Nazis, World War II-era comics also emphasized the need for Americans to work together for victory on the home front. In "The Justice Society of America Fights for a United

America," (*All Star Comics* April 1943), Gardner Fox told the story, in his words, about how "the Nazis were trying to weaken America by turning native-born Americans against immigrants, whites against blacks and Orientals (especially the Japanese-Americans), and the men against the women. In the end, they all realized that *all* people had to work together." Pulling together, even in the comic books, was the overriding media message from 1942 to 1945.

Kids were expected to do their part in the war effort. Along the bottom margin of comic book pages in the war years were messages like "Too Young To Enlist—Buy War Stamps and Bonds!" and "For Victory—Save Fats, Waste Paper and Old Rubber!"

Young readers were encouraged by superheroes to buy war stamps and bonds. On the winter 1942 cover of *World's Finest Comics*, Superman, Batman, and Robin exhort a gang of cheering kids to "Sink the Japanazis with Bonds and Stamps!"

Advertisements in comic books starring Captain Marvel, Mary Marvel, and Captain Marvel, Jr., showed youngsters how to participate in paper salvage drives and save scrap metal. (Ironically, the kids were so successful with their World War II paper collections, they destroyed almost all of the comic books from that time period.)

Even as the war was winding down by early 1945, the comic books and their heroes were still helping shape young attitudes. On the cover of *Action Comics* (July 1945), Superman makes his last wartime appearance. Under a blurb on the cover which encourages Americans to "Back the 7th War Loan," Superman is burying a Japanese officer alive beneath a pile of war bonds. "It isn't Superman who is doing this," the Man of Steel says as he dumps a load of bonds on the soldier's head, "it's the American people!"

A story entitled "This Is Our Enemy" (*All Star Comics*, Spring 1945) was rushed into print just weeks before Germany surrendered. In the book-length story, author Gardner Fox uses the heroes in the Justice Society of America to deliver a propaganda story about Germany's long history of militarism and warfare, in an effort to encourage popular support for the formation of a United Nations organization.

The months between Germany's defeat (May 7, 1945) and the end of the war with Japan (August 14, 1945) saw comic book heroes resolutely wiping up Japs on Pacific islands and kamikaze saboteurs at home. By the time comic books dated October–November 1945 appeared on the newsstands, the war was over.

ATOMIC BLASTS AND HEROIC FALLOUT

After the war ended, the comic book industry went through a period of readjustment and growth which, ironically, led to the ultimate decline and demise of the superheroes of the Golden Age.

With the war over, paper shortages became a thing of the past and comic book publishers unleashed their pent-up production. During 1945, more than 1,100 different comic book issues were published. The next year, there were more than 1,500 comic books, the largest increase since the beginning of the decade.

A *New York Times* article from June 25, 1946, stated that the sales of National Comics Group (DC Comics) rose for its twenty-six comic magazines from 20,011,000 issues during the first quarter of 1945 to 26,340,000 by the first quarter of 1946. By the last year of the decade, there would be twice as many comic books published as in any year during the war.

With the war over and paper readily available, first-time publishers were able to enter the comic book industry. Among the new and mostly small publishers producing comic books in the postwar years were Charlton Comics, Croyden Publishing, Rural Home, St. John Publishing, Spark Publications, and O. W. Publishing. Although these new publishers were dwarfed by established companies like DC Comics, Fawcett Publishing, and Quality Comics, they too signaled a vital growth in the field.

Max Gaines was a familiar face among the new comic book publishers of 1946. Having sold his interest in All-American Comics to Harry Donenfeld at DC Comics in 1945, Gaines began his own company called Educational Comics. The company, which published comics like *Picture Stories from the Bible* and *Picture Stories from American History*, would become better known as

Sun Girl #1 © 1948 Marvel Entertainment Group, Inc.

Entertaining Comics (EC) under the editorship of Gaines's son William, who would popularize the notorious 1950s horror comics.

The advent of the new publishers and the increased number of comics from established companies after the war was helped by the return of artists, writers, and editors from the service. Joe Simon, Jack Kirby, Bill Everett, Will Eisner, Reed Crandall, Ogden Whitney, Gill Fox, Bob Powell, and dozens of other experienced artists returned from the war, anxious to begin a freelance career. After the war years, the old comic book shops were no longer as influential. Many artists who worked in the shops before the war returned as freelancers or worked for companies like Quality or DC. Some, like Bob Powell, started small shops of their own.

New artists also came from the ranks of veterans who returned to art school on the G.I. Bill, such as Wally Wood and Roy Krenkel. Carmine Infantino, Joe Kubert, and Alex Toth began working for DC Comics right after the war. Infantino recalled that "we were the kids of that period, the new look—a new wave into the field."

While there was postwar growth in the comic book industry, superhero comics had reached a plateau around the end of the war years. No major new superhero character was introduced after the war. The few superhero titles introduced after 1944 were short lived and inconsequential. Even more telling, major heroes like Doctor Fate, the Hangman, Steel Sterling, and the Spectre made their last appearances in 1944.

Startling Comics #33
© *1945 Better Publications, Inc. Alex Schomburg.*

"All the G.I.s who'd been buying comics by the arm load in PXs were home living on twenty dollars a week in the real world."

While overall comic book sales increased after the war and into the early 1950s, it was because of the popularity of the new humor, crime, western, and romance comic books and not the superheroes. For example, during the war years more than 90 percent of the comic books published by DC Comics featured superheroes. Immediately after the war, however, superhero comics accounted for less than two-thirds of DC's business. By the end of the 1940s, they would make up barely half of DC's output.

Just as superheroes lost a large audience when servicemen became civilians, they also lost some of their inherent appeal by the war's end. The most obvious casualty of peace suffered by the superheroes was the disappearance of such satisfying villains as the Nazis and the Japanese. After four years of fighting spies, saboteurs, and

One of the most popular superhero comics of all times, *Captain Marvel Adventures*, hit its all-time high circulation in 1944 but then dropped steadily every year until it was selling at 50 percent of its war-years' high by 1949. Captain Marvel artist C.C. Beck blamed the decline in part on the postwar economy: "Gone were the huge sales of comic books to soldiers and sailors everywhere and to children of war industry workers who had been making big wages. Out of uniform, young men and women had to find jobs; they had no time to sit around reading comic books any more."

Writer Joe Gill, who began working for Marvel Comics in 1945, echoed Beck's observation that the decline of superhero comics was due in part to a loss of its most avid readership:

Then the war ended. As for the comic book heroes and heroines, they had nothing to do. They had become so humanized that they could no longer fly around, chase outlandish villains, or fight impossible monsters as they once had done; nobody believed in that old fairy tale stuff any more. The comic book industry, which had grown to enormous proportions during the war, collapsed like a punctured balloon and by the early 1950s, it was a dying relic of what it had once been. The Golden Age was over.
— *C.C. Beck,
Captain Marvel artist*

all the soldiers of Germany and Japan, comic book heroes had to turn to more prosaic villains like common criminals and street thugs—certainly not as exciting as despicable Axis agents.

In addition to fighting domestic crime, comic book heroes became social reformers and dealt with postwar ills. The Justice Society of America and its junior members, for example, tackled the problem of juvenile delinquency in a story called "The Plight of a Nation" (*All Star Comics*, April 1948).

Daredevil and the Little Wise Guys (*Daredevil Comics*, March 1948) also tried to address the problems of juvenile crime brought about by poverty and broken families. Daredevil tells a group of concerned parents:

> Some say combating juvenile delinquency is a problem for the schools—others say it belongs to the community—still others say, let the police and reform schools worry about it! While it is chiefly a problem for the parents and guardians, I believe all the adults of the community must share the responsibility of setting a good example for the children!

Other postwar problems were addressed in *Contact Comics* (September 1945). Black Venus, a costumed heroine who is actually physical therapist Mary Roche, concerns herself with the plight of disabled veterans: "Back from the wars come our heroes, to the world they saved from destruction! What does the future hold for them? Is there a place for the wounded, or will they become the casualties of peace as well as of the war?"

The question, in this case, might just as easily have been asked about the Golden Age superheroes, who also appeared on their way to becoming war casualties. By 1946, publishers were dropping long-running heroes like Starman, Magno, Angel, and Sandman. Over the next three years, the Black Hood, Black Owl, the Shield, Fighting Yank, Black Terror, Captain America, Human Torch, and the Sub-Mariner made their last Golden Age appearances before fading into limbo. Their titles were canceled or their books converted into more popular western and romance comics.

In one respect, the decline and eventual demise of the Golden Age of superheroes began with the dawning of the Atomic Age. The atomic bomb, with its real powers of awesome destruction, overshadowed the imaginary superheroics of costumed men and women. Could even Cap-

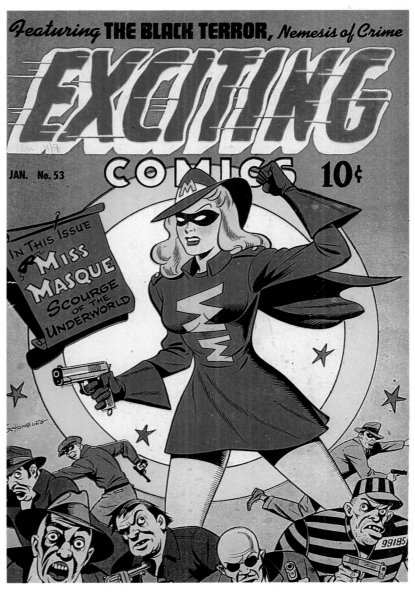

Exciting Comics #53
© 1947 Better Publications, Inc. Alex Schomburg.

tain Marvel, for example, protect us from the destruction we unleashed on Hiroshima on August 6, 1945?

On the front cover of the October 1946 issue of *Captain Marvel Adventures*, the world's mightiest mortal faces a rain of atomic missiles in the story "Captain Marvel Battles the Dread Atomic War!"

As the story begins, America's major cities are under an atomic attack by an unknown enemy. Captain Marvel first races to Chicago, but is too late: "Not one soul is alive in Chicago! Four million people—wiped out like flies! It's horrible . . . horrible . . . horrible! I'll go mad if I keep thinking about it!"

Before Captain Marvel can prevent other atomic bombs from exploding, "greed, confu-

Captain Marvel Adventures #66 © 1946 Fawcett Publications, Inc.

family replies: "I guess we'd all better learn to live and get along together—one nation with all nations and one person with all other persons—so that the terrible atomic war will never occur!"

Like all Americans, superheroes tried to come to grips with the Atomic Age. Superman dutifully checked out the latest weapon of mass destruction in a story entitled "Superman Covers the Atom Bomb Test!" (*Action Comics*, October 1946). Captain Marvel, Jr. helped out by tracking down "The Atomic Bomb on the Loose." Superheroes in general were busy all through 1946 and 1947 with keeping the atomic bomb out of the hands of enemy agents. In many respects, however, the heroes themselves seemed dwarfed by the greater consideration of the Bomb. When heroes like Captain Marvel and the Fighting Yank worried about nuclear proliferation, it diminished their omnipotence.

One way of dealing with the Atomic Age was to embrace it. Within months after Hiroshima, a wave of new atomic-created superheroes appeared on the scene, their awesome powers somehow derived from atomic energy itself. Atomic Man, who made his debut in *Headline Comics* (November 1945), emits gamma rays through his lead-gloved right hand. The Atomic Thunderbolt, who appeared in his own magazine

sion, and madness sweep through the world—and then all the nations release their atomic bombs at each other!"

"This is horrible," Captain Marvel cries. "I can't stop it! By now every major city on Earth is bombed! And later, the radioactive rays will spread out like a creeping plague and . . . groan!" Captain Marvel was helpless to prevent us from destroying ourselves.

Fortunately, at the end of the story we learn it was only a television documentary to show people the perils of atomic war. A relieved family clicks off their TV set and Dad turns to the children: "The world just can't afford another war, because it would wipe out all civilization and human life! Remember that, kids!"

To which the precocious little tyke of the

Captain Marvel, Jr. #53 © 1947 Fawcett Publications, Inc.
Bud Thompson.

Headline Comics #17 © 1946 Prize Publications

superheroes (and these were usually either Superman or Batman), compared to 96 percent of its titles ten years earlier.

Not only DC Comics but all comic book companies were experiencing lackluster sales of their superhero characters. At Fawcett Publishing, home of Captain Marvel, all of the Marvel superhero family was outsold by western comic books like *Tom Mix* and *Hopalong Cassidy*. Even the *Gabby Hayes* comic book out-performed *Captain Marvel, Jr.* by better than a million issues in 1949.

Besides poor sales, however, a longstanding lawsuit also threatened the survival of Captain Marvel. DC Comics, which had initially brought a copyright lawsuit against Captain Marvel and Fawcett Publishing in 1941, unsuccessfully fought its case in court through several years and ap-

Comic Cavalcade #14
© 1946 DC Comics, Inc.
Everett Hibbard.

(February 1946), had his atomic structure altered so that he was "immune to radioactivity and atomic explosions." Atoman, a new character from a new company (February 1946), is a superhero whose own body has become so radioactive "with radium and uranium that it can explode atoms" *inside* his body for "atomic strength." The new atomic heroes, however, faded within months of their introduction. Seemingly, the only comic book hero to benefit from the Atomic Age was the Atom, DC Comic's diminutive hero from *All-American Comics*, who enjoyed greater name recognition after the Bomb.

Even the Atom, however, was not immune to the tides of change. By the end of 1949, he had lost his regular series in *Flash Comics* and was only appearing in *All Star Comics* as a member of the Justice Society of America. Similarly, other JSA members were being phased out by the end of the 1940s. The Flash, Hawkman, and Green Lantern no longer had their series or comic book titles by the end of 1949 and were making appearances only in *All Star Comics*. By early 1951, the Justice Society of America itself made its last appearance. DC Comics gradually moved away from costumed heroes to other titles and genres. With the demise of *All Star Comics*, less than one-fourth of DC Comics's early 1950s titles featured

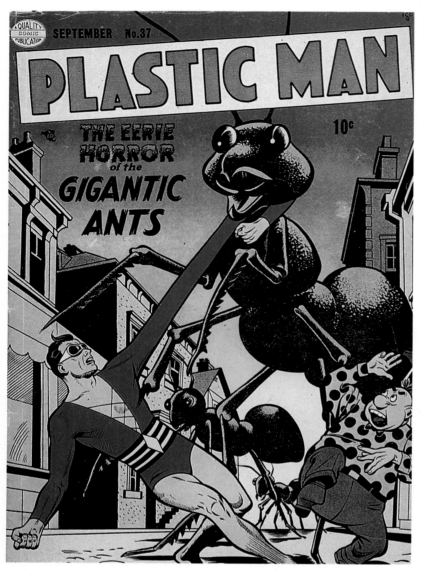

*Plastic Man #37 © 1952
Comic Magazines, Inc.*

Chief Captain Marvel artist C.C. Beck recalled that he never read the Superman comics. "I didn't have them on my desk. I never looked at them. There was no need to." Beck recalled that he did not believe the judge in the copyright trial ever read a Superman comic book either, or any comic books, for that matter. "The judge didn't read comics, never looked at one. He didn't want to be connected with such a sordid affair anyway—like one whorehouse suing another. Didn't do his reputation any good."

Faced with mounting legal costs, declining comic book sales, and a precedent ruling that Captain Marvel did infringe on Superman's copyright, Fawcett Publishing gave up the fight. In June 1953, Otto Binder got the word as he began the first chapter of a new Marvel Family story. Captain Marvel was dead.

With the end of the Marvel Family, Plastic Man was the only non-DC Comics's superhero left from the Golden Age of Comics. At DC Comics in 1953, titles were rearranged and editorial positions shuffled. When the dust settled, only Wonder Woman, Superman, Batman, Aquaman, and Green Arrow were left of what had once been the world's largest stable of superheroes.

The Golden Age of Superheroes had ended.

peals. Finally, in 1951, DC Comics was granted a new trial.

The artists and writers who worked on Captain Marvel insisted that there had never been any intentional attempt to copy Superman. Rod Reed, an editor and writer at Fawcett, recalled that "one thing I do remember is that during my tenure, we never copied Superman. It was stressed that there should not be even a kidding reference to anything Supermanly."

Otto Binder, who described himself as Captain Marvel's "chief writer and idea-man from mid-1941 till the end," saw no similarities between the "dead-serious grimness and plodding consistency of Superman" and the "humor, fantasy, and whimsy" of his character. "This I can state categorically—not one story idea was ever lifted from Superman!"

The Heroes

There were more than 700 costumed comic book characters in the Golden Age of Comics (1938–1954).

Some of these characters, like the Ferret, Green Ghost, Boogeyman, and Spider Woman appeared once or twice and then disappeared in the flood of superheroes on the newsstands. Other costumed characters of the Golden Age are more properly classified as aviators, magicians, cowboys, detectives, jungle men, or space men than superheroes.

The fifty heroes profiled in this section are among the best-remembered, historically significant, or simply most representative of a publisher or type. Their origins, as well as their appearances in the Golden Age of Comics, are noted, along with background information on their creation and history.

Facing Page: *Cat-Man Comics Vol. 3 #2* © *1944 Holyoke Publishing Company*

AMAZING MAN

September 1939 *Amazing-Man Comics* #5
Centaur Publications

John Aman, "an orphan of superb physical structure," was adopted by a secret Council of Seven masters located in the mountains of Tibet. They instilled in the boy "all the qualities of one who would dominate the world of men" and gave him the "power to make himself disappear in a cloud of green vapor." With his strenuous physical and mental training completed at the age of twenty-five, Aman is sent to America as Amazing Man to battle crime. A-Man (as he quickly became known) not only had to fight criminals but also had to defend himself from mystic mental attacks of a renegade member of the Council

Amazing-Man Comics #23
© 1941 Centaur Publications

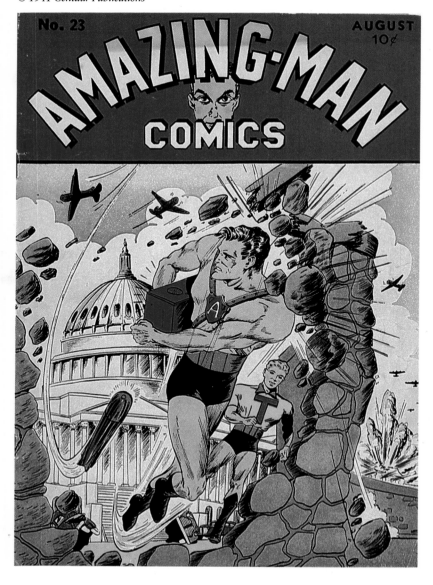

of Seven known as the Great Question. His other-worldly battles with the "Great Que" (as A-Man calls him) spilled over into World War II, with the evil Council master taking the side of the Axis and A-Man fighting for democracy. Other continuing characters included A-Man's girlfriend Zona and a Johnny-come-lately sidekick, Tommy The Amazing Kid (August 1941).

Amazing Man was one of the most unusual early comic book characters. Created months before the great outpouring of superheroes in 1940 and 1941, Amazing Man had few precedents and no set rules to follow. He did not wear a costume for the first six months and possessed an interesting amorality for a superhero. In one episode, he steals an airplane from the police and "coldly drops bombs on every building in sight."

Amazing Man was the most popular superhero from Centaur Comics, a small company which played a pivotal role in the development of the young comic book industry. Many early comic books consisted of reprinted Sunday comic strips. Joe Hardie and editor Lloyd Jacquet of Centaur Publishing, however, were looking for artists who could draw *original* material for their growing line of comic books. A gangly twenty-year-old with wire-rim glasses and a pipe clenched between his teeth applied for the position: Bill Everett.

Everett recalled that he created Amazing Man with Lloyd Jacquet and Joe Hardie, "but I don't remember the circumstances, how his creation came about." Everett wrote and drew the hero for the first seven issues before his time was taken up by another new hero, the Sub-Mariner.

Golden Age Appearances
Amazing Man Comics 5–27 (9/39–1/42)
Stars and Stripes Comics 2–6 (5/41–12/41)

THE ANGEL

November 1939 *Marvel Comics* #1
Marvel Comics

The Angel was Marvel Comics's unofficial captain of its second string of superheroes. Although a distant fourth in popularity behind Captain America, the Human Torch, and the Sub-Mariner, the Angel appeared in more than 100 stories during the 1940s—twice as many as any other "minor" Marvel superhero.

Originally appearing in the first Marvel comic book, along with the Human Torch and the Sub-Mariner, the Angel had neither secret identity nor superpowers, although he could soar through the air by the special properties of his cape. He appeared in both civilian clothes and in his wing-emblazoned, blue bodysuit and was recognized as the Angel in both cases. He also apparently had no last name and no formal occupation.

What the Angel did have was class. Nattily dressed, the dashing blond Angel sported an Errol Flynn mustache and occasionally savored a bowl of tobacco. He devoted all his time to helping out anyone in distress—particularly the ladies. He doubled as a suave private investigator and costumed vigilante.

He actually bore a not coincidental likeness to another urbane fictional detective hero, the Saint, as written by Leslie Charteris. The first Angel story was loosely based on Charteris's *The Saint in New York*. The similarities between Charteris's Simon Templar, the sophisticated personage known as the Saint, and the Angel were intentional, according to the character's creator, artist Paul Gustavson.

Gustavson, who drew and usually scripted the Angel for its first two years, was only twenty-two-years old at the time, but that didn't mean he was inexperienced. After breaking into the Chesler Shop in 1938 with one- and two-page gag strips, he drew several costumed adventurers for Centaur Publishing, such as the Arrow, a masked archer with no identity who began in the *Funny Pages* (September 1938). The Arrow was the first costumed adventurer in the comic books after Superman. Gustavson would also help originate another early masked comic book hero, the Fantom of the Fair, for *Amazing Mystery Funnies* (July 1939).

The Angel, like some of the other features that Gustavson drew and wrote, owed a heavy debt to the pulp magazine heroes and detectives. Like the Shadow and the Spider, the Angel had few compunctions about operating outside the law and using severe measures—especially if it meant scaring the hell out of criminals.

In his first appearance (*Marvel Comics*, October 1939), the Angel hides in the back seat of a thug's car. As the bad guy drives off, the Angel jumps him from behind and strangles him. He pins a note on the dead man's chest for the police to discover: "Six big men went for a ride—one took a dive—and then there were five!!"

The Angel always went for dramatic lighting. Whenever possible, he would cast a shadow of a giant winged angel over the eyes of evildoers. Like the pulp heroes, he was a guardian angel of the weak, the helpless, and usually the blonde. And, like the pulp novels, the Angel stories were

Marvel Mystery Comics #69 © 1946 Marvel Entertainment Group, Inc.

heavy on horror and macabre villains with titles like "The Banquet of Blood," "The Wolfman Terror," "The Case of Professor Torture," and "The Haunted Heritage of the Gobbling Ghost." Besides Gustavson, other artists who drew the character included George Mandel, Mike Roy, and Jimmy Thompson.

Reportedly a favorite of Marvel Comics publisher Martin Goodman, the Angel appeared for seven years in *Marvel Mystery Comics*, was the secondary feature in *Sub-Mariner Comics*, and had the lead in the second series of *Mystic Comics*. Nevertheless, the Angel had winged his way into oblivion by the end of 1946.

Golden Age Appearances
Marvel Comics 1 (11/39)
Marvel Mystery Comics 2–79 (12/39–12/46)
Sub-Mariner 1–21 (Spring/41–Winter/46)
All Winners Comics (1) 1 (Summer/41)
Mystic Comics (2) 1–3 (10/44–Winter/44)
Daring Comics 10 (Winter/45)

THE ATOM

October 1940 *All-American Comics* #19
DC Comics

Al Pratt, a five-foot-tall college student, is nicknamed "Atom Al" by his teasing friends:

All Star Comics #37
© 1947 DC Comics, Inc.
Alex Toth. The Atom,
as a member of the Justice
Society of America.

The Atom was created by Bill O'Connor and Ben Flinton for *All-American Comics*. Editor Sheldon Mayer recalled that the two men wrote and drew the feature interchangeably. Flinton and O'Connor, like many aspiring young comic book artists in the late 1930s, came to New York and promptly began to starve. Their first assignments through the Funnies Incorporated studio included stories for *Blue Bolt Comics* ("The Phantom Sub") and *Mystic Comics*.

The Atom was their first and only "big" feature. The two men were in the service by 1942 and story editor Ted Udall and artist Joe Gallagher continued the adventures of the "Mighty Mite."

Sheldon Mayer, the editor at *All-American Comics*, was not particularly impressed with the Atom. He was considered a definite second-string superhero. "I think the only reason anyone remembers him is that we also squeezed him into *All Star Comics* with Green Lantern and Hawkman."

In fact, the decision had been made to phase the Atom out of the Justice Society of America and he was dropped from *All Star Comics* with the Winter 1945 issue and replaced by Wildcat. Similarly, the Atom's last story was scheduled for *All-American Comics* #72 and his replacement was an adventure strip, the Black Pirate, who transferred from *Sensation Comics*.

After one absence, however, the Atom was back in the April 1946 issue of *All Star Comics*, where he would remain until its end in 1951. Within a few months, he would also be scheduled as a regular series for *Flash Comics* starting in 1947.

What occurred between the time the Atom was dropped and then reinstated took place on August 6, 1945, at Hiroshima. The atomic bomb made the word "atom" a household word. While other comic book publishers rushed out atom-bomb-inspired superheroes like Atomic Man and Atoman, DC Comics exploited the name of its existing hero. The Atom traded on his now trendy name and, unlike most superheroes, actually enjoyed more popularity after the war than before.

He received a bright new costume in August 1948 and was soon enjoying the capable artwork of Alex Toth and Paul Reinman.

Golden Age Appearances
All-American Comics 19–46, 48–61,70–72
 (10/40–4/46)
All Star Comics 3–26, 28–35, 37–57
 (Winter/40–2/51)
Big All-American Comic Book 1 (12/44)
Flash Comics 80, 82–85, 87, 89–95, 97–100,

"Hello little man—say 'Atom' are you standing in a hole or what?"

Pratt shuffles off, hanging his head, thinking: "Gee! How can I help being so small—I'll show them yet!"

After he is mugged in front of his girlfriend by a thug who calls him a "squirt," Pratt becomes obsessed with overcoming his small size. In a depressed state, he buys a meal for a bum down on his luck.

The bum is a former championship fight trainer and Pratt asks him if he could build him up. "Sure I could—you're not so bad—jus' a little soft—why I could make a li'l *Superman* out of you in less'n a year!"

With Al's determination and his trainer's program, he develops the strength of a giant. He decides to use his powers to fight crime and he wryly adopts the name of the Atom for his costumed alter ego.

102–104 (2/47–2/49)
Comic Cavalcade 22, 23, 28 (8/47–8/48)
Sensation Comics 86 (2/49)

BATMAN

May 1939 *Detective Comics #27*
DC Comics

Bruce Wayne, whose parents are murdered by a gunman, becomes a costumed, crime-fighting vigilante known as the Batman to avenge their deaths. Unlike Superman, Wayne has no unusual superpowers or extraterrestrial capabilities to help him in his mission of justice. He has only his natural athletic abilities and keen mental powers, which he develops through intensive training and self-discipline.

Not only is Batman a self-made superhero, he is a self-appointed judge, jury, and—in his early adventures—executioner of criminals. His dark motives of vengeance and punishment put him on equal footing with the evildoers he pursues. Like them, he works best under darkness and away from the scrutiny of law and order.

"I thought it would be more exciting," artist Bob Kane recalled, "for Batman to work outside the law rather than inside it. I guess growing up in the Bronx, we used to be vigilantes to survive."

Batman #38 © 1946 DC Comics, Inc. Dick Sprang.

Batman #65 © 1951 DC Comics, Inc. Winslow Mortimer.

The early Batman character was a loner who hid beneath a costume to strike fear into the hearts of his enemies. He came from the pulp magazine tradition of 1930s costumed avengers like the Shadow, the Phantom Detective, and the Spider. If there were two lineages of the superhero family, Batman came from the night and Superman from the day. Even their costumes, one bright red and blue and the other gray and black, belied their different approaches to life—and death. Batman even used a gun to kill a criminal in the first issue of his magazine—an unthinkable option for Superman.

After the first year Batman appeared, Kane recalled that the editors felt the character should be brought more onto the side of the law. "The policy was to make him an honorary member of the police force who was outside the law but still working in it. The whole moral climate changed

Batman #25 © 1944 DC Comics, Inc. Jerry Robinson.

after 1940—you couldn't kill or shoot villains."

Batman slowly changed from a pulp vigilante to a heroic detective during the course of his first year. By the April 1940 issue of *Detective Comics,* the "humanization" of Batman was complete with the addition of his youthful sidekick and ward, Robin the Boy Wonder. Batman was now a mentor and a protector.

Bob Kane remembered adding Robin to the strip specifically to "lighten" it up and also to give the younger readers someone to identify with. "I visualized that every kid would like to be a Robin . . . a laughing daredevil, free—no school, no homework, living in a mansion above the Batcave, riding in the Batmobile. It appealed to the imagination of every kid in the world."

As Jerry Robinson, Kane's early art assistant on Batman recalled, "Robin completed the basic cast, the basic appeal. He gave the kids a character they could directly relate to. A kid might imagine himself growing up to be the Batman, but in a realistic fantasy, he'd imagine himself meeting the Batman, helping him, like Robin."

The other supporting characters in the Batman strip included Police Commissioner Gordon, who controlled the Batsignal-spotlight, and Alfred, the loyal butler at Wayne mansion. It was the villains, however, who were the most memorable.

The Penguin, a whimsical character partially inspired by a Kool Cigarette ad, was "The Man of the Thousand Umbrellas." Two-Face, a

schizoid who made every decision by flipping a coin, was based on the Frederic March movie *Dr. Jekyll and Mr. Hyde* (1932). The slinky Catwoman, Kane recalled, was added to give the feature a little "sex appeal" and he remembered basing the character partially upon actress Jean Harlow. The ultimate Batman villain was, of course, the Joker.

Kane recalled that the Joker ("the best villain ever created, outside of Moriarity in Sherlock Holmes [stories]") was the product of writer Bill Finger's imagination and was based upon a photograph of Conrad Veidt from a 1928 movie *The Man Who Laughs.* Finger actually had a hand in the creation of almost all the Batman villains, as well as much of the other mythos and trappings, from Batplane to Batcave.

Artist Jerry Robinson, who gradually took over much of the art chores on Batman, including drawing the covers, recalled that "Bill Finger was a fantastic writer; perfect for the medium. Unlike most of the writers in the early comic book industry, Finger wrote very visually. If the story took place aboard an ocean liner, Bill would've researched the physical makeup of the ship and staged the action around that particular set. His stories were well-plotted and paced."

Editor Jack Schiff, who guided Batman's fortunes for a while in the 1940s, described Finger's

Detective Comics #96 © 1945 DC Comics, Inc. Jack Burnley.

Batman stories as possessing "an excellent pulp and comic sense. His stories had that schmaltz, those nice little touches of humor."

As Batman appeared in other comics, as well as in his own daily and Sunday newspaper strips, other writers and artists worked on the feature. In addition to Jerry Robinson, other 1940s artists on Batman included George Roussos, Jack Burnley, and Dick Sprang. Besides Bill Finger, other writers on Batman included Don Cameron (who created the Alfred the butler), Gardner Fox, Alvin Schwartz, Jack Schiff, and William Woolfolk.

Batman would be one of the half dozen Golden Age superheroes to survive beyond the early 1950s.

Golden Age Appearances

Detective Comics 27–216 (5/39–2/55)
Batman 1–89 (Spring/40–2/55)
New York World's Fair Comics 2 (1940)
World's Finest 1–74 (Spring/41–1/55)
All Star Comics 7, 36 (10/41–8/47)
Real Fact Comics 5 (11/46)
Superman 76 (5/52)

THE BLACK CAT

August 1941 *Pocket Comics* #1
Harvey Comics

"Linda Turner, Hollywood Star and America's Sweetheart, becomes bored with her ultra-sophisticated life of movie make-believe and takes to crime-fighting in her most dynamic role of all as the . . . BLACK CAT!"

Linda Turner, a successful movie star, is becoming bored with her life until she suspects that one of her movie directors may be a Nazi spy. She decides to solve the mystery herself.

Her dad, an amateur sleuth, encourages his daughter in her new role as a Hollywood detective. Linda receives the intense training that a movie stunt girl must undergo. She learns how to ride a motorcycle, throw a lariat, and take a fall. She is a judo expert. Since her suspected Nazi movie director has a phobia about black cats, Linda devises a Black Cat costume to disguise her true identity and to strike terror in his heart.

The Black Cat ("Hollywood's Glamorous Detective Star") was Harvey Comics's most popular superhero. The Hollywood starlet's name—Linda Turner—was a combination of two movie stars, Linda Darnell and Lana Turner. Al Gabriele was the original artist and Pierce Rice and Arturo Cazeneuve drew some of the early stories.

Black Cat #13 © 1948
Harvey Features Syndicate.
Lee Elias.

Linda, in her Black Cat alter ego, enjoyed having a secret dual-relationship with newpaper columnist Rick Horne. As a movie actress, she helped make the two a glamorous couple. As the Black Cat, she could be his rescuing heroine.

The Black Cat, however, was certainly more than just a costumed romance comic. While Linda Turner may have been "The Darling of the Comics," she packed a lovely wallop as the Black Cat. In a regular feature called "Black Cat's Judo Tricks," she taught young comic readers different ways to defend themselves in a series of step-by-step cartoons: "Swing the upper part of your body forward while slamming the edge of your left hand against his larynx. The impact will knock him down."

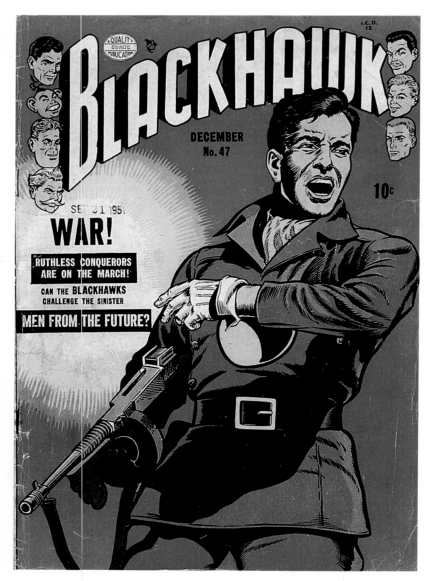

Blackhawk #47 © 1951
Comic Magazines, Inc.

The major artist on Black Cat during the late 1940s, Lee Elias, was described by the editors as "a fiend for authenticity" who "enacts all the judo stunts he illustrates, and swears by their credibility."

Movie star and vigilante, the Linda Turner and Black Cat combination appealed to both male and female readers for different reasons. As artist Lee Elias admitted in a 1948 interview: "Give me Linda Turner . . . sweet and clinging for a real life companion, but the adventurer in me can't help get a bang out of the more dynamic side of her character."

Golden Age Appearances
Pocket Comics 1–4 (8/41–1/42)
Speed Comics 17–38, 44 (4/42–1/47)

All-New Comics 6, 9, 15 (1/44–3/47)
Black Cat 1–29 (6/46–6/51)

BLACKHAWK
August 1941 *Military Comics #1*
Quality Comics

"History has proven that whenever liberty is smothered and men lie crushed beneath oppression, there always rises a man to defend the helpless, liberate the enslaved, and crush the tyrant. Such a man is Blackhawk. Out of the ruins of Europe and out of the hopeless mass of defeated people he comes, smashing the evil before him."

Poland, 1939. Nazi troops advance on the besieged city of Warsaw. The only defense left against the crushing German army are the few remaining planes of the Polish air force.

Airplane after airplane, however, is shot from the skies by the Nazi "butcher squadron," headed by the ruthless German, Captain Von Tepp. Finally, only one black plane remains to challenge Von Tepp and his squadron but the Polish pilot is forced to the ground beside a farmhouse. As the pilot runs for cover, Von Tepp bombs the farmhouse and destroys his plane.

Ironically, the demolished farmhouse is also the home of the Polish pilot. He runs inside the ruins, only to have his brother die in his arms. The pilot swears vengeance over his family's graves and works fervently to assemble his own renegade air force to combat the Nazis.

"Ours is a mission of *justice* and *death*."

The Polish pilot, who has adopted the name of Blackhawk, gathers aviators from around the free world who share his hatred of the Nazis. The men form a multinational squadron of fighters that answer to no man or country. They are the Blackhawks—an independent air force that flies from battlefield to battlefield wherever it is needed.

Over the next several months, the members of the Blackhawks—each with his own fighter plane (a modified "Grumman skyrocket")—are introduced to the readers. There is Andre from France, a womanizer *mais oui*, and Olaf from Sweden, friendly and big. Stanislaus, like Blackhawk, is also Polish. Hendrick, the elder gray-haired pilot, is initially Dutch but later turns into a Nazi-hating German named Hendrickson. Chuck is the blond all-American who comes onto the scene after two earlier Blackhawks, Boris and Zeg, have been shuffled off. Chop-Chop (as in chop suey) is their Chinese cook who soon becomes a full-fledged fighting member of the Blackhawks.

Blackhawk (who later becomes Polish-American) and his crew of international patriots struck a nerve in the 1941 American psyche. They were comrades in arms, sharing adventure, fighting together, and living together. They even had their own island—Blackhawk Island—for a special base. Complete with barracks, airport, signal tower, lighthouse, "disappearing forts," and a "zeppelin shed which can be lowered and revolved," Blackhawk Island was the ultimate clubhouse fantasy for boys and young men who daydreamed about war.

The fighting team spirit of the Blackhawks was almost contagious. Although they spoke in different accents and languages, the Blackhawks fought together with the same battle cry on their lips: "HAWKAAAA!"

"Like an angel of vengeance, Blackhawk and his men swoop down out of nowhere, their guns belching death, and on their lips the dreaded song of the Blackhawks . . . "

Yes, the Blackhawks even sang as they went into battle, like warrior Vikings or vengeful Valkyries:

Over land, over sea,
We fight to make men free,
Of danger we don't care . . . .
We're . . . .Blackhawks!

The Blackhawks dressed alike in somber blue-black storm trooper uniforms (except for Chop-Chop, who wore an Oriental green pantsuit

Military Comics #1 © 1941 Comic Magazines, Inc. Chuck Cuidera.

Military Comics #37 © 1945 Comic Magazines, Inc.

with a red bow in his erect pigtail). When the men had their hats on, it was sometimes hard to distinguish one Blackhawk from another—until they opened their mouths:

"By yumpin' yiminy! What ban go on here? Ay ban smack somebody's ears off, by Yupiter!"

"Ach du lieber! Dey have weapons that can look through der walls! Donnerwetter!"

"Zut alors! Mon dieu—ze woman weel show us!"

"Lookee see! Oh, gollies! Woe is everybody!"

The distinctive characters and consistently well-rendered artwork made the Blackhawks the best-selling comic book from Quality Comics. They originally appeared in the first issue of *Military Comics,* which was created by the Will Eisner studio for publisher "Busy" Arnold. Eisner drew

Blackhawk #13 © 1946 Comic Magazines, Inc.

the cover for the comic book, which featured the first appearance of Blackhawk, and roughed out the story.

Eisner recalled his usual working methods for creating new comic book features back in those days: "What I would do was design and develop and do the first sort of rough drawing or the first, final, finished drawing and usually did the cover after creating the character." Eisner passed the character design and story over to Chuck Cuidera, who drew the first Blackhawk adventure for *Military Comics.*

The two men who would shape much of the Blackhawk mythos, however, was writer William Woolfolk and artist Reed Crandall. Crandall, who had worked on Doll Man for Quality Comics, did some of his best work of the 1940s on the Blackhawks. He drew the feature from 1942 to

1948, with a several-year break for war service. Woolfolk, who wrote Blackhawk scripts for Crandall and the other artists, recalled that Crandall "was the out-and-out best artist I knew at the time. It was a great pleasure, indeed, to write those bold words on the page and see it come out so fully fleshed."

Other artists who worked on Blackhawk in a career that spanned three comics and lasted well into the 1950s (and beyond) included Bill Ward, Alex Kotzky, Al Byrant, Jon Cassone, John Belfi, Dick Dillin, and Chuck Cuidera.

After the war years, the Blackhawks battled tyrants, dictators, and weapons manufacturers who sought to enslave the populations of small and fictitious countries. By the early 1950s, communists had replaced Nazis and megalomaniacs as the Blackhawks's opponents of choice. During the Cold War years, the Blackhawks starred in stories like "Slavery in Siberia," "The Red Executioner," and "Trapped in the Kremlin."

The Blackhawks prospered all through the Cold War and beyond. Even after Quality Comics went out of business in 1956, the still-fighting Blackhawks got a transfer to DC Comics and a new lease on life.

Golden Age Appearances
Military Comics 1–43 (8/41–10/45)
Hit Comics 26 (2/43)
Blackhawk 9–86 (Winter/44–3/55)
Modern Comics 44–102 (11/45–10/50)

THE BLACK HOOD
October 1940 *Top-Notch Comics* #9
MLJ Publications

"I, the Black Hood, do solemnly swear that neither threats nor bribes nor bullets nor death itself—shall keep me from fulfilling my sacred vow . . . to erase crime from the face of the earth!!"

Harry Shorten, an editor and writer for the newly formed MLJ Comics, used the detective pulp magazine cliché of a wronged-cop-turned-vigilante as a springboard for a costumed comic book character he called the Black Hood.

Police patrolman Kip Burland discovers a robbery in progress at the Woodrow Mansion. Surprising the thief, Burland is himself surprised to discover the robber looks like an emerald skeleton!

The green-skulled criminal knocks Burland unconscious, puts some stolen jewels in his hands as a frame-up, and escapes with the rest. The policeman recovers, only to be arrested and charged with burglary.

Out on bail, Burland is determined to catch the criminal who framed him—the Skull. Unfortunately, the Skull finds him first, riddles his body with bullets, and then dumps the policeman in the woods.

A hermit finds the injured man and nurses him back to health. With the hermit's help, Kip Burland undergoes an extensive physical regimen to build his strength to nearly superhuman capacity. He also learns "all of science and all of knowledge, in order to make himself the world's greatest fighter against crime!" Finally, he dons a costume with a black hood to hide his identity from both the Skull and the police.

As the Black Hood, Burland captures the Skull and is exonerated of the robbery charge. Although Burland's reputation is cleared, his alter ego—the Black Hood—remains a suspicious character in the eyes of the law, especially to police Sergeant McGinty, Burland's supervisor.

When McGinty throws the Black Hood behind bars, Barbara Sutton, a reporter for the *Northville Courier,* writes an exposé which portrays the costumed vigilante as a hero and thus gains both his release and lifelong friendship. For the next five years, the Black Hood would rescue

Black Hood Comics #14 © 1945 Archie Comic Publications, Inc. Irv Novick.

Black Hood Comics #16 © 1945 Archie Comic Publications, Inc. Everett Raymond Kinstler.

Barbara from slobbering fiends and a host of villains equally as bizarre as the Skull, such as the Panther Man, the Crow, and the Mist.

Along with these macabre villains, Harry Shorten, Bill Woolfolk, and other writers of the Black Hood borrowed additional elements from popular pulp detective-horror magazines of the late 1930s, such as eerie atmospheric settings and scenes of bondage and torture. The pulp origins of "The Man of Mystery" (as he was billed) were so self-evident that the character made an unprecedented move *from* comic books *to* pulp magazines within a year of his first appearance. He starred as a fictional character in the *Black Hood Detective Magazine* and also enjoyed a brief career on radio.

Prize Comics #16 © 1941
Prize Publications

THE BLACK OWL

April 1940 *Prize Comics* #2
Prize Publications

Doug Danville is a society glamor boy—a millionaire gadfly who lives in a tuxedo. In fact, Doug uses his tux and an owl mask and a cape to create his Black Owl costume—an identity he assumes to fight crime. Later, Danville designs a more impressive blue bodysuit and adds boots and gloves to create an ensemble more fitting a playboy-turned vigilante.

The Black Owl appeared in *Prize Comics*, the first comic book venture of a pulp magazine publisher whose titles included *Double Detective* and *Detective Fiction Weekly*. The hero fought typical pulp novel villains in his early career, including characters like Madame Mystery, Doctor Devil, the Whistler, and Chief Skullface—an Indian with a green skull ("Me scalpum dark bird!").

In the September 1943 issue, a "first" occurred in comic books. Doug Danville, a patriotic sort despite his indolent lifestyle, enlists in the army and must abandon his superhero identity as the Black Owl. He passes his costume on to Walt Walters, who just happens to be the father of two young costumed heroes. His teenage twin sons, Rick and Dick, are the patriotic team of Yank and Doodle.

Yank and Doodle, or "America's Fighting Twins," as they were known, first appeared in *Prize Comics* in August 1941 and were drawn by Paul Norris.

By making the Black Owl the father of Yank and Doodle, the editors found a logical way to combine their best heroes into one popular feature with intriguing results. For the first year after assuming the mantle of the Black Owl, Walt Walters never told his sons his secret identity. After they learn their father is the Black Owl (*Prize Comics*, September 1944), the boys and dad are just one happy crime-fighting family—a healthy outlet for any father-son or sibling rivalry.

Some early Black Owl stories were produced by Jack Binder's art studio, with scripts by brother Otto Binder. The Black Owl was Binder's first script sale to a "big publisher," in late 1940. Wendell Crowley, an improbable six-foot, eight-inch delivery boy for Binder's studio, also broke in as a writer for the Black Owl. Crowley would later become editor of the Captain Marvel comics. Pete Riss, an artist who worked for the Binder shop under the name Pete Nebird, drew the Black Owl's early adventures. George Storm, whose di-

The Black Hood was second only to the Shield as MLJ's most popular hero, appearing in more than 80 stories. After the war years, the popularity of all superheroes was sinking fast. In the last issue of his comic book (Summer 1946), the Black Hood revealed his secret identity and discarded his crime-fighting costume. He made two more appearances in *Pep Comics* in 1947 as a plainclothes private investigator for the "Black Hood Detective Agency."

Golden Age Appearances
Top-Notch Comics 9–44 (10/40–4/44)
Jackpot Comics 1–9 (Spring/41–Spring/43)
Black Hood Comics 9–19
   (Winter/43–Summer/46)
Pep Comics 48–51, 59, 60 (5/44–3/47)

verse 1940s comics work included the Hangman, Bugs Bunny, and Buzzy (a teenage title he helped create for DC Comics), also drew the feature for a while, as did Bud Koste, another Binder shop artist.

Jack Kirby, who had already worked for a half dozen comic publishers, drew the Black Owl in late 1940 before landing a job at Fox Features Syndicate. The character was Kirby's first of the more than twenty-five superhero features he drew in the 1940s.

Golden Age Appearances
Prize Comics (as Doug Danville) 2–33
   (4/40–8/43)
(as Walt Walters) 34–53, 55–64, 66, 67
   (9/43–12/48)

THE BLACK TERROR

May 1941 *Exciting Comics* #9
Better Publications

Late at night, pharmacist Bob Benton is experimenting with "formic ethers" in the back of his drugstore. The concoction, however, overpowers him and changes the druggist into a super-powered being who can punch holes in concrete and deflect bullets off his chest.

Black Terror #7 © 1945 Better Publications, Inc. Alex Schomburg.

Black Terror #12 © 1945 Better Publications, Inc. Alex Schomburg.

In order to strike terror into the hearts of criminals, Benton constructs a solid black costume and decorates it with the druggist's symbol for poison—a white skull and crossbones. The mild neighborhood pharmacist is now the Black Terror!

He takes his drugstore assistant, young Tim Roland, into his confidence and gives him the same powers and identical costume he has. The two lookalikes fight crime and Nazis under the name of the Terror Twins. Jean Starr, the mayor's secretary, usually tags along as a help or hindrance and provides the bare romantic interest.

The Black Terror, Better Publications's most popular superhero, appeared in his own quarterly comic book and was usually the lead feature in *America's Best Comics* and *Exciting Comics* as well.

Blonde Phantom #15
© 1947 Marvel Entertainment Group, Inc.

THE BLONDE PHANTOM

October 1946 *All Select* #11
Marvel Comics

Louise Grant, girl Friday for the Mark Mason Detective Agency, wears her hair pulled up in a bun and hides behind a pair of owlish glasses. Mason, her eligible bachelor boss, tells her: "Personally, I like secretaries to dress conservatively!"

Louise Grant, as the costumed crime fighter, the Blonde Phantom, lets her golden hair cascade to her waist and slips into a long, red evening dress generously split to the thigh.

As the Blonde Phantom, Louise surreptitiously helps her boss solve his detective cases. When she gets a clue, she slips away from work and changes outfits:

"MEMO—Had to leave in a hurry, Mark! I'll transcribe my notes tomorrow!—Louise"

The Blonde Phantom was one of several comic book heroines to make a post-World War II debut and was also a reverse play on the typical superhero girlfriend/boyfriend relationship. Like Superman rescuing Lois Lane, the Blonde Phantom often had to save her boss and would-be boyfriend Mark Mason. When Mark was jumped by thugs, she would wade in the middle of the fistfight and deliver a vicious roundhouse punch to the crook's nose ("Just so I don't lose my touch . . .").

And, like Clark Kent, Louise Grant had a difficult time with a love life. Her boss ignores her and thinks only of her alter ego ("Gosh, if only I could find where the Blonde Phantom lives! We could have a night of it together!").

The lovelorn secretary thinks to herself: "What's the use? He never notices me! All he thinks of is the Blonde Phantom!"

Otto Binder wrote the initial Blonde Phantom stories. Syd Shores handled the art chores on the feature, which turned out to be Marvel's most popular superheroine of the 1940s. The blonde bombshell appeared in nearly fifty stories and, for a few months in 1948, readers could find her in seven titles on the newsstand.

Golden Age Appearances

All-Select Comics 11 (Fall/46)
Blonde Phantom 12–22 (Winter/46–3/49)
Marvel Mystery Comics 84–91 (10/47–4/49)
Sub-Mariner 25–28, 30 (Spring/48–2/49)
Blackstone, the Magician 2–4 (5/48–9/48)
All Winners Comics (2) 1 (8/48)
Namora 2 (10/48)
Sun Girl 2, 3 (10/48–12/48)

His popularity was due in part to his menacing "skull and crossbones" black costume, which fit in well with the series' offbeat villains of world-conquering zombies, maniacal monks, and Chinese dragons.

Editor and writer Richard Hughes came up with the early stories for the Black Terror and his origin was drawn by artist Dave Gabrielson. Later artists on the feature included Ed Hamilton, Edvard Moritz, George Tuska, and Mort Meskin.

Golden Age Appearances

Exciting Comics 9–69 (5/41–9/49)
America's Best Comics 1–31 (2/42–7/49)
Black Terror 1–27 (Winter/42–6/49)

THE BLUE BEETLE

August 1939 *Mystery Men Comics* #1
Fox Features Syndicate

The Blue Beetle was the most popular superhero published by Victor Fox. He was the second hero, right after Superman, to receive his own comic book. He was also right behind the Man of Steel in making the transition from comic book hero to the star of his own radio show and syndicated newspaper strip.

The character did have a striking visual appeal, but it was probably his name alone that ensured his success. The *Green Hornet*, one of the most popular adventure radio shows at the time, was reaching a national audience by spring 1938. An insect of a different color, the Blue Beetle tapped right into the same market that followed the Green Hornet's adventures. The similarity in names was calculated; he, too, was a masked crime fighter. He was also in the hands of huckster and promoter, publisher Victor Fox.

Fox formed his own syndicate (Fox Features Syndicate) and peddled the Blue Beetle daily comic strip to newspapers. He also pushed his hero onto a twice-weekly (and short lived) radio program and hyped it as a coast-to-coast event. When not promoting his comic book characters, Fox was planning to launch a new soft drink called "Kooba—A Refreshing Cola Drink With A New Thrill—*Vitamin B$_1$!*" Although extensively advertised on the back covers of his own comic books, Kooba never materialized.

Regardless, however, another vitamin-powered drink did play an important role in the development of Fox's big blue hero. Rookie policeman Dan Garret gains his strength to become the Blue Beetle when he gulps down a dose of "Vitamin 2X." With his chain-mail blue outfit, Dan Garret is nearly invulnerable and neatly disguised as the Blue Beetle.

The Blue Beetle, in his early appearances in *Mystery Men Comics*, behaved more like the Green Hornet than Superman. He had no super-powers, but he did drive around in a hot car and frequently projected his beetle insignia with a lamp on darkened walls. Like the Hornet, he loved to frighten the pants off criminals.

Like Clark Kent, however, Dan Garret had his Lois Lane—of a sort. Joan Mason, a lovely blonde newspaper reporter for *The Bulletin*, seemed to have a knack for snooping in the wrong places for her scoops. Fortunately, the Blue Beetle was always there to help out.

As Garret's career unfolded in 1940, he

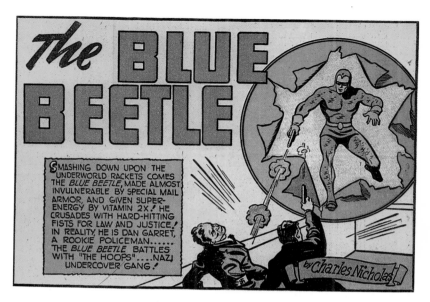

Mystery Men Comics #25
© 1941 Fox Features
Syndicate. Charles
Nicholas.

gained more and more powers—thanks to a vitamin discovery by his neighborhood pharmacist, Dr. Franz. Dr. Franz and Garret enjoyed one of the more unusual relationships between a superhero and his confidant.

Whenever Dan wanted to gain the powers of the Blue Beetle, he would run into Dr. Franz's drugstore and ask for a shot of the Doc's special discovery, "Vitamin 2X." ("Here's your vitamin 2X! Good for you but death to the forces of injustice!")

After swallowing this under-the-counter medication, Dan would change his clothes in Franz's back room behind a wooden screen and run out as the Blue Beetle. Evidently, gulping down powerful illegal drugs and undressing in a pharmacist's office was acceptable behavior for an early 1940s superhero.

Garret's secret identity as a seemingly permanent rookie cop allowed him easy access to crime as it happened. His partner on the beat, officer Mike Mannigan, never suspected that Dan was in fact the costumed crime fighter whom he considered to be a public menace.

Like all the early Fox features, the Blue Beetle was born in the studio of Will Eisner and Jerry Iger. Artist Charles Wojtkowski, better known as Charles Nicholas, drew the early adventures of the Blue Beetle. With his own comic book and a new newspaper strip, the Blue Beetle fell into the hands of several other artists, including Louis Cazeneuve, Al Carreño, Sam Cooper, and Jack Kirby, who drew the newspaper strip under Charles Nicholas's byline. (Ironically, two years later, Nicholas would work anonymously as Kirby's assistant on *Captain America*.)

*Blue Beetle #40 © 1945
Fox Features Syndicate*

After the war years, the Blue Beetle stories written by other writers became darkly adult and violent. Stories drawn by Jack Kamen from 1947 to 1948 were filled with underdressed women and homicidal Peeping Toms.

Dr. Fredric Wertham, author of the anti-comic book manifesto *The Seduction of the Innocent*, selected an illustration from *Blue Beetle #54* as an example of what children called "headlight comics" because of the exaggerated breast development of the women who swayed through the stories. Wertham particularly objected (on the grounds of both morality and good grammar) to one line in a 1948 *Blue Beetle* story in which a "sexy blonde female dressed in a string of beads and a scrap of material says: 'A gentleman, he never blackjacked a woman. He hit them with his fists.'"

By 1950, rookie cop Dan Garret would retire his Blue Beetle costume—a victim of both a declining interest in superhero comics and the end of Victor Fox's flamboyant publishing career.

Golden Age Appearances
Mystery Men Comics 1–31 (8/39–10/42)
Blue Beetle 1–60 (Winter/39–8/50)
Big 3 1–7 (Fall/40–1/42)
Phantom Lady 13 (8/47)
All Top Comics 8–13 (11/47–9/48)
Famous Crimes 1 (6/48)
Tegra, Jungle Empress 1 (8/48)
Zago, Jungle Prince (9/48)

BLUE BOLT

June 1940 *Blue Bolt* #1
Novelty Press

One of the early writers of the Blue Beetle was Robert Kanigher, who landed his first comic book writing job at Fox Features Syndicate. He recalled that one of the editors at the time, W. W. Scott, "ordered Blue Beetles by the yard after my first script."

Kanigher was impressed with his first encounter with a comic book editor: "Mr. Scott had a wispy mustache down which a rivulet of saliva flowed from a corncob pipe clenched in his teeth; his eyes were like bouncing marbles; he wore high-button shoes; and in his steambath office in New York in July, without air conditioning, he always wore longjohns." Kanigher turned out his Blue Beetle scripts in workmanlike isolation from the Fox offices. "We never plotted. One summer I wrote 100 pages a week."

Fred Parrish, Harvard football star, is struck by lightning while practicing with his teammates in a remote area. Barely alive, he climbs into an airplane and flies for help. Unfortunately, his plane is also struck by lightning and he crashes into a lost valley—deep *inside* the earth. The football player recovers in the subterranean laboratory of Dr. Bertoff, who has revived the young man "with the aid of my radium deposits."

The combination of lightning bolts and the doctor's radioactive treatment give Fred the powers of lightning itself. The doctor furnishes Fred with a light blue costume and lightning gun and he is transformed into Blue Bolt. After battling mindless subterranean hordes led by the exotically beautiful Green Sorceress, Blue Bolt turns his attention to world affairs back on Earth's surface.

On the doctor's "telescreen," he sees the rise to power of Hitler and Mussolini and their destruction of Europe: "Great Scott! War's broken out . . . those planes are machine-gunning refugees!"

After joining the army and battling the Nazis for several issues, Blue Bolt got some feminine help in the form of Lois Blake, who received a similar costume and powers in the December 1941 issue.

By March 1942, with America at war, Blue Bolt was now called Blue Bolt—The American. To further validate his patriotism, he reported to Army headquarters for special assignments. Yet with the September 1942 issue of *Blue Bolt Comics*, Fred discarded his blue costume and hood in favor of civilian clothes. He became a straight adventure character with no special powers or abilities. Although he would appear in the comic until 1949, his days as a superhero were over.

Joe Simon created Blue Bolt for the Funnies, Incorporated, comic book studio shortly after beginning as a freelance artist. Several months later, Funnies, Incorporated, used the feature to sell Curtis Publications, the publisher of the *Saturday Evening Post*, a package of materials for its new comic book line, Novelty Press. Impressed with Simon's creation, Curtis named their first comic book *Blue Bolt*.

By the time his first Blue Bolt story was scheduled for publication, Simon had become a full-time comic book editor at Fox Features Syndicate. To help him produce additional Blue Bolt stories, Simon asked an artist at Fox comics to be his partner.

Jacob Kurtzberg, a twenty-one-year-old artist who had drawn the "Blue Beetle" newspaper strip, was Simon's choice to moonlight with him on the Blue Bolt feature. They rented a one-room office and turned out nine Blue Bolt stories on weekends and lunch hours. Soon after, Kurtzberg legally changed his name to Jack Kirby and the Simon-Kirby art team was born.

After Simon and Kirby moved on to other features, Blue Bolt was drawn by a number of artists, including George Mandell, Alan Mandell, and Dan Barry.

Barry remembered that when "I was hired to do the pencils on Blue Bolt, they put me in an office with a writer, a handsome, cocky Irishman who seemed to be out all the time. Search parties were always out looking for him at the great bars around 45th Street. He was my writer on Blue Bolt. He was good."

The "handsome, cocky Irishman" who wrote Barry's Blue Bolt stories would eventually

Blue Bolt Vol. 2 #8
© 1942 Novelty Press

be better known as one of America's best-selling mystery writers, Mickey Spillane.

Golden Age Appearances
Blue Bolt 1–27 (6/40–8/42)

BULLETMAN

May 1940 *Nickel Comics* #1
Fawcett Publishing

When gangsters murder police Sergeant Pat Barr, his orphan son Jim vows to devote his life to eradicating crime. Too frail to pass the police physical, the studious Barr instead battles crime by becoming a police chemist and ballistics ex-

No. 7 — SEPT. 16

A FAWCETT PUBLICATION
10¢

In this Issue
BULLETMAN and BULLETGIRL battle
THE REVENGE SYNDICATE!

Bulletman #7
© 1942 Fawcett Publications, Inc.

pert (which earns him the teasing nickname "Bullet" from the police officers). Barr hopes to discover a chemical, "a germ-destroying serum," which will drive all the "poisons and toxins" out of a criminal's system—a "crime cure" as he describes it.

"Bullet" Barr tests the serum on himself one night. When he wakes the next morning, he discovers his muscles have grown so big his pajamas are splitting. He accidentally kicks a hole completely through his bedroom wall. The former weakling has become a "hard-muscled, steel-strong giant." The chemical also increases Barr's brain power and enables him to invent a gravity-regulator helmet which gives him the ability to fly. Barr puts on the bullet-shaped helmet and a costume to "terrify evil doers." The weak, test-tube police scientist has become the powerful Bulletman.

Barr's distinctive bullet-shaped helmet also attracts any bullets aimed at the hero and bounces them harmlessly away. A flying human projectile, he uses his bullet-shaped head to crash through walls like an exploding shell.

Barr's girlfriend Susan Kent, the daughter of a police sergeant, discovers he is Bulletman and wants in on the action. Barr invents a gravity-regulating helmet just Susan's size so she can join him in the air as Bulletgirl (*Master Comics*, April 1941). Bulletman and Bulletgirl were one of the first man and woman superhero duos in comics, appearing before such couples as Hawkman and Hawkgirl, Lash Lightning and Lightning Girl, or Flame and Flame Girl. Although there were many super men in the 1940s comic books, most of their similarly aged female accomplices seem to be forever girls.

Bulletman and Bulletgirl made a formidable fighting team against such villains as the Black Spider, the Black Rodent, Dr. Riddle, and the usual gang of Nazi saboteurs. The "Flying Detectives," as they were called, were Fawcett's most popular superheroes outside the Captain Marvel family.

Jon Small, who would later draw such heroes as Batman, Superman, and the Star Spangled Kid for DC Comics, drew the first Bulletman story. The Jack Binder shop provided most of the artwork over the years, with many scripts by Otto Binder.

Golden Age Appearances
Nickel Comics 1–8 (5/40–8/40)
Master Comics 7–82, 84–106 (10/40–8/49)
Bulletman 1–16 (Summer/41–Fall/46)
America's Greatest Comics 1–8
(Fall/41–Summer/43)
Mary Marvel 8 (Bulletgirl) (12/46)
Whiz Comics 106 (2/49)

CAPTAIN AMERICA

March 1941 *Captain America* #1
Marvel Comics

War was in the air. In the newspapers, in the movies, and in the minds of Americans during late 1940, there was a growing sense of patriotism as they prepared for a war that seemed inevitable. Hitler was the villain, Germany was the enemy, and the Allies were the heroes—but they needed our help. What they needed was a hero—an American hero—who could smash the Nazis and put Hitler in his place.

Joe Simon was a man who worked with

Captain America #1 © 1941 Marvel Entertainment Group, Inc. Jack Kirby.

heroes—comic book heroes—and he came up with an idea that was perfect for the times: Super American. Simon went to his studio and began designing his new comic book character:

"I stayed up all night," Simon recounted in his memoirs, *The Comic Book Makers*, "sketching

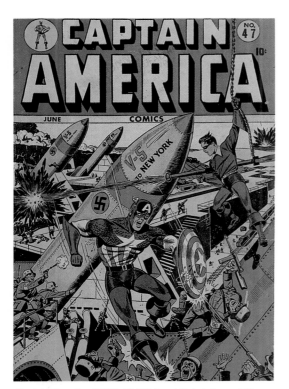

Captain America #47 © 1945 Marvel Entertainment Group, Inc. Alex Schomburg.

the usual athletic figure: mailed armor jersey, bulging arm and chest muscles, skin-hugging tights, gloves, and boots flapped and folded beneath the knee. I drew a star on his chest, stripes from the belt to a line below the star, and colored the costume red, white, and blue. I added a shield. The design seemed to work; the muscles of the torso rippled gallantly under the red and white stripes."

Looking at his character, Simon decided that Super American wasn't the proper name. There weren't too many "Captain" comic book heroes—yet. Captain Marvel had only been around for a few months. Captain America. The name fit; after all, he would be a super-soldier, so why not give him a rank?

Simon showed publisher Martin Goodman of Marvel Comics his patriotic superhero and suggested that they pit Captain America against no less a villain than Adolf Hitler. Goodman agreed, but with some trepidation—what if Hitler was killed before the comic book hit the news-stands? He ordered Simon to come up with a *Captain America* comic book as soon as possible while the idea was still timely.

The first issue of *Captain America*, dated March 1941, hit the newsstands December 1940—a full year before America's entry into the war. The front cover, which showed Captain America pushing his way through a room of Nazi thugs in order to personally smack Hitler in the face, was the wish fulfillment fantasy of millions of Americans.

Captain America #51
© 1945 Marvel Entertain-
ment Group, Inc. Alex
Schomburg.

the irritation of his training officer, Sergeant Duffy. One night when he is changing into his Captain America costume in his tent, he is surprised by young Bucky Barnes, the boy "mascot of the regiment."

"You little rascal! I ought to tan your hide! I guess you got me dead to rights—I am CAPTAIN AMERICA!"

"Gosh . . . Gee whiz . . . golly!! I . . . I never thought!"

"From now on we must both share this secret together . . . that means you're my *partner*, Bucky!"

Bucky was added to the strip to give Captain America someone to talk to, according to Simon, and he was named after one of Simon's high school basketball chums. The young boy gave school children an exciting role model. Bucky, after all, was in the thick of the action, defeating spies and saboteurs, and fighting like an adult. As an added appeal, Bucky and Captain America began a fan club for youngsters called "The Sentinels of Liberty." For ten cents, a child received a shield-shaped badge with pictures of Bucky, Captain America, and Betty Ross (Cap's platonic and patriotic girlfriend), as well as a membership card which read: "I solemnly pledge to uphold the principles of the Sentinels of Liberty and assist Captain America in war against spies in the U.S.A."

The club quickly got out of hand and hundreds of young members started reporting suspicious neighbors and relatives as potential fifth columnists and traitors. The offices of Marvel Comics in New York City were threatened by German sympathizers. Eventually, Mayor Fiorello LaGuardia phoned editor Joe Simon to tell him not to worry—he was ordering extra police protection for the publishers of *Captain America*.

Captain America was the right symbol for a nation poised for war. Steve Rogers, an army private, represented all of America's present and future soldiers who were being asked to become heroes for their country. The comic book was soon selling nearly a million copies a month and rivaled *Batman* and *Superman* in popularity. Besides lending patriotic appeal, Jack Kirby's dynamic artwork helped assure the comic's success.

Kirby's Captain America seemed to actually *move* across the static comic book page. Leaping, pirouetting, crashing, and then slamming his shield against the gun barrel of a Nazi spy, Captain America pulled the reader right into the middle of the action.

"Captain America was real," Kirby observed. "When Captain America got into a fight with a

"A nation thrills to his daring exploits! His name becomes a symbol of courage and a byword of terror in the shadow-world of spies! Who is Captain America?"

Captain America was originally Steve Rogers, a "frail young man" who is deemed unfit for military service. Rogers volunteers for a government experiment to test the effects of a superserum which can build body and brain tissues to "an amazing degree!" The serum transforms the army reject into a superior soldier—a "superagent."

Rogers keeps his new powers a secret and goes undercover as a private in the U.S. Army at Camp Lehigh. He feigns incompetence to protect his secret identity as Captain America, much to

dozen guys he could lick those guys, and anybody who read the book could see how he did it. I'd arrange it so that a wonderful fight scene would come out almost like a ballet, and it wouldn't be the kind of fight that we'd ordinarily see."

Kirby recalled that "the first issue was meant to look more like a movie than a traditional comic book. Movies were what I knew best, and I wanted to tell stories the way they did. I guess I'm just a frustrated director."

Kirby experimented with the panel layouts for Captain America, striving to inject more movement, more drama, and more impact into his storytelling. In the fourth issue of Captain America, he used an entire page for one panel—an almost unheard of use of comic book space in the early days, when six to nine panels per page was the tradition. Two issues later, in the September 1941 issue, Joe Simon suggested to Kirby that they use the centerfold of Captain America to create the first double-page illustration in comic books. Taking advantage of the comic's natural centerfold, where it is stapled in the middle, Simon and Kirby made the dramatic two-page illustration a trademark of *Captain America* which was continued even after their departure from the feature.

Kirby recalled that "after the strip took off, we enlisted the help of Al Avison and Al Gabriele

to ink. I discovered a kid named Syd Shores. He inked, too. Guys like Reed Crandall, Mort Meskin, George Klein, and Mike Sekowsky inked on later issues. After their pages were in, I'd pick up a brush and go over their work to make the strip look consistent."

Editor Joe Simon also brought in other writers for *Captain America*. Ed Herron, who worked with Simon at Fox Features Syndicate as one of the first full-time comic book writers, created Captain America's archfoe and one of the greatest menaces in comics: the Red Skull. Herron's villain, a seemingly unbeatable Nazi madman dressed in a swastika-emblazoned robe, was as merciless as he looked terrifying—even Hitler was reportedly afraid of him.

Otto Binder, who was tapped by Joe Simon to write scripts for the November and December 1941 issues, continued working on Captain America stories through the war years and beyond. Other writers on the comic included Manly Wade Wellman, Joe Gill, Bill Finger, and Gerry de la Ree.

After Simon and Kirby left Marvel Comics in late 1941 in a dispute over royalties and their emerging working relationship with DC Comics, Stan Lee took over briefly as editor and writer before entering the service. Artists who worked on Captain America after Kirby's departure included Al Gabriele, Al Avison, Syd Shores, Don Rico, Dan Barry, and Harry Anderson.

The writers and artists guided Captain America and Bucky through the war years and into peacetime. In the years following the war, the red-white-and-blue hero tried to adapt to the less nationalistic mood of the times. Steve Rogers turned in his army uniform and tried his hand at being a police officer and a school teacher. Bucky was written out of the strip in 1948 and was replaced by Betty Ross when she became Captain America's costumed companion, Golden Girl.

With the October 1949 issue, the comic book was retitled *Captain America's Weird Tales*, and horror stories soon replaced the heroic adventures of America's favorite fighting patriot.

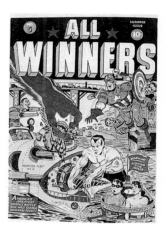

All Winners Comics #5
© 1942 Marvel Entertainment Group, Inc.

Golden Age Appearances
Captain America 1–74 (3/41–10/49)
All Winners Comics (1) 1–19, 21
   (Summer/41–Winter/46)
Young Allies 1–5 (Summer/41–Fall/42)
USA Comics 6–17 (12/42–Fall/45)
All-Select Comics 1–10 (Fall/43–Summer/46)
Marvel Mystery Comics 80–84, 86–92 (1/47–6/49)
Blonde Phantom 16 (Winter/47)
All Winners Comics (2) 1 (8/48)

Captain America #1 © 1941 Marvel Entertainment Group, Inc. Jack Kirby.

Human Torch 33, 35 (11/48–3/49)
Sub-Mariner 31 (4/49)

CAPTAIN MARVEL

February 1940 *Whiz Comics #2*
Fawcett Publishing

Billy Batson, a homeless orphan boy, sleeps in the subway and sells newspapers to survive. A faceless stranger summons the boy to follow him into an unknown subway tunnel. There they are met by a driverless train and whisked to a secret underground hall carved from solid rock. At the end of the hallway is an "old, old man" who sits on a marble throne: "Welcome, Billy Batson."

"How did you know my name?" asks the surprised boy.

Captain Marvel Adventures #53 © 1946 Fawcett Publications, Inc. C.C. Beck.

"I know everything. I am SHAZAM!"

A blinding flash of lightning thunders out of nowhere and an inscription appears magically on the wall behind the old man. It explains the significance of each letter in SHAZAM's name:

Solomon (Wisdom)
Hercules (Strength)
Atlas (Stamina)
Zeus (Power)
Achilles (Courage)
Mercury (Speed)

Shazam explains that "for 3,000 years I have used the wisdom, strength, stamina, power, courage, and speed the gods have given me to battle the forces of evil." Now the old man tells the boy that it is time for someone else to continue the good fight by using the powers of his name. He knows that Billy Batson has been cheated out of his inheritance by his evil uncle and believes that the boy would stand up against injustice and cruelty.

Shazam tells Billy: "You shall be my successor. Merely by speaking my name you can become the strongest and mightiest man in the world—CAPTAIN MARVEL!" The old man then commands the boy: "Speak my name!"

"SHAZAM!"

Like magic, the young Billy Batson turns into a super-powered adult—a handsome and muscled hero. Every boy and girl who ever read a *Captain Marvel* comic book in the 1940s whispered, at least once, that magic word "Shazam" to see if it, too, might work for them.

In the first story, Billy, in his new identity of Captain Marvel, foils a gang of radio saboteurs led by the fiendish scientist Sivana (who, incidentally, would return countless times as the Captain's archfoe). Sterling Morris, the owner of the Amalgamated Broadcasting radio station, offers Billy a job as a radio reporter in gratitude for his heroics against the saboteurs. The orphan boy now has a secret identity as a superhero and a good-paying job. Anytime he hears about danger as reporter, he can become the world's mightiest superhero simply by saying the word "Shazam!"

Captain Marvel was created by Bill Parker, an editor at Fawcett Publishing, for its new line of comic books. Ralph Daigh, Parker's managing editor, helped design the gold-and-red uniform with the button-down flap and lightning bolt insignia. With the cape, Captain Marvel's costume made him look like a cross between a light Italian operetta soldier and a girls' club band leader. Parker and Daigh turned the character over to artist C.C. Beck, who drew the superhero as a good-natured strongman, polite and muscle-bound.

Beck's simple and cartoony artwork was perfectly complemented by the stories of the writers who made Captain Marvel the most personable and popular of all the 1940s superheroes. In particular, writer Otto Binder helped fashion much of the Captain Marvel mythos. From 1941 and the character's demise in 1953, Binder wrote 986 of the 1,743 Marvel Family tales (which included Captain Marvel, Jr. and Mary Marvel), as well as other Fawcett features. "New titles were launched in that dizzying period with machine-gun rapidity," Binder recalled. "I personally launched (by writing the original scripts) *Mary Marvel*, *The Marvel Family*, and others for Fawcett, not to mention a dozen or more for other publishers."

Beck remembered Binder as "even-tempered, down-to-earth, plain, honest, fond of fishing, gardening, and playing poker. He worked out of his home and took great delight in puzzling the wives of his commuter-type neighbors by walking about in a dressing gown at home. They could never understand why Otto didn't have to shave, put on vest, coat, and tie, and dash off to catch the 8:03 every morning as their husbands did. 'They think I'm a kept man,' Otto once told me. 'I don't dare tell them what I really do for a living.'"

Even with Binder's prolific output, other writers had to help with the great demand for Captain Marvel stories. From 1943 to 1944, Robert Kanigher developed the popular series in which Captain Marvel visits various cities around the United States and bumps into real-life local politicians and celebrities ("Captain Marvel Battles Doom to Detroit," "Captain Marvel Finds Action in Indianapolis"). Rod Reed, who became editor of Captain Marvel (1941–1943) after Bill Parker's entry into the Army, was the second Captain Marvel writer and was responsible for many of the more humorous and "corny" stories. William Woolfolk, who wrote dozens of Captain Marvel stories as part of his huge output for several companies, also recalled that his stories for the Captain were usually more cheerful and funny than those for the other grim superheroes he wrote.

Even the villains and supporting characters were more often like cartoons than "real" comic book people. For example, the evil Mr. Mind, who fought Captain Marvel for two years in a serial called "The Monster Society of Evil," turned

Captain Marvel Adventures #98 © 1949 Fawcett Publications, Inc.

out to be nothing more than an oversized garden worm who barked orders through a magnifying voice box. One of Captain Marvel's most trusted friends was Mr. Tawny, a talking *tiger* who looked like he belonged in *Winnie the Pooh* instead of a superhero comic book.

Besides the intentional humor in Captain Marvel, Beck also felt that one of the things that made the character so popular was the character of Billy Batson. He was one of the first boy-hero role models in comics and the envy of millions of readers. Beck recalled that "the part that I liked best was Billy Batson, and so did Otto Binder and so did Wendell Crowley, the editor. To us Captain Marvel was a necessary evil, insisted on by the publishers. And we could have done very well without him. If we could have kept him more in the background as a threat and a presence, it would have been better."

While Billy may have been the favorite of the artists and writers, it was Captain Marvel who became the most popular and beloved of all the 1940s superheroes.

Golden Age Appearances
Whiz Comics 1–155 (2/40–6/53)
Special Edition Comics 1 (8/40)
Captain Marvel Adventures 1–150
 (Spring/41–11/53)
America's Greatest Comics 1–8
 (Fall/41–Summer/43)
Master Comics 20, 21, 48, 50 (11/41–5/44)
Wow Comics 9 (1/43)
Marvel Family 1–89 (12/45–1/54)

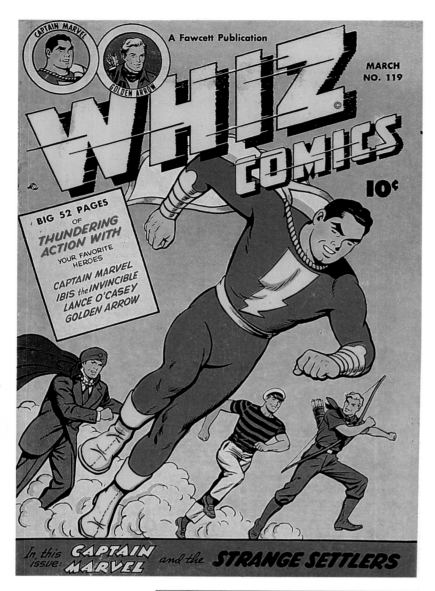

Whiz Comics #119 © 1950 Fawcett Publications, Inc. C.C. Beck.

CAPTAIN MARVEL, JR.

December 1941 *Whiz Comics #25*

America was at war. Captain Marvel, on the latest covers of *Whiz Comics*, pushed back German tanks, rescued RAF pilots, and boomeranged a Nazi torpedo. It was only a matter of time before the Third Reich would strike back at America's champion with their version of a super man.

Captain Nazi, the "vaunted champion of the German war lords," first appeared in the pages of the December 1941 issue of *Master Comics*. A superpowered agent of Hitler, he knocks Bulletman around and then leaves a note for Fawcett's biggest hero: "You'd better keep your snooping nose in *Whiz Comics*, Captain Marvel, because I'm coming over there next month to beat your brains out!"

True to his word, Captain Nazi continues his campaign of terror against "weak-livered Yankees" in the next Captain Marvel story in *Whiz Comics*. In the midst of a fierce air battle, Captain Marvel knocks the Nazi down into an ocean bay.

On a small fishing boat in the bay are teenager Freddy Freeman and his grandfather. They see the man fall into the water and cruise over to rescue him. The old man pulls the Nazi agent into their boat and tells him: "Easy me boy! You're in good hands now!"

The revived Captain Nazi repays their kindness by immediately killing the boy's grandfather and throwing him overboard! When Freddy tries to defend himself, Captain Nazi seizes the boat's oar and breaks the boy's back in half and leaves him to drown: "Cursed Yankees! We'll kill them *all* some day!"

Fortunately, Captain Marvel sees the drowning boy and rushes him to the hospital. Freddy, however, will be crippled for life—if he lives at all.

Taking a desperate chance, Captain Marvel (in his identity as Billy Batson) carries the unconscious Freddy down into the hidden subway tunnel to the ancient underground hall and summons forth the wizard Shazam with his plea:

"There's a man loose up above—a man called Capt. Nazi, who is destroying everything. I've brought you a boy who is dying as a result of Capt. Nazi's cruelty. You must help him as you once helped me!"

The wizard Shazam tells Billy he can pass some of his powers over to the injured boy if he will only say his name. Billy says "Shazam!" and turns into Captain Marvel. Freddy is awakened by the transformation and exclaims "Captain Marvel!" in surprise.

Suddenly there is a flash of lightning and the crippled boy is transformed into a teenage superhero:

"I'm well again! I'm strong—I—I'm like you!"

"That's right," the good Captain says. "You're Captain Marvel Junior!"

He tells Freddy that he can become Captain Marvel, Jr. at any time by simply saying his name. "You have all the powers I have. Use them to fight the forces of evil wherever they appear!"

The first force of evil to deal with is, of course, Captain Nazi. "I'm going to send you into *Master Comics* to take care of Capt. Nazi!" Captain Marvel tells his junior companion.

In the meantime, Captain Nazi "speaks on a secret trans-Atlantic phone, to his wicked dictator boss . . . "

"Herr, Hitler, I haff killed an old man and

crippled a little boy . . . it iss so eassy beating these Yankee pigs . . . "

But, as the story reminds us, "what Capt. Nazi doesn't know is that the innocent lad he crippled is now the most powerful boy in the world!"

Moving over to *Master Comics* in January 1942, Captain Marvel, Jr. defeats, if only temporarily, the heinous Captain Nazi. The super-villain, however, would return again and again, along with other war foes, such as Captain Nippon (who came on the scene after Pearl Harbor) and the deadly Mr. Macabre.

As good (or bad) as the villains were, it was the youthful appeal of Captain Marvel, Jr. that kept readers coming back for more. The idea of making Freddy Freeman, a crippled newspaper boy, into one of the world's strongest teenagers was a brilliant stroke by the staff at Fawcett Comics, particularly by then-editor Ed (France Edward) Herron.

Herron broke into the comic book business in 1939 by selling scripts to Victor Fox for five dollars per story and then spent the next few months at the Harry "A" Chesler comic book shop as a writer and editor. He landed a position as editor at Fawcett Comics in October 1940 after selling them several exciting *Captain Marvel* stories which were distinguished by their long fight scenes.

Captain Marvel, Jr. #77 © 1949 Fawcett Publications, Inc. Kurt Schaffenberger.

Master Comics #58 © 1945 Fawcett Publications, Inc. Mac Raboy.

In 1941, Herron decided to give Fawcett comic book readers the longest superhero fight in history. He structured a battle that raged over three issues of *Master* and *Whiz Comics* with Fawcett's two most popular superheroes—Captain Marvel and Bulletman—and then threw in one of the vilest Nazi villains in the comics, Captain Nazi. And, as an added bonus, he introduced a new hero right in the middle of the fracas: Captain Marvel, Jr.

The decision to create a teenage version of Captain Marvel was not Herron's alone; during the previous year, dozens of pint-size and teenage superhero sidekicks had joined their older mentors. The Fawcett staff did not want a Captain Marvel look-alike that would dilute the impact of the original. The decision was made to give the character a bright blue costume distinctive from Captain Marvel's red union suit. To further ac-

Master Comics #68 © 1946 Fawcett Publications, Inc.
Mac Raboy.

centuate the difference, an artist was selected for Captain Marvel, Jr. whose illustrative style would contrast with the cartoony approach of the Captain Marvel stories as drawn by C.C. Beck.

Mac (Emanuel) Raboy, who had worked with Herron in the Chesler shop in 1940, was drawing the Bulletman stories for Fawcett's *Master Comics* in 1941. Raboy, who was heavily influenced by Alex Raymond's *Flash Gordon* strip, combined an eye for anatomy and figure work with a drive for painstaking draftsmanship. His finely-lined and realistically rendered art was deemed perfect for the new Captain Marvel, Jr.

Raboy drew the teenage superhero in his origin story in *Whiz Comics* and then illustrated both the covers and stories for the Captain Marvel, Jr. series in *Master Comics* for nearly two years.

Raboy's care and detail to his art slowed him down to the point that he had to take on assistants, such as Gene McDonald and Ruby Zuboff. When Captain Marvel, Jr. got his own comic book in late 1941, Raboy could not handle the extra work and the title was given to Al Carreño to illustrate.

In an effort to keep up with production without compromising his quality, Raboy even drew his art on smaller pages—some of his covers were drawn actual printed size instead of the standard "twice-up" size. The deadline pressures, however, were still too much, and the now chain-smoking Raboy left the series in 1944.

Other artists followed Raboy and Al Carreño on Captain Marvel, Jr. stories, most notably Bud Thompson, who worked on the series from 1945 to 1952, and Kurt Schaffenberger who remembered cutting his artistic teeth on Captain Marvel, Jr. right after World War II.

A few months after launching Captain Marvel, Jr., Ed Herron left Fawcett Comics over an explosive conflict of interest caused by his writing and editing the same series. Robert Kanigher, a writer and editor who worked with Herron, recalled the man as "an authentic Hemingway character. Doomed. And laughing."

After Herron, editor Rod Reed and writers William Woolfolk, Irving Schuffman, and Otto Binder guided the adventures of the world's mightiest boy. More than 600 Captain Marvel, Jr. stories appeared from 1942 to 1953. By the 1950s, superheroes were falling from favor; the sales of *Captain Marvel, Jr.* was less than half of their war years peak. The last issue of his comic book, dated June 1953, had the self-fulfilling blurb on its cover: "Captain Marvel, Jr.—Condemned To Die!"

Golden Age Appearances
Whiz Comics 25 (12/41)
Master Comics 22–133 (1/42–4/53)
Captain Marvel, Jr. 1–119 (11/42–6/53)
Wow Comics 9 (1/43)
All Hero Comics 1 (3/43)
America's Greatest Comics 8 (Summer/43)
Marvel Family 1–89 (12/45–1/54)
Captain Marvel Adventures 52 (1/46)

CAPTAIN MIDNIGHT

March 1941 *The Funnies* #57
Dell Publishing/Fawcett Publications

The clock tower bell tolls the hour of midnight. An airplane roars through the air. The radio dial glows and the voice of the announcer crackles and thunders two words which echo "ka-boom" around your living room: "CAP-TAINNN MID-NIGHHHT!"

The Captain Midnight radio show began in late 1939 on a Chicago station and was nationally syndicated by September 30, 1940. Captain Albright, a World War I pilot, saves the free world when he captures an enemy mastermind by the midnight deadline. The fearless aviator becomes a special agent known as Captain Midnight. He is joined by two teenage aides, Joyce Ryan and Chuck Ramsay, and a grease-monkey sidekick named Ichabod Mudd, who make up his Secret Squadron.

Captain Midnight quickly became the most popular radio aviator hero in a class that included such high-flying stalwarts as Hop Harrigan, Smilin' Jack, and Sky King. In 1942, he starred in a fifteen-chapter movie serial from Columbia Pictures and also began a series of adventures in both the daily and Sunday newspaper comic strips.

The Captain's comic book career began in Dell Comics's *The Funnies* and continued in *Popular Comics*. These early comic book adventures were drawn by Dan Gormley, Robert Brice, and Bob Jenney, who specialized in writing and drawing aviation comic series for Dell such as Sky Ranger, Stratosphere Jim, Sky Hawk, Masked Pilot, and New Flying Fortress.

With the popularity of the Captain Midnight movie serial, Fawcett Publishing decided it was time for the aviator to join its ranks of comic book heroes. In late summer 1942, Captain Marvel introduced Fawcett comic book readers to Captain Midnight on the front cover of his new magazine. Readers probably needed the formal introduction because Fawcett's Captain Midnight was noticeably different from his radio and earlier comic book counterparts.

No longer dressed in a khaki airman's suit, Captain Midnight sported a bright red costume with a steel-blue helmet and cowl, complemented by matching gloves and boots, and topped off with a pair of goggles. On his chest was his special emblem: a yellow-winged clock with the hands pointing to midnight. The aviator looked like a superhero and that was no accident.

The Captain Midnight stories came from the Jack Binder art studio and many of his adventures were written by Otto Binder. Binder changed the origin so that Captain Albright became a crime fighter after World War I and later an inventor on the same level as Thomas Edison:

"Captain Midnight is not only a mighty fighter, he is not only America's ace trouble-shooter, he is not only the headache of the Axis spies, he is also one of the world's keenest inventive minds!"

Captain Midnight has a secret laboratory "somewhere in Nevada" and, at "his Menlo Park of the desert," devises a collection of crime-fighting weapons. Included in his arsenal of gadgets are Blackout Bombs (for chemically inducing darkness as black as midnight), a Doom-Beam Torch (an infra-red branding iron), a Belt Transmitter (for calling members of his Secret Squadron), and a Gliderchute (a silk, web-wing parachute attached between the armpits and bodysuit that allows the Captain to glide through the air like a flying squirrel).

Captain Midnight quickly became one of Fawcett's most patriotic heroes during the war years. As an ace aviator and brilliant inventor, he used his talents to fight Japanese and Germans in such stories as "Smashing the Jap Juggernaut,"

Captain Midnight #3
© 1942 Fawcett
Publishing, Inc.

Cat-Man Comics Vol. 3 #4 © 1942 Holyoke Publishing Company. Charles Quinlan.

"The Terror of the Tokyo Turkey," and "Nazi Theft of the Giant Glider."

After the war years, Binder slowly changed the Captain into a science fiction hero. In 1947, he became known as "The Space Sentinel" and fought alien monsters like Jagga the Space Raider and Xog the Evil Lord of Saturn. In the February 1948 issue, Binder has Captain Midnight battling the menace of Flying Saucers—one of the first comic book stories to come out of "flying saucer scare," which seized newspaper headlines and riveted public attention in the late 1940s and early 1950s.

Other writers who worked on the Captain Midnight comic book included William Woolfolk, Joe Millard, and editor Stanley Kauffman. Leonard Frank drew the majority of the stories; other artists included Al Bare, Clem Weisbecker, and Lincoln Cross.

Golden Age Appearances
The Funnies 57–64 (7/41–5/42)
Popular Comics 76–78 (6/42–8/42)
Captain Midnight 1–67 (9/42–9/48)
All Hero 1 (3/43)
America's Greatest Comics 8 (Summer/43)

CAT-MAN

August 1940 *Crash Comics* #4
Holyoke Publications

An American caravan is ambushed by bandits in the jungles of Burma. The only survivor is young David Merrywether, who is protected and reared by a tiger. The boy develops catlike powers and can see in the dark, leap and climb anywhere, and hear the quietest sound.

As an adult, Merrywether returns to America and is so offended by the evil he sees, he dons a costume and becomes the Cat-Man. He is watched over by the spirit of his guardian tigress, who grants him the gift of nine lives.

With war in the making, Merrywether enlists in the Army as a lieutenant. Just to make his life more complicated as a U.S. soldier, he gains an unlikely crime-fighting sidekick—an eleven-year-old girl named Katie Conn.

After Katie's parents are killed in a train wreck, the soldier informally "adopts" her. Since the girl is a trained acrobat, he makes her his aide and mascot. With a similar, cute cat-suit, Katie becomes Kitten. Although Katie takes to calling the Cat-Man her "Uncle David," the innocent relationship progresses as Kitten grows up in a big way. By the end of the series, the coquettish and fully developed Kitten and her Uncle David could certainly provide rich fodder for small-minded gossips.

Irwin Hasen drew the early appearances of Cat-Man in *Crash Comics*. Charles Quinlan drew the majority of the stories in *Cat-Man Comics*, with later art by Bob Fujitani and others. The feline hero was the most popular character from Holyoke Publications and was its longest running title.

Golden Age Appearances
Crash Comics 4, 5 (8/40–11/40)
Cat-Man Comics 1–32 (5/41–8/46)

DAREDEVIL

September 1940 *Silver Streak Comics* #6
Lev Gleason/Comic House

Bart Hill's father is an engineer who has created an amazing new invention. Unfortunately, the invention attracts the notice of thieves, who break into the Hill home and "ruthlessly kill" both of Bart's parents. Next, they grab the young boy and, using a branding iron, torture him so he won't talk. Bart is left with a boomerang-shaped burn on his chest and "speechless by the torture inflicted upon him."

The mute boy grows into manhood, determined "to destroy the forces of crime and evil." He becomes an expert acrobat and, in a grim reminder of the boomerang-shape branding he suffered, learns to use the boomerang as a weapon of vengeance. Armed only with his strength, agility, and a boomerang, he becomes a silent costumed avenger—the Daredevil.

The original eight-page story took place in the middle of *Silver Streak Comics*—a comic book named after publisher Arthur Bernhard's automobile. Jack Cole was the editor and he got the art for Daredevil from Jack Binder, who was shop foreman at the Chesler studio. Cole looked at Binder's hero and got an idea.

Before Daredevil's arrival, the most popular character in *Silver Streak Comics* was Cole's villainous creation, The Claw. Possessing the cunning of Fu Manchu and the temperament of Godzilla, the Claw was a caricature of all the Oriental madmen who dominated the pulp literature of the 1930s. With talons for hands and razor-sharp tusks for teeth, the Claw could also grow *several stories high* and eat battleships for breakfast. The seemingly unbeatable Claw tore through the first two issues of *Silver Streak* in his effort to "domi-

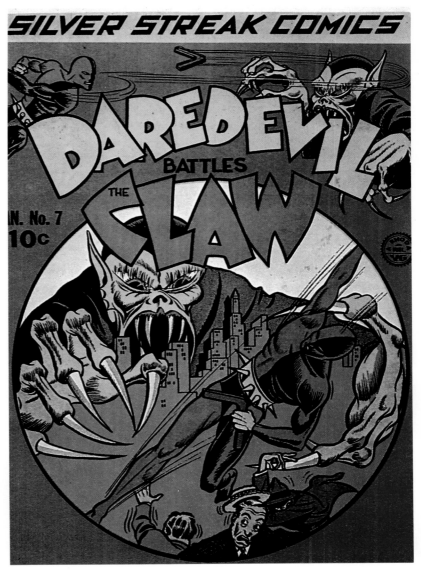

Silver Streak Comics #7 © 1941 Lev Gleason Publications. Jack Cole.

Daredevil #47 © 1947 Lev Gleason Publications. Charles Biro.

nate the universe." Cole had been planning to bring his monstrous villain back again, but he needed a worthy opponent to make the story interesting. Daredevil came along at the right time.

Cole changed Daredevil's original blue and yellow costume to a more striking red and black one. Split down the middle in two contrasting colors, the costume made the character more "devilish," dark, and distinctive. Completing the costume's effect was a giant, metal-spiked belt, which made the character a walking weapon. The mute hero also got his voice back, without explanation, and was propelled from a secondary feature to front cover star: "DAREDEVIL BATTLES THE CLAW!"

For the next five issues, the Claw and Daredevil engaged in a running battle of massive

Daredevil #6 © 1941 Lev Gleason Publications

destruction. Daredevil would hurl his body like a boomerang at the towering Claw, who was always hissing "Die, swine!"

Cole's art was both "cartoony" and violent, and it caught the attention of Everett Arnold, the publisher of Quality Comics, who was looking for an artist for his new masked detective feature, Midnight. Arnold hired Cole away from *Silver Streak Comics* in early 1941 and artist Don Rico stepped in to draw the last chapter of the battle royal between Daredevil and the Claw in the June 1941 issue.

The very next month, however, Daredevil would be matched against an even more monstrous villain—a real one—and in his own magazine: *Daredevil Battles Hitler*. There, on the front cover of the comic book, was Daredevil throwing his boomerang at a retouched photo of a frightened Führer's face.

The Daredevil-Hitler matchup (which came right on the heels of Adolph's first major appearance as a comic book villain in *Captain America*) was the brainchild of publisher Arthur Bernhard, who freely admitted to possessing strong antifascist views, and his editor and business partner, Lev Gleason. Gleason, who began his comic book career in 1936 as a packager for *Tip Top Comics,* would take over later in 1941 as the company's publisher.

Gleason gave Daredevil his own comic book and brought in two new writer/editors, Charles Biro and Bob Wood. Biro, who had created Steel Sterling for MLJ Comics, wrote and drew the early Daredevil stories. He gave the character a new origin (August 1943) in which Bart Hill, lost in the Australian outback, is adopted by a tribe of aborigines and instructed in the fine art of boomeranging. His costume was a gift from an aborigine chieftain who certainly had a wry sense of fashion.

Biro's biggest contribution to the Daredevil mythos, however, was introducing a gang of supporting kid characters known as the Little Wise Guys (October 1942). Two runaway boys, with the street names of Meatball and Scarecrow, fall in together and later form a gang with two other unsupervised kids, Peewee and Jocko. Daredevil takes the kids under his wing, and the Wise Guys help him fight crime on the street.

In a bold move for the early comics, Biro kills off Meatball and replaces him with Curly, a refugee from a street gang called the Steamrollers. Biro delighted in writing hard-hitting stories which tore at the reader's heartstrings and delivered a strong moral message. He used the Wise Guys more and more in *Daredevil Comics*, developing their personalities and frequently making them the heroes of the story.

After the war years, Daredevil took an increasingly minor role and gradually appeared only at the end or the beginning of the story to help the Wise Guys tie up loose ends. By 1950, Daredevil was booted out of his own comic by the Wise Guys, who prospered for another six years on the newsstands.

After Biro, stories for Daredevil were handled by the husband-and-wife team of Carl and Virginia Hubbell, as well as by other artists, including Dan Barry, Norman Mauer, John Belfi, and Mike Roy.

Golden Age Appearances
Silver Streak Comics 6–17 (9/40–12/41)
Daredevil Comics 1–69, 79, 80 (7/41–11/50)

DOLL MAN
December 1939 *Feature Comics #27*
Quality Comics

"By an immense effort of will, Darrel Dane, a mild-mannered young scientist, can compress the molecules of his body to midget size . . . until he has transformed himself into Doll Man, the

Doll Man #40 © 1952 Comic Magazines, Inc.

Feature Comics #48 © 1941 Comic Magazines, Inc. Lou Fine.

miniature menace to all evildoers! Only Dr. Roberts and his daughter Martha, Darrel's fiancée, know that Doll Man and Darrel Dane are one and the same!"

Doll Man had a sissy-sounding name and an unlikely superpower. After all, making yourself itty-bitty and teensy-tiny hardly seemed the smartest thing to do if you wanted to clobber somebody. Nevertheless, over his fourteen-year career, Doll Man outlasted Captain America, Flash, Green Lantern, Sub-Mariner, Human Torch, and most 1940s superheroes.

Darrel Dane, a research scientist, works with his elder colleague, Dr. Roberts, to create a chemical solution that will "shrink a human being to the size of a doll!" When Martha Roberts, the doctor's daughter, is kidnapped, Darrel uses the shrinking formula to become a doll-sized spy and rescues her.

The scientist discovers that by "exerting my will power, I can condense the molecules of my body." Similarly, he can also will himself to return to his normal adult size. Depending upon the artist, Doll Man was from five to eight inches tall—"pint-size" as he was often called.

Doll Man turned his diminutive size into a fighting advantage—a message not lost on the pint-sized readers who read his adventures. Surprise was on his side because he could hide anywhere. Popping out of pockets, purses, and even pie pans, Doll Man proved that there was indeed "no crime too big for a mite so small!"

When his girlfriend is about to be abducted, Doll Man hops unobtrusively onto her shoulder and whispers: "Let them take you and your dad . . . we can find out more about this plot . . . I'll hide in your hair."

Doll Man got around in the most imaginative way of any superhero. Unable to fly, too small to run very fast, and too short to hail a cab, Doll Man frequently resorted to flying on the backs of birds or hopping on a roller skate to get to the scene of the crime.

During the patriotic war years, he traveled via an American bald eagle he had freed from the local zoo. Later, he gets his own "tiny Dollplane," which he disguises as a model airplane in his study. Toward the end of his career, Doll Man gains a canine companion named Elmo, which he rides like a horse by holding onto its spiked collar.

Feature Comics #48 © 1941 Comic Magazines, Inc. Lou Fine.

Feature Comics #96
© 1946 Comic Magazines,
Inc. Al Bryant.

book publisher in the spring of 1939, Arnold also wanted a costumed hero. Will Eisner was just the person to give him one.

With a full six months of superhero-making behind him (Wonder Man, the Flame, the Green Mask), the twenty-two-year-old Eisner was the most experienced supplier for the burgeoning "long-underwear" hero marketplace. He sketched a costume design for Doll Man, wrote an origin story, and then gave some rough sketches to perhaps the best artist in his studio, Lou Fine.

Eisner's inspiration for his Lilliputian-sized hero might have been sparked by Max Fleischer's feature-length 1939 cartoon movie *Gulliver's Travels*, or perhaps by the appearance of an earlier pint-sized comic book hero called Minimidget (*Amazing Man Comics*, September 1939). Regardless, Lou Fine's art on Doll Man in *Feature Comics* soon propelled the tiny hero to star status and his own comic magazine.

Eisner recalled that Lou Fine was "the epitome of the honest draftsman. No fakery, no razzle-dazzle—very direct, very honest in his approach. His work was in the style of the old classic heroic painters and sculptors."

After Fine left Doll Man, other artists handled the feature, including John Cassone (who drew the first issue of *Doll Man Comics*), Max Elkan, Mort Leav, Fran Matera, Rudy Palais, Alex Kotzky, John Spranger, and the prolific Al Bryant. The only other artist, however, who approached Fine's success with the character was Reed Crandall, who drew Doll Man from 1942 to 1943.

Bill Woolfolk, who wrote several Doll Man stories illustrated by Crandall, recalled that he "was the out-and-out best artist I knew at the time—and I didn't know anybody who drew more dimensional figures with more realism than he did."

Other writers who came before and after Bill Woolfolk on Doll Man included Gwen Hansen, an assistant editor at Quality Comics who pinch-hit on the early stories, Robert Hyatt, and Joe Millard.

The writers and artists deserve a lot of credit for keeping Doll Man popular through the late 1940s and early 1950s, when other superheroes were disappearing on a monthly basis. Colorful villains, such as the Undertaker (a guy who camps out in a mausoleum) and Tom Thumb (a publicity-seeking evil midget), certainly helped the series, as did the proliferation of monster-type stories during the horror-loving 1950s.

Ultimately, however, Doll Man's popularity probably came from that simple childhood

Martha Roberts, Darrel's fiancée, is also his research assistant. Together, they work on such worthwhile projects as developing growth vitamin extracts and breeding exotic narcotic plants which "paralyze the will to exist." He also slips her a dose of the shrinking solution, and in the December 1951 issue of *Doll Man Comics*, Martha Roberts becomes Doll Girl. The Doll Duo makes an effective fighting team, and the two always seem to run into trouble just when they're going out on a date.

The "World's Mightiest Mite" first appeared in late 1939 in the pages of *Feature Comics*, a comic book which initially consisted of mostly newspaper strip reprints. Everett Arnold, the publisher of *Feature Comics*, contracted with the art studio of Will Eisner and Jerry Iger to supply his line of Quality Comics with original humor and adventure comic stories. Like almost every comic

belief that just being small doesn't mean you can't be great.

Golden Age Appearances
Feature Comics 27–139 (12/39–10/49)
Doll Man 1–47 (2/41–10/53)

DOCTOR FATE

May 1940 *More Fun Comics* #55
DC Comics

"High on a hilltop in ghost-haunted Salem stands a lonely stone tower. Some say the Vikings built it before Columbus discovered America. It has windows—but no doors. Within this strange edifice lives Doctor Fate, Man of Mystery. Possessor of lost secrets, his face is unknown but his deeds are legion wherein he fights these present-day sorcerers against whose Black Magic law officers are powerless."

Doctor Fate was a master of the ancient magics and eldritch powers. He can levitate, fly through the air, and turn his body into pure energy at will, which renders him invulnerable and nearly ageless:

"No force on earth or in the air can harm pure power such as my body becomes when I so desire it! Lead or steel, or fire or sound! I am—immortal!"

Doctor Fate's origins began in the ancient valley of Ur, where a young Kent Nelson is accompanying his archeologist father to uncover the secrets of the pyramids. Nelson's father is killed by a poisonous gas as he tries to enter a secret chamber in one of the pyramids. The boy, unaware of his father's death, triggers another gas in the pyramid, which awakens an alien man—Nabu—who has been in suspended animation for a million years.

Nabu becomes the young boy's guardian and teaches Kent the ancient knowledge his race possesses, such as the secret of molecular control. Nabu also gently ages Kent so he turns into a young man, and then slows his aging process so he will remain a young man for a long time. He gives Kent a yellow and blue costume and a helmet that completely and mysteriously covers his face. As Doctor Fate, he uses his magical powers against the forces of evil and darkness.

"Doctor Fate was my own invention," writer Gardner Fox recalled. To my knowledge, I wrote all the Doctor Fate yarns that appeared. I always liked the supernatural; I read H.P. Lovecraft, August Derelth, Sax Rohmer, Robert Howard, Clark

Ashton Smith, all the others. Fate was a derivation from my imagination influenced by those writings. I give full credit to the artist for visually designing the character, but I remember the mask was my idea."

Howard Sherman was the artist who brought Fox's creation to life. Sherman broke into the comics by way of illustrating pulp magazine covers for the *Thrilling* magazine line run by publisher Ned Pines of Better Publications. When Pines entered the comic book business, Sherman drew a strip for an early issue of *Thrilling Comics*. "I wrote it, lettered it, drew it and colored it. I think I received ten dollars per page," Sherman recalled.

Sherman went over to DC Comics when he heard it was looking for new artists. "I contacted Whit Ellsworth, who was the head editor at the time. He gave me the script for Doctor Fate to

More Fun Comics #61
© 1940 DC Comics, Inc.

All Star Comics #3 © 1941 DC Comics, Inc. Howard Sherman.

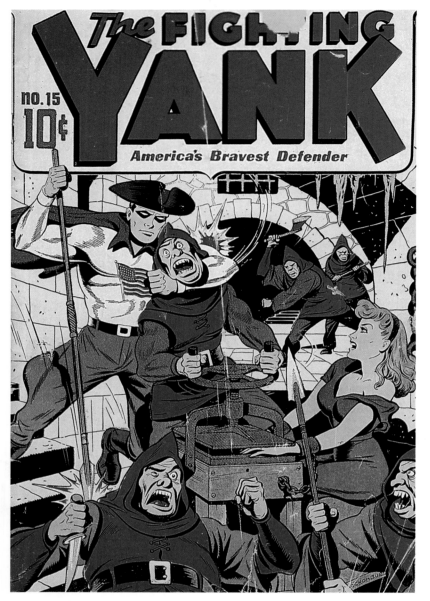

Fighting Yank #15
© *1946 Better Publications,*
Inc. Alex Schomburg.

from the world behind his golden mask. In the April 1941 issue of *More Fun Comics*, however, Doctor Fate removes his helmet and shares his secret identity with Inza Carmer, his girlfriend of nearly a year ("Surprised? I'm overwhelmed! What—why—how??").

Fate fought a few recurrent villains in *More Fun Comics*, including Wotan, his first enemy, and Mr. Who, an insane collector who uses a serum called "Z Solution" to grow, shrink, and disappear. His other adventures took place in *All Star Comics* as a member of the Justice Society of America.

In summer 1943, artist Howard Sherman ended his association with Doctor Fate in both *More Fun Comics* and *All Star Comics*. Jon Kozlak continued the Doctor's adventures in *More Fun* and drew some of the stories for *All Star* as well. In early 1944, the decision was made to drop the supernatural Doctor from the DC lineup.

Golden Age Appearances
More Fun Comics 55–98 (5/40–7/44)
All Star Comics 3–12, 14–21
 (Winter/40–Summer/44)

THE FIGHTING YANK

September 1941 *Startling Comics* #10
Better Publications

Bruce Carter III discovers that he is the spitting image of his ancestor, Bruce Carter I, who fought and died in the Revolutionary War. Bruce's ancient ancestor comes to him in spirit form during the early days of the second World War and tells the young man that he, too, must be willing to fight for his country's freedom.

The spirit of his Revolutionary War ancestor tells Bruce where he can find an ancient cloak which will give him awesome powers and make him invulnerable to bullets. Bruce puts on the cloak and makes a uniform in the eighteenth-century colonial fashion, complete with a tri-cornered hat and square-buckled boots. Dressed as an early American Yankee, he adopts the name of the Fighting Yank and vows to protect the United States from the enemies of democracy.

Bruce soon confides his secret identity to his girlfriend and traveling companion, Joan, a college graduate student. Whenever the two are overwhelmed by Nazis, Japanese infiltrators, or cattle rustlers, the spirit of Bruce's ancestor appears in gigantic form and rescues them: "I was at Valley Forge—and Shiloh . . . and the Marne . . . I was at Bataan . . . and Iwo Jima . . . and I am here!"

start with, at $12 a page." For the next three years, Sherman would draw a Doctor Fate story every month. "I was slower in production than some of the other artists. It took me about ten to fourteen days to pencil and ink six pages."

Sherman's dark and moody drawings, coupled with Gardner Fox's supernatural settings and allusions, made the omnipotent Doctor Fate a sometimes frightening hero. ("Helen, reveal your innermost thoughts to me! I want to see *your soul!*") Lightning bolts emit from his eyes and his fingertips when he calls upon the powers of magic: "Floors open! Dyaleth mytharp! Reveal to me the secrets of the tomb!"

Little was hidden from Doctor Fate ("I have the ability to read men's minds! Now, you shall use your tricks no more!"), yet he himself hid

Editor and writer Richard Hughes came up with the early stories for the Fighting Yank, and his origin was drawn by artist Jon Blummer. The patriotic hero persevered for nearly five years after the war ended, due in part to the interesting relationship he had with his otherworldly ancestor.

Golden Age Appearances
Startling Comics 10–49 (9/41–1/48)
Fighting Yank 1–29 (9/42–8/49)
America's Best Comics 9, 11, 13–25 (4/44–2/48)

THE FLASH

January 1940 *Flash Comics* #1
DC Comics

The Flash, the fastest man alive, brought to life the universal fantasy of superhuman speed. Since the days of ancient Greece, with its heroes like Perseus, who wore winged sandals, and Hermes, the fleet-footed messenger of the gods, everyone has dreamed what it would be like to move faster than anyone else alive. The Flash showed us.

"Swifter than the speed of light itself—faster than a bolt of lightning in the sky—is the Flash! Dedicating his speed to the cause of justice, the Flash triumphs over crime because of the magical swiftness of his movements—at times his incredible speed renders him invisible to the human eye!"

The Flash can outrun bullets, overtaking them in mid-flight and then plucking them out of the air as if they were floating in space. In a whirlwind of flying fists, he can punch and jab a

Flash Comics #1 © 1940
DC Comics, Inc.
Sheldon Moldoff.

Flash Comics #1 © 1940 DC Comics, Inc. Harry Lampert.

dozen crooks in split-second intervals. He can create a swirling vortex by running around a pair of crooks so that the threads in their pants unravel and fall to their feet. "By moving his body back and forth so swiftly that he cannot be seen, the Flash is able to be in the same room with a person without being detected."

Like many other superheroes, the Flash began as a person who was not blessed with any outstanding physical abilities. Jay Garrick, "an unknown student at Midwestern University," is a "scrub" on the college football team. His girlfriend, Joan Williams, snubs him for a date with the football captain ("A scrub is just an old washwoman!!").

Garrick, however, is not a total failure: "in the research laboratory, the football dub is a

All-Flash #22 © 1946 DC Comics, Inc. Martin Naydel.

by three supporting characters: Winky, Blinky, and Noddy, known collectively as the Dimwits. The Dimwits, loosely inspired by the Three Stooges, provided comic relief with wisecracks and slapstick humor. They frequently involved themselves, uninvited, with the Flash as he tried to solve crimes in spite of their interference.

The Flash was popular enough to receive his own comic book, *All-Flash Comics,* as well as regular appearances in *Flash Comics, Comic Caval-cade,* and *All Star Comics.* Only Superman, Batman, and Wonder Woman bettered his record as DC Comics's most prolific superhero of the 1940s.

The Flash was dreamed up by editor Sheldon Mayer and writer Gardner Fox for Max Gaines's new comic book. Fox, who was twenty-eight-years-old at the time he created the Flash, remembered Mayer (who was then twenty-two) as his "boy-editor" who instructed him to come up with a complete line of features for a new comic book. Fox became a full-time comic book writer that day.

Harry Lampert, a former animator at the Fleischer Studios, drew the first two Flash stories. Lampert gave the character his most distinctive trademark—the winged helmet, based upon the petasos of the Greek god of speed, Hermes.

Everett E. Hibbard succeeded Lampert as the principal artist on the Flash and drew the majority of his adventures from 1940 to 1947 (assisted by Hal Sharpe and Louis Ferstadt). Editor Mayer recalled that Hibbard "had been a commercial artist and illustrator, never a cartoonist, but he understood what I was after and accommodated me. He learned to draw the way he would have if he had started out as a cartoonist, and when good craftsmanship was needed, he could provide it. Most important, he did learn to tell the story."

By the late 1940s, other writers (Robert Kanigher, John Broome) and artists (Carmine Infantino, Joe Kubert) handled the adventures of the Scarlet Speedster. The Dimwits were dropped from the strip by 1947, and there was less comedy and more heroics as the Flash fought villains like the Thinker, the Fiddler, Star Sapphire, and Thorn. The times, however, caught up with Flash. His own magazine was discontinued by 1949, and his last appearance was at the final meeting of the Justice Society of America in 1951.

Golden Age Appearances
Flash Comics 1–104 (1/40–2/49)
All Star Comics 1–7, 10, 24–57
   (Summer/40–2/51)

brilliant student." Garrick has been conducting experiments with the gases given off by hard water. Late one night, he accidentally breaks the glass retorts in his lab, and the powerful gases from his experiment knock him unconscious.

The comatose student struggles for his life in a hospital while extensive tests are run. Finally, a scientist announces that the results of his tests show Garrick to be "the fastest thing that ever walked on earth!!" Garrick will be able to "walk, talk, run and think swifter than thought . . . He is a freak of science!!"

Garrick delights in his new-found powers and uses them to win a football game and land a date with his fickle girlfriend. Interestingly, his girlfriend Joan knows about Garrick's secret identity as the Flash from the very beginning.

After college, Garrick settled down with his own research laboratory in Keystone City joined

All-Flash 1–32 (Summer/41–12/47)
Comic Cavalcade 1–29 (Winter/42–10/48)
Big All-American Comic Book 1 (12/44)

GREEN ARROW

November 1941 *More Fun Comics* #73
DC Comics

Oliver Queen, a wealthy collector and student of Indian artifacts and lore ("There was little about Indian life that I hadn't mastered, including archery . . . "), travels to Lost Mesa, where he hopes to discover "valuable Indian remains" to help with his archeological research. He is followed there by crooks who mistakenly think that the wealthy Queen is looking for gold.

Also on Lost Mesa are two survivors of an airplane crash, a young boy named Roy Harper and his family Indian servant, "old Quoag." Marooned there for several years, the boy has perfected his archery skills under Quoag's tutelage.

The boy, his Indian companion, the crooks, and Oliver Queen all run into each other and a fight ensues. After Quoag is killed by Queen's would-be robbers, the boy teams up with Queen to capture the murderers. Using the only weapons at hand, bows and arrows, the two attack the crooks with good results:

"Watch out for the big guy! He shoots a mean *green arrow*!"

"Golly, that kid's *speedy*! We can't get 'im!"

Oliver Queen (now dubbed "Green Arrow") devises an "arrow-line" made from rawhide strips, which he uses to help him and Roy (now christened "Speedy") escape. During their escape, the murderers are killed and Quoag's death is avenged.

"Speedy, I've learned a lesson," Green Arrow tells the young boy. "You can't run away from evil men! You must turn and fight them . . . as we have, with weapons we understand! We must always fight them!"

Within four months of their debut in *More Fun Comics* (November 1941), the Green Arrow and Speedy had replaced Dr. Fate and the Spectre as the most popular heroes in the title. Their front cover star status was probably due to Speedy's appeal—teenage sidekicks were the current rage. The arrow-slinging duo was also given an immediate spot in *Leading Comics* and secured a second series in *World's Finest* within the first year of their debut.

The first Green Arrow story for *More Fun Comics* was written by Mort Weisinger and drawn by George Papp. Weisinger was formerly the editor of *Thrilling Wonder Stories* and *Startling Stories*, the two most aggressively juvenile science fiction pulp magazines of the late 1930s.

He had a knack for making young pulses pound and quite naturally entered the rapidly growing comic book field in 1941 as a story editor for DC Comics. His first assignment was an initiation by fire: Come up with three new superheroes for the November 1941 issue of *More Fun Comics*.

Weisinger obliged with Aquaman, Johnny Quick, and Green Arrow. Aquaman was a dressed-up version of the Sub-Mariner, without anger or soul. Johnny Quick was a gimmicky Flash-type hero with a super-speed formula. Green Arrow was the classic hero of folklore, the archer. He was a "streamlined Robin Hood—a law-abiding Robin Hood," according to Weisinger. With an array of fantastic arrows, unlimited wealth, a sleek

More Fun Comics #89
© 1943 DC Comics, Inc.

Arrowmobile to cruise in, and a happy-go-lucky kid sidekick, Green Arrow presented an attractive picture of a 1940s crime fighter.

George Papp, who was twenty-five when he drew Green Arrow in 1941, became the artist most associated with the character. Papp broke into comics three years earlier by drawing fillers like "Fantastic Facts" for what was to become DC Comics. His first regular feature was Pep Morgan for *Action Comics*, a strip about an all-American athlete. Before Green Arrow, Papp was drawing two other early *Action Comic* series, Congo Bill and Clip Carson.

Papp dropped all his comic book assignments, including Green Arrow, in 1942, when he entered the service. During the war years, the primary art team on Green Arrow was Cliff Young and Steve Brodie, followed by brothers Arturo and Louis Cazeneuve. Papp returned to the feature in 1946 and then drew almost every Green Arrow story published during the next twelve years.

Green Arrow managed to survive the waning postwar years of the superheroes when more popular characters vanished. Editor Mort Weisinger kept his creation alive by running it as a secondary feature in *World's Finest Comics* and *Adventure Comics,* which were headlined by such company stalwarts as Superman and Superboy. Along with Aquaman, Wonder Woman, Batman, and Superman, Green Arrow was published uninterrupted from the 1940s to the 1960s.

Golden Age Appearances
More Fun Comics 73–107 (11/41–1/46)
Leading Comics 1–14 (Winter/41–Spring/45)

World's Finest 7–74 (Fall/42–1/55)
Adventure Comics 103–205, 207–209 (4/46–2/55)

GREEN HORNET

December 1940 *Green Hornet Comics* #1
Helnit Publishing/Harvey Comics

"He hunts the biggest of all game—public enemies that even the G-Men cannot reach!"

The Green Hornet was one of the most popular costumed adventurers of the 1930s. Beginning as a radio series in 1936 on station WXYZ in Detroit, the Green Hornet was a nationally syndicated success by 1938. Played originally by Al Hodge (who would later star as TV's Captain Video), the Green Hornet radio show aired twice every week until 1952.

The Green Hornet was primarily the creation of Fran Striker, a radio script writer who also had a big hand in the birth of another multimedia hero, the Lone Ranger. Hoping that success might rub off, Striker made the Green Hornet (Britt Reid) the grand-nephew of his famous cowboy hero. Moreover, Reid used his inheritance from the Lone Ranger's silver mine (the source of his bullets) to underwrite his dual lifestyle of newspaper publisher and masked vigilante.

Like the Lone Ranger, the Green Hornet was given a faithful companion of color—Kato—who shared his secret identity. Originally Japanese, Kato became a Filipino for obvious reasons after December 7, 1941.

In 1940, the masked detective and his man-servant followed the footsteps of other successful radio heroes such as the Shadow and Captain Midnight, and made the transition to both the movie screen and comic book page. Kids packed the Saturday morning movie houses for three months running so they could watch the thirteen-chapter serial *The Green Hornet*. Later that same year, they returned to see another thirteen weekly chapters of *The Green Hornet Strikes Back*.

The popularity of the radio show and the movie serials caught the attention of artist Bert Whitman, who was putting together comic book packages for small publishers in New York City. George W. Trendle, the radio show's producer, granted Whitman the rights to do a comic book package featuring the Green Hornet as part of his national publicity campaign:

"On the AIR, in the MOVIES, and in your favorite COMIC MAGAZINE!"

Working with artists like Irwin Hasen and Dan Gormley (who would work on another radio-turned-comic book hero, Captain Midnight), Whitman put together six issues of *Green Hornet Comics*, loosely based on the radio scripts, for Helnit Publishing. After a year's suspension, the title was sold to Harvey Comics in 1942, which published it for the next seven years using the talents of Arturo Cazeneuve, Pierce Rice, Al Avison, and Jerry Robinson. Robinson, who began his career as an assistant on Batman and later drew such diverse characters as the Vigilante, Atoman, and Lassie, recalled that he "tried to establish a

Green Hornet Comics #31 © 1946 Green Hornet, Inc. Al Avison.

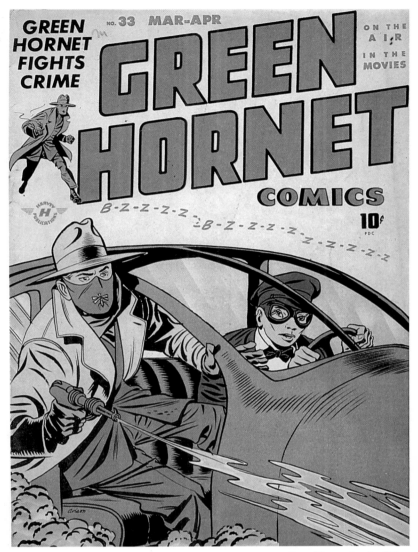

Green Hornet Comics #33 © 1947 Green Hornet, Inc. Al Avison.

'style' for *The Green Hornet* which suited its concept."

For the most part, the Green Hornet comic book did manage to capture the flavor of the original radio show. Kato chauffeured the Hornet around town in the sleek, hot car known as The Black Beauty. The masked man wielded a pistol which shot sleep-inducing gas capsules. And, as in the radio show, the police in his comic book adventures suspiciously regarded the Green Hornet as a clever gangster.

Although never a major comic book character, the Green Hornet played a role in the development of other 1940s comic book superheroes and perhaps inspired the names of characters like the Blue Beetle and Yellowjacket. His gas gun weapons turned up in the hands of the Sandman in *Adventure Comics* and his midnight black, crime-fighting car surely influenced Bob Kane as he sketched the Batmobile for the first time in late 1940.

SEPT.-OCT. No. 68

ALL-AMERICAN COMICS

Hop Harrigan

AA ALL-AMERICA PUBLICATION

48 PAGES IN FULL COLOR

10¢

GREEN LANTERN meets NAPOLEON and JOE SAFEEN

Also in this issue:—A NEW HOP HARRIGAN ADVENTURE

All-American Comics #68 © 1945 DC Comics, Inc. Paul Reinman.

Golden Age Appearances
Green Hornet Comics 1–47 (12/40–9/49)
All-New Comics 13–14 (1/46–1/47)

GREEN LANTERN

July 1940 *All-American Comics* #16
DC Comics

Aladdin and his lamp: a person gains amazing powers from a magical object. It was an old story but still fresh enough to launch a new superhero in 1940. Alan Scott, a young construction engineer, is the sole survivor of a train-and-bridge explosion set up by a jealous competitor. As he staggers away, Scott pulls a green lantern

from the demolished train cab. As Scott collapses from his injuries, the lantern begins to glow with an "eerie green light."

Lying by the wreckage, Scott hears a voice from the green lantern! The lantern is a conscious entity and it tells Scott that it originally existed as a green meteor which fell to Earth hundreds of years ago. Over the years, its green energy had been transformed into an old Chinese lamp and, finally, into a modern train lantern. The energy tells Scott that it is ready to fulfill the prophesy of bringing power to its next owner—Scott!

"You, who are to have this power, must use it to end evil! The light of the Green Lantern must be shed over the dark, evil things . . . for the dark evil things cannot stand light! Power shall be yours, if you have faith in yourself. Lose that faith and you lose the energetic power of the green lantern, for *will power* is the flame of the green lantern!"

The lantern tells Scott he should construct a ring from the lantern itself and renew the ring's energy by touching it to the lantern every twenty-four hours.

With his ring, Scott can will himself to fly through the air, materialize through walls, and make his body impervious to bullets. He uses his new powers to avenge the deaths of the train passengers killed by saboteurs. Then he realizes: "Somehow I feel as if destiny has taken hold of my life . . . that this is only the beginning . . . that I must continue to fight against evil!"

Green Lantern was the brainchild of a young artist named Martin Nodell. He submitted a sketch of the proposed hero to Sheldon Mayer, editor of *All-American Comics*. Mayer recalled that "Nodell's drawing was very crude. His idea for the Green Lantern appealed to us as a possibility but I didn't want to take it . . . I preferred to invent titles and characters myself and assign them to people who were more 'ready' than Nodell was at the time."

Still, there was an almost desperate need for new superhero features. Publisher Max Gaines wanted another costumed character for his All-American line which now included only the Flash and Hawkman. He pushed Mayer to give Green Lantern a spot in *All-American Comics*. Mayer huddled with writer Bill Finger, the cocreator of Batman, to flesh out the concept and develop the characters.

Mayer was savvy enough to realize the strong underlying appeal of the new hero—he got his powers from a magical ring. "It's a talisman," Mayer explained. "A St. Christopher's medal. The kids could visualize themselves actually owning the ring."

Since the character with a magical ring could easily become all-powerful, Mayer decided to "give him an Achilles heel; his powers didn't work against wood." As a result, baseball bats, falling tree limbs, and carefully hurled chairs proliferated throughout the strip.

Finger eventually staged the action of the feature in Gotham City and made Scott a radio announcer. He originally toyed with the idea of naming the hero Alan Ladd, as in "Aladdin," but rejected the choice "as too obvious." He wrote all the Green Lantern stories during its first two years.

One year into the feature, Finger wrote a story for *All-American Comics* (June 1941) which introduced Doiby Dickles, a comic sidekick who drove a taxi named "Goitrude" and always wore a bowler. Brooklyn-born and well-seasoned, the scrappy taxi driver was always ready to enter a fray to help his buddy—Green Lantern. ("Youse okay Lantrin? I didn't chase 'em on account I hadda help you!")

Doiby learns that Alan is actually Green Lantern (*All-American Comics*, February 1942) and for a short while thereafter, he wears a costume à la his hero. Doiby also rigs his cab Goitrude with a supersonic horn so he can silently alert Alan at his home when he sees trouble on the streets.

All-American Comics #92
© 1947 DC Comics, Inc.
Alex Toth.

The first Doiby Dickles appearance was drawn by Irwin Hasen, who broke into the super-hero business by drawing the Fox for *Blue Ribbon Comics* and the Cat-Man for *Crash Comics*. Hasen drew almost sixty adventures of the Emerald Crusader, second only to creator Nodell's nearly 100 stories. Paul Reinman would also draw Green Lantern for *All-American Comics* and *Comic Cavalcade,* as would, eventually, Alex Toth.

Other writers succeeded Bill Finger on the feature, such as science fiction writers Alfred Bester and Henry Kuttner. Kuttner's wife, science fiction author C.L. Moore, loved Doiby Dickles, and a preponderance of Doiby-oriented stories appeared between 1944 and 1946 ("Doiby Dickles Enters," "Doiby Dickles, The Human Bomb," "Doiby Dickles, Da Distrik Attoiney," and "Dickles Vs. Fate"). Bester, on the other hand, professed a strong dislike for Green Lantern's cherubic foil:

"When Shelly (Mayer) gave me complete control," Bester recalled, "I dumped Doiby Dickles . . . with that cockamamie derby hat, driving his cockamamie cab." Bester also railed against another well-established tradition in the feature, Green Lantern's Oath:

All-American Comics #17 © 1940 DC Comics, Inc.

> In brightest day, in blackest night,
> No evil shall escape my sight.
> Let those who worship evil's might
> Beware my power—Green Lantern's light!

Green Lantern invariably recited the awe-inspiring oath every time he recharged his ring, which always seemed to be at least once each issue. Bester thought it had become trite. "I did not like the oath. I thought it was pretty corny. Pretty tired." Nevertheless, it was part of the allure of the feature and it persevered through several changes in its text.

Green Lantern matched wits with regular worthy opponents, including the Icicle, the Gambler, Sportsmaster, and Solomon Grundy. His most memorable and popular antagonist, however, was a woman.

The Harlequin first appeared in the September 1947 issue of *All-American Comics* and would return nine times to try to defeat Green Lantern. Created by story editor Robert Kanigher, a self-professed admirer of womankind in general, the Harlequin was one of the most intriguing females in a 1940s comic book.

Kanigher, who would later handle the *Wonder Woman* comic book as writer and editor, created a strong-willed woman in the character of Molly Mayne, the Harlequin's alter ego. Mayne, who, coincidentally, was Alan Scott's secretary at the radio station WXYZ, was frustrated by being a female in a male-dominated society. "I never had a date because I was too athletic," the woman explained. "No man could beat me in sports. I have to hide my talents and become a mousy secretary."

When she meets Green Lantern, the imposing woman realizes that here is a man who will not be intimidated by her strength and presence. She becomes frustrated, however, when he ignores her in favor of fighting crime. To get his attention, she disguises herself as a harlequin and starts a one-woman crimewave. Using a mandolin stuffed with gimmicks and wearing a pair of blinding spectacles, the Harlequin was one of Green Lantern's most formidable foes. Eventually, the Harlequin, who was never completely bad, began to fight *with* instead of *against* Green Lantern. In the end, Mayne goes straight and becomes a government agent.

Kanigher also created another character for the Green Lantern series that eventually rivaled the Emerald Crusader himself in popularity. Streak the Wonder Dog appeared in the February 1948 issue of *Green Lantern* and was drawn by Alex Toth. After a few more heroic canine stories, Streak bumped Green Lantern from the cover of his own comic book. By the end of 1948, Green Lantern lost both his series in *All-American Comics* and *Comic Cavalcade*. Although his own magazine was canceled in 1949, he remained a member of the Justice Society of America until its end in 1951.

Golden Age Appearances
All-American Comics 16–102 (6/40–12/48)
All Star Comics 2–7, 10, 24–57 (Fall/40–2/51)
Green Lantern 1–38 (Fall/41–5/49)
Comic Cavalcade 1–29 (Winter/42–10/48)
All-Flash 14 (Spring/44)
Big All-American Comic Book 1 (12/44)

THE HANGMAN

July 1941 *Pep Comics* #17
MLJ Publications

John Dickering is a superhero called the Comet. He has a girlfriend, Thelma Gordon, who is a newspaper reporter, and a brother named Bob. When vengeful criminals attempt to kidnap the Comet, they grab his brother by mistake. As John Dickering swoops in as the Comet to save his brother, he is felled by a volley of bullets. Bob takes his wounded brother to Thelma's apartment. On his deathbed, the Comet turns to his brother and his girlfriend and tells them: "My turn now . . . You two stick together . . . Kind of a memorial to me . . . Goodbye Bob—Bye Thel . . . Aahh!"

Hangman Comics #4
© 1942 Archie Comic
Publications, Inc.

Bob Dickering stands over his murdered brother and takes a vow before the dead man's girlfriend: "I'll carry on for him, Thel! I'll bring his murderers to the hangman . . . I'll be their *Hangman*!!"

The Hangman was one of the more cold-blooded superheroes. Motivated by revenge instead of a sense of moral righteousness, he rarely showed compassion as he tracked down killers and maniacs. He often projected the shadow of a gallows and a hangman's noose to terrorize his foes: "Like a harbinger of doom, a beam of light cuts through the murky darkness, and the soul-chilling symbol of the Hangman is vividly etched across the man's face—the gallows."

Within a few months of his origin, the Hangman turned his attention from thugs to Nazis. His arch-enemy was Captain Swastika—the kind of guy who tries to steal a U.S. battleship. The Captain's henchman, a fellow called the Executioner, has an icepick in place of a missing hand.

The Hangman also takes the war to Germany's home front when he goes overseas to fight another Nazi villain called The Hunter—"arch sleuth of the Gestapo."

The Hangman stories were often dark and violent. George Storm, who drew one of the first newspaper adventure strips in the 1920s (*Phil Hardy*), was the first artist. Harry Lucey, a former pulp cover artist, introduced the elements of horror into the strip. Lucey's assistant, Bob "Fuje" Fujitani, eventually took over the strip and made the Hangman an even darker character. In one story drawn by Fujitani, a madman strangles a mother in front of her son ("I've long wanted to do this, Mary! Kill you . . . KILL YOU!") and then decides to kill the young boy as well ("I can break his thin neck so easily . . . ").

Cliff Campbell, who had written detective and horror stories for the pulp magazines, wrote the first adventure of the Hangman and gave the character a hardboiled edge. He was succeeded on the feature by writers William Woolfolk and Otto Binder, who kept the dark characterization and blood flowing.

Golden Age Appearances
Pep Comics 17–47 (7/41–3/44)
Special Comics 1 (Winter/41)
Hangman Comics 2–8 (Spring/42–Fall/43)
Black Hood Comics 9, 10 (Winter/43–Spring/44)

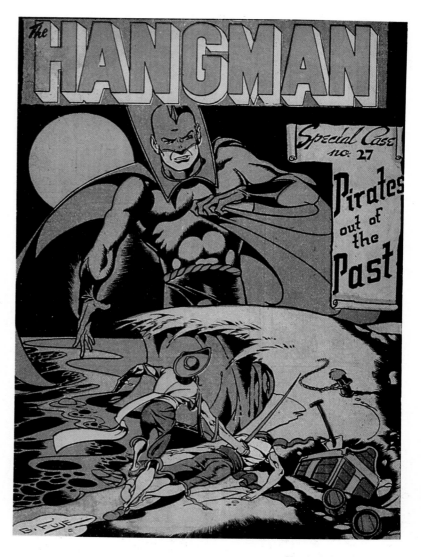

Hangman Comics #8
© 1942 Archie Comic Publications, Inc. Bob Fujitani.

HAWKMAN

January 1940 *Flash Comics* #1
DC Comics

Carter Hall, "a wealthy collector of weapons and research scientist," acquires an ancient Egyptian sacrificial knife made of glass for his collection. The mere presence of the knife, however, causes Hall to have a hypnotic vision of his previous life when he was the ancient Prince Khufu.

In this past life, Hall as the prince was fighting for the life of his lover, Shiera, who had been "betrayed by the hawk-god Anubis." Unfortunately, before he can rescue Shiera, the prince is killed by the glass knife which is wielded by Hath-Set, a priest of the hawk-god. As he dies, Prince Khufu (who looks like Carter Hall) makes an oath:

Flash Comics #5 © 1940 DC Comics, Inc. Sheldon Moldoff.

"I shall live again . . . and then I shall be the victor!"

As Hall snaps out of the vision, he realizes he must be the reincarnated spirit of the Egyptian prince. He also speculates that Shiera, too, has been reincarnated in the twentieth century.

Indeed, several hours later, Hall literally runs into Shiera on the street. The woman looks exactly like the vision of his past-life lover. Shiera confesses to Hall that she, too, has had similar visions of a past life where she was persecuted by the hawk-god Anubis ("Only I thought them nightmares!").

As the reincarnated lovers pick up the pieces of a relationship suspended for several thousand years, Hall decides he must continue his centuries-long battle against the forces of evil. He embarks on his mission by using weapons from his own collection and dressing up, "as a grim jest," in the garb of his archrival, the hawk-god Anubis.

Hall uses a webbing for his hawk wings made from a substance he discovered in his laboratory—"the ninth metal which defies the pull of earth's gravity." With his antigravity wings, Hall realizes one of the oldest dreams—human flight.

"And so Carter Hall goes to his weapon room and emerges . . . the Hawkman—the winged phantom of the night who fights the evils of the present with the weapons of the past!!"

Carter Hall would not have all the fun himself, however. This was the twentieth century and, reincarnated girlfriend or not, Shiera was not about to sit on the sidelines for long. When the couple attend a masquerade party (*Flash Comics*, December 1941), Carter makes a feminine version of his hawk costume for Shiera to wear, complete with working wings. When a crime ensues, Shiera naturally "flies" into action just as she has seen Carter do several times before. Although she botches her first fight and must be saved by Hawkman, Shiera prevails upon her boyfriend to let her keep the costume. He reluctantly agrees and Shiera becomes his partner, Hawkgirl.

Hawkman and Hawkgirl were the creation of writer Gardner Fox, who was busily writing most of the features for the new *Flash Comics* (January 1940). Where Fox's lead character for the comic, the speedy Flash, was an obvious borrowing from Roman mythology, Hawkman owed his existence to the writer's interest in Egyptian mythology. "I've always liked the supernatural," Fox admitted, and he delighted in filling the Hawkman stories with midnight scenes ("Like a fabled bird, the Hawkman flies against the moon . . . ").

Fox was also influenced by "Flash Gordon," Alex Raymond's newspaper strip of heroic derring-do on the planet Mongo. As early as 1934, Raymond populated his science fiction series with a race of flying men known as the Hawkmen. He also seemed to prefer arming his hero Flash with ancient weapons in his battles against Ming the Merciless.

The influence of Raymond's "Flash Gordon" on Hawkman became more apparent when artist Sheldon ("Shelly") Moldoff took over the strip from Dennis Neville after the first three stories. Moldoff, like many comic artists at the time, was an admirer of both Alex Raymond and Hal Foster, the artist of "Tarzan."

When publisher Max Gaines asked the nineteen-year-old Moldoff to draw Hawkman, he was an assistant for Bob Kane, drawing backgrounds and lettering panels for *Batman*.

With no time to learn on the job and a minimal art background, Moldoff used Raymond and Foster for his mentors, incorporating their compositions and imitating their shadings from "Flash Gordon" and "Tarzan." Moldoff succeeded in giving Hawkman the perfect look for Fox's heroic exploits and became the Winged Wonder's principal artist for the first five years.

Moldoff was succeeded on the Hawkman feature by teenager Joe Kubert with the February 1945 issue of *Flash Comics*. "By the time I got out of high school," Kubert recalled, "I had started doing Hawkman and the Flash. Shel Mayer, who was editor of those books before they both became part of the Detective Comics group, was the one who gave me my first chance to do covers, and I did Hawkman covers for him. I was doing that in my second, third, and fourth years of high school."

Kubert continued Moldoff's homage to Alex Raymond when drawing Hawkman, but he also added his own sense of dynamic motion to the heavily shaded panels. By late 1948, Hawkman had traded in his distinctive hawk headgear for a cowl mask which made him look like a cheap wrestling hero. After Gardner Fox left DC Comics in 1947, John Broome and Robert Kanigher wrote the series.

Flash Comics #5 © 1940 DC Comics, Inc. Sheldon Moldoff.

Despite the consistent quality in stories, Hawkman made his last appearance in his own feature in 1949. For the next two years, however, Hawkman would maintain his status as the chairman of the Justice Society of America in *All Star Comics* until its demise.

Golden Age Appearances
Flash Comics 1–104 (1/40–2/49)
All Star Comics 1–57 (Summer/40–2/51)
Big All-American Comic Book 1 (12/44)

Flash Comics #33 © 1942 DC Comics, Inc. Sheldon Moldoff.

THE HUMAN TORCH

November 1939 *Marvel Comics* #1
Marvel Comics

The Human Torch, a blazing red character who streaked through the air like a ball of flame, was the perfect hero for the "picture-action-story" in the first issue of *Marvel Comics* ("Jumping through space like a comet, the Human Torch lands on the car and melts the body as if it were made of butter!").

The idea for a hero made of fire came from artist Carl Burgos. In the first issue of *Marvel Comics*, a purported interview called "Carl Burgos's Hot Idea" reveals that the artist came up with the

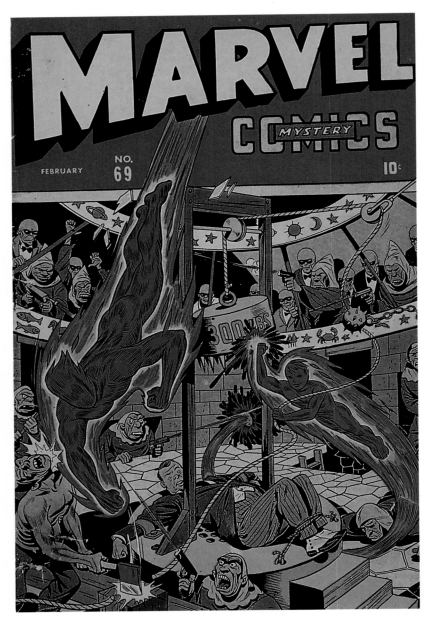

Marvel Mystery Comics #69 © 1946 Marvel Entertainment Group, Inc. Alex Schomburg.

Everett, his colleague at Funnies, Incorporated, and creator of the Sub-Mariner, found it pleasurable to hold their brainstorming meetings at a much-visited Manhattan bar. Everett recalled that he and Burgos had been "asked to develop new characters, and Carl and I were quite close friends. Between us somewhere we came up with two elements [fire and water] and what we could do with them."

Everett chose water for his heroic medium and came up with the Sub-Mariner. The natural complement for an aquatic hero was one made of fire, and Burgos took his cue.

Earlier that year, Burgos had created a character for Centaur Publishing called the Iron Skull, which appeared in *Amazing Man Comics*. The Iron Skull was a super-powered android, and Burgos decided to recycle the idea for the Human Torch.

Professor Phineas Horton creates "a synthetic man—an exact replica of a human being" in his laboratory. The only problem with Horton's creation is that it bursts into flames when exposed to oxygen, so he must keep his "human torch" inside an "air-tight glass cage."

The android, however, escapes and eventually learns to control his flame so he can turn it on and off at will. After being exploited by gangsters and later his own creator, the android decides to become a crimefighter and adopts a human identity. For a while, the Human Torch operated under the identity of Jim Hammond, police officer, but quickly dropped the pretense of an alter idea of a Human Torch after a nightmare filled with screaming kids and a demanding publisher who wanted him to come up with a new comic book character. In his dream, Burgos himself catches on fire and becomes a living human torch:

"The roar of the fire was filling my ears. A hot draft fanned the flames and I could feel myself being drawn up into the chimney. I seemed to float, my body was lighter than air, and for a horrible minute I found myself hurtling up through the sooty black chimney . . ."

In reality, the inspiration for the Human Torch was much more prosaic and was induced by a bottle instead of a nightmare. Burgos and Bill

Marvel Mystery Comics #19 © 1941 Marvel Entertainment Group, Inc.

ego. After the first year, little mention was made of his android origins, and for all practical purposes, he was treated as truly a "human" torch.

The humanizing of the Torch continued with the debut of his own magazine in late 1940, which introduced a boy sidekick with the unlikely name of Toro. Toro was adopted by a traveling circus after his parents were killed in a fiery train accident.

Toro, it seems, has a natural immunity to fire ("I used to pull baked potatoes outta the fire for the gang!") and was perfect for a fire-eating act in the circus. One day, as the Human Torch flies by the circus, he sees the young fire-eater inexplicably burst into flames!

Sympathetic to the boy's predicament, the Torch helps him learn to control his flame powers just as he himself had learned a few months earlier. Together, they make quite a fighting team, trapping crooks in a volley of searing fireballs ("YEOW! My moustache! I-I-It burned off!") and crisscrossing the sky in a net of flames. Toro would later become a star in his own right in such comics as *Young Allies* and *Kid Komix*.

By late 1948, the Human Torch dumped Toro in favor of Sun Girl, the newest addition to the growing line of good-looking Marvel heroines. Sun Girl first appeared in her own magazine in August 1948, where she distinguished herself as a natural fighter accomplished in judo and acrobatics. The woman with the sunbeam device played a more subservient role, however, in her appearances with the Human Torch, and often ended up as the beautiful damsel in distress.

Perhaps the Human Torch made a mistake in tossing aside his flaming sidekick for a pretty face. In any case, he was rewarded for his capriciousness by having all his magazines canceled by the spring of 1949.

Arguably, the Human Torch was the most popular Marvel Comics superhero of the 1940s. He was on more Marvel covers than any other hero of the 1940s, appeared regularly in six titles by 1944, and nearly ties Captain America (259 versus 262) for the greatest number of stories published during the 1940s for a Marvel hero.

Golden Age Appearances
Marvel Comics 1 (11/39)
Marvel Mystery Comics 2–92 (12/39–6/49)
Human Torch 1–35 (Fall/40–3/49)
All Winners Comics (1) 1–13, 17–19, 21
   (Summer/41–Winter/46)
Captain America 19, 21–67, 69 (10/42–11/48)
All-Select Comics 1–10 (Fall/43–Summer/46)
Mystic Comics (2) 1, 2 (10/44–Fall/44)

Marvel Mystery Comics #19 © 1941 Marvel Entertainment Group, Inc.

Daring Comics 9–12 (Fall/44–Fall/45)
Sub-Mariner 23, 29 (Summer/47–12/48)
All Winners Comics (2) 1 (8/48)

HYDROMAN

August 1940 *Heroic Comics #1*
Eastern Color Printing

Harry Thurston, "a young chemist who devotes all his spare time to constructive invention," creates a chemical solution which can turn human flesh to water. He accidentally spills the chemicals on his hand with alarming results and summons his friend Bob Blake to his laboratory:

"Glad you came, Bob. I think I made an important discovery! I just mixed a chemical that transformed my hand into a *waterspout*—yet there's no pain."

As Bob examines the water spurting from the stump of the scientist's arm, he is accidentally splashed with the chemical solution and "instantly goes up in a geyser of water!"

After being changed into a puddle of water, Blake is restored to human form by a chemical antidote. He decides to let the chemist inject the solution into his bloodstream so that at will he can turn his body into a stream of living water. In his "watery" form, he can surge through the air like a stream or travel like a waterspout. He can turn his body into water and drown his enemies or hide from them inside a water pipe.

*Heroic Comics #4 © 1941
Eastern Color Printing Co.
Bill Everett.*

His chemist friend tells Blake, "Look, I've got some full-length tights here, part of a masquerade costume—why don't you wear them with a pair of high boots? Might as well look 'in character!' You can have my service automatic and the aviator's helmet and goggles—they'll help with the disguise."

Bob's girlfriend, Joyce Church, watches him dress up in his new costume and in a burst of refreshing realism tells him: "You're a nut, Bobby!"

"It's not so funny, Joyce! This discovery is really revolutionary. Wait'll you see what I do with it! From now on you can call me HYDROMAN!"

Bill Everett, working in the Funnies, Incorporated, studio, created Hydroman for the first issue of *Heroic Comics*. Everett recalled that when a boyhood friend suggested the idea of Hydroman to him, "I thought it was utterly preposterous. It was so ridiculous that I couldn't do anything with it. And he said, 'Why sure! He could change

himself into water, he can run through the sewers of New York and water mains. You could turn on the tap in the kitchen, and out comes Hydroman!'"

Steve Douglas, the editor of *Heroic*, liked the idea, and Everett came up with the first Hydroman story. "I used the name Bob Blake for Hydroman's alter ego, because the guy that created the idea, his name was Bob. It was one way I could give him credit for giving me the story without having to pay him." His hero's last name, Blake, was taken from Everett's middle name.

After drawing the first nine adventures of Hydroman, Everett turned the strip over to fellow Funnies, Incorporated, artist Ben Thompson, the artist on Ka-Zar The Great (an early Tarzan imitation) for *Marvel Comics*. Thompson and editor Steve Douglas introduced a new character in the Hydroman strip, a kid sidekick called Rainbow Boy.

Golden Age Appearances
Heroic Comics 1–29 (8/40–3/45)

IBIS THE INVINCIBLE
February 1940 *Whiz Comics #2*
Fawcett Publishing

At the Egyptian wing of a famous American museum, the mummified form of young Prince Amentep lies on display in a glass case. Inscribed on his casket is the ancient Egyptian symbol for rebirth and eternal life, the sacred Ibis bird. "We call him Old Man Ibis," a museum guard remarks to a visitor. "The inscription means—'I will live again.'"

That very night, the inscription comes true, and the mummy form of "old man Ibis" comes back to life. In his bandaged hand "he holds the Ibistick—the most powerful weapon ever devised." He points the Ibistick (an eight-inch wand with a jeweled Ibis talisman at the end) at the restraining glass case and murmurs a command:

"Melt!"

The glass melts away and the mummy points the Ibistick at his body: "Clothe me!"

The ancient bandages fall away to reveal a young man in a red turban and black business suit. The resurrected Egyptian prince uses his Ibistick to materialize such things as money, houses, and food. He even uses the stick to create a bombproof glass dome over an endangered city. The Ibistick, which can "do mighty magic for good purposes and fails only against other magic," even allowed the Egyptian magician to locate and revive his ancient lover, Princess Taia. Separated by death 4,000 years ago in ancient Egypt, Ibis and Taia are reunited in twentieth-century Europe.

Magician heroes were popular in the 1940s comic books and most were inspired by Lee Falk's successful newspaper strip *Mandrake the Magician* (1934). Such masters of magic as Zatara (*Action Comics*), Zambini (*Zip Comics*), Zanzibar (*Mysterymen Comics*), Blackstone (*Super Magician Comics*), and Yarko the Great (*Wonderworld Comics*), cast spells and gestured hypnotically at dragons, Nazis, vampires, and jewel thieves. Ibis the Invincible, however, was the longest-lasting and perhaps the best conceived of the comic book magicians.

Editor and writer Bill Parker created Ibis the Invincible, along with Captain Marvel and Spy Smasher, for *Whiz Comics*. Parker indulged his fondness for the ancient classics and took his hero from the twelfth dynasty of Egypt. What made Ibis (pronounced "eye-biss," not "ib-ess," according to Parker) outlast all the other comic book magicians was the imaginative writing of Otto Binder, Manly Wade Wellman, Irwin Schoffman, and William Woolfolk.

Elements of horror, the occult, and the grotesque ran through every Ibis story courtesy of artists like Kurt Schaffenberger, Carl Pfeufer, and Alex Blum. The writers (all admirers of the pulp fiction magazine *Weird Tales*) made Ibis and Taia the supernatural stars of the Fawcett comics line and filled the pages with scenes of walking corpses, human sacrifices, and mysteriously appearing body parts. After a sunshiny story featuring Captain Marvel, readers of *Whiz Comics* always turned to Ibis with shivery expectation.

"Great Zoth! Ibistick, hear my commands!"

Golden Age Appearances
Whiz Comics 2–155 (2/40–6/53)
Ibis, the Invincible 1–6 (1/42–9/48)
America's Greatest 4 (Summer/42)
All Hero 1 (3/45)

JUSTICE SOCIETY OF AMERICA

Winter 1940 *All Star Comics #3*
DC Comics

The Flash, Green Lantern, Hawkman, Hourman, Sandman, Doctor Fate, the Spectre, and the Atom were all together—in the same comic book, in the same room, for the first time. For comic book readers in 1940, so many superheroes had never appeared in one place together.

The idea of putting all the superheroes together in one comic book came from publisher Max Gaines. According to writer Gardner Fox, Gaines called him and editor Sheldon Mayer and said that he wanted to do "a companion comic book" called *All Star Comics* to go with his other superheroes who were coming out in *Flash Comics* and *All-American Comics*. "The books were selling so well, he wanted to make even more money," Fox recalled. "We decided to take all the superheroes that we had and form them together into a society."

Fox and Mayer formed a team of superheroes they called The Justice Society of America. In the first story, the eight superheroes gather around a hotel dining table and each relates a past adventure. At the end of this superhero bull session, the Flash makes the announcement that the F.B.I. wants to meet with the Justice Society for a special assignment. It was the prewar years, and the

All Star Comics #13
© 1942 DC Comics, Inc.
Jack Burnley.

government wanted the JSA to break up espionage rings and monitor possible saboteur activity.

The Justice Society of America developed at a time when the idea of teamwork and pulling together was a vital part of the war effort. Early prewar and wartime Justice Society of America adventures included "For America and Democracy," "Hemisphere Defense," "The Bomb Defense Formula," "Food For Starving Patriots," and "One Million Dollars for War Orphans."

The JSA was originally an opportunity for DC Comics to showcase heroes who were appearing in only one other comic book. Batman and Superman, who already starred in two comic books, with a third title planned, did not need the extra exposure afforded by membership in the Justice Society.

As charter members like the Flash and Green Lantern received their own comic books, they

All Star Comics #3
© 1941 DC Comics, Inc.
Everett E. Hibbard.

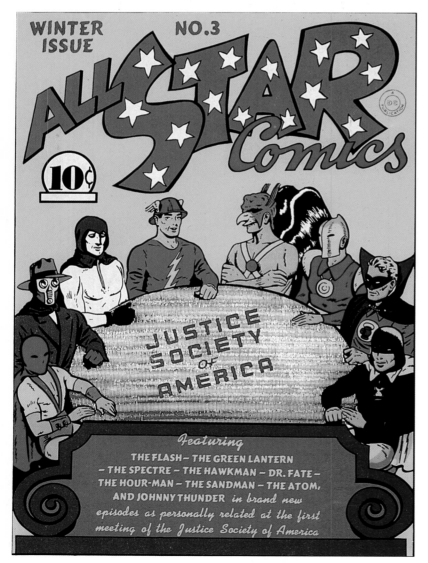

All Star Comics #37 © 1947 DC Comics, Inc.

were replaced by up-and-coming heroes such as Johnny Thunder from *Flash Comics* and Dr. Midnite from *All-American Comics*. Other heroes like the Spectre and Hourman were dropped from the rolls as their popularity faded, and were replaced by Starman from *Adventure Comics* and Wonder Woman (who served as secretary) from *Sensation Comics*.

Other heroes who took part in the JSA included Mr. Terrific, Wildcat, and the Black Canary. Even Batman and Superman made their first joint appearance in a story as honorary members. Hawkman was the only member who appeared in every adventure and eventually became the team's chairman.

With so many heroes in each issue, the book-length stories had to be carefully structured and plotted. Gardner Fox, who wrote the first thirty-two JSA adventures, recalled working on the early stories with editor Sheldon Mayer: "Shelly and I would plot the whole story. He would come up to my house for dinner, and right after it, we would sit down and go to work. After a time, of course, he let me go at it by myself, but in the beginning, he wanted to have a hand in the story line; to make sure, I imagine, that when I sent in the finished product, he could just send it off to the artist without any fussing over it."

Mayer recalled that during his dinner meetings with Fox, "we'd finish plotting a book-length *All Star* before I'd leave at night. To me, the collaborations were just a way of two guys doing more writing together than they could possibly do separately. By the time we finished a script, it was impossible to tell who wrote what. The ideas grew while we sat there."

The ideas which grew were dazzling. Some of the best-written and socially conscious comic book stories of the 1940s were in *All Star Comics.* In their superhero fables, Mayer and Fox tackled such issues as juvenile delinquency, racial intolerance, attitudes toward the handicapped, and even the need for a strong United Nations in a postwar world. There were also plenty of comic book villains as well, such as Brain Wave, who mentally projected false images; Psycho-Pirate, who used emotions to confound and confuse; and the infamous Injustice Gang of the World.

All Star Comics, with the Justice Society of America, proved to be one of the most venerable titles of the Golden Age and remained the last refuge for the failing DC superheroes of the 1940s. In many respects, the demise of the JSA and *All Star Comics* marked the end of many a reader's "Golden Age" of comics.

Golden Age Appearances
All Star Comics 3–57 (Winter/40-2/51)

KID ETERNITY

December 1942 *Hit Comics* #25
Quality Comics

"To make up for his untimely death, extraordinary powers were bestowed upon Kid Eternity . . . powers no other mortal ever had! Under the guardianship of Mr. Keeper, he can revisit

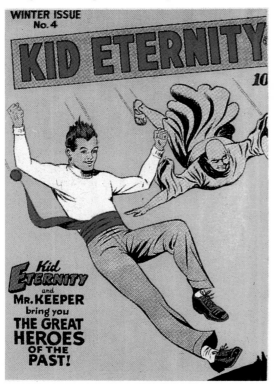

Kid Eternity #4 © 1946 Comic Magazines, Inc.

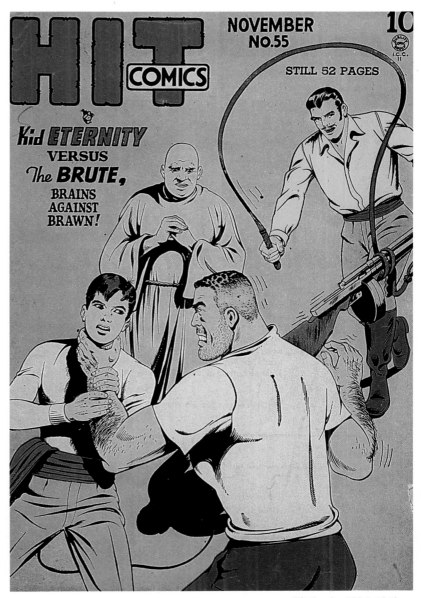

Hit Comics #55 © 1948 Comic Magazines, Inc. Al Bryant.

earth in his mortal form . . . can make himself visible or invisible at will . . . and can summon all the great men and women of the past to his aid by uttering the single word—ETERNITY!"

Another chance at life, a hero who returns from the dead, and a guardian angel. The concept for Kid Eternity and his afterlife aide, Mr. Keeper, may have come from the popular 1941 movie *Here Comes Mr. Jordon,* which starred Robert Montgomery as a prizefighter who dies in an airplane crash before his allotted time on Earth is up. Accompanied by a celestial guide called Mr. Jordon, Montgomery gets a chance at another life on Earth.

The idea of a hero returning from an untimely death had also been used in the comic books before Kid Eternity's late 1942 appearance, as witness the success of the Spectre (February 1940) and the Spirit (June 1940). What made Kid Eternity special, however, was simple: he was a kid and only a kid—he had no other name, no identity. Just a kid who died, as always, too soon.

It's 1942, and the kid is with his grandfather on a merchant marine ship carrying war supplies in the North Atlantic. A German submarine torpedoes the ship and kills the kid's grandfather. Then the U-boat surfaces and machine-guns the kid.

Next, the kid and his grandfather are standing on a bank of clouds with a golden archway stretching toward the heavens. They join other disembodied spirits as they move toward a gate. The kid is stopped at the gate, however. Something is wrong. It's not his time. He is allotted another seventy-five years on Earth. His death was a mistake.

To make up for the mistake, the kid is allowed to return to Earth under the guardianship of the ethereal Mr. Keeper, a bald and portly eunuchlike fellow who wears only a robe and rope sandals. Mr. Keeper always accompanies the kid and turns invisible (represented in the comic book by light-blue coloring) when he is on Earth. Mr. Keeper tells the kid that he has the power to either be invisible or be in his physical body while on Earth. All he has to do to change back and forth is to say the magic word, "Eternity!"

As an extra bonus for biting the bullet so early, the kid also gains another power:

"When you speak the magic word, you shall be able to call on any person in mythology or history! They shall come and you shall enter their body and battle in that form. Your powers are unlimited, kid—and we know you will use them to the best advantage! Say it, kid—speak the magic word! For you are KID ETERNITY!"

With this one power, Kid Eternity could call upon "the strength and power of all great men of the past." For example, if the kid needed some heavy lifting done, he could say "Eternity" and summon forth Hercules or Atlas. When he's finished, he can send them back to eternity by repeating the magic word. Fortunately, all the resurrected heroes spoke English.

In one story, Kid Eternity first summons forth Phidippedes, the original Olympic marathon runner, to take a warning message to a bank about to be robbed ("Fear not, Kid Eternity! I will do my utmost!"). When the famous Greek athlete, dressed in an Olympian wreath and tiny yellow running shorts, arrives at the bank, he is told: "Listen, screwball! Go home—or I'll run you in for indecent exposure!"

Undaunted, the Kid summons forth the Roman warrior Horatius from eternity to help catch the crooks and next brings back Dr. Frederic Mesemer, the discover of hypnotism, to hypnotize one of the captured criminals. Finally, Kid Eternity wraps up the whole affair by bringing in Samson.

The first Kid Eternity story was drawn by Shelly Moldoff, who was also busily drawing the first appearance of Hawkgirl for *Flash Comics* that month. Moldoff was followed by a string of artists, including Ruben Moreira, Al Bryant, Mort Leav, and Alex Kotzky, who drew the Kid in his original series in *Hit Comics,* as well as in his own comic book *Kid Eternity.*

Golden Age Appearances
Hit Comics 25–60 (12/42–9/49)
Kid Eternity 1–18 (Spring/46–11/49)

MAGNO, THE MAGNETIC MAN
July 1940 *Super Mystery Comics* #1
Ace Magazines

When Aaron A. Wyn (Ace Magazines) decided to add comic books to his line of pulp magazines, he invested heavily in superheroes.

Four Favorites #24 © 1946 Ace Magazines, Inc. Rudy Palais.

More than a dozen costumed characters appeared in *Sure-Fire Comics*, *Banner Comics*, *Our Flag Comics*, and *Super Mystery Comics*. While most of the early Ace comic book heroes were unabashedly patriotic (Captain Courageous, The Unknown Soldier, The Flag), the company's most enduring superhero, Magno the Magnetic Man, was actually more of a playboy than a patriot.

Possessing no secret identity, Magno passes himself off as an idle socialite who just likes to wear blue tights, a red bodyshirt, and a high-collared yellow cape. Magno possesses extraordinary magnetic powers which can divert trains and attract objects from miles away. Bombs bounce off his chest and he can fly through the air.

With his fourth adventure (*Super-Mystery Comics*, November 1940), Magno acquires a youthful crime-fighting partner called Davey, who also has the powers of magnetic attraction and repulsion. The two are often referred to as the "Dynamic Duo" and are called upon by the government for secret war missions.

An early enemy was the Cobra, a snakelike saboteur who battled the polarized pair for four consecutive issues. The Clown was another recurrent archvillain who escaped from the duo time and time again as the result of some deadly prank.

Magno appeared in both *Super Mystery Comics* and *Four Favorites* and was featured on the cover of all but seven issues. Artists who worked on the feature included Jim Mooney, Rudy Palais, Harvey Kurtzman, and L.B. Cole.

Golden Age Appearances
Super Mystery Comics 1–33 (7/40–12/45)
Four Favorites 1–26 (9/41–11/46)

Wow Comics #21 © 1944 Fawcett Publications, Inc.

MARY MARVEL

December 1942 *Captain Marvel Adventures* #18
Fawcett Publishing

"But why should I be scared? Naturally, the bullets just bounce off! That's the final proof—*I'm just like Captain Marvel!!*"

Imagine you're a very bright teenage girl with parents in the social registry. Imagine you one day discover that you actually are an orphan—switched at birth—and that your long-lost brother is no other than Billy Batson—better known as Captain Marvel!

Mary Bromfield discovers her true identity after she appears on Billy's "Mental Marvel Quiz" program at radio station WHIZ. When the two teens compare their matching sets of broken lockets, they realize they are twins—separated since birth.

After Mary sees her brother turn into the world's mightiest mortal—Captain Marvel—simply by saying the magic word "Shazam," she wonders: "Billy, I'm your twin sister—so maybe if I said the magic word, I'd change into something too!"

Mary gets her chance when a group of kidnappers threaten them and she says the word—"Shazam!" "Instantly there is an answering roll of thunder . . . a blinding flash of lightning. . . and a new figure appears in the place of Mary Batson!!"

"It happened!" says the teenager. "I changed! I feel strong—powerful!"

Dressed in a thigh-high red skirt, yellow boots, and a high-collar cape, Mary Marvel takes

Mary Marvel #17 © 1947 Fawcett Publications, Inc.

Wow Comics #49 © 1946 Fawcett Publications, Inc.

Zephyrus (spirit of the West Wind), Aurora (goddess of the Dawn), and Minerva (goddess of Wisdom).

Rod Reed, the executive editor of Fawcett comics at the time that Mary Marvel was created, recalled that, originally, the letter "S" in Shazam was to have stood for *Sappho*. Rather than give his young heroine the questionable powers of a Greek poet from the isle of Lesbos, Reed suggested that Selena, goddess of the moon, might be a more wholesome choice.

And Mary was wholesome. Ever cheerful, fresh, and pleasant, Mary Marvel was the perfect Girl Scout of the superheroines. None of that bondage and bikini stuff you saw in Sheena or Wonder Woman.

Artist Marc Swayze of the Jack Binder studio drew the first adventure of Mary Marvel for the December 1942 issue of *Captain Marvel Adventures*. He helped design the character by first doing a series of portraits which, according to editor Rod Reed, ended up "as beautiful covers on the early issues."

As Mary began her series in *Wow Comics*, *Marvel Family*, and her own comic book, Jack Binder and other artists from his shop like Bob Butts, John Spranger, Pete Riss, Kurt Schafenberger, Clem Weisbecker, Andre LeBlanc, Ken Bald, Harry Anderson, and Bob Boyajian had a hand in drawing the adventures. Jack's brother, Otto Binder, wrote the majority of the Mary Marvel stories, with other scripts contributed by Rod Reed and Bill Woolfolk.

Otto Binder lays claim to "personally launching Mary Marvel by writing the original script." Binder, and the other writers, kept Mary Marvel chaste and removed from any serious romantic encounter. She never had a boyfriend, kissed only her Uncle Marvel, and channeled her libido into raising money for war orphans.

For girls growing up in the 1940s, Mary Marvel may not have had the feminist slant afforded by Wonder Woman but she was alluringly more accessible. The powers of Mary Marvel were only a magic word away. Boys and girls both whispered "Shazam" and dreamed about the super-powered teenager who might, perhaps, someday turn out to be their long-lost sister.

time to make a feminine observation ("My! What a lovely costume!") before she jump-kicks and punches out her would-be kidnappers.

"Captain Marvel couldn't have done it better himself," gushed Billy Batson. "Boy, what a sister I have!"

Billy, Mary, and Freddy Freeman (also known as Captain Marvel, Jr.) next visit the old seer known as Shazam, who gave Captain Marvel his original powers. Shazam tells the kids that "Mary derives her powers from a different group of my old friends than you, Billy."

Instead of the powers of Solomon, Hercules, Atlas, Zeus, Achilles, and Mercury, Shazam gives Mary the powers of grace, strength, skill, fleetness, beauty, and wisdom, derived from women: Selena (goddess of the Moon), Hippolyta (queen of the Amazons), Ariadne (spirit of Skill),

Golden Age Appearances

Captain Marvel Adventures 18, 19, 37, 43, 65, 69 (12/42–2/47)
Wow Comics 9–58 (1/43–9/47)
Mary Marvel 1–28 (12/45–9/48)
Marvel Family 1–89 (12/45–1/54)
Master Comics 118 (12/50)

MISS AMERICA

November 1943 *Marvel Mystery* #49
Marvel Comics

Miss America, a fair sex homage to Captain America, was Marvel Comics's longest-running superheroine of the 1940s. The red-white-and-blue patriot was originally Madeline Joyce. She gained her super-powers during a thunderstorm at a lighthouse when an electrical charge surged through her body. Knocked unconscious, Joyce awakens one week later and discovers she now has the power to fly, X-ray vision, the "strength of a thousand men," and the "wisdom of the ages."

Since this is 1943, Joyce devises a costume with a red, white, and blue shield on the chest and gets busy fighting Nazis as Miss America. Madeline did have an advantage over Captain America; she could smack women without dishonor and had no compunctions about smashing female villains right in the face:

"Sorry, sister! Hate to do this, but you invited it!"

The Captain and Miss America never met during the war years. In 1946, however, Miss America was made a member of the short-lived All Winners Squad, which consisted of Captain America and Bucky, the Human Torch and Toro, Sub-Mariner, and the Whizzer. It was the first time all the major Marvel heroes appeared in the same story.

Miss America was created by veteran comic book writer Otto Binder. The art on the first *Miss America* comic book was by Pauline Loth, an animator who originally worked in the Fleischer Studio and was the voice of the Honeybee in the feature-length 1942 cartoon *Mr. Bug Goes To Town*. Loth also worked in the Jack Binder comic art studio in 1942 as a replacement artist for the young men who entered the service. There, she drew the Fighting Yank, Captain Midnight, Captain Marvel, Jr., and Mary Marvel—another Otto Binder heroine.

Marvel editor Vince Fago remembered Loth from her animation days and felt that her style was perfect for Miss America, a feature he hoped would have a strong appeal to girls. Fago was right. Within two weeks after the first issue of *Miss America Comics* appeared, he received 20,000 subscription requests.

Golden Age Appearances
Marvel Mystery Comics 49–85 (11/43–2/48)
Miss America 1–2 (1944–11/44)
All Winners 19, 21 (Fall/46–Winter/47)

All Select 11 (Fall/46)
Blonde Phantom 12–14
  (Winter/47–Summer/47)
Sun Girl 1 (8/48)

Marvel Mystery Comics #69
© 1946 Marvel Entertainment Group, Inc.

PHANTOM LADY

August 1941 *Police Comics* #1
Quality Comics/Fox Features

"Sandra Knight, daughter of the famous Senator Knight, and Washington society's pampered darling, is none other than PHANTOM LADY, challenger and terror of lawbreakers everywhere! Not even her boyfriend, Don Borden, is aware of this . . . so let's keep her secret safe as we follow her breathtaking adventures!"

Phantom Lady #14
© 1947 Fox Features
Syndicate

comic book shop of Will Eisner and Jerry Iger. She was originally drawn by Arthur Peddy, who worked on such heroes as Doll Man (*Feature Comics*) and the Human Meteor (*Champ Comics*).

Sandra Knight began her road to heroics and bondage on the steps of our nation's capitol, when she thwarted an assassination attempt on her father, Senator Henry Knight. Feeling empowered by her success, she next discovers a "black-out ray" invention that was given to her father by an old family friend, Professor Davis.

Sandra modifies the blackout-ray projector so that it can fit on a bracelet. She operates the blackout-ray like a reverse flashlight so that it spreads darkness around crooks and temporarily blinds them. Next, she fashions a one-piece, yellow bodysuit and a green cape to wear in her role as a crimefighter.

Her costume became a little less modest in 1943, when artist Frank Borth took over the strip. Borth, who was already drawing another costumed heroine, the Spider Widow (*Feature Comics*), dropped the Phantom Lady's neckline and gave the senator's daughter a shove toward womanhood. Evidently, Borth's embellishments did not make the character any more popular because the Phantom Lady disappeared from Quality Comics by late summer of 1943.

By 1947, the Iger studio was supplying publisher Victor Fox with characters and stories for his revived line of comic books. Since the Phantom Lady was in retirement from Quality Comics, Jerry Iger decided to bring her back for his client. Iger maintained that he had a proprietary interest in the characters his studio had created and no one seemed to object when he delivered the Phantom Lady to the clutches of Victor Fox.

The job of drawing the resurrected Phantom Lady went to Matt Baker, who had already established his reputation as the best pinup artist in the Iger studio. For Fiction House Comics, another Iger client, Baker was drawing the luscious adventures of Tiger Girl (*Fight Comics*) and Sky Girl (*Jumbo Comics*).

Baker's physically exaggerated heroines, and Phantom Lady especially, fell into the category of what critic Dr. Fredric Wertham called "headlights comics." The term, supposedly coined by Wertham's juvenile psychiatric patients, referred to comic books which featured women with torpedo-shaped breasts.

"One of the stock mental aphrodisiacs in comic books," Wertham told concerned parents, "is to draw girls' breasts in such a way they are sexually exciting. Whenever possible they protrude and obtrude."

The Phantom Lady was a woman with two pasts, innocent and notorious. In her early appearances (*Police Comics*) with guys like Plastic Man, Firebrand, and the Human Bomb, she was simply the attractive, female costumed hero. By the late 1940s, Phantom Lady was appearing in stories rife with bondage, bosoms, and blood.

The front cover of the April 1948 *Phantom Lady* comic book, which showed the heroine trussed with ropes yet looking sultrily at the reader, provoked the accusation from comic book critic Dr. Fredric Wertham of "sexual stimulation" by pandering to "the sadist's dream of tying up a woman."

So, how did a nice girl like Sandra Knight get herself all tied up like this?

The Phantom Lady, like many other early Quality comic book characters, came from the

While Baker's Phantom Lady was guilty on both counts of protrusion and obtrusion, the feature was more than just a vulgar excess. Baker's use of perspectives, clever figure work, and action pacing made Phantom Lady the most "breathtaking" superheroine of the 1940s.

Golden Age Appearances
Police Comics 1–23 (8/41–10/43)
Feature Comics 69–71 (7/43–9/43)
Phantom Lady 13–23 (8/47–4/49)
All Top Comics 8–17 (11/47–5/49)

PLASTIC MAN

August 1941 *Police Comics* #1
Quality Comics

Eel O'Brian and his gang are robbing the Crawford Chemical Works one night when a guard surprises them. Eel catches a slug in his shoulder and then a vat of acid spills over him. His frightened gang abandons him in the getaway car:

"Hey, ya putrid punks! Wait up!!"

"Adios, Eel!"

The wounded criminal staggers away to hide. "Curse this acid! It's in the wound and stingin' like blazes!"

After crashing through a swamp and up a mountainside, Eel falls unconscious. He awakens in a monastic retreat and recovers from his wound. As he stretches out his arms in bed, he discovers that they keep growing! Not only that, his face and entire body have become elastic and pliable. "Great guns!! I'm stretchin' like a rubber-band!"

The acid entered the man's bloodstream and caused a permanent physical change. He can stretch and shape his body into any form. He has become a Plastic Man.

"What a powerful weapon this would be *against* crime! I've been *for* it long enough! Here's my chance to atone for the evil I've done!"

Eel decides that the first order of business is to "clean up the rats who deserted me on the Crawford job . . . but first I'll need a costume of rubber!"

Dressed in red trunks with bare legs and an open, black, mesh-neck body shirt, Eel O'Brian completes his secret disguise with a pair of wrap-around goggle sunglasses.

When he meets up with his old gang, he flattens out like a rug and then wraps his body around them when they walk over him. He chases them down a flight of stairs by doubling his body into a rubber ball and *bouncing* down the street.

He stretches his arm out like a rope and then lassos the crooks into a police net. "I never knew fighting for the law could be so much fun," muses the stretchable superhero.

Fun was the operative word for Plastic Man. Readers were delighted and surprised to see a superhero who could flatten himself into a parachute, turn into a suitcase, roll like a hoop, stretch like a fire hose, or mold his features into anything from a flying squirrel to a Broadway showgirl. He could stand on the ground and send his neck stretching up twenty stories high to look inside a window, or he could lengthen his body into a string that could slip through a keyhole.

Jack Cole, who wrote and drew nearly all of the early Plastic Man adventures, originally wanted to call his hero the India Rubber Man. Quality Comics publisher "Busy" Arnold suggested instead that they take advantage of the public's

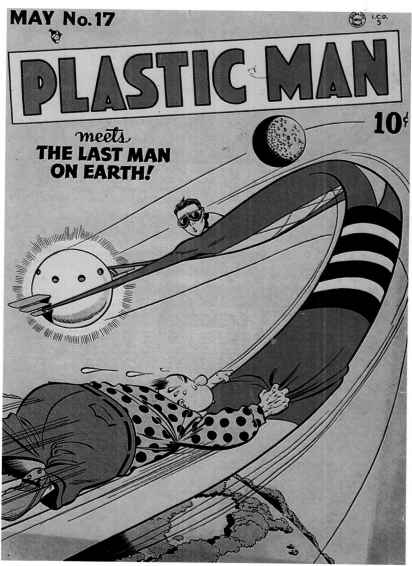

Plastic Man #17 © 1949 Comic Magazines, Inc.

Police Comics #1 © 1941 Comic Magazines, Inc.

Alex Kotzky and John Spranger successfully imitated Cole's style, while writers like William Woolfolk and Manly Wade Wellman penned some of the adventures. Still, it was Jack Cole's uniquely comic vision and energetic drawing which made Plastic Man one of the most unusual, popular, and enjoyable superheroes of the 1940s.

Golden Age Appearances
Police Comics 1–102 (8/41–10/50)
Plastic Man 1–52 (Summer/43–2/55)
Hit Comics 32 (Summer/44)

THE SANDMAN

April 1939 *New York World's Fair Comics #1*
DC Comics

Wesley Dodds, former athlete and playboy, lives in a mansion on Park Drive and is attended by his butler Humphries. Behind a secret panel in his bedroom is a passage to his underground laboratory. There, Dodds develops a sleeping gas and a gas gun which he uses in his "relentless war on the underworld and crime."

fascination with plastic, which had just been dubbed the "miracle material." During the late 1930s, there were dozens of new household and industrial items made from plastic. Now there was a man made of plastic as well.

A little more than a year after Plastic Man's debut in *Police Comics*, Cole introduced an unlikely sidekick for the stretchable hero in the November 1942 issue. Woozy Winks, perennially dressed in a straw hat, lime-green polka dot shirt, and baggy trousers, was a round lump of humanity who also happened to be an ex-con with super-powers. When Woozy saves a mystic from drowning, he is granted the power of nature's protection, which causes thunderstorms, earthquakes, and tornadoes to come to his aid should he ever be threatened.

Woozy and Plas (as he was affectionately called) made a redoubtable duo. Woozy usually barged right into trouble and got himself "strategically" captured until he was finally rescued by his pliable friend ("Plas is here! Oh, boy! Now we'll show you what it means to fool around with us!").

As Plastic Man's popularity increased, he was given more room to stretch out in *Police Comics* from six to fifteen pages each issue. He also earned his own magazine, which ran from 1943 to 1956. With the increase in the number and length of Plastic Man stories, Jack Cole had to use other writers and artists on the feature. Artists

Plastic Man #21 © 1950 Comic Magazines, Inc.

Sought by police and criminals alike, accused of crimes that he never committed, foe of evil and all wrongdoing, "THE SANDMAN wages relentless war upon the underworld and crime!

Hiding his features behind a gas mask, cloak, gloves, and a snap-brimmed green hat, Dodds becomes the Sandman—"the foe of evil and all wrongdoing." The Sandman tracks down criminals and then mercifully shoots them with his sweetly scented, sleep-inducing gas gun ("I smell flowers—violets? Guess . . . gee . . . I . . . I'm . . . fallin' . . . asleep . . . ").

Over his sleeping victim, the Sandman sprinkles sand and intones: "The sands of deep sleep fill his eyes." When the police arrive, the Sandman is gone and only the lingering smell of violets and grains of sand remain. His gas gun, mysterious appearance, playboy alter ego, and obligatory trademark left at the scene of each retribution were elements borrowed from such radio and pulp heroes as the Green Hornet, the Shadow, and the Spider. Like these heroes, the Sandman is also seen as being on both sides of the law ("sought by police and criminals alike"). Dodds was sometimes assisted by girlfriend Dian Belmont, the district attorney's daughter, who kept his Sandman identity a secret.

The first Sandman stories were drawn and occasionally written by Bert Christman, who broke into the comic book field in 1936 by drawing adventure stories for *Detective Picture Stories*. Christman had also drawn *Scorchy Smith*, a newspaper strip about a heroic pilot, from 1936 to 1937. In 1938, Christman followed in Scorchy's

footsteps and became a Navy flying cadet. The following year, while working for DC Comics on *Action* and *Adventure Comics*, he helped create the first Sandman story ("Theft at the World's Fair!") which appeared in the 1939 issue of *New York World's Fair Comics*.

Writer Gardner Fox worked with Christman and later with artist Creig Flessel on the early Sandman series in *Adventure Comics*. Flessel succeeded Christman on the series when the Naval pilot enlisted in early 1941 with the American Volunteer Group to fight the Japanese in China. Flessel recalled that "I met Bert just before he left to fly for General Chenault and his Flying Tigers. He had long blond hair, a leather jacket and a faraway, adventure-bound look in his eye. He flew several missions and was shot down, only to be machine-gunned in his parachute." Flessel recalled that he also wrote and colored some of the early Sandman stories during the first year of the strip.

When Flessel left the comics for the advertising field, Chad Grothkopf followed him on the Sandman series. Grothkopf, who had been drawing for DC Comics since 1938, discussed the idea with editor Whitney Ellsworth of turning the gas-mask-wearing Sandman into more of a superhero-type character. Ellsworth agreed.

In the December 1941 issue of *Adventure Comics*, the Sandman exchanged his 1930s cloak-

Left: Adventure Comics #51 © 1940 DC Comics, Inc.

Right: Adventure Comics #40 © 1939 DC Comics, Inc. Creig Flessel.

and-hat outfit for a pair of yellow tights and a purple cape and cowl with matching boots. Grothkopf and Ellsworth also gave Sandman a kid sidekick, Sandy Hawkins, also known as the Golden Boy.

Grothkopf left Sandman after initiating his transformation into a full-fledged superhero in order to create Hoppy The Marvel Bunny, one of the first "funny animal" superhero characters, for Fawcett Publishing. Paul Norris, who was drawing Aquaman in *More Fun Comics*, drew Sandman for a couple of issues and then moved over for the arrival of Joe Simon and Jack Kirby to DC Comics.

Fresh from their success with Captain America and Bucky, Simon and Kirby brought their sense of dramatic storytelling to Sandman and Sandy. Full-page panels, foreshortened action figures, and acrobatic staging marked the Simon and Kirby stories. Kirby recalled that when he started drawing and writing the Sandman, he brought his own vision to the character: "To me, he represented something entirely different. I'd get him into dreams and into nightmares."

The Simon and Kirby Sandman stories often revolved around dreams with titles like "Dreams of Doom," "The Unholy Dreams of Gentleman Jack," and "The Man Who Couldn't Sleep." The last story, in which an insomniac masterminds a crime wave, causes the Sandman

to observe: "It's a sure thing there's some deep psychological reason why he likes to spoil people's rest. And that makes this case right down Sandman's alley!"

Simon and Kirby drew most of the Sandman stories in *Adventure Comics* until the series ended in early 1946. The character also appeared as a member in the Justice Society of America in *All Star Comics*. His adventures there were drawn by Creig Flessel, Cliff Young, Joe Simon, and Jack Kirby.

Golden Age Appearances
New York World's Fair Comics 1, 2 (4/39–1940)
Adventure Comics 40–102 (7/39–2/46)
All Star Comics 1–21 (Summer/40–Summer/44)
World's Finest 3–7 (Fall/41–Fall/42)
Boy Commandos 1 (Winter/42)
Detective Comics 76 (6/43)

THE SHADOW

March 1940 *Shadow Comics* #1
Street & Smith Publications

"The weed of crime bears bitter fruit! Who knows what evil lurks in the hearts of men? The Shadow knows!"

The Shadow evolved from a 1930 mystery radio show called *The Detective Story Magazine Hour,* which featured a host known as the Shadow who had a mysterious high and chilling laugh.

The publishers of *Detective Story Magazine* paid Walter B. Gibson, a thirty-three-year-old writer of crime tales for pulp magazines, five hundred dollars to write a 75,000-word manuscript based on the Shadow character for a new series called *The Shadow Magazine.* The first issue (April 1931) sold out immediately and Gibson's new pulp detective hero, the Shadow, was an assured success. Street and Smith, the publisher of *Shadow Magazine,* brought the magazine out every two weeks during the 1930s to meet audience demand.

For the next fifteen years, Gibson wrote 282 Shadow novels by keeping three typewriters busy (allowing the manual machines time to "cool off" so the keys wouldn't stick) and taking time off only to let his bruised fingertips heal.

In 1937, a revamped Shadow radio show was launched starring Orson Welles as the voice of the man of mystery. The radio show introduced Margo Lane, the Shadow's friend and companion, and established Lamont Cranston as the Shadow's secret identity (a point on which the early pulp magazines were deliberately vague).

Adventure Comics #51 © 1940 DC Comics, Inc.

The radio show also gave the character the power of invisibility—"to cloud men's minds so that they could not see him."

After the radio show, a comic strip featuring the Shadow appeared in newspapers and was drawn by Vernon V. Greene. Greene, who had illustrated mystery magazines, as well as ghosting such newspaper strips as *Bringing Up Father* and *Polly and Her Pals* in the late 1930s, incorporated much of the radio show elements in the comic strip, including the Shadow's ability to turn invisible.

When Street and Smith decided to follow other pulp magazine publishers into the comic book business in 1940, it chose *Shadow Comics* (March 1940) as an obvious good bet. Greene continued drawing the Shadow for the comic book with some of his newspaper strip adventures used in the early issues.

Walter B. Gibson, the author of the Shadow's prose adventures, recalled the Shadow comic book was part of the burgeoning merchandising growing up around a character he helped popularize. "Street and Smith was treating comics as promotional items," Gibson remembered. "As soon as they began, I went in and insisted that they use my scripts for all the *Shadow Comics*."

Gibson had a hand in many of the Shadow's comic book adventures until he temporarily ended his association with the character in 1946. As in his pulp magazine stories, Gibson populated the early comic book adventures with Oriental villains, including the Shadow's archfoe, the evil Shiwan Khan, and Hoang Hu, "the Dreaded Leader of the Orient."

After Vernon Greene left the comic book to enter the war as a USAF medical photographer, Jon Blummer, Al Bare, and Jack Binder stepped in. Charles Coll followed them and drew many 1944–1946 stories.

The later issues of the *Shadow* comic book were its best, with art and stories from the Bob Powell art studio. Powell, a veteran of the Eisner-Iger comic shop, had drawn Sheena Queen of the Jungle for *Jumbo Comics* and Mr. Mystic for Will Eisner's *Spirit* comic section. In 1947 he began his own comic art studio with Street & Smith as a client. With the assistance of Howard Nostrand and other artists and writers, Powell created comic stories for a half dozen publishers in the late 1940s.

The Shadow comic book disappeared in the summer of 1949, along with the original pulp magazine as well, when Street & Smith left the comic book business.

Shadow Comics Vol. 8 #8 © 1948 Street & Smith Publications, Inc. Bob Powell.

Golden Age Appearances
Shadow Comics 1–101 (3/40–8/49)
Super Magician Comics 13 (5/43)

THE SHIELD

January 1940 *Pep Comics* #1
MLJ Publications

The Shield, premiering two years before America entered World War II, was the first patriotic comic book superhero. The red-white-and-blue character was MLJ Publications's most successful hero and appeared in nearly one hundred stories in *Pep* and *Shield-Wizard Comics*.

The Shield began as an idea in the mind of

Shield-Wizard Comics #10 © 1943 Archie Comic Publications, Inc.

Harry Shorten, an editor two years out of college and already seasoned by his one-year career as an adventure pulp magazine writer. Irving Novick, still a young artist even for such a young field, got the assignment to draw the Shield, his first big feature. Novick would also become well-known for his work on MLJ's two other big heroes, the Black Hood and Steel Sterling.

Our story begins as Lieutenant Tom Higgins of the U.S. Army Intelligence receives his orders to supervise the loading of an ammunitions ship. Higgins, who is also a research chemist, and his son Joe have been searching for a chemical solution which would turn an ordinary person into a super-being. Higgins leaves his son at the laboratory and heads down to the ammo ship.

Saboteurs, however, have already planted explosives on the ship and Tom Higgins is caught in the explosion. At the hospital, Higgins passes on his secret chemical research to his son Joe in the form of an anatomical formula: S-H-I-E-L-D.

After his father dies, Joe refines the secret chemical formula but is unsure how to use it. While leafing through a medical book, he suddenly understands the meaning of his father's coded message—each letter in the formula stood for an anatomical area: S for the Sacrum, H for Heart, I for Innervation (nerve center), E for Eyes, L for Lungs, and D for Derma (the skin covering).

He applies the solution to the areas of his body specified by the formula and bathes himself in fluoroscopic rays for twelve hours to force the chemicals into his organs. He also devises a skintight "fibro-metallic" suit to help his body retain the chemicals. Joe Higgins has now become the super-powered Shield.

Higgins reports to J. Edgar Hoover and is given a special commission as the "G-Man Extraordinary" so he may battle America's enemies on the home front. During his first year in *Pep Comics*, the Shield got a steady girlfriend, Betty Warren, the daughter of a U.S. senator murdered by enemy agents.

When Higgins and Betty investigate reported sabotage in an airplane factory (*Pep Comics*, January 1941), they discover a burning plane and only one survivor: a red-headed boy named Dusty. When the saboteurs attack Betty, Dusty jumps to her defense and he is quickly joined in action by Higgins, now dressed as the Shield.

The Shield tells Dusty that they would make a great team and takes the orphaned boy to his laboratory, where he makes him a uniform. Although possessing no super-powers (and evidently no last name), Dusty was dubbed the "Boy Detective" and eventually earned his own comic book feature.

As war officially started for America, the Shield and Dusty fought both Japanese (The Fang) and German (The Strangler) henchmen, but their all-time foe was the Hun, a merciless super-Nazi and descendant of Atilla himself. The Hun, "symbol of sabotage and lord high master of cruelty," fought the Shield in a sixty-page knockdown-dragout fight over two issues. Just when they put the bad guy away, the Shield and Dusty had to face his offspring, the Son of the Hun ("that super-Nazi rat") in the pages of *Shield-Wizard Comics*. During their first brawl, the Shield tells the cowering Son of the Hun:

"Get up and fight! I don't need any Nazi tricks to lick you!"

"Spineless fool," spits back the Hun's son as he waves his own swastika-emblazoned shield.

"Do you think I respect your weakling code of fair play? Dere iss only vun law ve Nazis respect . . . survival of the strong . . . und death to der veak!"

And speaking of "der veak," the Shield underwent a transformation in the July 1942 issue of *Pep Comics* that would leave him without his super-powers. When Japanese spies shoot the Shield, the seemingly impossible happens:

"Ooooh—I've been hit! Every—everything is going black!"

The Shield, no longer all-powerful, tells Dusty: "I suspect that the formula of my father's which gave me my strength is wearing off."

The Shield is unable to restore his powers, but he and Dusty still continue their patriotic crusade. The loss of his powers, however, was an omen for the Shield. A few months earlier, a teenager named Archie Andrews appeared in the back pages of *Pep Comics*. By the February 1943 issue, the red-haired teen was sharing the cover with the Shield. With the September 1944 issue of *Pep*, Archie had dislodged the superhero from the cover for good.

As superheroes fell in popularity, Archie became the lead feature in *Pep*. The Shield G-Man Club, which had been advertised in *Pep Comics*, was turned into the Archie Fan Club. After appearing as a back feature during its last year, the Shield left the comic book to its gang of teenagers at the end of 1947.

Golden Age Appearances
Pep Comics 1–65 (1/40–1/48)
Shield-Wizard Comics 1–13
 (Summer/40–Spring/44)
Top-Notch Comics 7 (8/40)

THE SPECTRE

February 1940 *More Fun Comics* #52
DC Comics

"No one knows that Jim Corrigan, hard-fisted detective, is in reality the Earth-bound Spectre, whose mission is to rid this world of crime . . . "

"Gat" Benson and his gang of criminal thugs finally get their hands on a bothersome detective named Jim Corrigan and his girlfriend Clarice Winston. In true gangster fashion, they stick Corrigan in a barrel of cement and dump him into the river. The murdered detective arrives at the gates of the Hereafter but he is turned away by a voice which tells him: "Your mission on Earth is unfinished . . . You shall remain earthbound battling crime on your world, with supernatural powers . . . "

Corrigan's body returns to the land of the living, but now it is inhabited by a spirit known as the Spectre. The Spectre, through astral projection, leaves Corrigan's body in a supernatural state to fight crime. As the white-and-green-garbed Spectre, he can fly, dematerialize, walk through walls, expand his body so he is larger than Earth itself, transmute matter, paralyze foes, read minds, look into the past or future, and cause time itself to stand still. Nothing could harm the Spectre. He was already dead.

The macabre origin and early supernatural tales of the Spectre were written by Jerry Siegel, the cocreator of Superman. Siegel made the Spectre an even more powerful character than Superman, giving the hero almost godlike powers over life and death, time and space. Siegel admitted that he had been a great fan of the *Weird Tales* pulp magazine and the Spectre was his opportunity to interject the elements of horror and supernatural which were too disparate for his science-fiction-oriented Superman.

More Fun Comics #57 © 1940 DC Comics, Inc.

All Star Comics #1 © 1940
DC Comics, Inc.

Siegel based the Spectre on Dr. Occult, a supernatural investigator he and Joe Shuster created for *New Fun Comics* in 1935. Like the Spectre, Dr. Occult is a ghost who uses his unusual powers to battle evil. Siegel wrote the script for the Spectre in late 1939. Shuster was busy with the Superman stories and the new feature was assigned to a young artist named Bernard Baily.

Baily recalled that he "went over to DC Comics after Harry Donenfeld took over from Nicholson. I was offered a job as editor, but I could make more money drawing so I didn't take it. I must've been eighteen or nineteen. When I was there at DC, Siegel came up with the feature the Spectre. The look of the character I created, the script he wrote. Siegel did the writing on the Spectre the whole time. The thing I created in the Spectre was his sidekick, Percival Popp the Super Cop."

The Spectre was one of the earlier DC Comics heroes, appearing even before Batman received his own comic book. He appeared in the first issue of *All Star Comics* and was a founding member of the Justice Society of America. In 1941, the Spectre was under consideration for his own comic book, right after the Flash and Green Lantern had received their second titles (*All-Flash Comics, Green Lantern Comics*), but it never occurred. Instead by the end of 1944, the Spectre was among the first of the Golden Age superheroes to be retired by DC Comics.

Golden Age Appearances
More Fun Comics 52–101 (2/40–1/45)
All Star Comics 1–23 (Summer/40–Winter/44)

THE SPIRIT
June 1940 Register and Tribune Syndicate

Denny Colt, "criminologist and private detective," tries to stop an evil scientist named Dr. Cobra from injecting a chemical formula into the city's water supply which will induce "suspended animation." In the ensuing struggle with the scientist's henchmen, Colt is knocked into the vat of chemicals and apparently dies. The crimefighter is buried and mourned by his friends, including Police Commissioner Dolan. Two days later, a mysterious figure who calls himself the Spirit shows up at Commissioner Dolan's office and announces he intends to bring Dr. Cobra to justice.

When Dolan presses him for his identity, the Spirit reveals that he is Denny Colt: "When I tried to capture Cobra, the vat with some chemicals in it, smashed! I was put in a state of suspended animation! Believing me dead, you fellows buried me . . . I came to several hours later and broke out of my grave!"

Colt tells Dolan that he has decided to remain "dead" and pose as the Spirit in order to operate "without the normal restrictions" imposed upon a living crime fighter. As the Spirit, he'll live off the rewards for capturing criminals. He sets up an underground apartment at Wildwood Cemetery (his original burial site) and, dressed in a blue business suit and blue snap-brim hat, embarks on his career as a beyond-the-living and above-the-law crime fighter.

The Spirit, like many comic detective heroes, enjoyed the company of both a girlfriend, Ellen Dolan (the Commissioner's daughter) and a sidekick, Ebony White, who drove a cab and spoke in a dialect that confirmed his Southern black heritage ("Yassuh, Mr. Spirit Boss!").

Will Eisner created the Spirit as the star for a newspaper comic book supplement in 1940. After working on costumed characters like the Flame and Doll Man for comic books, Eisner relished the opportunity to create a more adult hero for a newspaper audience. "For the first time," Eisner recalled, "I would be able to address myself to an audience other than that ten-year-old cretin in Kansas City."

Eisner, who wrote and drew the Spirit for the first year and a half before entering the service, introduced elements from the movies into his art, and poetic imagery into his scripts. He used the Spirit to tell wry stories of justice, retribution, love, hate, and irony. Eisner's writing on the Spirit was often reminiscent of works by his favorite short story authors—O. Henry, Ambrose Bierce, and Ben Hecht. His nearly cinematic artwork reflected perspectives and pacing borrowed from his favorite movie directors. "I felt a very strong kinship to Orson Welles in those days," Eisner recalled. He was also heavily influenced by the films of Alfred Hitchcock and the early experimental works by director Man Ray.

The Spirit reached the more adult audience that Eisner was seeking. Eventually, twenty Sunday newspapers distributed the Spirit comic sections to an audience of five million—nearly five times as many readers as the most popular comic books. The character also appeared in a daily newspaper strip (1941–1944) and in a short-lived radio show.

During the war years, other artists in Eisner's studio took over the Spirit, including Lou Fine, Alex Kotzky, and Bob Powell. Writers who worked on the Spirit after Eisner left included William Woolfolk, Bill Millard, and Manly Wade Wellman. Eisner returned to the Spirit in 1946 and created some of the most memorable comic work of the postwar years. During the last years of the Spirit comic section, Eisner was assisted by other writers and artists, including Jules Feiffer, Tex Blaisdell, and Wally Wood.

The Spirit stories from the Sunday supplement sections were eventually reprinted in comic books from 1942–1954.

Golden Age Appearances

The Spirit (weekly newspaper comic book)
   6/2/40–10/5/52
Police Comics 11–88, 90, 92, 94–102
   (9/42–10/50)
The Spirit (Quality Comics) 1–22 (1944–8/50)
Modern Comics 83, 102 (3/49–10/50)
The Spirit (Fiction House Comics) 1–5
   (Spring/1952–1954)

The Spirit © 1940 Will Eisner. Will Eisner.

SPY SMASHER

February 1940 *Whiz Comics #2*
Fawcett Publishing

"Death to spies in America!"
Two years before America entered World War II, spies were thought to be everywhere. Bill Parker, the writer and editor of *Whiz Comics*, used the country's preoccupation with fifth columnist terrorists as the inspiration for the Spy Smasher, one of the first comic book heroes to become involved in the early war efforts. Parker began his story at a dinner party given by U.S. Naval intelligence officer Admiral Corby for his daughter Eve

and her fiancé Alan Armstrong ("a wealthy young Virginia sportsman"). Corby has received reports of what appears to be a rash of military accidents, but he confides to the young man: "I tell you Alan, these things were not accidents! I am positive that those ships and aircrafts were deliberately destroyed—by spies!"

Turner takes the admiral's hint and decides to fight the spies on his own as Spy Smasher. Wearing a cape and what appears to be a leftover World War I cavalry officer's uniform, the Virginia horse breeder becomes a costumed aviator in the tradition of pulp and radio heroes like *G-8 and His Battle Aces* and *Captain Midnight*.

Turner uses his wealth to invent a flying gyro-sub—"a super-craft combining the functions

Spy Smasher #3 © 1942 Fawcett Publications, Inc.

of an airplane, auto gyro, speedboat, and submarine." Traveling in his gyro-sub, Turner as the Spy Smasher can effectively foil sabotage and espionage attempts on land, water, and in the air.

As World War II approached, the Spy Smasher became a more visible symbol of American patriotism. He ditched his drab khaki costume for a bright green suit with a diamond-shaped red emblem and matching cloak (December 1941). With scripts by Otto Binder and art by Charles Sultan and Emil Gershwin, Spy Smasher now looked more like a superhero than a vigilante aviator. After the war began, Spy Smasher enjoyed increased popularity in both his own comic book and *Whiz Comics*. Republic Features made the costumed aviator the star of a 1942 movie serial and he became the second original comic book character (after Captain Marvel) to be adapted as a live-action feature.

Although all superheroes dropped in popularity with the war's end, peace was catastrophic for the Axis-smashing Spy Smasher. His very reason for existence was jerked away when Japan unconditionally surrendered on August 14, 1945. Refusing to give up, however, Spy Smasher was still fighting "Jap treachery in Tibet" as late as March 1946.

With the July 1946 issue of *Whiz Comics*, Turner faced reality and became the Crime Smasher. He turned his attention from fighting foreign agents to battling common criminals. Without spies to smash, however, the gyro-sub-riding sportsman was really no longer needed

Adventure Comics #67 © 1941 DC Comics, Inc.

and he disappeared within a year.

Golden Age Appearances
Whiz Comics 2–75 (2/40–3/47)
America's Greatest Comics 1–6, 8
  (Fall/41–Summer/43)
All Hero Comics 1 (3/43)
Spy Smasher 1–11 (Fall/41–2/43)

STARMAN

April 1941 *Adventure Comics #61*
DC Comics

"For thousands of years, men have spoken of the mysterious powers of the stars—but I am the first to discover that radiated starlight can be harnessed and used scientifically!"

Ted Knight, an amateur astronomer and "bored playboy," possesses an amazing invention called the gravity-rod, which "utilizes the powerful infra-rays from the distant stars." Knight's gravity-rod, operated by control buttons, "overcomes the forces of gravity and launches bolts of energy!"

The world-weary playboy uses the powers of the gravity-rod to become Starman and he dons a red and green costume with a yellow star on chest and cape. Knight's invention allows him to fly through the air and intimidate criminals as well: "The magnetic current of the gravity-rod draws the frightened thug back to Starman!"

Many of Starman's adventures took place at night when he could easily tap into the "cosmic rays" of the "mysterious stars." By day, Ted Knight kept the company of his fiancée Doris Lee ("niece of the famous G-Man, Woodley Allen") and he assumed the guise of an effete hypochondriac, afraid of a cold draft or a dark room:

Whiz Comics #62 © 1945 Fawcett Publications, Inc.

"Just as I feared! One of my dizzy spells has hit me! This excitement is too much for me!"

While his feigned illness and weaknesses often provoked his girlfriend's exasperation ("Why don't you act like the man you *could* be?"), they also provided the playboy with an excuse to slip off and assume his secret identity as Starman.

Starman was the creation of Jack Burnley, an artist who began his career at seventeen as a sports cartoonist for King Features Syndicate. His first comic book job was a 1940 Superman story for *Action Comics*. Whitney Ellsworth, an editor at DC Comics, liked Burnley's work and asked him to come up with another character along the lines of Superman and Batman. Ellsworth's assistant Murray Boltinoff, who was writing stories for the Crimson Avenger in *Detective Comics*, was asked to help with the original story.

After designing "all kinds of costumes," Burnley came up with Starman. Burnley borrowed the Superman uniform (with color schemes reversed and changed) and then added a Buck Rogers-type helmet to go along with the hero's science fiction-sounding name. The bored playboy alter ego, reminiscent of Bruce Wayne (Batman) and Wesley Dodd (Sandman), was developed by other writers, including Gardner Fox, who had written for both the Batman and Sandman series. Burnley recalled, however, that "Fox was not the principal early Starman writer. The best scripts were done by Alfred Bester, an award-winning science fiction author."

Adventure Comics #67
© 1941 DC Comics, Inc.
Jack Burnley.

After Burnley left the character, Mort Meskin and George Roussos drew Starman in *Adventure Comics* while later stories were by Emil Gershwin, an artist who had worked on Captain Marvel, Jr. and Spy Smasher.

Golden Age Appearances
Adventure Comics 61–102 (4/41–2/46)
All Star Comics 8–23 (12/41–Winter/44)

STEEL STERLING

February 1940 *Zip Comics #1*
MLJ Publications

"In one breathless moment, John Sterling wagered the faint hope of possessing a body of human steel against horrible mutilation and death! He emerged from his bath of molten metal as Steel Sterling, enemy of the underworld, a man immune to all known implements of death! Now, posing as his own twin brother, he operates his own private detective agency!"

After his father is killed by gangsters, John Sterling devotes his life to learning about chemistry so he can develop a formula to help fight crime. He finally discovers a chemical solution that *may* make his body impervious to bullets, *but* to make it work, he must first coat himself with

Adventure Comics #66 © 1941 DC Comics, Inc. Jack Burnley.

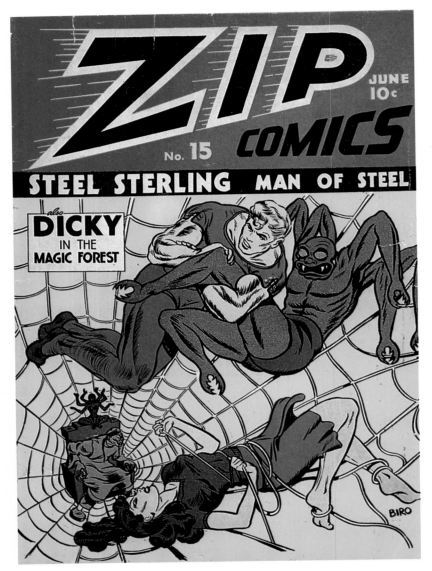

Zip Comics #15 © 1941
Archie Comic Publications,
Inc. Charles Biro.

Laughs aside, however, most of Steel's time was spent dealing with conmen, saboteurs, and costumed villains like the Black Knight and the Rattler. Like every superhero from MLJ Publications, Steel had a super Nazi archenemy—Baron Gestapo: "A menace so gigantic that man's mind reels at the thought, a dread monster whose name strikes terror into the hearts of the bravest."

Steel Sterling was originally written by MLJ editor Abner Sundell and drawn by Charles Biro, who was with MLJ from its beginnings in 1939. Biro previously had worked in Harry "A" Chesler's comic book studio as early as 1936.

Although Steel Sterling was Biro's first superhero strip, he injected a raw-energy toughness into the feature that made it an early favorite with readers. After Biro left Steel Sterling, artists Carl Hubbel and Irving Novick, among others, handled the art chores. Steel's script writers included William Woolfolk, Robert Kanigher, and Otto Binder.

Golden Age Appearances
Zip Comics 1–47 (2/40–Summer/44)
Jackpot Comics 1–9 (Spring/41–Spring/43)

SUB-MARINER

April 1939 *Motion Picture Funnies Weekly* #1
Marvel Comics

"Hate you? Yes, I hate you—and with good reason! You white devils have persecuted and tormented my people for years!"

The Sub-Mariner, born of rage, fueled by hate, and living for revenge, was the offspring of an ill-crossed marriage. His father was Commander Leonard McKenzie, the American captain of an Antarctic research ship. His mother was the beautiful Fen, a member of an undersea race known as the Sub-Mariners.

Our story begins when the American expedition led by McKenzie inadvertently blasts and destroys a part of the underwater kingdom of the Sub-Mariners. Fen boards McKenzie's ship disguised as a spy to stop the carnage, but unexpectedly falls in love and marries the Captain. When the American ships blast through the ice sheets and destroy most of her remaining people, the embittered (and pregnant) woman deserts her husband. For the next twenty years, she raises their child in the remnants of her underwater kingdom and plots her revenge.

At the age of twenty, her son Namor (whose name means "Avenging Son") kills two deep-sea divers without provocation. His mother tells him:

the chemical and then plunge naked into a cauldron of hot, bubbling steel!

Sterling's molten metal bath causes the chemicals to harden his body until he is a "Man of Steel." To protect his new identity as Steel Sterling, he pretends that he has a twin brother. After several months, he drops the pretense of an alter ego twin in favor of a less schizophrenic life. Sterling's trademark as a superhero is that he always leaves a sonic trail behind him, brightly indicated by the letters "ZIP."

Steel starts out with a girlfriend, Dora Cummings, who is tossed aside to make room for two comic-relief characters: Clancy, a bumbling cop with a bulbous nose, and Looney, an affable idiot with a pencil neck. The comedy team of Clancy and Looney was popular enough to rate its own strip in *Jackpot Comics*.

"Congratulations, my son! You have made a good beginning in our war of revenge!" She explains that "since you are the only one of us left who can live on land and in the water, and who can also fly in the air, and because you have the strength of a thousand Earth-men, it is your duty to lead us into battle . . . Go now to the land of the white people!"

Namor, soon to be known to the world as the Sub-Mariner, leaves his underwater world and begins an attack on the hated world of the Earth-men. After destroying a lighthouse, the Sub-Mariner uses the wings on his feet to leap onto a low-flying airplane. He coldly tosses the pilot overboard to his death. With a superhero like that, who needed a villain?

"His only message was that he wanted to get even with the human race," observed Bill Everett, the creator of the Sub-Mariner. "He thought they were trying to destroy his race. So it was all retaliatory; all his ideas were."

Everett was twenty-one when he wrote and drew the first Sub-Mariner story for a promotional movie theater giveaway comic called *Motion Picture Funnies Weekly*. An admittedly "cocky" and angry young man, Everett had spent 1938 listening to his stomach growl after ending a two-year stretch of doing newspaper advertising art. He broke into comics by writing and drawing a science fiction strip called Skyrocket Steele for Centaur Publishing (*Amazing Mystery Funnies*, September 1938) for editor Lloyd Jacquet.

When Jacquet left Centaur to form his own comic book studio, Funnies, Incorporated, Everett followed. While at Funnies, Incorporated, Everett developed the Sub-Mariner story on his own with no rules or editorial interference. "In the begin-

ning, I did it any way I wanted to because I had no supervision," Everett recalled.

The angry Sub-Mariner, who was nearly the same age as his creator, served perhaps as a voice for the frustration and fears of Everett's generation, caught between a Depression and a World War:

"What fools these mortals be! Warring among each other to satisfy the arrogant egos of a few stupid governments! I'll show them what war is like—war to preserve the safety and happiness of the civilian population!"

Everett remembered that "I made up the dialogue as I went along—usually when I lettered it."

Everett drew from several sources for his inspiration for the Sub-Mariner. A lifelong love of

the ocean, the sea adventure novels of James Conelly and Jack London, Samuel Taylor Coleridge's poem *The Rime of The Ancient Mariner*, and a passing familiarity with mythology all played a role in the creation of his aquatic hero. The wings on Sub-Mariner's feet were drawn from Roman god Mercury while the character's name "Namor" was chosen by writing the word "Roman" backwards. By making his character a sympathetic yet angry product of miscegenation, Everett also tapped into the ancient Greek tragedy of a hero cursed by his birth.

The Sub-Mariner became part of a package offered by Funnies, Incorporated, to publisher Martin Goodman for his very first comic book, *Marvel Comics.*

Everett developed the character of the Sub-Mariner as he wrote and drew stories for the first several issues of Goodman's *Marvel Mystery Comics.* Everett shows a softer side of his vengeful hero in his second story, when Sub-Mariner saves a woman's life.

Gradually, he became less an anti-hero bent upon revenge and more the crusader for justice— especially during the war years and afterwards. Before his transformation from bad boy to good guy, however, the Sub-Mariner would fight the Human Torch in what Marvel Comics billed in 1940 as "The Comic Battle of the Century!"

The Human Torch, who shared the pages of *Marvel Mystery Comics* with the Sub-Mariner, was a man of fire and flame. What better foe for a man who came from the world of water? Everett and Burgos, who drew the Torch, suggested the idea of a battle royal between what were then Marvel Comics's most popular two characters. Martin Goodman, the publisher, loved the idea. He liked it so much, he wanted it done in time for the next issue of the comic book, which meant the book-length story had to be done over the weekend.

Everett quickly marshaled a team of artists, writers, and letterers from the Funnies, Incorporated, studio and proceeded with his battle plan. In a published 1961 letter to Jerry DeFuccio, Everett recalled that "we turned out the first combination Sub-Mariner–Human Torch volume—48 pages of writing, layout, drawing and lettering, in three days. All done in my apartment on 33rd St., with six writers, four artists, and a case of booze. Sandwiches sent in, Joey Piazza lying in the bathtub, fully clothed, writing up a storm, reams of paper littering the floor, everybody yelling at each other, neighbors complaining, the radio and record player going full blast, and the telephone ringing constantly. But we got the job done, and it sold out completely."

During the war years, the Sub-Mariner got with the superhero program and was fighting side-by-side with the Human Torch and Captain America on covers of comics like *All Winners* and *All-Select Comics.* Everett himself went to war in February 1942, and other artists, including Mike Roy, Carl Pfeufer, and Jimmy Thompson, drew the character in *Marvel Mystery Comics* and in *Sub-Mariner Comics.* Most of the covers during this period featured the Sub-Mariner destroying submarines, battleships, and any other nearby machine or member of the Axis navy.

After the war, the Sub-Mariner became a regular crime-buster, working with the police and generally behaving himself. Other changes occurred as Everett returned in 1946 to draw most of the remaining Sub-Mariner stories that decade.

In 1948, Namora, the long-lost cousin of the Sub-Mariner, became a co-star. Everett recalled that he "had wanted to feature a girl counterpart of the Sub-Mariner, almost from the very beginning." Although he didn't draw the first appearance of Namora (*Marvel Mystery,* May 1947), Everett designed her costume and stated that "I always felt it was my character."

Namora and the Sub-Mariner co-starred in more than two dozen late 1940s adventures. The "Sea Beauty" even got her own magazine in 1948. By the following year, however, she would be gone. In fact, all the Marvel superheroes would be off the newsstands by the summer of 1949, in-

Marvel Mystery Comics #7 © 1940 Marvel Entertainment Group, Inc. Bill Everett.

cluding the Sub-Mariner.

Golden Age Appearances
Motion Picture Funnies Weekly 1 (4/39)
Marvel Comics 1 (11/39)
Marvel Mystery Comics 2–91 (12/39–4/49)
Human Torch 1–33 (Fall/40–11/48)
Sub-Mariner 1–32 (Spring/41–6/49)
All Winners Comics (1) 1–19, 21
   (Summer/41–Winter/46)
Captain America 20, 68, 70 (11/42–1/49)
All-Select Comics 1–5, 10 (Fall/43–Summer/46)
Kid Komics 4 (Spring/44)
Daring Comics 9–12 (Fall/44–Fall/45)
Blonde Phantom 13–15, 17–22 (Spring/47–3/49)
All Winners Comics (2) 1 (8/48)
Namora 1–3 (8/48–12/48)

SUPERBOY

January 1945 *More Fun Comics* #101
DC Comics

   "Superman, what were you like when you were a boy?"

   "If that's what you'd like to know," Superman replies to the young boy on the cover of the first issue of *Superboy Comics*, "look inside!"

   In the pages of *Superboy Comics*, *More Fun Comics*, and *Adventure Comics*, readers got to see what Superman's childhood was like. He lived with his foster parents, went to high school, and performed super-deeds in his secret identity as Superboy. He had all the powers of an adult Superman yet all the pleasures afforded a boy in small-town America. He even got a chance to meet a younger version of Lois Lane (*Adventure Comics*, May 1948), who would later play a big role in his life as Superman.

   Gradually, the Superboy stories reconstructed a rich past life for America's first comic book superhero. Readers even got to see the Man of Steel in his earliest incarnation as Superbaby (*Superboy Comics*, May 1950). Lana Lang, a high school classmate who suspects Clark Kent of being Superboy, became an important supporting character in the series (*Superboy Comics*, September 1950). A bright, snoopy, and would-be girlfriend, Lana was Lois Lane's predecessor.

   In 1944, DC Comics editor Jack Schiff remembered that "Jerry [Siegel] was off in the Army and we put out Superboy (in *More Fun Comics*)." Joe Shuster was called in. "We sat him down. For about two or three hours, he was drawing different sketches until finally we got what we felt was right. Then he drew those first Superboys." Schiff

Superboy #22 © 1952 DC Comics, Inc. Curt Swan.

assigned the script for the first Superboy story to Don Cameron, who was also scripting Superman and Batman stories.

   An editorial decision was made to make the Superboy adventures part of Superman's boyhood instead of making the character a junior version or teenage sidekick of the adult Superman. Superboy and Superman would be the same person, existing separately in past and present, and would never share adventures together, unlike Captain Marvel and Captain Marvel, Jr. or Batman and Robin.

   By making Superboy part of Superman's past, DC Comics hoped to avoid diluting the original character's impact while also establishing copyright ownership. Since they already maintained all rights to Superman, and Superboy was just a younger version of the same character, then DC Comics should also own Superboy.

   Superman's creator, Jerry Siegel, however, thought differently. In a 1947 issue of *Newsweek*, an article summarized a lawsuit which Siegel brought against DC Comics over Superboy:

   "Superboy, Siegel contends, was his brain child and was submitted to Donenfeld but rejected by him as far back as 1938. Then in 1945, when Siegel was in the Army, Superboy made his debut under the double byline. Siegel claims he never authorized such use of his name and has never received a cent for the strip."

Adventure Comics #117
© 1947 DC Comics, Inc.
Jack Burnley.

Siegel and Shuster were eventually awarded a settlement over Superboy. In the eyes of the law, he was not just Superman with a few years shaved away, but also a separate comic book character.

By 1949, Superboy was appearing in two comic books and was the most successful comic book character of the Golden Age introduced after the war. Over the years several artists drew the Boy of Steel, including Johnny Sikela, Stan Kaye, Marvin Stein, Curt Swan, and Al Plastino.

Golden Age Appearances
More Fun Comics 101–107 (1/45–1/46)
Adventure Comics 103–209 (4/46–2/55)
Superboy 1–38 (3/49–1/55)

Action Comics #48 © 1942 DC Comics, Inc.

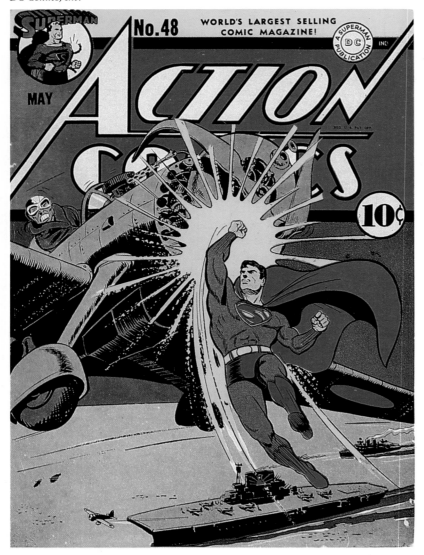

SUPERMAN

June 1938 *Action Comics* #1
DC Comics

"Far from Earth rotated the planet Krypton whose highly evolved inhabitants were capable of incredible feats of strength: leaping great heights and distances, lifting and smashing mighty weights, possessing impenetrable skins. As this amazing planet erupted, a scientist launches his infant son toward Earth in a small space ship."

The rocket lands near a farm and the young boy is discovered by an elderly couple, the Kents. They adopt the child and soon discover he possesses superhuman powers and can "hurdle skyscrapers, leap an eighth of a mile, raise tremendous weights, run faster than a streamline train, and nothing less than a bursting shell could penetrate his skin!"

They name the boy Clark and tell him: "This great strength of yours—you've got to hide it from people or they'll be scared of you! But when the proper time comes, you must use it to assist humanity!"

Upon his foster parents' deaths, Clark decides to "turn his titanic strength into channels that would benefit mankind" and he assumes the costumed identity of Superman, "champion of the oppressed." He applies for a job as newspaper reporter at the office of the *Daily Star* (later to become the *Daily Planet*): "If I get news dispatches promptly, I'll be in a better position to help people!"

As reporter Clark Kent, he works with love-lorn columnist Lois Lane, who regards him as a bespectacled and ineffectual milksop. When a thug harasses Lois in front of Clark, he feigns meekness and declines to defend her. She dumps him as an "unbearable coward" and storms away. Minutes later, he would come to Lois's rescue, but as the invincible Superman.

Lois is smitten with Superman's heroic strength and manliness. When she sees Clark Kent later in the office, she thinks: "The spineless worm! I can hardly bear looking at him, after having been in the arms of a *real* he-man!"

The spineless worm and real he-man were, of course, one and the same. The meek and mild newspaper reporter Clark Kent was also the mightiest person on the face of the Earth. Invincible and omnipotent, Superman was the ultimate wish-fulfillment fantasy for every reader who ever dreamed of being someone greater and stronger than he or she was. Perhaps it was no surprise that

Superman was created by two daydreaming adolescents who shared a love for the fantastic and heroic: Jerry Siegel and Joe Shuster.

"Back in 1931," Siegel recalled, "cartoonist Joe Shuster and I (a would-be writer) met. Both of us were students at Glenville High School in Cleveland, Ohio. The other thing we both had in common was that we wanted to be comic creators. We teamed up together. We had eagerness, we had enthusiasm. We wanted to create a hit strip. Eventually, we co-created Superman."

Superman was a combination of mythological strongmen and Siegel and Shuster's favorite fictional and movie heroes. The name of Superman's hometown, Metropolis, was taken from the Fritz Lang science fiction movie of the same name. The name Clark Kent was taken from movie actors Clark Gable and Kent Taylor.

According to Siegel, "Clark Kent grew not only out of my private life, but also out of Joe's. As a high school student, I thought that some day I might become a reporter, and I had crushes on several attractive girls who either didn't know I existed or didn't care if I existed . . . It occurred to me: What *if* I was real terrific?"

Both Siegel and Shuster were shy and awkward teenagers and uncomfortable around girls. When Shuster needed a female model for his early cartooning work, he advertised in the *Cleveland Plain Dealer*. Joanne Carter answered the ad and modeled Saturdays at his house for sketches. When Shuster first saw Joanne Carter, he recalled "to me she was Lois Lane." The name for Superman's girlfriend was taken from a Glenville High School classmate, Lois Amster, whom Shuster secretly admired. Joanne Carter, whose face inspired Shuster's depiction of Lois Lane, kept in touch with the two creators of Superman. In 1948, in a case of life surpassing art, Jerry Siegel (the model for Clark Kent) married Joanne Carter, the model for Lois Lane.

Siegel's happiness, however, was tempered by the treatment that he and Joe Shuster had received from the publishers of *Superman*. The previous year, the two had filed a $5 million lawsuit against National Comics Publications (formerly known as Detective Comics, Inc.), which contended they had been unfairly denied their share of the profits being realized on Superman.

According to the April 14, 1947, issue of *Newsweek*, in 1938, publisher Harry Donenfeld bought the first Superman story, "a thirteen-page, colored sequence at $10 a page and talked Siegel and Shuster into releasing all rights to Superman to his Detective Comics, Inc." For $130, the two young men sold their claim to a character

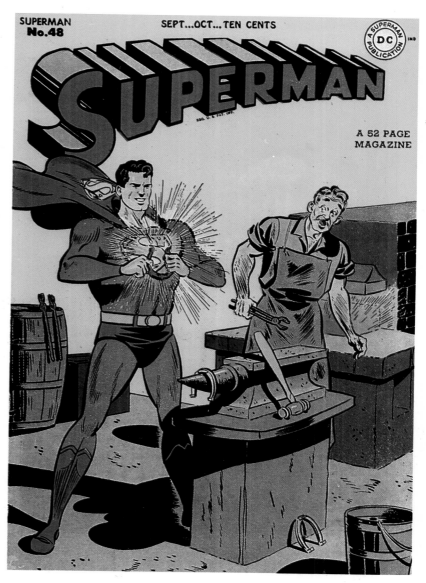

Superman #48 © 1947
DC Comics, Inc. Al Plastino.

which eventually became one of the most popular fictional heroes of all time and the star of radio, screen, and countless merchandising efforts. Under their initial ten-year contract with Donenfeld, Siegel and Shuster received $500 for each thirteen-page Superman story and a small percentage of the merchandising. In 1940, they made more than $60,000 from Superman, but by 1947, their earnings had fallen to $46,000. Siegel and Shuster blamed the decline in their Superman earnings on competition from other DC Comics superheroes, such as Batman, Superboy, Flash, and Aquaman, who were inspired by the initial success of their character.

Siegel and Shuster lost the lawsuit and were dismissed from working on their own character. Their absence, however, did not seem to diminish the popularity of Superman. As early as 1938,

Superman #2 © 1939 DC Comics, Inc. Joe Shuster.

Shuster had hired assistants to help with the art chores. By the 1940s, artists like Wayne Boring, Paul Cassidy, Leo Nowak, Dennis Neville, John Sikela, and Jack Burnley were drawing the bulk of the stories. Other writers replaced Siegel, such as the prolific William Woolfolk and Al Schwartz, who wrote under the name of Vernon Woodrum.

Although dropping from a wartime high circulation, the Superman comic books remained on DC Comics's best-selling list through the late 1940s and early 1950s. While not immune to the declining interest which befell all Golden Age superheroes in the late 1940s, Superman did prove to be a viable media character beyond the comic

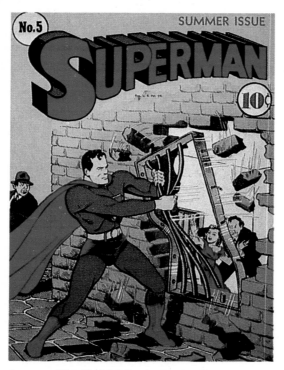

Superman #5 © 1940 DC Comics, Inc. Joe Shuster.

books. A successful radio show (1940–1952) had already popularized the character of Jimmy Olsen and introduced the catch phrase: "Look! Up in the sky! It's a bird! It's a plane! It's . . . SUPER-MAN!"

By 1948, the comic book hero was appearing in the movie theaters in a Columbia serial starring Kirk Alyn. Another serial, *Atom Man Vs. Superman*, was released in 1950. In 1953, at the end of the Golden Age, Superman gained a new lease on life with the success of a syndicated television show starring George Reeves that introduced the Man of Steel to millions of homes.

The first comic book superhero of them all had also proven to be the most resilient and successful of the Golden Age superheroes.

Golden Age Appearances
Action Comics 1–201 (6/38–2/55)
New York World's Fair Comics 1, 2 (4/39–1940)
Superman 1–95 (Summer/39–2/55)
World's Finest 1–74 (Spring/41–1/55)
All Star Comics 7, 36 (10/41–8/47)

WONDER WOMAN

December 1941 *All Star Comics* #8
DC Comics

"Wonder Woman's story is the story of her race. It reaches far back into the Golden Age when proud and beautiful women, stronger than men, ruled Amazonia and worshipped ardently the immortal Aphrodite, goddess of love and beauty. Out of that legendary glory, which present-day Amazons still preserve in secret, comes Wonder Woman, the most powerful and captivating girl of modern times . . ."

The most popular comic book superheroine of the 1940s had her origin on Paradise Island, the secret twentieth-century home of the Amazons where no man may set foot. Queen Hippolyte, the ruler of Paradise Island, makes a statue of a baby girl. The goddess Aphrodite endows the statue with life and gives the queen a young daughter, who grows up to be the Princess Diana, "as lovely as Aphrodite, as wise as Athena, with the speed of Mercury and the strength of Hercules."

Although time has seemingly stood still for the Amazons on Paradise Isle (fashion and architecture is utterly Homeric Greek), there is a world war on the horizon in 1941. The goddess Athena appears before Queen Hippolyte and tells her that "American liberty and freedom must be preserved! You must send your strongest and wisest Amazon—the finest of your wonder women—for America, the last citadel of democracy, and of equal rights for women, needs your help!"

An Amazonian contest, with such events as fencing, high-rope jumping, and deflecting bullets off bracelets, is held to select the best "wonder woman." Princess Diana, in disguise, wins the contest and the right to help America. She is given a costume of star-spangled shorts and a red halter top with a gold eagle emblem. She is also given a magic lasso made from the girdle of Aphrodite. Her mother tells her, "The magic lasso carries Aphrodite's power to make men and women submit to your will! Whoever you bind with that lasso must obey you!"

Princess Diana, now dressed as Wonder Woman, leaves Paradise Island in her "silent invisible plane" to help not only America but American women in the war for freedom. In the United States, Wonder Woman adopts the secret identity of army nurse Diana Prince. She later becomes a secretary to Colonel Darnell, who is also the commanding officer of her boyfriend, Captain Steve Trevor.

During the war years and after, Diana Prince would slip in and out of her Wonder Woman clothes over and over again to help her adopted country, rescue Steve Trevor, or give aid and support to women in need. In a 1943 story titled "Battle For Womanhood," Wonder Woman rescues a woman whose life has been destroyed by the evil ambitions of her husband. The wife tells Wonder Woman: "Submitting to a cruel husband's domination has ruined my life! But what can a weak girl do?"

The Amazon princess tells her: "Get strong! Earn your own living—join the WAACS or WAVES and fight for our country! Remember the better you can fight the less you'll have to!"

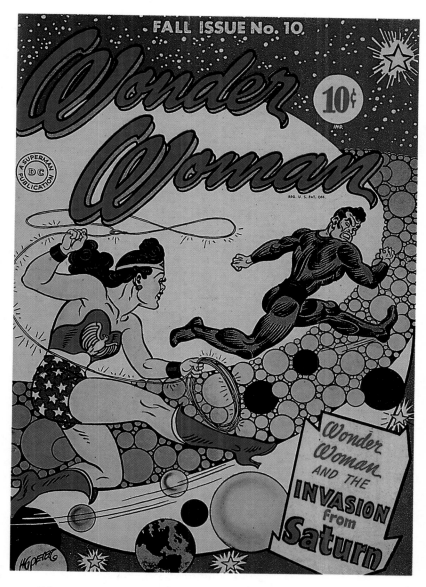

Wonder Woman #10
© 1944 DC Comics, Inc.
H.G. Peter.

The underlying message in all the Wonder Woman stories of the 1940s was the same: "You see, girls, there's nothing to it—all you have to do is *have confidence in your own strength*!"

Wonder Woman, the most vocal feminist hero to appear in popular fiction ostensibly for children, was the product of a man.

William Moulton Marston discovered the systolic blood-pressure test in 1915 at the age of twenty-two. His youthful discovery would lead to the invention of the lie detector. A doctor of psychology from Harvard, Marston was a frequent lecturer at universities, a member of several government study committees, and the author of several books on psychology as well as a string of popular articles for newspapers and magazines.

Marston, as a result of his lie detector experiments, was convinced that women were more honest and reliable than men and could work

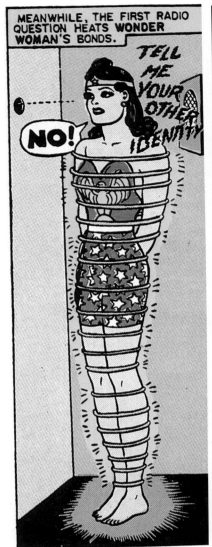

Left: *Sensation Comics #46* © *1945 DC Comics, Inc.* H.G. Peter.

Right: *Wonder Woman #13* © *1945 DC Comics, Inc.* H.G. Peter.

faster and more accurately. During the early war years when the role of women was rapidly changing, Marston championed their cause.

Max "Charles" Gaines, the publisher of All-American Comics, had retained Marston as an educational consultant. Gaines was toying with the idea of a line of educational comic books. Marston looked at Gaines's comic book titles with their images of supermen like Flash and Green Lantern and wondered why he wasn't publishing any comics with a woman as the hero.

Gaines was intrigued and a bargain was made. Marston undertook to create a female comic book hero, a "Wonder Woman," for Gaines under the pen name of their combined middle names, Charles Moulton.

According to his wife, Marston "wrote the first and every subsequent strip" with the idea of making Wonder Woman "a personal expression of the female character." He wanted his creation, a comic book superheroine for children, to fill a void in a society whose mythology and culture was dominated by masculine images.

Writing in a 1943 issue of *The American Scholar*, Marston stated that "Not even girls want to be girls so long as our feminine archetype lacks force, strength, and power. Not wanting to be girls, they don't want to be tender, submissive, peace-loving as good women are. Women's strong qualities have become despised because of their weakness. The obvious remedy is to create a feminine character with all the strength of a Superman plus all the allure of a good and beautiful woman."

Marston's "good and beautiful woman" made her debut in Gaines's most popular superhero comic at the time, *All Star Comics* (December 1941). Following such exposure, Wonder Woman became the lead feature in a new title *Sensation Comics* (January 1942), received her own magazine, and regularly appeared in *Comic Cavalcade*.

Marston kept tight control over his Amazon. He personally selected Harry G. Peter to draw Wonder Woman because he liked his "simplicity" in style and the way he drew women. He set up an art studio for Peter and his assistants (some of them women) so he could closely supervise his creation. According to his wife, Marston "made suggestions for layouts—how the panels should go—and then he edited the drawings very, very closely."

Marston's scripts and ideas gave *Wonder Woman* its emotional heart, but it was the artwork of H.G. Peter (as he signed his work) that made her the most popular superheroine of the 1940s. Peter's quaintly dated style was perfect for Marston's feminist fairy tales.

Peter developed his drawing skills while serving as a staff artist for a San Francisco newspaper in 1906. A product of *fin de siècle* influences, Peter exaggerated rather than modernized his nineteenth-century art style for the dozens of caricatures he drew for early twentieth-century humor magazines. By the time Peter came to comic books in 1940, he had perfected a heavy line that was ideal for cartoon storytelling.

After drawing a feature for *Hyper Mystery Comics*, Peter illustrated the adventures of Man O'Metal and Fearless Flint, two early superheroes who appeared in *Heroic Comics* and *Famous Funnies*, respectively. Peter's characters—even his heroes—often looked awkward, frozen at uncomfortable moments, and frequently sized to the proportions of fun-house mirror reflections. Yet it was also Peter's flat and hieroglyphic art which gave Marston's Wonder Woman stories a childhood dreamlike quality.

Only a few other artists besides Peter worked on Wonder Woman in the 1940s (notably illustrator Frank Godwin). After Marston's death in 1947, Peter continued to draw Wonder Woman for another ten years.

Robert Kanigher, who succeeded Marston as the principal writer and editor on *Wonder Woman*, remembered Peter as "a white-haired elf from Staten Island. When I jokingly asked for a crowd of 100 people in a single panel, he actually drew a hundred. I counted them. But no matter what kind of villain I painstakingly described, he drew them all like Hitler, with wet moustache and shiny black hair parted dead center. Peter was impervious to my yelling. Years later I realized that his mythic style was perfect for the mythic Wonder Woman. My apologies, Harry."

Whether or not the mythic Wonder Woman accomplished Marston's original purpose of favorably influencing anyone's views about the female character is difficult to say.

Gloria Steinem, a founding editor of *Ms.* magazine, remembered her girlhood experiences with the 1940s comic book character: "Here was a heroic person who might conquer with force, but only a force tempered by love and justice. She was beautiful, brave, and explicitly out to change 'a world torn by the hatreds and wars of men.'"

Dr. Fredric Wertham, who wrote a scathing indictment of the comic book industry in his 1954 book *Seduction of the Innocent*, was not so taken with Marston's Amazon: "If it were possible to translate a cardboard figure like Wonder Woman into life, every normal-minded young man would know there is something wrong with her."

Wertham thought that Wonder Woman and all the other superwomen in comics presented a perverted image of American womanhood to young readers: "They do not work. They are not homemakers. They do not bring up a family. Mother-love is entirely absent. Even when Wonder Woman adopts a young girl there are Lesbian overtones . . . "

The charge of implicit homosexuality in the Wonder Woman stories was an easy one to make, but also easily dismissed. In one story, Wonder Woman sits on a bed with a woman whom she holds in her lap. She has her hand on the woman's thigh while the woman has her arms looped around Wonder Woman's neck. The underlying emotional message, however, was one of comfort, not seduction. "Don't be afraid," Wonder Woman tells her. "He can't hurt you—

he has no power over you except what you *give* him!"

Critics also pointed suspiciously to Wonder Woman's relationship with the Holliday Girls, a bunch of sorority sisters from Holliday College. Wertham noted that the very name Holliday Girls implied the following—"Holliday girls, the gay party girls, the gay girls." The all-girl gang, led by a chunky short redhead known as Etta Candy, was ostensibly Wonder Woman's cheerleaders and helpmates.

Etta and her Holliday girls maintained contact with Wonder Woman through an Amazonian contraption called the "mental radio." Looking vaguely like an art-nouveau, Grecian fishbowl with a stethoscopic headband attachment, the mental radio can receive and broadcast a

Wonder Woman #1
© 1942 DC Comics, Inc.
H.G. Peter.

Sensation Comics #51 © 1945 DC Comics, Inc. H.G. Peter.

Sensation Comics #76
© 1948 DC Comics, Inc.
H.G. Peter.

Sensation Comics #83
© 1948 DC Comics, Inc.
H.G. Peter.

person's image and voice via thought waves. When Wonder Woman needs help, she sends a mental transmission to Etta and her Holliday girls:

"Woo woo! The chief's in hot water again an' calling her trusty cohorts! Come kids—we got work to do!" Etta Candy, a rough-and-tumble girl with a fondness for sweets, always prefaced her remarks the same way: "Woo woo! Wonder Woman that was a close shave!" and "Woo woo! Watching new girls arrive is so exciting!"

While Etta did seem to have an eye for the girls, she had an interest in the opposite sex as well ("Woo woo! Get your man, girls!"). Many of Wertham's perceived "Lesbian overtones" in Wonder Woman amounted to his failure to distinguish between romantic love (as exhibited by Wonder Woman toward Steve Trevor) and the *emotional* bonding which occurs between women.

It was the *physical* bonding, however, that concerned the moral guardians of the times. Bondage, domination, humiliation, and a host of other fetishes abounded in the early stories. In a Wonder Woman story, women (and occasionally men) were invariably bound in ropes, wires, chains, and manacles.

In a typical sixteen-page story from 1943, there are a dozen incidents of bondage: a blindfolded woman is chained to a bed, several women are handcuffed in their underwear, another woman is bound with ropes in a chair and gagged, women are handcuffed and strip-searched, and one woman has an iron ball and chain locked around her leg. Even Wonder Woman is strung up with her hands over her head, shackled to a cage, and finally manacled to a wall.

Wonder Woman herself also binds people with her "magic lasso" to make them obey her commands. On the other hand, if a man is able to bind Wonder Woman's bracelets together, then she will become powerless.

Supposedly, the bondage was used by Marston to illustrate the psychic domination and control of one sex over the other. As a villain in a Wonder Woman story wraps a rope around and around his female captive, the young woman pleads: "Oh, I hate to be bound—can't I please remain free?" The man crisply replies: "Certainly not, my dear! No woman can be trusted with

freedom—you ought to know that!"

Marston himself easily slipped into his bondage and domination metaphor when talking about his superheroine. "Give men an alluring woman stronger than themselves to submit to," Marston wrote in a scholarly journal, "and they'll be proud to become her willing slaves."

As Wonder Woman herself observed in a 1945 story: "Some girls love to have a man stronger than they are make them do things. Do I like it? I don't know—it's sort of thrilling. But—isn't it more fun to make the man obey?"

For the most part, Wonder Women did make them obey. Although she had feminine rivals, like the cat-suited Cheeta or Nazi agent Paula van Gunther (who later reformed), most of Wonder Woman's time was spent fighting twisted misogynists like Dr. Psycho and Mars, god of war.

Dr. Psycho, a dwarflike man with a bushel-basket-sized head, uses his powers over ectoplasm to assume any form—including that of a woman—in order to defeat Wonder Woman and "to enslave the women of the world!"

Mars, the male god of war and destruction, was the archenemy of Wonder Woman and all womankind: "Summon my war staff—I won't tolerate giving women the slightest freedom! If women gain power in war, they'll escape man's domination completely! They will achieve a horrible independence!"

After the war years, Marston backed away from male-bashing and toned down the bondage scenes in the stories. Wonder Woman, however, was still very much a woman's woman—despite her sometimes exasperating relationship with the now-promoted Major Steve Trevor.

After Marston's death in 1947, editor Robert Kanigher wrote the adventures of Wonder Woman for the remainder of the 1940s and into the 1960s. Her popularity made her the longest-lived of all the female superheroes.

Golden Age Appearances
All Star Comics 8, 11–22, 24–57 (12/41–2/51)
Sensation Comics 1–106 (1/42–11/51)
Wonder Woman 1–72 (Summer/42–2/55)
Comic Cavalcade 1–29 (Winter/42–10/48)
Big All-American Comic Book 1 (12/44)

The Comics

Nearly 7,000 comic books make up the Golden Age of Superheroes (1938 through 1954). What follows are descriptions and a collector's checklist of the 200-plus comic book titles which contain costumed Golden Age heroes.

In addition to title, publisher, publication dates, and issue numbers, there is also a listing of major costumed heroes in each title. The highlights of each title are given, along with a brief description of the superheroes who starred in the comic. When known, artists and writers who worked on the superhero series are listed.

Collecting the original Golden Age superhero comic books can be difficult and expensive because of their overall scarcity. World War II paper drives, postwar resettlement, the cleaning zealousness of mothers, and the fragile nature of the product itself have all conspired to deprive the historian and collector of these cultural artifacts. Fortunately, DC Comics and Marvel Comics have reprinted some of their superhero comics from the 1940s in comic books and in hardback collections. Collectors may wish to obtain these reprints before investing in the original issues.

Facing Page: *Wonder Comics #12 © 1947 Better Publications, Inc.*

Action Comics #27
© 1940 DC Comics, Inc.

Adventure Comics #48
© 1940 DC Comics, Inc.
Bernard Baily.

ACTION COMICS

DC Comics
Published 6/38–2/55   **Issue #s** 1–201
Major Characters
Superman 1–201
Mr. America 33–74
The Star Spangled Kid and Stripesy 40
The Vigilante 42–198

The birthplace of the superhero, *Action Comics* produced only a few costumed heroes, although it did launch Superman into his own magazine and newspaper strip. Tex Thomson, who began in the first issue of *Action* as a modern-day cowboy adventurer, became the early patriotic hero Mr. America (February 1941). While supervising a transatlantic shipment of food to Europe as part of the war relief effort, Tex is caught in an explosion set by saboteurs. He escapes as the sole survivor and vows to battle spies on the home front. He dons a red, white, and blue uniform and becomes Mr. America. His ineffectual sidekick, Bob Daley, becomes a costumed helper known as Fat Man (November 1941). Mr. America and Fat Man were collectively known as the Americommandos after the war was under way (September 1942). Bernard Baily drew the stories.

The Vigilante, a costumed cowboy hero, was created by writer Mort Weisinger and artist Mort Meskin. Greg Sanders, a Wyoming born cowboy and son of a county sheriff, pursues a crime-fighting career after his father is killed in a stagecoach robbery. Moving east, he becomes a singing radio star called the "Prairie Troubadour." He dresses the part of a drugstore cowboy to hide his identity as the Vigilante so he can operate outside the law. He has a girlfriend, blues singer Betty Stuart, and rides a motorcycle instead of a horse ("Get goin', you gas–eating bronco!"). The Vigilante was also a member of the Seven Soldiers of Victory in *Leading Comics*.

ADVENTURE COMICS

DC Comics
Published 11/38–2/55   **Issue #s** 32–209
Major Characters
The Sandman 40–102
The Hourman 48–83
Starman 61–102
The Shining Knight 66–125, 127, 128, 131, 132,
    137–139, 142–145, 148, 150, 151, 153, 155, 157,
    159, 161, 163, 165, 166
Manhunter 73–92
Superboy 103–209
Aquaman 103–117, 119–152, 154, 156, 158,160, 162,
    164, 167, 168, 170–206, 208, 209
Green Arrow 103–205, 207–209
Johnny Quick 103–204, 206, 207

Adventure Comics was the home of several superhe-

roes. Hourman, as his name might lead you to believe, was super for only one hour at a time, thanks to a supply of "Miraclo pills" he invented in his alter ego of Rex Tyler, research chemist. Drawn by Bernard Baily, Hourman ran out of time and pills by 1943.

The Shining Knight was originally Sir Justin, a knight of King Arthur's Round Table who rode a flying horse named Winged Victory. Sir Justin and his steed fall into an ice pit and remain frozen for 1,500 years. They thaw out in time for World War II and Sir Justin adopts a modern day identity of an assistant museum curator. Dressed in golden mail armor and wielding an enchanted sword and lance (given to him by Merlin), Sir Justin becomes the Shining Knight and fights twentieth-century criminals and enemy soldiers while mounted on Winged Victory. Drawn initially by Creig Flessel, the Shining Knight was also a member of the Seven Soldiers of Victory in *Leading Comics*.

Joe Simon and Jack Kirby created the Manhunter, a costumed hero who turns from big-game hunting to tracking down the "beasts of civilization." Simon recalled that the 1941 movie *Man Hunt*, about a man attempting to kill Hitler, provided the inspiration for this character.

When *More Fun Comics* was canceled, Superboy, Green Arrow, Aquaman, and Johnny Quick moved over to *Adventure Comics* and replaced Starman and Sandman.

AIRBOY COMICS

Hillman Periodicals
Published 12/45–5/53   **Issue #s** 23–111
Major Characters
Airboy 23–111

After making his debut in *Air Fighters Comics*, Airboy officially took over the retitled magazine at the end of 1945. Even with the end of the war, the adolescent aviator was still quite popular (due in part to the artwork by Fred Kida and Dan Barry).

Editor Ed Cronin acted out the Airboy stories for his writers, grabbing himself around the throat, punching and kicking imaginary villains, and sometimes smacking himself in the nose until he bled.

AIR FIGHTERS COMICS

Hillman Periodicals
Publication Date 11/41–Fall/45   **Issue #s** 1–22
Major Characters
Airboy 2–22
Black Angel 2–20, 22

Kids loved airplanes and pilots in the 1940s and *Air Fighters Comics* was full of high-flying heroes. Among the best were Airboy and Black Venus, a female freelance combat pilot.

Professor Nelson, a government scientist, hides

his son Davy in a monastery to protect him from enemy agents. Davy learns about aeronautics from Martier, a monk who builds a batlike plane which flies by flapping its wings. When Martier dies after his "sinister batlike ship" is sabotaged, Davy vows to carry on the monk's work and rebuilds the plane. He also dons a costume handed down through the monk's family since the French Revolution and becomes the costumed aviator, Airboy. Airboy's black-winged plane, which is christened Birdie, has a thirty-two-foot wingspan, a duraluminum fuselage, and plenty of .50-caliber machine guns for World War II dogfights. His most persistent opponent was Valkyrie who led the Air Maidens, a Nazi squadron of women pilots. Charles Biro and Ed Cronin created the popular boy hero who later took over the title.

Sylvia Manners, a beautiful English pilot, lives with her aunt Lady Lawton in a medieval castle. She decides to fight back against the Nazis, who attack her country in daily air raids. She constructs an airplane hangar under her castle for her jet-black plane. Piecing together a skin-tight and purple-black satin suit, Miss Manners takes to the skies as the costumed vigilante, the Black Angel. "Black death on wings . . . wrapped in dazzling beauty, her name spells horror to swaggering Nazis."

ALL-AMERICAN COMICS

DC Comics
Published 4/39–10/48   **Issue #s** 1–102
Major Characters
Green Lantern 16–102
The Atom 20–46,48–61,70–72
Dr. Mid-Nite 25–102

Although Green Lantern was the star of *All-American Comics* from his debut, both the Atom and Dr. Mid-Nite were popular enough to also rate a membership in the Justice Society of America.

Dr. Charles McNider is blinded in an explosion while trying to aid the victim of a racketeer. Unable to practice surgery, the sightless doctor becomes a writer for detective pulp magazines. When an owl crashes through his window one night, the alarmed McNider rips away the bandages from his eyes and discovers he has developed night vision! Encouraged by his new power, he develops a pair of infra-red goggles to allow him to see in the daytime as well. He also develops an arsenal of black-out bombs to blind evildoers and devises a superhero costume from some old masquerade gear. Aided by his pet owl Hooty, Dr. Mid-Nite delights in taking on after-hour cases ("If there's danger in the dark, you'll find Dr. Mid-Nite around to brighten things up!"). Pretending to be a sightless writer in order to protect his secret identity, McNider makes a living by writing about the exploits of Dr. Mid-Nite with the help of his secretary-typist, Myra Mason.

Written initially by Charles Reisenstein (who also helped create Mr. Terrific for *Sensation Comics*) and drawn primarily by Stan Asch, Dr. Mid-Nite

followed a tradition of costumed blind vigilantes. The Mask, who appeared exactly one year earlier in *Exciting Comics* (April 1940), was a vengeful district attorney who had lost his sight to criminals. The Black Bat, a 1934 detective pulp magazine hero, also took the law into his own hands after being blinded by acid.

ALL-FLASH

DC Comics
Published Summer/41–12/47   **Issue #s** 1–32
Major Characters
The Flash 1–32
Green Lantern 14

When it became evident that the Flash was the most popular superhero of the All-American comic book line, the next natural step was to put him into a second title. Writer Gardner Fox took advantage of the new title and wrote a dozen book-length Flash stories. Another Fox creation, the sidekick comedy team of Winky, Blinky, and Noddy, began as a secondary series in issue #5.

ALL HERO COMICS

Fawcett Publications
Published 3/43   **Issue #s** 1
Major Characters
Captain Marvel, Jr. 1
Spy Smasher 1
Ibis the Invincible 1
Captain Midnight 1

This 100-page comic book was bound in cardboard covers and sold for fifteen cents. Captain Marvel appeared on the cover only.

ALL-NEW COMICS

Harvey Publications
Published 1/43–3/47   **Issue #s** 1–15
Major Characters
The Black Cat 6, 9, 15
Shock Gibson 8
Zebra 7, 10
Green Hornet 13,14
Stuntman 13

This anthology starred Harvey heroes from several other titles (*Speed Comics, Pocket Comics, Green Hornet, Stuntman*). Many issues (#s 5–12) featured Captain Red Blazer (from *Pocket Comics*) and his sidekick Sparky on the front cover. The two costumed heroes, however, did not appear in any story inside the comic. Instead, their adventures appeared in a regular text feature, "The Story Behind The Cover."

All-American Comics #17 © 1940 DC Comics, Inc. Sheldon Moldoff.

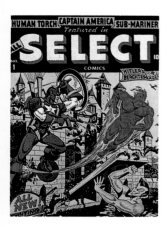

*All-Select Comics #1
© 1943 Marvel Entertainment Group, Inc.*

*All Star Comics #4
© 1941 DC Comics, Inc.
Everett E. Hibbard.*

ALL-SELECT COMICS

Marvel Comics
Published Fall/43–Fall/46   **Issue #s** 1–11
Major Characters
Black Widow 1
The Human Torch 1–10
Captain America 1–10
Sub-Mariner 1–5, 10
Whizzer 3–5, 7
Destroyer 6, 10
The Blonde Phantom 11
Miss America 11

The Human Torch, Sub-Mariner, and Captain America—Marvel's top three heroes—were featured in this comic book. With the March 1945 issue, Sub-Mariner was dropped from the lineup. With the last issue (Fall 1946), however, Captain America and the other super guys were replaced by two women: Miss America from *Marvel Mystery Comics* and the brand-new Blonde Phantom. The Blonde Phantom took over the title under her own name with issue #12.

ALL STAR COMICS

DC Comics
Published Summer/40–2/51   **Issue #s** 1–57
Major Characters
The Flash 1–7, 10, 24–57
The Hourman 1–7
The Sandman 1–21
The Spectre 1–23
Hawkman 1–57
Green Lantern 2–7, 10, 24–57
The Atom 3–26, 28–35, 37–57
Dr. Fate 3–12, 14–21
Justice Society of America 3–57
Superman 7, 36
Batman 7, 36
Dr. Mid-Nite 8–57
Starman 8–23
Wonder Woman 8, 11–22, 24–57
Wildcat 24, 27
Mr. Terrific 24
Black Canary 38–57

Originally an anthology featuring the Flash, Hawkman, Sandman, Hourman, and the Spectre, *All Star Comics* became the first superhero team title with the appearance of the Justice Society of America (Winter 1940). The JSA, as it was known, consisted of DC Comics heroes who were not already starring in their own comic books. Membership changed as characters advanced to their own title and less popular members were replaced.

 Several artists worked on each issue, each one drawing a different character and chapter in the story. Artists included Stanley Asche (Doctor Fate, Dr. Mid-Nite, Green Lantern, Mr. Terrific, Starman), Bernard Baily (Hourman, Spectre), John Belfi (Flash),

Jack Burnley (Starman), Ed Dobrotka (Starman), Lee Elias (Flash), Lou Ferstadt (Starman), Creig Flessel (Sandman), Ben Flinton (Atom), Joe Gallagher (Atom, Flash, Spectre, Sandman, Wildcat), Frank Harry (Dr. Mid-Nite), Irwin Hassen (Batman, Superman, Atom, Green Lantern), Everett Hibbard (Flash), Carmine Infantino (Flash), Bernard Klein (Doctor Fate), Jon Kozlak (Atom, Doctor Fate, Hawkman, Green Lantern, Wildcat), Joe Kubert (Doctor Fate, Hawkman), Harry Lampert (Atom), Sheldon Moldoff (Hawkman), Martin Naydel (Flash, Green Lantern), Martin Nodell (Green Lantern), Harry G. Peter (Wonder Woman), Paul Reinman (Atom, Green Lantern, Starman), Pierce Rice (Spectre, Sandman, Starman), Howard Sherman (Doctor Fate), Joe Simon and Jack Kirby (Sandman), Alex Toth (Atom, Dr. Mid-Nite), and Cliff Young (Sandman, Spectre). Gardner Fox wrote #s 3–34, Robert Kanigher scripted #36–38, and John Broome authored #s 35,39–57.

ALL TOP COMICS

Fox Features Syndicate
Published 11/47–3/49   **Issue #s** 8–18
Major Characters
Phantom Lady 8–17
The Blue Beetle 8–13

After seven issues of funny animal strips like "Cosmo Cat" and "Flash Rabbit," publisher Victor Fox filled *All Top Comics* with racy women, bondage scenes, and—if anti-comic book crusader Fredric Wertham is to be believed—"sadistic racism." Rulah the Jungle Goddess was the star of the book, although the newly revamped Phantom Lady certainly helped sales. Fox also added the Blue Beetle to the title in hopes of attracting the superhero fan.

ALL WINNERS COMICS (1)

Marvel Comics
Published Summer/41–Winter/46   **Issue #s** 1–19, 21
                                                   (No 20)
Major Characters
The Angel 1
Black Marvel 1
Captain America 1–19, 21
The Human Torch 1–13, 17–19, 21
Sub-Mariner 1–19, 21
The Destroyer 2–12
Whizzer 2–5, 7–11, 13–19, 21
Miss America 19, 21
All Winners Squad 19, 21

Marvel Comics publisher Martin Goodman launched a comic book that would have no second-string heroes or losers—just "all winners." Captain America, who had appeared in four issues of his own comic book, was selected to star in this title along with the Human Torch and the Sub-Mariner. For the last two issues (Fall 1946), they formed a team called the All Winners Squad consisting of Captain America, Human Torch, Sub-Mariner, Bucky, Toro, Whizzer, and Miss America.

ALL WINNERS COMICS (2)

Marvel Comics
8/48
1
The Blonde Phantom 1
Captain America 1
The Human Torch 1
Sub-Mariner 1

This second version of the All-Winners Squad featured the three Marvel headliners plus their most popular female superhero at the time, the Blonde Phantom. As superheroes lost ground to the growing popularity of movie and comic cowboys, the magazine was retitled *All-Western Winners* with its second issue.

AMAZING COMICS

Marvel Comics
Published Fall/44 **Issue #s** 1
Major Characters
Destroyer 1
Whizzer 1
Young Allies 1

The Young Allies, who appear in a three-chapter story, are the stars of this book. Both the Destroyer (who was appearing in *USA Comics* at the time) and the Whizzer (from *All-Winners Comics*) got some secondary exposure as well. With the second issue, the magazine was retitled *Complete Comics*.

AMAZING-MAN COMICS

Centaur Publications
Published 9/39–1/42 **Issue #s** 5–27 (No 1–4)
Major Characters
Amazing Man 5–27
The Iron Skull 5–11, 14–22
Mighty Man 5–27
Minimidget 5–25
Shark 6–22

Amazing-Man was the second superhero (after Superman) to have a comic book named after him. Bill Everett drew the first seven issues and the character was continued by artist Louis Glanzman and writer Allen Kirby. Glanzman also created the Shark for *Amazing-Man Comics*. This early sea-going hero ("the son of Father Neptune") began one month before the Sub-Mariner appeared on the newsstand. The webbed-footed Shark was assisted by Neptune, or "Pop," as he was known in the stories.

Carl Burgos drew the Iron Skull, the first android superhero ("Bullets won't penetrate his iron body! Acts as a human torpedo to sink an enemy boat"). The android's only vulnerable spot is the "main artery in his left forearm." Burgos later created two other android heroes, the Human Torch for *Marvel Comics* and the White Streak for *Target Comics*.

Mighty Man ("Has the ability to become small or large! First a midget then a giant!") was drawn by Martin Filchock. Assisted by his friend Super Ann, Mighty Man (who was originally a twelve-foot giant) later acquires the power to make any *specific* part of his body grow! Minimidget ("No larger than your hand—can ride on a carrier pigeon!") was lucky enough to have a super-midget girlfriend named Ritty. The diminutive couple, victim of a mad scientist's shrinking ray, cruises through life in a tiny sports car and little airplane in stories drawn by John Kolb.

AMAZING MYSTERY FUNNIES

Centaur Publications
Published 8/38–9/40 **Issue #s** 1–24
Major Characters
Fantom of the Fair 11–23
Fantoman 24
Speed Centaur 12–24

After several science fiction series, including Bill Everett's Skyrocket Steele, *Amazing Mystery Funnies* presented a costumed hero known as the Fantom of the Fair. An unnamed masked genius constructs an elaborate hideout underneath the grounds of the 1939 New York World's Fair in order to protect it from would-be saboteurs. Partially inspired by the 1925 movie *Phantom of the Opera*, the Fantom of the Fair also used a series of tunnels and developed his own weapons to fight racketeers and criminals. The art and stories, which were all staged with 1939 New York Fair landmarks in the background, were usually by Paul Gustavson, who visited the fair to authenticate details. As the World's Fair came to an end, the character changed his name to Fantoman and moved over to his own comic book.

The other *Amazing Mystery* hero actually made the Fantom of the Fair seem like a normal guy. Speed Centaur was half-human and half-horse and doubtless inspired by the name of his publishing company. Originally from the Arctic wastelands, this survivor from a lost race teamed up with newsman "Reel" McCoy to fight crime on the streets of New York City (including investigating a fixed horse race!). This equine superhero was written and drawn by Malcolm Kildare, who perhaps might wish to be remembered more for his work on Classic Comics's *The Three Musketeers*.

Amazing-Man Comics #17 © 1940 Centaur Publications. Lew Glanzman.

America's Best Comics #24 © 1947 Better Publications, Inc. Alex Schomburg.

Atoman #1 © 1946 Spark Publications. Jerry Robinson.

AMERICA'S BEST COMICS

Better/Standard Publications
Published 2/42–7/49   **Issue #s** 1–31
Major Characters
The Black Terror 1–31
Captain Future 1–3, 5, 22
Doc Strange 1–23, 27
The Woman in Red 1, 2
The Liberator 1, 3–5, 8
The American Eagle 2, 6, 7, 10–12, 14
Pyroman 3–8, 10, 12, 13, 17–22, 24, 28, 29
American Crusader 6
The Fighting Yank 9, 11,13–25
Miss Masque 23–31

Better Publications's first attempt at comic books was the short-lived *Best Comics* (November 1939), which consisted of western, adventure, and humor stories. *America's Best,* published two years later at the height of the superhero boom, put Better's successful new heroes into one title: Black Terror (*Exciting Comics*), Doc Strange (*Thrilling Comics*), and Captain Future (*Startling Comics*). Pyroman, a popular hero from *Startling,* was soon added and then Captain Future was eased out by the more patriotic American Eagle. The American Eagle made his first appearance in the September 1942 issue and was drawn by Ken Platt and written by Richard Hughes. Tom Standish dons a blue suit with red-and-white stripes and becomes "Democracy's Champion—The American Eagle!" The month after his debut, the American Eagle (known simply as "Eagle" to his friends) moved over to *Exciting Comics* and got a kid sidekick, Bud Pierce, who became known as the Eaglet. The last major hero to join the rest of "America's Best" was the Fighting Yank, who soon became the title's resident patriotic hero with the departure of the American Eagle, American Crusader, and the Liberator.

AMERICA'S GREATEST COMICS

Fawcett Publications
Published Fall/41–Summer/43   **Issue #s** 1–8
Major Characters
Bulletman 1–8
Captain Marvel 1–8
Minute-Man 1–7
Mr. Scarlet 1–7
Spy Smasher 1–6, 8
Ibis the Invincible 4
Commando Yank 4–7
Captain Marvel, Jr. 8
Captain Midnight 8

This 100-page comic book with soft cardboard covers retailed for fifteen cents and featured the top heroes from Fawcett publishing.

ARROW, THE

Centaur Publications
Published 10/40–10/41   **Issue #s** 1–3
Major Characters
The Arrow 1–3
Dash Darwell, the Human Meteor 3
The Rainbow 3

After making his debut in the *Funny Pages* (and a brief stop in *Fantoman Comics*), the Arrow received his own magazine. The stories in the first two issues, however, were reprints from earlier comics. By issue #3, the Arrow was drawn by a new artist, Bob Lubbers, and had assumed the secret identity of Ralph Payne, U.S. intelligence agent. The Rainbow was the creation of writer Ed Herron and artist Al Plastino. Jim Travis got the idea of becoming a costumed hero by reading a comic book. Determined to outdo the fictional heroes, Jim creates a green, red, yellow, and blue costume and becomes the Rainbow.

ATOMAN

Spark Publications
Published 2/46–4/46   **Issue #s** 1, 2
Major Characters
Atoman 1,2

Barry Dale, one of the world's first nuclear scientists, discovers he has absorbed enough radioactivity to give him the power to "explode atoms." The scientist muses: "I can smash mountains, wipe out whole cities, leap into the air and travel for thousands of miles at one leap. I can move faster than thought. There's no limit to my atomic power! Perhaps I am the new type of man who will come into existence as the Atomic Age develops . . . but in the mean time, I am the only ATOMAN on earth!" Dale decides to use his Atoman identity to protect the weak: "Atomic power belongs to the whole Earth. My own power must be used to help all people, regardless of race or creed or nationality!"

This idealistic superhero was created by Joseph Greene, who wrote several *Batman* stories in the early 1940s. The art was by Jerry Robinson, another *Batman* alumnus.

ATOMIC THUNDERBOLT

Regor Company
Published 2/46   **Issue #s** 1
Major Characters
Atomic Thunderbolt 1

It's the year after the first atomic bomb. Professor Josiah Rhonne is searching for a way to end the threat of nuclear war with his "experiment in transmutation." By subjecting people to "neutron bombardment," the professor hopes "to change the atomic structure of the human body and make the tissue immune to radioactivity and atomic explosions!" The professor, however, needs a guinea pig for his experiment ("I must have a human subject— even if I have to become a kidnapper and a murderer!"). Fortunately, the professor runs across William Burns, better known as Willy the Wharf Rat ("a cross between a beach–comber and a bum . . . a Nazi torpedo exploded too close to him"), who has nothing to lose by volunteering for the experiment. An explosion in the lab, however, accidentally turns Willy into the Atomic Thunderbolt, an atomic hero who can radiate energy and fly through the air. This early nuclear-age hero was drawn by Mort Lawrence.

BANG-UP COMICS

Progressive Publishers
Published 12/41–6/42   **Issue #s** 1–3
Major Characters
Cosmo Mann 1–3
Lady Fairplay 1–3

Cosmo Mann, a scientist, harnesses the rays of the sun and invents a "G-Ray Gun" which can dissolve objects and paralyze people. He also devises a sun suit which allows him to fly. Armed with his sun-ray gun, Cosmo matches wits each issue with a would-be German conqueror. Lady Fairplay was orginally mild-mannered school marm Mary Lee. After Professor Amazo gives Mary some unusual treatments, she becomes the super-charged Lady Fairplay. She slips into a costume, complete with diadem, and earns a reputation as the "goddess of chastisement." All three chastising adventures of the Lady were drawn by Jack Ryan, who also assisted Chester Gould on the *Dick Tracy* comic strip.

BANNER COMICS

Ace Magazines
Published 9/41–1/42   **Issue #s** 3–5
Major Characters
Captain Courageous 3–5

Captain Courageous, "Defender of America and Champion of Liberty," fought Nazi saboteurs in his earliest adventures before turning his attention to the Pacific battlefront. His archenemy was Captain Nippon, a Japanese commander with a hook for a hand. Appearing both in costume and in "civies," Captain Courageous had the powers of super strength and flight. The early adventures were drawn by Harry Sahle, who was later known for his work for Archie Comics, and Jim Mooney, whose work in comics included such characters as Supergirl and Batman. The sixth issue of *Banner Comics* was retitled *Captain Courageous Comics* in March 1942 but lasted for only one issue.

BATMAN

DC Comics
Published Spring/40–2/55   **Issue #s** 1–89
Major Characters
Batman and Robin 1–89

After originally appearing in *Detective Comics*, Batman received his own magazine at the same time he was joined by Robin the Boy Wonder. The comic book featured the first appearance of the Joker (#1), the Catwoman (#3), the Batmobile (#5), and Alfred the butler (#16), who went from fat to thin over the years. For a couple of years, Alfred had his own strip in the comic.

BIG 3

Fox Features Syndicate
Published Fall/40–1/42   **Issue #s** 1–7
Major Characters
The Blue Beetle 1–7
Flame 1–7
Samson 1–6
Stardust 2
V-Man 7

The "Big Three" consisted of the Blue Beetle, the Flame, and Samson. With this title, Fox's biggest heroes were each appearing in three titles: Blue Beetle (*Mysterymen* and *Blue Beetle Comics*), the Flame (*Flame Comics* and *Wonderworld*), and Samson (*Samson Comics* and *Fantastic*).

BIG ALL-AMERICAN COMIC BOOK

DC Comics
Published 12/44   **Issue #s** 1
Major Characters
The Atom 1
The Flash 1
Green Lantern 1
Hawkman 1
Little Boy Blue 1
Mr. Terrific 1
The Whip 1
Wildcat 1
Wonder Woman 1

Max Gaines, the publisher of the All-American line of comic books, put his four most popular superheroes—Flash, Green Lantern, Hawkman, and Wonder Woman—in one book, along with his other characters from *All-American, Flash,* and *Sensation Comics*. The resulting 132-page comic book, coming out at a time when a regular fifty-two-page comic sold for a dime, retailed for a quarter.

Gaines timed the book's release for the Christmas holidays in hopes that its extra pages and higher price would put it in the "gift" comic category, much like Fawcett Comics had done with

Banner Comics #3 © 1941 Ace Magazines, Inc. Jim Mooney.

Batman #15 © 1943 DC Comics, Inc. Jack Burnley.

*Black Cat #4 © 1947
Harvey Features Syndicate*

*Black Hood Comics #14
© 1945 Archie Comic
Publications, Inc.*

its extra-long and similarly priced *Xmas Comics.* Unlike Fawcett's anthology, however, the *Big All-American Comic Book* contained all original stories with no reprints. The issue also marked the first time Joe Kubert drew Hawkman—a feature he would be associated with through the 1940s and again in the 1960s.

BIG SHOT COMICS

Columbia Comics Group
Published 5/40–8/49   **Issue #s** 1–104
Major Characters
The Face 1–62, 73, 74, 80
Skyman 1–41, 43–101
The Cloak 11–28

The first comic book from the Columbia Comic Group, headed by ex-DC Comics editor Vincent Sullivan, featured reprints from the "Joe Palooka" newspaper strip as well as two original costumed heroes: Skyman and the Face. Skyman was the second costumed aviator hero to appear in comic books after Spy Smasher (*Whiz Comics*). He was originally drawn by Paul Reinman and written by Gardner Fox. Within a year, he had his own comic book.

Tony Trent, a radio announcer, is distressed by the crime reports he broadcasts. He takes matters into his own hands and designs a green rubber mask so "weird and gruesome" that his very appearance will frighten evildoers. Wearing his false face and a green tuxedo, Trent becomes a masked vigilante known as The Face. Editor Vincent Sullivan came up with the idea for the character and writer Gardner Fox and artist Mart Bailey launched the series. Bailey drew most of the Face's appearances and wrote the later stories. By 1946, Trent discarded his rubber mask and ended his career as the Face.

BLACK CAT

Harvey Publications
Published 6/46–6/51   **Issue #s** 1–29
Major Characters
The Black Cat 1–29
Red Demon 4–7
Scarlet Arrow 5, 6
Stuntman 9

Although Black Cat made her debut in the August 1941 issue of *Pocket Comics,* she did not receive her own magazine until after the war. While the first issue was drawn by Jill Elgin, Lee Elias drew the majority of the Black Cat adventures. As for the short-lived features in the comic, Bob Powell was the artist on the Scarlet Arrow (otherwise known as Alan Bidel), while Bill Draut drew the adventures of the Red Demon (the costumed alter ego of Judge Straight).

BLACK HOOD COMICS

MLJ/Archie Comics
Published Winter/43–Summer/46   **Issue #s** 9–19
(no #s 1–8)

Major Characters
The Black Hood 9–19
Boy Buddies 9, 11
The Hangman 9, 10
Dusty, Boy Detective 10

Originally appearing in *Top-Notch Comics,* the Black Hood was awarded his own comic book after his series ended in *Jackpot Comics.* In issue #19, the Hood reveals his secret identity and quits the business. The next issue (Fall 1946) was retitled *Laugh Comics* and the Black Hood was replaced by a red-headed teenager named Archie.

BLACK TERROR

Better/Standard Publications
Published Winter/42–6/49   **Issue #s** 1–27
Major Characters
The Black Terror 1–27
Miss Masque 21
Spectro, The Mind Reader 25
The Scarab 20

After his debut in *Exciting Comics,* the Black Terror and his identically dressed, boy sidekick Tim Roland (known collectively as The Terror Twins) starred in fifty-two stories in this title and in ninety-two stories in other Better comics. Artists included Ken Platt, Ed Wexler, George Tuska, Mort Meskin, Ed Moritz, Jerry Robinson, George Roussos, Ruben Moreria, and Ralph Mayo.

BLACKHAWK

Quality Comics Group
Published Winter/44–3/55   **Issue #s** 9–86
(No #s 1–8)

Major Characters
Blackhawk 9–86

The Blackhawks, a multinational squadron of airborne freedom-fighters, received their own magazine in 1944 after appearing in *Military Comics* for three years. Most issues of *Blackhawk Comics* featured three Blackhawk adventures and a humorous Chop-Chop story as the secondary feature. The Blackhawks were popular enough to survive after most 1940s costumed heroes had vanished. Quality Comics continued publishing the comic until the end of 1956 and then turned the Blackhawks over to DC Comics, which would continue the title uninterrupted for another twenty years.

BLAZING COMICS

Rural Home/Enwill Publishing Company
Published 6/44–4/45 **Issue #s** 1–6
Major Characters
The Green Turtle 1–4

The Green Turtle was perhaps the most mysterious of all the 1940s superheroes. Not only was his secret identity never revealed to readers, but even his (her?) face was never shown in any adventures! He (she?) possessed no special super-powers and used a "Turtle Plane" to get around. The Green Turtle was accompanied by a sidekick known as Burma Boy and many of the adventures took place in China. The character was created by one of the first Chinese-American comic book artists, Chu F. Hing.

BLONDE PHANTOM

Marvel Comics
Published Winter/46–3/49 **Issue #s** 12–22 (no 1–11)
Major Characters
The Blonde Phantom 12–22
Miss America 12–14
Sub-Mariner 13–15, 17–22
Captain America 16

Marvel's most popular superheroine, the Blonde Phantom, first appeared in *All Select Comics,* and the comic was renamed after her with the next issue. There were two or three Blonde Phantom stories in each issue, with a Miss America or Sub-Mariner story usually rounding out the book.

BLUE BEETLE

Fox Features Syndicate/Holyoke
Published Winter/39–8/50 **Issue #s** 1–60
Major Characters
The Blue Beetle 1–60
Dynamite Thor 7,8
Dynamo 7, 8
Black Fury 12
V-Man 13–19

The Blue Beetle was the second superhero after Superman to earn his own comic book after appearing first in another magazine. Publisher Victor Fox pushed the Blue Beetle into star status after premiering the hero in *Mystery Men Comics* (August 1939). When Fox suspended publication of his comics in 1942, Holyoke Publishing took over and a new set of writers and artists worked on the feature, including a young Joe Kubert and Charles Quinlan, the artist on the *Cat-Man*. During this period, the Beetle picked up a short-lived sidekick named Sparky, who vanished by 1943.

Fox picked the title up again in June 1944 and with the August 1946 issue, he turned the comic book into a blood-and-sex serial. Jack Kamen, an artist who would later work for EC Comics, filled the stories with guns, bondage, and lingerie.

The early 1940s issues of *Blue Beetle* featured farewell performances by several minor Fox superheroes from other titles: Dynamo (*Science Comics*), Dynamite Thor (*Weird Comics*), V-Man (*V Comics*), and the Black Fury (*Fantastic Comics*).

BLUE BOLT

Novelty Press
Published 6/40–3/44 **Issue #s** 1–44
Major Characters
Blue Bolt 1–27
Sub-Zero Man 1–37, 39, 44
The Twister 13–19

Blue Bolt #1 © 1940 Novelty Press

Named after Joe Simon's costumed character, this comic featured several other superheroes. Sub-Zero Man was a Venusian spaceman who looks like an ordinary Earthman. The alien crash-lands on Earth after colliding with an asteroid which encases him in ice. The icy extraterrestrial makes it to a laboratory where scientists bombard him with gamma rays. The radiation gives the frozen alien the powers to freeze anything he touches or looks at. Bullets freeze and crumble when they hit his sub-zero body. Sub-Zero Man was the first of the super-cold heroes, predating Stan Lee's Jack Frost at Marvel Comics by more than a year. Sub-Zero Man was drawn by Larry Antonette, Bill Everett, and John Daly. Writer Ray Gill took over the strip in 1941 and gave Sub-Zero an Eskimo crime-fighting companion named Freezum (October 1941).

The Twister, originally drawn by Paul Gustavson and written by Ray Gill, is born when a young man is swept up in a tornado and becomes a part of it. He can control and create a cyclone at will, fly through the air, and blast Manhattan criminals with jets of air from his Cyclone Gun.

BLUE CIRCLE COMICS

Rural Home Publishing Company
Published 6/44–4/45 **Issue #s** 1–6
Major Characters
Blue Circle 1–5
The Steel Fist 1–5

The Blue Circle is secretly Len Stafford, a costumed avenger with links to the underworld. When he has to solve a case, he calls a meeting of the Blue Circle Council, which consists of "past masters in crime." The Blue Circle usually spends his time busting up small-time rackets like counterfeit war ration books and crooked horse racing.

Timothy Slade is a machine worker in an industrial war plant. His right hand and upper arm have been replaced by metal, which gives him a "steel fist." Whenever sabotage threatens his plant, Tim slips into a yellow-and-blue costume and unleashes the power of the Steel Fist.

Blue Ribbon Comics #9 © 1941 Archie Comic Publications, Inc. Sam Cooper.

Boy Comics #59 © 1950 Lev Gleason Publications

BLUE RIBBON COMICS

MLJ/Archie Comics
Published 11/39–3/42   **Issue #s** 1–22
Major Characters
Bob Phantom 2, 3
The Fox 4–22
Green Falcon 4–15
Mr. Justice 9–22
Inferno, the Flame Breather 13–19
Captain Flag 16–22

Blue Ribbon Comics was the first comic from MLJ Publications, a company which would become better known as Archie Comics.

Mr. Justice, a supernatural hero written by Joe Blair and drawn by Sam Cooper, was the most popular character in *Blue Ribbon*. During the Rogers Rebellion in eleventh-century Scotland, Prince James of England is lured to Rogers Castle and murdered. His spirit, however, lives on to fight for justice. In 1940, the spirit of Prince James comes to America in the form of Mr. Justice, a blue ectoplasmic figure who is known as "The Royal Wraith." Mr. Justice (dressed in ghostly white gloves, cape, and trunks) frequently aids Pat Clark and her dad by battling villains like the Green Ghoul and even Satan himself.

Tom Townsend, a dissipated playboy who lives off his inventor father, is kidnapped by a master criminal who wants the plans for a new invention. When his father refuses to talk, he is tortured and strangled while Tom watches helplessly. The young man is saved, however, when an an eagle crashes through a window and carries him off to its aerie. The eagle nurses Tom back to health until he develops his muscles and strength in the thin mountain air. When the eagle returns one day with an American flag in its beak, Tom takes that as an omen and makes a costume from it. He becomes the patriotic fighter for justice known as Captain Flag. Joe Blair scripted the series which was drawn by Lin Streeter and Warren King.

Paul Patten, a photographer, becomes a costumed hero known as the Fox so he can be first on the scene when crime happens. The hero, who drove a Fox-Car and lived in a Fox Den, was drawn by Irwin Hasen, Warren King, and Bob Montana.

BOUNCER, THE

Fox Features Syndicate
Published 9/44–1/45   **Issue #s** 11–14, No Number
Major Characters
The Bouncer 11–14, No Number

Adam Anteas, Jr. is an artist and sculptor as can be discerned by his beret, smock, floppy bow-tie, and pointed mustache. He molds a statue of the Greek god Antaeus, his namesake, and discovers that the god comes to life whenever danger threatens.

Together with his animated statue, Adam can "bounce" through the air and squash bad guys by landing on top of them. Adam and the statue (now known as the Bouncer) obtain their strength through contact with the earth, just like the Greek god from ancient myth. The original Antaeus was an unbeatable wrestler who was defeated only after Hercules held him aloft from the earth and squeezed him to death. Similarly, the Bouncer is also vulnerable when he is in a mid-air bounce.

Robert Kanigher created the mythologically inspired Bouncer. Four issues (#s 11–14) were published by Fox Features. The fifth unnumbered issue was issued by R.W. Voight of Chicago in early 1945.

BOY COMICS

Lev Gleason Publications
Published 4/42–3/56   **Issue #s** 3–119
Major Characters
Crimebuster 3–111
Bombshell 3–7

The star of *Boy Comics* was just that—a teenager named Chuck Chandler who was the costumed hero Crimebuster (or "C.B." to his friends). Chuck is a cadet student at the Custer Military Academy at the beginning of World War II. His father, a reporter, dies in a vicious Nazi plot (dissected on the surgeon's table) and his mother is killed when her boat is sunk by a German U-boat. Chuck vows vengeance for the death of his parents and adapts his school hockey uniform into a costume for his mission of justice. He adds a cape and calls himself Crimebuster.

Crimebuster discovers that the Nazi who killed his father is an archfiend known as Ironjaw—so named because his entire mouth had been replaced with a steel trap. Chandler finally defeats Ironjaw. Along the way, he picks up a pet monkey named Squeeks (who would eventually be popular enough to rate his own comic book).

This popular boy hero was created by Charles Biro and Bob Wood. Artists who worked on the long-running feature included Norman Mauer, Dan Barry, Mike Roy, Frank Bolle, John Belfi, Joe Kubert, and George Tuska. With issue #112, in deference to the 1954 Comics Code backlash against the use of the word "crime" in a comic book title, the name "Crimebuster" was dropped and the comic was retitled simply *Chuck Chandler*.

BOY COMMANDOS

DC Comics
Published Winter/42–11/49   **Issue #s** 1–36
Major Characters
Liberty Belle 1,2
The Sandman 1
Boy Commandos 1–36

After first appearing in *Detective Comics* (June 1942) in a story by Joe Simon and Jack Kirby, the Boy Commandos received their own comic book. This World War II "kid gang" fought the Axis powers on their own turf in Europe and the Pacific. Simon recalled that he and Kirby came up with the idea for the group as a combination of the real-life British commandos and an international "street gang." For a while the comic book about the young boy allies was one of DC's best-selling titles.

While it was strictly "men-only" in the Boy Commandos, a patriotic woman hero named Liberty Belle also got her start in the first two issues of the comic. The "fabulous feminine fighter for freedom" was secretly a blonde "all-American girl" named Libby Belle Lawrence who was a "noted woman reporter and radio commentator." Libby becomes the costumed Liberty Belle whenever she receives a summons on her miniature liberty-bell lapel pin. Her boyfriend, Ricky Cannon, a military intelligence officer, helps her thwart Nazi plots and saboteurs. After her debut in *Boy Commandos*, Liberty Belle pealed over to a regular series in *Star Spangled Comics*, which was drawn by Chuck Winter and written by Don Cameron.

BULLETMAN

Fawcett Publications
Published Summer/41–Fall/46 **Issue #s** 1–16
Major Characters
Bulletman 1–16

After making his debut in *Nickel Comics* and beginning a series in *Master Comics*, Bulletman received his own magazine. The flying detective hero with the "gravity regulating helmet" was joined by Bulletgirl in the first issue.

BULLS-EYE COMICS

Harry "A" Chesler
Published 1944 **Issue #s** 11
Major Characters
Green Knight and Lance 11
Lady Satan 11
Yankee Doodle Jones 11

The Green Knight, secretly Denis Knight, was accompanied by young Lance Cooper, his medieval-costumed cohort. Rafael Astarita ("John Martin") was the artist.

CANNONBALL COMICS

Rural Home
Published 2/45–3/45 **Issue #s** 1,2
Major Characters
The Crash Kid 1,2

Rusty Adams, a copy boy for the Daily Herald,

becomes the Crash Kid ("boy nemesis to gangdom") when he dresses up in cape, gauntlets, tight short-shorts, and mid-thigh leather boots. Other than being able to supersede all rules of fashion and good taste, the Kid has no special powers.

CAPTAIN AERO COMICS

Holyoke Publishing Company
Published 12/41–8/46 **Issue #s** 1–26 (No 18–20)
Major Characters
Flag-Man 1–13
Miss Victory 6–17, 21–26
Red Cross 8–17, 21–25

Captain Aero, World War II aviator, fights the Japanese in the air with the assistance of "his little Chinese pal, Chop Suey." This "king of the sky trails" headed a comic with three costumed superheroes. Major Hornet adopts the disguise of Flag-Man in order to fight the Axis without the restrictions of military regulations. The red, white, and blue Major was later aided by a similarly dressed sidekick named Rusty (April 1942). Flag-Man was first drawn by Alan Ulmer and then by Joe Kubert and George Mandel. Miss Victory, who made her debut in *Captain Fearless*, picked up her series in this title, with art by Charles Quinlan and later by Nina Albright. Dr. Peter Hall is an army medic who decides to wage a one-man war for mercy. Dressed as the Red Cross, Hall uses his fists and a revolver to make sure medical supplies and patients get through enemy lines: "I should have known you Japs wouldn't respect a flag of truce!" Charles Nicholas and Sol Brodksy, fellow alumni from the *Blue Beetle* comic, created the Red Cross, who was later drawn by Jack Alderman and Maurice Whitman.

CAPTAIN AMERICA

Marvel Comics
Published 3/41–10/49 **Issue #s** 1–74
Major Characters
Captain America 1–74
Hurricane, Master of Speed 1–11
Fathertime 6–12
The Human Torch 19, 21–67, 69
Sub-Mariner 20, 68, 70
Golden Girl 66–68,70–73
Namora 68, 70
Sun Girl 69
The Witness 71

One of the most popular comic book heroes of the early war years, Captain America was created by editor Joe Simon and drawn by Jack Kirby. While not the first patriotic superhero, Captain America was the best realized. Simon and Kirby's first ten issues achieved immediate success and prompted dozens of flag-wearing and flag-waving imitators.

Simon and Kirby also reworked an earlier hero,

Captain America #15
© *1942 Marvel Entertainment Group, Inc.*

Captain Flight Comics #10 © 1946 Four Star Publications, Inc. L.B. Cole.

Captain Marvel Adventures #51 © 1946 Fawcett Publications, Inc. C.C. Beck.

Mercury, from *Red Raven Comics,* into a secondary feature called Hurricane, Master of Speed. Hurricane (secretly Harry Kane) was the last descendant of the Greek gods and, like the super-fast Mercury, continued his running battle with Pluto.

Another original hero who appeared in Captain America was Simon's Fathertime, which was written by Stan Lee and drawn by Al Avison and Al Gabriele. Larry Scott, who is trying to prove his convicted father's innocence, loses a race against time and his dad is wrongly executed. Scott takes an oath to make time work against criminals instead of the innocent and, donning a mask and hood, becomes Fathertime. The seconds-obsessed vigilante also appeared in *Mystic Comics* and *Young Allies.*

Betty Ross, Captain America's longtime girl companion and sometime girlfriend, became a costumed crime fighter known as Golden Girl (May 1948). She replaced Bucky as Cap's fighting sidekick and added a bit of glamor to the fading title. In issue #74 (now retitled *Captain America's Weird Tales*), the star-spangled hero appears amidst a mix of horror stories.

CAPTAIN FEARLESS

Holyoke Publishing Company
Published 8/41–9/41 **Issue #s** 1, 2
Major Characters
Captain Fearless 1, 2
Miss Victory 1, 2

Army private John Fearless VI is the descendant of Captain John Fearless, a Revolutionary War hero. He meets the ghost of his ancestor in a Boston graveyard. The spirit gives him a magic horn and a buckskin uniform and tells him that he can summon his help by blowing the horn. Working together, the buckskin private and his ancestral spirit defeat the powers of the Axis. Created by Charles Quinlan, Captain Fearless came out within a month of Fighting Yank and Major Liberty, two other patriots who also gained their powers from the spirit of a Revolutionary War hero.

Miss Victory, also drawn by Charles Quinlan, was a suitable patriotic backup for the Captain. Joan Wayne, a Washington, D.C., stenographer, helps the FBI in an unofficial capacity as Miss Victory. Having no special powers, one could surmise that Miss V may have been so named in honor of her costume's neckline, which ended somewhere past the navel.

CAPTAIN FLIGHT COMICS

Four Star Publications
Published 3/44–2/47 **Issue #s** 1–11
Major Characters
The Red Rocket 5–11
Black Cobra 6, 8, 9, 11
Torpedo Man 8, 11

Captain Flight followed the flight path of dozens of leather-jacketed aviator heroes who flew through comics in the war years. The comic book also featured costumed heroes. The Black Cobra (secretly Jim Hornsby) teams up with his younger brother Bob (who dresses up as Kid Cobra). The Cobra brothers originally appeared in *Dynamic Comics* from another publisher. The Red Rocket (aka Rod Page) wore a costume suspiciously like the Blue Beetle—a coincidence perhaps explained by the presence of publisher Robert Farrell, who originally worked with Victor Fox to promote the Blue Beetle. Don Wallace becomes the flying, costumed hero Torpedo Man and appears in only three advenures—two in the comic's last issue.

CAPTAIN MARVEL ADVENTURES

Fawcett Publications
Published 3/41–11/53 **Issue #s** 1–150
Major Characters
Captain Marvel 1–150
Mary Marvel 18, 19, 37, 43, 65, 69
Captain Marvel, Jr. 52

After his debut in *Whiz Comics* and appearance in *Special Edition Comics*, Captain Marvel received his own magazine. Most issues contained at least three and often four Captain Marvel stories. The comic book introduced Mary Marvel (December 1942) and was also distinguished by a two-year serial (1943–1944) which featured Mr. Mind and the "Monster Society of Evil." Captain *Marvel Adventures* was one of the best-selling superhero titles of the 1940s. Its total annual circulation of 2,600,000 issues in 1941 increased to more than 14,000,000 copies in 1944. Artists C.C. Beck, Pete Costanza, and Kurt Schaffenberger drew many of the stories, while Otto Binder and William Woolfolk wrote more than eighty percent of all the scripts.

CAPTAIN MARVEL, JR.

Fawcett Publications
Published 11/42–6/53 **Issue #s** 1–119
Major Characters
Captain Marvel, Jr. 1–119

After his debut in *Master Comics*, Captain Marvel, Jr. became the first teenage superhero to receive his own magazine. *Captain Marvel, Jr.* sold about forty to fort-five percent as many issues as *Captain Marvel Adventures* (the company's most popular title) and was often one of Fawcett's five top-selling comic books during the 1940s.

CAPTAIN MIDNIGHT COMICS

Fawcett Publishing
Published 9/42–Fall/48 **Issue #s** 1–67
Major Characters
Captain Midnight 1–67

This popular aviator from radio flew into his own comic book after first appearing in *The Funnies* and *Popular Comics*. Transformed into a comic book superhero with the addition of a bright red costume, secret hideout, and an arsenal of crime-fighting gadgets, Captain Midnight appeared in 227 stories in his own comic. For a brief period, he was aided by his sidekick and mechanic, Ichabod Mudd, who assumed the secret identity of Sergeant Twilight.

CAPTAIN WIZARD COMICS

Rural Home
Published 1945 **Issue #s** 1
Major Characters
Captain Wizard 1

After previous appearances in *Meteor* and *Red Band Comics*, Captain Wizard appears in his own magazine with a new costume.

CATMAN COMICS

Holyoke Publishing Company
Published 3/41–8/46 **Issue #s** 1–32 (Two #26)
Major Characters
The Catman 1–32
The Deacon 1–32
Little Leaders 8–29,31,32
The Hood 5–26,29
Volton 8–12
The Reckoner 25, 27–32

When *Crash Comics* folded, its resident superhero, the Cat Man made his move over to his own book. He received a new costume, got a preteen girl for a sidekick, named Kitten, and changed his occupation from private eye to U.S. Army officer. His double–word name also became hyphenated and then eventually just one word—the Catman. The Catman and Kitten shared their book with a high-collared crime-fighter named the Deacon, who also had a young aide, Mickey Matthews.

Mickey and Kitten eventually got together and formed their own kid team called the Little Leaders. This new feature, drawn by Charles Quinlan and later by Jack Alderman, began in the June 1942 issue. Jack Grogan wrote the feature and tried to make it a patriotic citizenship strip: "If more and more children of today would look to the simple and clean pastimes of life, instead of the vulgar or sophisticated, they would help win the war on the home front . . . "

Grogan also wrote the adventures of the Hood. Drawn by George Mandel and later by Jack Alderman, the Hood (aka Major Craig Reynolds) is an FBI agent who dons a hooded costume to fight war saboteurs and enemy agents. An interesting aside is that the Hood has a girlfriend named Rae Herman—an in-joke reference to a woman comic book writer (and later editor and publisher) of the same name.

Joe Kubert drew Volton, his first comic book hero, at the age of fifteen.

CHAMPION/CHAMP COMICS

Worth Publishing/Harvey Publications
Published 12/39–3/44 **Issue #s** 2–29
Major Characters
The Human Meteor 6–24

The forerunner of the Harvey Comics empire, this unusual anthology title featured transdimensional Egyptian adventure stories (The Blazing Scarab, drawn by George Papp), the second Tarzan clone to hit the comic books (Jungleman), and an underwater feature (Neptinia, Queen of the Deep), which made its debut the same month as Sub-Mariner in *Marvel Comics*. Its first bona fide superhero began as an adventure feature, Duke O'Dowd of the Foreign Legion in issue #6. By issue #8, O'Dowd segues his legionnaire membership into a trip to Tibet. He meets an ancient master named Wah Le who bestows upon him a "wonder belt." The belt creates a "contra-magnetic field" around the body of the wearer, thus giving O'Dowd the power to repel knives, bullets, and other metallic objects. He is called the Human Meteor since he has super speed and cannot be deflected by anything metal. He can, however, be knocked out by a well-placed baseball bat or wooden club, each of which is impervious to his anti-magnetic powers. O'Dowd returns to the United States and goes undercover as a taxi driver. He entrusts his secret identity to Toby, an orphan shoeshine boy who spots any illicit activity that might require the attention of the Human Meteor. The comic title was shortened to simply *Champ Comics* with issue #11.

CLUE COMICS

Hillman Periodicals
Published 1/43–5/47 **Issue #s** 1–15
Major Characters
The Boy King 1–9, 12
Twilight 1–5, 7, 9
Micro–Face 1–7, 10, 11, 15
Nightmare and Sleepy 1–15

Clue Comics featured a strange mix of costumed heroes. The Boy King was the star of the bunch. A young boy named David had the services of a giant, Grecian-like statue at his command. Dressing in a king's costume, complete with crown and a ceremonial short sword, he becomes the Boy King. Along with his Giant, the royal boy fought such bizzare villains as Dr. Plasma, The Gold Mummy King, and worst of all, The Crane ("Hitler's Mechanical Man"). The Crane (so named because of his extendable metal arms) fought the Boy King over three issues. Alan Mandel and Dan Barry, the original artists, were followed by Fred Kida, Tony

Cat-Man Comics #8 © 1941 Holyoke Publishing Company

Clue Comics #6 © 1943 Hillman Periodicals

*Crack Comics #8 © 1940
Comic Magazines, Inc.*

DiPreta, Rudy Palais, and Jack Keller.

After being severely beaten in a steet fight, Terry Gardner receives a visit from a parrot. The bird delivers a card which reads: "At Twilight you will be Master." Taking this as an encouraging omen, the bruised Gardner buys a costume already monogrammed with the letter "T" and becomes the avenging hero, Twilight. Gardner adopts the parrot as his pet mascot, Snoopy, and uses him to gather information. Twilight and Snoopy were drawn by John Cassone, the artist on the Web for *Zip Comics*.

After his brother is murdered, Tom Woods invents a "micro-mask" which is fitted with photo-electrical eyes, amplified voice system, and supersensitive hearing. He devises a costume and becomes the masked vigilante, Micro-Mask. The hero was drawn initially by Alan Ulmer and then by John Belfi.

Nightmare and Sleepy (Bob White and Terry Wake) were also drawn by the "Boy King" art team of Alan Mandel and Dan Barry.

COMEDY COMICS

Marvel Comics
Published 4/42–9/42   **Issue #s** 9–11
Major Characters
The Fin 9
Silver Scorpion 9
The Vagabond 11

Formerly published as *Daring Mystery Comics,* Marvel Comics changed the title's name to *Comedy Comics* to appeal to the growing audience for humor comics. Along with the last appearances of Bill Everett's aquatic hero the Fin, and the Silver Scorpion by Harry Sahle, was the first appearance of the Comedy Kid.

COMIC CAVALCADE

DC Comics
Published Winter/42–10/48   **Issue #s** 1–29
Major Characters
The Flash 1–29
Green Lantern 1–29
Wonder Woman 1–29
Wildcat 1, 2
The Atom 22, 23, 28
Black Canary 25

By the summer of 1942, the appetite for superheroes had not yet peaked and publisher Max Gaines put his three top characters into one title—a cavalcade of heroes. Like *World's Finest Comics,* Gaines made *Comic Cavalcade* an extra-long (ninety-six-page) book with a square binding, which sold for fifteen cents— a nickel more than a regular comic. With issue #30 (December 1948), the Flash, Green Lantern, and Wonder Woman were usurped by the likes of Nutsy Squirrel, Dodo and the Frog, and the Fox and the Crow, who turned the title into a humor comic.

COMPLETE COMICS

Marvel Comics
Published Winter/44   **Issue #s** 2 (No #1)
Major Characters
Destroyer 2
Whizzer 2
Young Allies 2

Formerly titled *Amazing Comics,* the Young Allies continue their star status with a three-chapter story.

CONTACT COMICS

Holyoke Publishing Company
7/44–5/46
1–12
Black Venus 1–11

After fighting the Japanese in the Pacific air war, Mary Roche returns to civilian life as a physical therapist who rehabilitates wounded veterans: "I didn't come to offer sympathy—just to tell you that your new prosthetic leg is ready!" She secretly maintains a small black fighter plane which she uses in her role as Black Venus, a costumed defender of widows, orphans, and disabled war veterans ("I'll teach you to hit a man who can't defend himself!"). Black Venus was drawn by Frank Tomsey, L. B. Cole, Nina Albright, Harvey Kurtzman, and George Gregg.

CRACK COMICS

Quality Comics Group
Published 5/40–9/49   **Issue #s** 1–62
Major Characters
Black Condor 1–31
The Clock 1–35
Madame Fatal 1–22
Captain Triumph 27–62

The Black Condor was the best-drawn superhero in *Crack Comics.* Lou Fine drew the early adventures of an orphan boy raised by a flock of black condors after his family is killed on an archeological expedition. The boy imitates the birds and learns to fly on the air currents over the desolate steppes of Outer Mongolia. A hermit discovers the nearly grown boy and names him the Black Condor. When the monk is murdered, the young man travels to America to use his birdlike powers to fight crime. Upon his arrival, a Dr. Foster asks him (for national security reasons) to assume the identity of Thomas Wright, a recently assassinated senator to whom he bears an uncanny resemblance. Along with his senatorial privileges, the Black Condor inherits the ex-senator's girlfriend, Wendy Foster. Appearing with the Condor was Madame Fatal, the first transvestite superhero, who was secretly (and how!) Richard Stanton. Stanton, a retired actor who lives alone with a parrot called Hamlet, goes after his daughter's kidnappers by dressing up like an old lady to avoid attracting attention. After he rescues his daughter, he continues fighting crime while wearing a wig, brown jacket, and dowdy skirt.

When Michael Gallant is killed by saboteurs, his twin brother Lance vows revenge. The spirit of his murdered brother appears and tells Lance that whenever he rubs his "T"-shaped birthmark, he will become the super-powered Captain Triumph. The crime-fighting brothers were drawn by Alfred Andriola, Reed Crandall, Mort Leav, and Al Bryant.

CRACKAJACK FUNNIES

Dell Comics
Published 7/40–1/42 **Issue #s** 25–43
Major Characters
The Owl 25–43

Although newspaper strip reprints made up the majority of *Crackajack Funnies,* there was one memorable costumed hero. The Owl, created by Dell editor Oscar Lebeck, followed the tradition of Batman, the Shadow, and other after-dark heroes. Nick Terry, "a special investigator" by day, operated as the Owl by night. Wearing a purple costume with an owl-cowl, Terry sulked about in the shadows, posed in front of the rising moon, and flitted through the evenings in a somber Owlplane. His adventures were brightened considerably by his fiancée Belle Wayne, who was a newspaper reporter, as most superhero girlfriends were. Belle eventually put two and two together and figured out why her boyfriend stayed out all night. She became Owl Girl in February 1941.

Bill Baltz drew the first Owl story but was thereafter replaced by Frank Thomas, who did a complete makeover on the costume and designed the distinctive owl-face mask. Thomas, who had already written and drawn such heroes for Centaur Publishing as Dr. Hypno (*Amazing Man*) and the Eye (*Keen Detective Funnies*), also wrote some early Owl stories. After *Crackajack* was canceled, the Owl and Owl Girl moved to *Popular Comics* for another year of adventures.

CRASH COMICS

Holyoke Publishing Company
Published 5/40–11/40 **Issue #s** 1–5
Major Characters
Blue Streak 1–5
Strongman, the Perfect Human 1–5
The Cat Man 4, 5

Crash Comics was produced by a small comic book studio headed by Bert Whitman, who employed such artists as Jack Kirby, Frank Robbins, and Irwin Hasen. Whitman drew several covers and Hasen drew the book's most popular feature—Cat Man. A young boy who lost his parents in the jungle is raised by a tiger. A sort of "Tarzan of the Tigers," the grown boy first appears as the Cat Man in issue #4

(September 1940). In each adventure, the leopard-skin-clad hero dies but then returns miraculously alive. Like a cat, he has nine lives.

Playboy Percy Van Norton dabbles in yoga. After years of practice, he develops superhuman physical and mental capabilities to become "the world's most perfect man!" For all his yogic attainments, Percy never lacked for ego. He slipped on a skin-tight suit and promptly billed himself as "Strongman, the Perfect Human."

The Blue Streak was a little more modest. He was simply "the Defender of the People" and the "self-appointed foe of ruthless dictators." He had the requisite, trusty Oriental manservant who kept his blue-purple costume well-pressed.

DAREDEVIL

Lev Gleason Publications
Published 7/41–9/56 **Issue #s** 1–134
Major Characters
Daredevil 1–69, 79, 80
The Claw 1–31
Nightro 2–8

The first issue, which was titled *Daredevil Battles Hitler,* was a six-chapter book in which a different guest star from *Silver Streak Comics* joined Daredevil in each chapter to fight the Führer. In issue #13, Daredevil gets a "gang" of adolescent sidekicks known as the Little Wise Guys. After the war years, the Wise Guys began to dominate the stories and, by 1950, replaced Daredevil altogether.

The Claw, the infamous villain from *Silver Streak Comics,* had a series in the magazine which ran for four years. For the first two years, the Claw fought a running battle with another costumed hero, the Ghost (aka Brad Hendricks). The monstrous evildoer was finally killed in the July 1945 issue. Artists on the strip included Manny Stallman, Rudy Palais, and Bob Wood. Manly Wade Wellman wrote some scripts near the end of the series.

The other costumed character appearing in *Daredevil Comics* was yet another blind superhero (see The Mask and Dr. Mid-Nite). The visually impaired Hugh Goddard can only see at night unless he wears special glasses. He becomes the costumed hero Nightro ("the streamlined Robin Hood") and is assisted by his dog Blackie. The feature was drawn by George Roussos and Edd Ashe.

DARING COMICS

Marvel Comics
Published Fall/44–Fall/45 **Issue #s** 9–12
Major Characters
The Human Torch 9–12
Sub-Mariner 9–12
The Angel 10
Destroyer 11, 12

After a two-and-half-year suspension, Marvel

Crackajack Funnies #31 © 1941 Dell Publishing Co., Inc.

Daredevil #4 © 1941 Lev Gleason Publications

Detective Comics #33
© *1939 DC Comics, Inc.*
Bob Kane and Jerry
Robinson.

Doc Savage Comics #5
© *1941 Street & Smith
Publications, Inc.* Jack
Binder.

publisher Martin Goodman brought back *Daring Mystery Comics* under a shortened name. Instead of the minor league heroes who dominated the first incarnation of the title, Goodman put his two most popular characters—the Human Torch and the Sub-Mariner—on the front cover of every issue and also featured them in two stories in the first issue.

DARING MYSTERY COMICS

Marvel Comics
Published 1/40–1/42   **Issue #s** 1–8
Major Characters
Fiery Mask 1, 5, 6
The Challenger 7
The Blue Diamond 7, 8
The Fin 7, 8
Silver Scorpion 7, 8

The second Marvel comic book (named after publisher Martin Goodman's pulp magazine *Daring Stories*) got off to a shaky start, with only one notable costume hero in the first six issues. Joe Simon created the Fiery Mask, his first superhero, for twelve dollars per page.

With the seventh issue, Bill Everett tried to re-create his success with the Sub-Mariner with another aquatic hero called the Fin. Navy lieutenant Peter Noble survives a submarine accident and discovers he has supernormal strength as long as he is not removed from water for more than three hours. Noble constructs a costume with a shark fin cowl and, using a magic cutlass from an ancient shipwreck, wages a war against evil.

The Blue Diamond, drawn by Ben Thompson, was originally Professor Morrow, discoverer of a giant blue diamond in the Antarctic. When the diamond is blown up in a sabotage attempt, its chips become lodged in Morrow's body and transform him into the rock-hard Blue Diamond.

The Challenger, a master of weapons, went around "challenging" people to duel with weapons of their choice. This aggressive good guy, who also appeared in *Mystic Comics,* was drawn by Mike Sekowsky and George Klein.

Betty Barstow, a secretary for Detective Dan Hurley, discovers a crime while en route to a masquerade party. She uses her natural fighting abilities to send the crooks running and decides to continue wearing her party costume for after-hours work as the Silver Scorpion.

DETECTIVE COMICS

DC Comics
Published 3/37–2/55   **Issue #s** 1–216
Major Characters
Crimson Avenger 20–29, 37–89
Batman 27–216 (with Robin, #38 on)
Boy Commandos 64–150
The Guardian and the Newsboy Legion 76

The Sandman 76
Robotman 138–154, 156–202

Known primarily as both the home of Batman and the early flagship of the DC Comics line, *Detective Comics* was also one of the most successful anthology comic books. It featured several series about different kinds of "detectives," from the automated crime-solver known as Robotman to the mysteriously cloaked Crimson Avenger. Although Batman and Robin became the lead feature and cover stars, the Crimson Avenger actually predated the Caped Crusader by several months. Lee Travis, publisher of the *Daily Globe Leader,* wears a mask and a crimson cape to fight criminals while assisted by his faithful Oriental manservant, Wing. The Crimson Avenger was cut from the same cloth as the Green Hornet, a popular radio show hero who also published a newspaper, had an Oriental manservant, and fought crime under a cloaked identity. The Crimson Avenger was initially drawn by Jim Chambers. John Lehti took over the strip, and with the October 1940 issue, the character got a new costume and superhero make-over. His confidant, Wing, also received a costume and become his fighting sidekick (January 1942). The Crimson Avenger and Wing also appeared as members of the Seven Soldiers of Victory in *Leading Comics.*

DETECTIVE EYE COMICS

Centaur Publications
Published 11/40–12/40   **Issue #s** 1, 2
Major Characters
The Eye 1, 2
The Air Man 1, 2
The Masked Marvel 1

Centaur pulled together its three lead heroes from the recently canceled *Keen Detective Funnies* and put them in this short-lived title.

DOC SAVAGE COMICS

Street and Smith
Published 5/40–10/43   **Issue #s** 1–20
Major Characters
Doc Savage 1–20
Ajax, the Sun Man 2–17
Supersnipe 9

Doc Savage, the superman of pulp magazines since 1933, moved into the comic book medium in March 1940 as a backup feature in Street and Smith's *Shadow Comics.* The first Doc Savage story, adapted from a 1934 radio script, was drawn by Maurice Gutwirth and featured only one of Doc's intrepid companions from the pulp stories, a bullet-head chemist known as Monk. After two appearances in *Shadow Comics,* Doc moved into his own magazine and was joined by the second member of his team, "Ham" Brooks. Doc's other compatriots from the pulps—Renny, Long Tom, and Johnny—never made it to the comic book.

For the August 1941 issue of Doc Savage Comics, the Jack Binder studio gave the pulp magazine hero a new comic book look. Writer Carl Formes turned Doc Savage into a superhero character known as The Invincible, whose super-powers came from a Tibetan "sacred hood with a miracle-working ruby." Dressed in knee-length boots and jodhpurs, Doc Savage worked barechested as a hood-wearing superhero. The ruby emitted a beam which deflected bullets and hypnotized unwilling subjects. Interestingly, the superhero makeover of Doc Savage as the Invincible was carried over into a 1943 radio show.

After Doc's comic book was dropped, he returned to his secondary status in *Shadow Comics*. For the most part, he also dropped his bare-chested "sacred hood and magic ruby" routine and fought criminals in a sensible business suit.

Artists who drew Doc Savage included Jack Alderman, William A. Smith, Al Bare, Charles Coll, and Bob Powell. Writers included Otto Binder, Ed Gruskin, and Bruce Elliot.

DOLL MAN

Quality Comics Group
Published Fall/41–10/53   **Issue #s** 1–47
Major Characters
Doll Man 1–47
The Dragon 2–6

After his debut in *Feature Comics* (December 1939), Doll Man received his own magazine. The comic appeared on a quarterly basis the first two years and was suspended for two-and-a-half years during the paper rationing of World War II. Doll Man got a canine companion, Elmo the Wonder Dog, in the December 1950 issue. Joining Elmo and Doll Man one year later (December 1951) was Doll Girl—formerly his fiancée, Martha Roberts.

The Dragon (secretly Red McGraw), a costumed hero drawn by Fred Guardineer, appeared briefly as an early backup feature.

DYNAMIC COMICS

Harry 'A' Chesler
Published 10/41–3/48   **Issue #s** 1–24 (No 4–7)
Major Characters
Dynamic Man 1–3, 8–24
Major Victory 1–3
Dynamic Boy 2–3, 13
Lady Satan 2, 3
The Echo 8–23
The Master Key 8, 9, 24
Yankee Boy 8–12, 16–22
Mr. E 9–23
Yankee Doodle Jones 8
Green Knight 2, 3
Black Cobra 1

Harry 'A' Chesler, an early comic book packager, entered the booming superhero market in 1941 as a publisher. *Dynamic Comics*, his first title, introduced Chesler's longest-running superhero, Dynamic Man. Chesler's studio had already created another Dynamic Man for Marvel's *Mystic Comics*. This version of the hero, however, was an android. In later stories, Dynamic Man became the human Bert McQuade, a high school basketball coach who received his powers from an energy treatment courtesy of a Dr. Stahl. As Dynamic Man, McQuade can fly through the air, ignore speeding bullets, and knock people senseless. In the September 1944 issue, Bert's kid brother Ricky gets a dose of dynamic powers from the agreeable Dr. Stahl and becomes Dynamic Boy. (Another Dynamic Boy, Kent Banning, briefly appeared in the magazine but was not related to the other character.) Dyanamic Man was first drawn by Charles Sultan, who also drew Major Victory for this comic.

EAGLE, THE

Fox Features Syndicate
Published 7/41–1/42   **Issue #s** 1–4
Major Characters
Eagle 1–4
The Spider Queen 2–4

After his debut in *Science Comics*, the Eagle received his own magazine. Bill Powers, who wore a red-and-white-striped cape as the Eagle, has help from a young sidekick named Buddy. The Eagle also appeared in *Weird Comics* and was drawn by Alex Blum, among others. The Spider Queen, otherwise known as Sharon Kane, was the "sworn enemy of saboteurs, racketeers, gangsters—criminals of every sort!" The art was by Pierce Rice, who worked on many early Fox superheroes, including Samson, the Green Mask, and the Flame.

EXCITING COMICS

Better/Standard Publications
Published 4/40–9/49   **Issue #s** 1–69
Major Characters
The Mask 1–20
The Sphinx 2–14
The Black Terror 9–69
The Liberator 15–30, 34, 35
The American Eagle 22–27, 29–38, 40–47, 49, 50
The Scarab 42–48
Miss Masque 51–54

The first issue of *Exciting Comics* introduced The Mask, the first blind superhero. Drawn by Raymond Thayer, the Mask was secretly Tony Colby, who decided to become a hooded vigilante after being blinded by thugs. Ellsworth Forrester made his debut as the costumed Sphinx in the second issue. The first major hero in *Exciting*, however, was the Black Terror, who quickly earned his own magazine and a

Doll Man #19 © 1948 Comic Magazines, Inc. Lou Fine.

*Exciting Comics #28
© 1943 Better Publica-
tions, Inc. Alex
Schomburg.*

*Feature Comics #89
© 1945 Comic Magazines,
Inc. Al Bryant.*

regular spot in *America's Best Comics* as well.

The Liberator made his debut in the December 1941 issue—the same month America entered the war with Japan. Dr. Nelson Drew, a college professor at Clafin University, stumbles across an ancient Egyptian formula for a super potion. When he swills the secret sauce, the ectomorphic professor becomes the super-powered Liberator or, as he is soon known, "Fighter for Democracy." He affects a star-spangled blue pullover which is worn over year-round red trunks. Another Egyptian-inspired hero, the Scarab (aka Peter Ward) moved over to *Exciting* after his July 1945 origin story in *Startling Comics*.

In the September 1946 issue came Better's entry into the growing field of postwar superheroines— Miss Masque. "With society life as a camouflage, Diana Adams continues her secret role as Miss Masque—picking up the trail of crime as a kittenish debutante—and following through with the stalking skill of a tigress!" Miss Masque also appeared in *America's Best Comics*, *Fighting Yank*, and *Black Terror* and was drawn by pretty-girl expert, Bob Oksner.

FACE, THE (TONY TRENT)

Columbia Comics Group
Published 1942–1948   **Issue #s** 1–4
Major Characters
The Face 1–3

"Tony Trent, radio commentator of station WBSC is also THE FACE—whose gruesome mask brings an involuntary shudder to anyone who beholds it! This fact is unknown to all except Babs Walsh, Tony's secretary." After witnessing a murder by two men disguised as police officers, Tony Trent decides to investigate the matter himself by hiding his face under a hideous green rubber mask and false orange-red hair. The Face, who made his debut in *Big Shot Comics*, appeared in his own magazine for four issues (after two issues, the comic was retitled *Tony Trent, the Face*). With the third issue, Trent phased out his masked identity.

FAMOUS FUNNIES

Eastern Color/Famous Funnies
Published 6/34–7/55   **Issue #s** 1–218
Major Characters
Fearless Flint, the Flint Man 89–109

Famous Funnies, the first newsstand comic book, consisted primarily of newspaper comic strip reprints since its beginning. With costumed heroes becoming immensely popular by 1941, editor Stephen Douglas came up with Fearless Flint the Flint Man for *Famous Funnies*. He tapped artist H. G. Peter, who was drawing Man O'Metal for *Heroic Comics*, to draw the Flint Man's adventures beginning in the December 1941 issue.

The story by Douglas and Peter begins on top of

Mount Rushmore in the "black hills of South Dakota." Jack Bradley is busy drilling with his jackhammer on top of Abraham Lincoln's head as he helps create our national monument. Two disgruntled South Seas Islanders(!), however, want to sabotage the project and they cause Jack's jackhammer to explode. Bradley tumbles over the mountainside to what seems a certain death, but instead lands on a ledge—still alive: "Something amazing has happened—a human being is transformed into a MAN OF FLINT . . . particles of flint which dropped on the ledge from the drilling above become imbedded in Jack Bradley's skin and cause this unexplainable reaction. This strange phenomenon that should have killed is now changed into flint with the strength of ten men." Now, whenever metal touches his skin, Bradley becomes transformed into the rock-hard (and lobster-red) Fearless Flint, the Flint Man.

FANTASTIC COMICS

Fox Features Syndicate
Published 12/39–11/41   **Issue #s** 1–23
Major Characters
Samson 1–23
Stardust, the Super Wizard 1–16
Black Fury 17–23
Banshee 21–23

The star of *Fantastic Comics* was the descendant of the original strongman—Samson. The hero shared the name, strength, and weakness of the biblical character; he even lost his powers when his hair was cut. Wearing a red loin cloth and sandals, the bare-chested, long-haired hero was joined (September 1940) by a similarly attired boy sidekick named David (as in "Goliath") who carried a rope slingshot. Samson was originally drawn by Alex Blum, who had warmed up for the job of drawing half-naked he-men with his earlier work on Kaänga (a Tarzan imitation) for *Jungle Comics*. Samson earned his own comic book within a year after his debut.

Stardust the Super Wizard was inexplicably written and drawn by Hank Fletcher, who gave his hero unlimited powers and unbelievable anatomy. Stardust flew stiffly through space, his arms held flat against his sides and his head aimed resolutely at his destination. When he corners some "fifth columnists," he uses his powers to turn them into rats and then becomes a panther and chases them through the streets of New York.

John Perry, a gossip columnist for the *Daily Clarion*, goes undercover as the costumed Black Fury to get material for his crime exposés. He gains the help of Chuck Marley, the son of a murdered policeman, who becomes his costumed aide. The Black Fury also appeared in *V Comics* and the *Blue Beetle*.

Jim O'Donnel becomes the Banshee to avenge the death of his stepfather, who is killed on the Irish moors. This Irish hero (who wears a green costume) relocates to America and later engages in patriotic adventures in *V Comics*.

FANTOMAN

Centaur Publications
Published 8/40–12/40   **Issue #s** 2–4
Major Characters
Fantom of the Fair 2, 3
Fantoman 2–4
The Arrow 2

After his debut in *Amazing Mystery Funnies*, the Fantom of the Fair, who became known as Fantoman, continued in this title (which was itself a continuation of *Amazing Adventure Comics*). The Fantom of the Fair stories were reprints. Harry Sahle and George Kapitan contributed the new Fantoman stories.

FEATURE COMICS

Quality Comics Group
Published 6/39–5/50   **Issue #s** 21–144
Major Characters
The Clock 3–31
Doll Man 27–139
USA 42–48
Spider Widow 57–72
The Raven 60–71
Phantom Lady 69–71

Originally called *Feature Funnies*, the comic book slowly metamorphosized from newspaper strip reprints like Joe Palooka and Mickey Finn to an all–new adventure and humor comic. Doll Man was the first costumed hero introduced and was soon featured on every cover until 1950.

The second costumed hero in *Feature Comics* was a woman—USA, The Spirit of Old Glory. USA, as she was only known, sometimes appeared as a USO volunteer ("Remember . . . I dance only with *real* Americans!"). In her costumed identity, she wore an American flag as a cape and used her "liberty torch" to defeat Nazi saboteurs and infiltrators ("You fools—the flag is stronger than your bullets . . . it's an ideal!"). USA was drawn by Maurice Gutwirth.

Dianne Grayton, an accomplished sportswoman, has everything—wealth, good looks, boyfriends—but is unbearably bored. After discovering she can control black widow spiders, Dianne parlays that strange talent into becoming the Spider Widow. She adopts the disguise of a spinster hag and uses her arachnid helpers to dispense justice. She later gets some help from another costumed hero, the Raven, and also teams up with the Phantom Lady from *Police Comics*. The Spider Widow was originally drawn by Frank Borth.

FIGHTING YANK

Better/Standard Publications
Published 9/42–8/49   **Issue #s** 1–29
Major Characters
The Fighting Yank 1–29
The Grim Reaper 7
The American Eagle 18
Miss Masque 22, 24

As their most visible patriotic superhero, the Fighting Yank was the first character from Better Publications to receive his own comic book. Writer Richard Hughes, who professed a strong fondness for ghost stories, made the Fighting Yank a descendant of a Revolutionary War hero who was aided by his ancestor's spirit. Artists included Jon Blummer, Jack Binder, Mort Meskin, and Jerry Robinson.

Al Camerata drew the first appearance of the Grim Reaper before the character transferred to *Wonder Comics*.

FLAME, THE

Fox Features Syndicate
Published Summer/40–1/42   **Issue #s** 1–8
Major Characters
The Flame 1–8

After his debut in *Wonderworld Comics*, the Flame was arguably Fox's second most popular hero (after the Blue Beetle). The first issue reprinted stories from *Wonderworld* by Lou Fine. Other artists included Larry Antonette, Edd Ashe, Arturo Cazeneuve, Lee Harris, and Pierce Rice. Clyde Kleinert, a part-time writer for the Eisner-Iger studio, scripted some of the adventures. The Flame also appeared in *Big 3 Comics*.

FLASH COMICS

DC Comics
Published 1/40–2/49   **Issue #s** 1–104
Major Characters
The Flash 1–104
Hawkman 1–104
Johnny Thunder 1–91
The Whip 1–55
The Atom 80, 82–85, 87, 89–95, 97–100, 102–104
Little Boy Blue 81
Black Canary 86–88, 90–104

Although the Flash and Hawkman are the undisputed stars, three other costumed heroes got their start in *Flash Comics*.

The Whip, a costumed cowboy avenger drawn initially by George Storm and written by John Wentworth, was a Zorro clone. Rodney Gaynor, a polo-playing "Eastern dude," heads to the Southwest and dresses up as a masked Mexican horseman to right wrongs. Gaynor even affects a bad accent when he dons his Zorro-inspired mask and becomes El

*Fighting Yank #20
© 1947 Better Publications,
Inc. Alex Schomburg.*

*Flash Comics #10 © 1940
DC Comics, Inc. Sheldon
Moldoff.*

Four Favorites #22 © 1946 Ace Magazines, Inc. Rudy Palais.

Funny Pages Vol. 3 #7 © 1939 Centaur Publications. Paul Gustavson.

Castigo, the Whip: "Wan fonny move from anyone, I geev a leetle twitch to the whip."

Johnny Thunder, drawn initially by Stan Asch and also written by John Wentworth, has the magical power to command any person or thing, including the weather. Whenever he utters the magic words "cei-u" ("Say you!"), a pink thunderbolt with a humanoid head appears and does Johnny's bidding for an hour at a time.

The Black Canary was introduced in the Johnny Thunder strip and soon replaced the whimsical hero. Created by Robert Kanigher and drawn by Carmine Infantino, the Black Canary was second only to Wonder Woman as DC Comics's most popular 1940s superheroine. Dinah Drake, the brunette owner of a flower shop, has a private detective boyfriend named Larry Lance. Dinah dresses up in black net stockings, boots, and waistcoat and becomes the blonde Black Canary in order to help Larry solve his cases. The Black Canary, who was also a member of the Justice Society of America in *All-Star Comics,* was one of the better realized postwar heroines.

FOUR FAVORITES

Ace Magazines
Published 9/41–12/47 **Issue #s** 1–32
Major Characters
Lash Lightning 1–22
Magno, the Magnetic Man 1–26
The Raven 1–4
Vulcan 1–4
Unknown Soldier 4–20
Captain Courageous 5, 7–21
The Flag 6
Lightning Girl 14, 22

Ace Magazines featured its four "favorite" superheroes in one title and led off with Lash Lightning, Vulcan, the Raven, and Magno the Magnetic Man. While Ace's other superhero anthology, *Super Mystery Comics,* suspended publication for six months in 1942, *Four Favorites* continued uninterrupted until 1947. By 1947, however, superheroes were falling from favor and the last dozen issues featured mystery and humor stories. For example, Captain Courageous discarded his costume and joined the Marines in issues #22–28. The Unknown Soldier hero was turned into a narrator of suspense stories ("The Unknown") with issue #21. In issue #23, Lash Lightning (known simply as Lightning since issue #15) was replaced by teenager Hap Hazard.

FUNNIES, THE

Dell Comics
Published 7/40–3/42 **Issue #s** 45–63
Major Characters
Phantasmo 45–63

Captain Midnight 57–64

The first forty-four issues of *The Funnies* consisted of popular newspaper strip reprints. By 1940, however, editor Oscar Lebeck knew his young readers wanted superhero and costumed characters and he introduced two regular series.

Phil Anson travels to Tibet and spends the next twenty-five years learning the secrets of the yogis. He develops the power to separate his spiritual self from his physical body—a sort of super-powered astral projection. In his spirit state as Phantasmo, he can become an invisible phantasm, expand to gargantuan size, fly through space, and possess incredible strength. Anson's physical form, however, is virtually helpless and vulnerable to attack while he exists as Phantasmo. He makes friends with a young bellhop, Whizzer McGee, who looks after Anson's body when he is out fighting criminals in his spirtual state. Elmer Stoner was the artist of this spectral superhero.

Captain Midnight, a costumed aviator from a successful radio series, made his comic book debut in the July 1941 issue, with art by Dan Gormley.

FUNNY PAGES

Centaur Publications
Published 11/36–10/40 **Issue #s** 6–42
The Clock 6–11
Major Characters
The Arrow 21–42

Before there was a Superman, there was the Clock (November 1936). Brian O'Brien, former district attorney and part-time playboy, wears a blue tuxedo and a black silk mask to become the Clock, an anonymous crime fighter. O'Brien chose his name because he wanted to remind crooks that their last few minutes of freedom were "ticking off." Artist George Brenner, who would later become an editor at Quality Comics, created the Clock—the first original masked comic book detective. The Clock also showed up in *Keen Detective Funnies, Crack Comics, Funny Picture Stories,* and *Feature Comics.*

The Arrow, the first costumed comic book hero to appear after the debut of Superman, began in the September 1938 issue. A vigilante archer, the Arrow owed his origins to Robin Hood as well as pulp magazine heroes like the Shadow and the Spider. Hidden under a crumpled red suit and a face-covering cowl, the Arrow was a man of mystery without name or background. A no-nonsense fellow, the Arrow coldly shot arrows into hands, shoulders, and hearts of slobbering fiends who were always putting blondes into bondage. Paul Gustavson wrote and drew the series.

FUNNY PICTURE STORIES

Comics Magazine/Centaur Publications
Published 11/36–5/39   **Issue #s** 1–23
Major Characters
The Clock 1,2
An early anthology of original comic book features, *Funny Picture Stories* was the second title (after *Funny Pages*) to feature George Brenner's masked detective, the Clock.

GOLDEN LAD

Spark Publications
Published 7/45–6/46   **Issue #s** 1–5
Major Characters
Golden Lad 1–5
Shaman and Flame 5

Tommy Preston, who works in his grandfather's antique shop, comes across an ancient Aztec sacrificial totem—a Heart of Gold. Imbued with the strength of one thousand martyred warriors, the heart gives strength and courage to whoever holds it with a pure heart. By holding the heart and saying the words "Heart of Gold," Tommy can become Golden Lad with the power to fly. Tommy is later joined by Golden Girl (June 1946) when Peggy Shane finds a sliver of the gold heart and puts it in her locket.

Mort Meskin, who had warmed up by illustrating such features as Sheena, the Wizard, the Shield, and the Vigilante, helped create the character and drew most of the stories. Jerry Robinson and George Roussos lent their artistic talents to the title as well.

When the last issue of the comic was expanded to fifty-two pages, two new characters were introduced. Shaman and Flame, drawn by Louis Ravielli, were a costumed pair who were secretly Don Wickett, manager of radio station WWGL, and his secretary, Kandy Wilson.

GREEN GIANT COMICS

Pelican Publications
Published 1940   **Issue #s** 1
The Green Giant 1

This unusual title was put together by Lloyd Jacquet's studio Funnies, Incorporated. The hero's name was supposedly inspired by the brand-name of a canned vegetable. George Kapitan, who was writing such features as Air Man, the Black Widow, and the Fiery Mask, scripted the story. Harry Sahle, an ambidextrous artist who reputedly could pencil with one hand and ink with the other, did the art chores. With circulation evidently limited to the New York area, this single appearance of the Green Giant (aka Mr. Brentwood) was seen by few.

GREEN HORNET COMICS

Helnit/Harvey Publications
Published 12/40–9/49   **Issue #s** 1–47
Major Characters
The Green Hornet 1–47
The Spirit of '76 7–25, 27–37
The Zebra 7–24, 26, 28–30
Shock Gibson 37, 38
Stuntman 39

The popularity of the Green Hornet radio show and 1940 movie serial prompted a comic book about the masked detective and Kato. When publisher Alfred Harvey took over the *Green Hornet* comic book he added two superheroes from his recently canceled *Pocket Comics*: The Spirit of '76 and the Zebra. The Spirit of '76 was usually drawn by Bob Powell, while the Zebra enjoyed artwork by Arturo Cazeneuve, Pierce Rice, and Joe Kubert.

GREEN LAMA

Spark/Prize Publications
Published 12/44–3/46   **Issue #s** 1–8
Major Characters
Green Lama 1–8
Lieutenant Hercules 1–8

Jethro Dumont, a multimillionaire college student, travels to Tibet for postgraduate work in Buddhism. After several years of intense study and meditation, he becomes an ordained priest in the Lamaist sect. When he chants the Jewel Lotus mantra (Om mani padme hum), Dumont gains the powers of the Green Lama, rendering him invulnerable and able to fly through the air. As befitting an independently wealthy American-Buddhist priest, Dumont lives on Park Avenue and has an Oriental valet, Tsarong.

The Green Lama was originally created for the April 1940 issue of *Double Detective* magazine by editor Ken Crossen in an effort to compete with the Shadow, the most popular pulp hero at the time. Crossen's hero, with his proclivity for disguises and melodramatic costuming, appeared in fourteen pulp magazine stories and made an easy transition to the comic book medium, as the Shadow had done a few months earlier.

Crossen, a veteran pulp writer of more than a million words per year, also wrote the early comic book adventures of the Green Lama for *Prize Comics* from 1940 to 1943. The following year, he got a paper allowance from the government and started his own comic book company, Spark Publications. Crossen used the Green Lama to launch his company's fortunes and got Mac Raboy, the artist of Captain Marvel, Jr., to draw the covers and stories. Mac Raboy was assisted by Al Jetter, a former letterer who worked with him at Fawcett Comics.

A secondary feature, Lieutenant Hercules, was a superhero parody written by science fiction writer H. L. Gold.

Golden Lad #1 © 1945 Spark Publications. Mort Meskin.

Green Lama #3 © 1945 Spark Publications. Mac Raboy.

*Green Mask Vol. 2 #4
© 1945 Fox Features
Syndicate*

*Heroic Comics #8 © 1941
Eastern Color Printing Co.
Bill Everett.*

GREEN LANTERN

DC Comics
Published Fall/41–5/49   **Issue #s** 1–38
Major Characters
Green Lantern 1–38

After a successful run in *All-American Comics,* Green Lantern moved into his own magazine. Creator Martin Nodell drew the first twenty-five issues, with the remaining issues by Irwin Hasen, Howard Purcell, and Alex Toth. Streak the Wonder Dog has a series in issue #s 34–37.

GREEN MASK

Fox Features Syndicate
Published Summer/40–10/46   **Issue #s** 1–17
Major Characters
Green Mask 1–17

The Green Mask, who began in *Mystery Men Comics* as a hero with no secret identity or super-power, became more fleshed out in his own magazine. Now we learn that "Michael Shelby, placed in a vita-ray machine, discovers that the super-charged shocks make him a miracle man. He can zoom through the air and perform astounding super-human feats! He adopts a distinctive costume—and as THE GREEN MASK . . . wars against crime and rackets . . . assisted by his boy helper, THE DOMINO!" Domino ("The Miracle Boy") has a boomerang in his arsenal while Shelby relies on a no-nonsense revolver. The comic suspended publication from February 1942 until August 1944.

When the Green Mask returned, he was now a young boy named Johnny Green. In this second incarnation we learn that "little Johnny Green, whose fury against crime and injustice changes him, without his knowledge, into the amazing Green Mask, avenger of wrong!" Whenever Johnny gets angry over some perceived injustice, he lets loose a yell ("EEOWW!") and turns into the adrenalin-charged and adult-sized Green Mask. After battling crooks, the Green Mask becomes tired and then turns back into young Johnny Green as soon as he yawns.

The early issues were drawn by Walter Frehm, who would later draw "Ripley's Believe It or Not" for the newspapers. Jack Fisk drew the second version of the Green Mask.

HANGMAN COMICS

MLJ/Archie Comics
Published Spring/42–Fall/43   **Issue #s** 2–8 (No #1)
Major Characters
The Hangman 2–8
Boy Buddies 2–8

Formerly published as *Special Comics* #1, the comic

book was retitled to take advantage of the Hangman's growing popularity. Each of the Hangman stories was numbered sequentially by "Case Number" so that by the last issue, the Hangman was working on Case #24. Art was by Harry Lucey, Bob King, and Bob Fujitani, while stories were usually written by William Woolfolk.

Joining the Hangman in the back of the comic was a regular feature called the Boy Buddies, consisting of Dusty the Boy Detective (from the Shield series) and Roy the Super Boy (from the Wizard series). Woolfolk wrote many of the stories; the main artists were Bill Vigoda and George Harrison. With issue #9, the comic book underwent a title change to *Black Hood Comics.*

HEADLINE COMICS

Prize Publications
Published 2/43–9/46   **Issue #s** 1–21
Major Characters
Yank and Doodle 1
Blue Streak 13–15
Atomic Man 16–21

Although the main feature of *Headline Comics* was a multiethnic boy gang called the Junior Rangers, the comic also featured Atomic Man—an early nuclear-age superhero—in the November 1945 issue. Adam Mann, a research chemist at the Energy Research Laboratories, is involved in a uranium accident which charges him with "millions of ergs of nuclear energy." Mann discovers he can now radiate nuclear energy through his right hand. His new powers make him an Atomic Man. He wears a lead glove to control his powers but removes it whenever he wants to fly through the air "propelled by gamma rays."

Charles Voight, who had been drawing comics since 1901 as a fourteen-year-old cartoonist for the *New York Evening World,* handled the early art chores on Atomic Man. Gil Kane, still in his teens and also at the Baily shop, drew some Atomic Man stories as well.

Finishing up the superhero lineup was Jim Dare in his brief career as the Blue Streak as drawn by August Froehlich and a guest appearance by Yank and Doodle (the young brother crime-fighting team from *Prize Comics*) in the first Junior Rangers story.

HEROIC COMICS

Eastern Color/Famous Funnies
Published 8/40–7/45   **Issue #s** 1–31
Major Characters
Hydroman 1–29
Man O'Metal 7–28
The Music Master 12–26, 28–31
Rainbow Boy 14–20, 25

Eastern Color, the publisher of the first newsstand

comic book (*Famous Funnies*), instructed its editor Stephen Douglas to come up with a comic book about heroes. From artist/writer Bill Everett at Funnies, Incorporated, Douglas got the adventures of Hydroman—another watery superhero from the creator of the Sub-Mariner.

Douglas also created a hero called Man O'Metal for artist H.G. Peter to illustrate. Jack Dempsey, a foundry worker, gains a remarkable power after a vat of white-hot metal falls on him. Now, whenever heat touches Dempsey's skin, he burns with an indestructible blue flame.

The Music Master, also written by Douglas, featured a hero who can fly on the waves of music, leaving a jet trail of quarter-notes and half-notes behind him. John Wallace, a concert violinist, gains this and other powers when the "musical pipes of death" reveal to him the secrets of the ancients. As the Music Master, Wallace can materialize solid sheets of music to use as shields or weapons. Artists Bernard Bailey, Jim Thompson, and Alan Ulmer made the Music Master's adventures sing.

Jack Walton gains the powers to become Rainbow Boy whenever he is exposed to sun rays. For brief periods, he can fly at the speed of light and materialize solid rainbows, which he molds into useful objects and weapons. The hero, who made his debut as a sidekick for Hydroman, was written by Douglas and illustrated by Ben Thompson, another Funnies, Incorporated, veteran.

HIT COMICS

Quality Comics Group
Published 7/40–7/50   **Issue #s** 1–65
Major Characters
Hercules 1–21
Neon, the Unknown 1–17
Red Bee 1–24
Stormy Foster, the Great Defender 18–34
Kid Eternity 25–60
Blackhawk 26
Plastic Man 32

Although the most popular hero in *Hit Comics* was the back-from-the-dead Kid Eternity, other costumed characters also proved to be a hit with readers.

Joe Hercules, born the stongest man in history, works as a circus strongman. After his mother dies of a heart attack when a racketeer illegally forecloses on their home, Hercules goes out for revenge but is tossed into prison. His cellmate shows Joe a comic book which features Doll Man, another Quality Comics hero. The strongman gets the idea to become a superhero and crashes through the prison wall. Artists on Hercules included Joe Celardo, George Tuska, and Reed Crandall.

Rick Raleigh, an assistant district attorney, becomes frustrated when criminals go free on courtroom technicalities. He designs a red-and-yellow-striped costume so he can battle crime off the

books as the Red Bee. Raleigh keeps a pet bee named Michael, uses a stinger gun, and wears a weapon belt full of live bees ready to do his bidding.

Tom Corbett, a Foreign Legionnaire, is the only survivor of an African desert expedition. Dying of thirst, he discovers a pool of water which is covered with phosphorescent vapors. After he drinks the shiny liquid, he possesses "neonic power" which he can shoot out of his hands. As the superhero Neon, he can also fly on a ray of light. One of the few characters created by Jerry Iger of the Eisner-Iger studio, Neon was doubtless inspired by the bright lights of Times Square.

HUMAN TORCH

Marvel Comics
Published Fall/40–3/49   **Issue #s** 2–35 (Two #5s)
Major Characters
The Human Torch 2–35
Fiery Mask 2
Sub-Mariner 2–33
Patriot 4, 5
Namora 28, 31
Sun Girl 33–35
Captain America 33, 35

After appearing in a dozen issues of *Marvel Mystery Comics*, the Human Torch became the first major Marvel character to receive his own magazine. The title which began with issue #2 (picking up the numbering from *Red Raven Comics*) made up for lost time by having two #5 issues.

Sub-Mariner had a secondary spot in the comic. After their first succesful matchup in *Marvel Mystery Comics* (June 1940), Sub-Mariner and Human Torch continue their mammoth battles in issue #s 5, 8, 10. The war issues ended after #20 and the Human Torch returned to fighting criminals after the defeat of the Axis powers. With issue #36, the title was changed to *Love Tales*, and red-hot romance replaced the Human Torch.

HYPER MYSTERY COMICS

Hyper Publications
Published 5/40–6/40   **Issue #s** 1, 2
Major Characters
Hyper, the Phenomenal 1, 2

This first and only comic book from a small publisher featured a costumed hero modestly called Hyper the Phenomenal, who looked suspiciously like Buck Rogers in a body suit, complete with "zap" guns. Reginald Greenwood, who drew the Sparkman and Mirror Man for United Features, got his start in the superhero business as the artist for Hyper.

Hit Comics #53 © 1948 Comic Magazines, Inc. Al Bryant.

Human Torch #10 © 1942 Marvel Entertainment Group, Inc.

Ibis #5 © 1946 Fawcett Publishing, Inc.

Keen Detective Funnies #23 © 1940 Centaur Publications

IBIS THE INVINCIBLE

Fawcett Publications
Published 1942–Spring/48 **Issue #s** 1–6
Major Characters
Ibis the Invincible 1–6

After his debut in *Whiz Comics,* Fawcett's master magician received his own comic book with three or four stories in each issue. The comic book was irregularly published, with an issue coming out about once each year. Otto Binder wrote many of the stories in this series, including the origin story in the first issue.

JACKPOT COMICS

MLJ/Archie Comics
Published Spring/41–Summer/43 **Issue #s** 1–9
Major Characters
The Black Hood 1–9
Mr. Justice 1–9
Steel Sterling 1–9

The idea behind *Jackpot Comics* was simple: Give the readers their favorite superheroes in one comic book. MLJ Publications had tried this approach earlier with the Shield and the Wizard in *Shield-Wizard Comics.* For *Jackpot,* it took its most popular heroes from *Top Notch* (Black Hood), *Blue Ribbon* (Mr. Justice), and *Zip Comics* (Steel Sterling). From *Pep Comics* (home of the Shield), MLJ borrowed Sgt. Boyle for its fourth regular feature. Although without super-powers or costume, Sgt. Boyle represented the most popular emerging hero of the times—the American soldier.

KAYO COMICS

Harry "A" Chesler
Published 3/45 **Issue #s** 12
Major Characters
Green Knight 12
Captain Glory 12

Formerly a humor anthology comic called *Jest,* the comic was retitled for its last issue and featured two costumed heroes who previously appeared in other Chesler comics: Captain Glory from *Punch Comics* and the Green Knight from *Dynamic Comics.*

KEEN DETECTIVE FUNNIES

Centaur Publications
Published 7/38–9/40 **Issue #s** 8–24
Major Characters
The Clock 8, 9
The Masked Marvel 11–24
The Eye 16–24
The Air Man 23–24

Originally an anthology of G-Men ("Dan Dennis,

FBI") and private-eyes ("Dean Denton, Scientific Detective"), costumed heroes slowly infiltrated *Keen Detective Funnies.* The Masked Marvel—an accomplished pilot, expert marksman, and scientific genius—was one of the first (July 1939). Although he had no super-powers or secret identity, the hero did have a nifty glass-domed mountain hideout as well as three masked assistants (ZL, ZR, and ZY) who were former G-Men. Ben Thompson, who later drew the jungle hero Ka-Zar for *Marvel Comics,* was the original artist for the Masked Marvel.

Although not a costumed hero in the strictest sense, the Eye was one of the more unusual continuing characters in comics. Created by Frank Thomas, the Eye was just that—a huge flying eyeball that could shoot repelling rays. The Eye could spot evil as it unfolded and enlisted the aid of humans (notably Jack Barrister) to fight wrongdoers.

The Air Man, drawn by Harry Sahle and written by George Kapitan, followed the Hawkman as one of the earliest winged comic book heroes. When famous ornithologist Professor Claude Stevens is murdered, his son Drake wants justice. He constructs a pair of wings and fastens a jet pack on his back to give him the power of flight. Armed with "concentrated highly explosive" bombs and "fitted with lighter than air gas-filled wings of the famed albatross, Drake as the Air Man brings the power of mythology, the wonders of science and the might of his body to wreak vengeance."

KID ETERNITY

Quality Comics Group
Published Spring/46–11/49 **Issue #s** 1–18
Major Characters
Kid Eternity 1–18

Although Kid Eternity was the big star of *Hit Comics,* he did not receive his own comic book until the paper rationing of the war years was over. The Kid and his ghostly sidekick, Mr. Keeper, were popular enough to outlast several "big-name" 1940s superheroes but finally succumbed to the declining sales of all costumed hero comics.

KID KOMICS

Marvel Comics
Published 2/43–Spring/46 **Issue #s** 1–10
Major Characters
Captain Wonder 1, 2
Subbie 1, 2
Young Allies 2–10
Vision 3
Destroyer 4–6, 9,10
Sub-Mariner 4
Whizzer 7, 10

The popularity of the *Young Allies,* Marvel's original kid gang comic, prompted the first issue of *Kid*

Comics. Knuckles and Whitewash, two members of the *Young Allies,* appeared in the first issue and were joined the next issue by the rest of the team (Bucky, Toro, Tubby, and Jeff).

Subbie, a kid-sized version of the Sub-Mariner, showed up in both issues and then disappeared as an anomaly.

Captain Wonder made his debut in *Kid Komics* and came with a kid sidekick—Tim Mulrooney. Professor Jordan shows his young friend Tim a vial of a "wonder drug" which can multiply a person's strength twelve times. As he debates how to best test the drug, he accidentally breaks the vial. The professor and Tim are enveloped by fumes which give them the power of a dozen men (or boys, as the case may be). They both don costumes and Jordan becomes Captain Wonder while Tim remains Tim.

LADY LUCK COMICS

Quality Comics
Published 12/49–8/50   **Issue #s** 86–90
Major Characters
Lady Luck 86–90

Brenda Banks is a society girl bored with her life as a debutante. She uses her daddy's money to finance her career as a costumed crime fighter known as Lady Luck. Brenda cloaks herself in a green skirt and blouse, elbow-length opera gloves, and a wide-brimmed hat. She hides her identity behind a partial veil and is aided in her adventures by her chauffeur and confidant, the trustworthy Peecolo.

Will Eisner created Lady Luck as a secondary feature for his new *Spirit* comic section (June 2, 1940), which was distributed to newspapers. Artist Nick Cardy drew the early Lady Luck stories with a mix of glamor, intrigue, and light-hearted adventure. Klaus Nordling took over the art in 1942. Nordling, whose only previous brush with a costumed hero had been the Thin Man from *Mystic Comics,* drew Lady Luck for the next eight years in the weekly Spirit comic section. Nordling's cartoon style, which was honed by his many humorous features for the Quality Comics line, gave a sense of zany drama to the ex-debutante's adventures. Nordling's Lady Luck adventures from the *Spirit* comic sections were also reprinted in *Smash Comics.* The veiled lady adventurer took over *Smash Comics* with issue #86 and the comic book was retitled *Lady Luck Comics.* Nordling drew three new Lady Luck adventures for each issue of this comic book.

LEADING COMICS

DC Comics
Published Winter/42–Spring/45   **Issue #s** 1–14
Major Characters
The Seven Soldiers of Victory 1–14

The success of the Justice Society of America, a superhero team which appeared in *All-Star Comics,* prompted DC Comics to scrape together a second team for *Leading Comics.* The editors and writers, including Whitney Ellsworth, Mort Weisinger, Murray Boltinoff, and Jack Schiff, put together a group they called The Seven Soldiers of Victory (also known as The Law's Legionnaires). From *Star Spangled Comics* came the Star Spangled Kid and Stripesy. Green Arrow and his sidekick Speedy joined up from *More Fun Comics.* The Crimson Avenger (who was joined by his sidekick Wing in the sixth issue) appeared originally in *Detective Comics.* From *Adventure Comics* came the Shining Knight. The costumed cowboy called the Vigilante from *Action Comics* completed the group. Creig Flessel and Mort Meskin handled some initial art chores.

LIBERTY SCOUTS

Centaur Publications
Published 6/41–8/41   **Issue #s** 2, 3
Major Characters
Man Of War 2, 3
Vapo-Man 2, 3
The Fire-Man 2, 3
The Sentinel 3

Mars, the god of war, decides to create a superhero to help the Axis powers win World War II. Mars creates a Man of War—a hero with "the strength of Hercules, the speed of Mercury, the wisdom of Zeus"—and gives him a flaming sword to aid the Nazis. Fortunately for America, Mars has a lousy sense of geography and accidentally puts his hero down in Dayton, Ohio, instead of Nazi Germany. Being in a "peace-loving nation," the Man of War decides to throw his lot in with the Allies. Created and drawn by Paul Gustavson, the hero later had his own magazine.

Vapo-Man was originally chemist Bradford Cole who experiments with dissolving and expanding objects at will. When his lab is bombed by Nazi saboteurs, the blast causes Cole to be able to vaporize and travel through the air. This gaseous guy, originally dressed in just a pair of trunks, waited until his appearance in *Man of War Comics* before getting a costume. Vapo-Man was written and drawn by Sam Gilman.

The Fire-Man, who could extinguish fire just by touching it, also had the ability to fly. Drawn by Martin Filchock, he would do battle with a flaming man in *Man of War Comics* who looked suspiciously like the Human Torch.

The Sentinel was created by the "Spirit of America" and wears the costume of a minuteman from the Revolutionary War. Always appearing enveloped inside the flame of freedom, the Sentinel came on the scene almost simultaneously with three other revolutionary-spirited heroes: Captain Fearless, Major Liberty, and Fighting Yank.

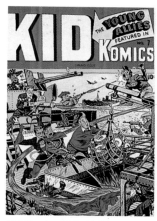

Kid Komics #7 © 1945 Marvel Entertainment Group, Inc.

Lady Luck Comics #88 © 1950 Comic Magazines, Inc. Gill Fox.

Lightning Comics Vol. 2 #5 © 1942 Ace Magazines, Inc. Jim Mooney.

The Mad Hatter #1 © 1946 O.W. Comic Corp. John Giunta.

LIGHTNING COMICS

Ace Magazines
Published 12/40–6/42 **Issue #s** 4–13
Major Characters
Flash/Lash Lightning 4–13
Raven 4–13
Dr. Nemesis 6–13
Lightning Girl 13
The Sword 13

Ace renamed *Sure-Fire Comics* after its most popular hero—Flash Lightning—who became the star of this title as well. Perhaps because of the similarity with DC Comics's character the Flash, the character was renamed Lash Lightning with issue #7. Jim Mooney drew all but the first and the last of Lightning's adventures. Lash finally got some help in issue #13 with the introduction of Lightning Girl (aka Isobel Blake). The Raven followed Lightning over from *Sure-Fire Comics* and his adventures were continued in part by Jim Mooney.

Doctor Nemesis was one of the more unusual heroes. Dr. James Bradley of the City Hospital has no super-powers, but that doesn't stop the plucky surgeon from hiding behind a trenchcoat and white doctor's mask to investigate medical foul play or a suspicious corpse. His only weapon was a hypodermic needle full of powerful truth serum which he liberally injected into suspected criminals and innocent bystanders alike in an effort to get at the truth. Doctor Nemesis was drawn by "Red" Holmdale and Harry Anderson.

MAD HATTER, THE

O.W. Comics Corporation
Published 1/46–9/46 **Issue #s** 1–2
Major Characters
The Mad Hatter 1, 2

The O. W. Comics Corporation consisted of William Woolfolk, one of the most prolific comic book writers of the 1940s, and John Oxton of Paramount Newsreel. The company published only two books: *The Mad Hatter* and *Animal Fables* (which was later sold to EC Comics). Woolfolk created the Mad Hatter as a "standard conventional feature, very much like Batman" (another character he had scripted). Grant Richmond, a junior law partner in the firm of Fuddy and Bustle, is the costumed crime fighter known as the Mad Hatter. His trademark is a purple top hat insignia which he shines against walls to strike terror in evildoers. He is also fond of leaving rhyming notes at the scene of his retributions such as: "A clever man who gave crooked advice, as free as a bird was he, till his counsel failed and now in a trice in a prison cage he'll be."

John Giunta drew the first issue while Mort Leav handled the art chores on the second issue.

MAJOR VICTORY COMICS

Harry 'A' Chesler
Published 1944–Summer/45 **Issue #s** 1–3
Major Victory 1–3
Spider Woman 1
Dynamic Boy 2
Rocket Boy 3

Major Victory, who first appeared in *Dynamic Comics,* headed up this title which reprinted his stories. Dynamic Boy, also a *Dynamic Comics* refugee, and Rocket Boy, who made his debut in *Scoop Comics,* also showed up. Helen Goddard had her one chance at fame with this issue, which marked her only appearance as Spider Woman.

MAN OF WAR COMICS

Centaur Publications
Published 11/41–1/42 **Issue #s** 1,2
Major Characters
Man Of War 1, 2
Vapo-Man 1, 2
The Fire-Man 1, 2
The Sentinel 1, 2
The Ferret 2

The four costumed characters introduced from the *Liberty Scouts* (Man Of War, Vapo-Man, Fire-Man, and the Sentinel) continued their series in this patriotic offering. The Ferret, making his only appearance in the last issue, has the dual honor of being Centaur's last costumed hero and surely the most ignominiously named. Cal Daltan, police commissioner, decides to work off the record to ferret out criminals. With super strength and the ability to fly, Daltan hides his identity behind a gray, fuzzy mask complete with little ferret ears.

MARVEL COMICS

Marvel Comics
Published 10/39 **Issue #s** 1
Major Characters
The Angel 1
The Human Torch 1
Sub-Mariner 1

The first comic book of the future Marvel Comics empire introduced three of its four top costumed heroes of the 1940s: the Human Torch by Carl Burgos, Sub-Mariner by Bill Everett, and the Angel by Paul Gustavson.

The first issue was originally dated "OCT." 1939 but many copies appeared with "NOV." printed over the October date, leading to speculation that two printings of the comic book *cover* occurred. The book actually appeared on most newsstands during the first two weeks of September 1939. The comic book was retitled *Marvel Mystery Comics* with the second issue.

MARVEL FAMILY

Fawcett Publications
Published 12/45–1/54 **Issue #s** 1–89
Major Characters
Marvel Family 1–89
Captain Marvel 2–10, 12, 13, 15–35, 37–39, 41–43, 45–47, 49–51, 53–55, 57, 58, 60, 61
Captain Marvel, Jr. 2–10, 13, 15–35, 37–39, 41–43, 45–47, 49–51, 53–55, 57, 58, 60, 84, 85
Mary Marvel 2–10, 13–35, 37–39, 41–43, 45–47, 49–51, 53–55, 57, 58, 60

Captain Marvel, Captain Marvel, Jr., and Mary Marvel teamed up to become the Marvel Family. The three Marvels were occasionally joined by Uncle Marvel, a pompous but endearing impostor, and the three Lieutenant Marvels. Each issue featured at least one story with all three Marvels battling a common foe. The heroes also often starred in stories of their own each issue. The title began the same month that Mary Marvel also received her own comic book, thereby giving the "marvelous" girl exposure in three magazines (including *Wow Comics*).

MARVEL MYSTERY COMICS

Marvel Comics
Published 12/39–6/49 **Issue #s** 2–92
Major Characters
The Angel 2–79
The Human Torch 2–92
Sub-Mariner 2–91
Vision 13–48
Patriot 21–45, 49–74
Miss America 49–85
Young Allies 75–83
Captain America 80–84, 86–92
Namora 82, 84–91
The Blonde Phantom 84–91
Golden Girl 87–92
Sun Girl 88–90

The flagship title of the Marvel Comics line featured the company's major heroes. For the first year, the Human Torch, Sub-Mariner, and the Angel rotated as front cover stars. By 1941, however, the Human Torch was the comic's lead feature. The flaming fiery hero was so visually striking and startling that he practically leapt from the covers and snatched the dimes from readers' hands.

Besides the Human Torch and the Sub-Mariner, two other characters from *Marvel Mystery* who later got their own comic books were Miss America and Namora. Other heroines in *Marvel Mystery* included the Blonde Phantom, Golden Girl, and Sun Girl.

The Vision (November 1940) was originally

drawn by Joe Simon and Jack Kirby. Inhabiting another dimension, the green-complectioned Vision enters our world via a path of smoke, "gateway to the supernatural." Other artists on the transdimensional character included Al Avison, Syd Shores, Ramona Patenaude, and Gil Kane.

The Patriot (July 1941) was reporter Jeff Mace, who either worked for the *Consolidated News* or the *Daily Planet*(!) depending upon the writer. Donning a red-and-blue costume with a big white "V" on his cowl, the Patriot dispatches saboteurs on the home front. His job is made easier when his companion Mary becomes Miss Patriot (December 1943). Ray Gill, who would later devote most of his time to writing and drawing Mighty Mouse and Terrytoon characters for Marvel, wrote the early episodes. Artists who worked on the Patriot included Sid Greene, Bill Everett, Al Fagaly, Art Gates, and Ray Houlihan.

MARY MARVEL COMICS

Fawcett Publications
Published 12/45–9/48 **Issue #s** 1–28
Major Characters
Mary Marvel 1–28
Mr. Scarlet 9

After a three-year run as the lead feature in *Wow Comics*, Mary Marvel received her own title. Actually, a Mary Marvel comic book had been planned as early as 1943 but wartime paper shortages delayed its release until late 1945.

The "World's Mightiest Girl" had two recurrent supporting characters. Her girlfriend Freckles was "a lovable tomboy and self-appointed cousin" who liked to wear a Mary Marvel costume. Although she had no special powers (except for "the knack of stirring a hornet's nest"), the young girl called herself Freckles Marvel and frequently joined Mary in her adventures.

Another familial imposter and "self-appointed" relative was Uncle Dudley, a charming buffoon who also liked to dress up in Marvel Family clothes. Uncle Dudley, who dubbed himself Uncle Marvel when he wore his ill-fitting costume, was a likeable and blustery character in the tradition of W.C. Fields. With no super-powers, Uncle Marvel often had to rely on his "niece" Mary to help him out whenever his trouble-shooting agency Shazam, Inc. ran afoul.

Although popular with girls, *Mary Marvel* only sold about two-thirds as well as the *Captain Marvel, Jr.* comic book. The last issue was an omen. Instead of her regular costume, Mary wears cowgirl clothes on the cover. With the next issue, the comic was changed to a cowboy comic, *Monte Hall Western*, and Mary lost her comic book.

Marvel Mystery Comics #9 © 1940 Marvel Entertainment Group, Inc. Bill Everett.

Mary Marvel #12 © 1947 Fawcett Publications, Inc. Jack Binder.

Master Comics #26 © 1942 Fawcett Publications, Inc. Mac Raboy.

Miss America #1 © 1944 Marvel Entertainment Group, Inc. Pauline Loth.

MASKED MARVEL

Centaur Publications
Published 9/40–12/40   **Issue #s** 1–3
Major Characters
Masked Marvel 1–3

The Masked Marvel (and his masked assistants—ZR, ZY, and ZL) received his own magazine the same month he lost his series in the canceled *Keen Detective Funnies*. Sam Gilman, who was assisting Bill Everett with the Sub-Mariner stories, wrote and drew some of the adventures.

MASTER COMICS

Fawcett Publications
Published 3/40–4/53   **Issue #s** 1–133
Major Characters
Masterman 1–6
Bulletman 7–82, 84–106
Minute-Man 11–49
Captain Marvel 20, 21, 48, 50
Captain Marvel, Jr. 22–133
Mary Marvel 118

The first six issues of *Master Comics* were larger than normal-sized comic books and the first three issues sold for fifteen cents. The title was part of Fawcett's early and largely unsuccessful experiments with different comic book formats and prices (for example, *Nickel Comics*).

Masterman, an early superhero who appeared one month after Captain Marvel, lasted for the first six issues until dropped due to a lawsuit by DC Comics. Bulletman from the canceled *Nickel Comics* replaced *Masterman*. Minute-Man (February 1941), an early patriotic hero who predated Captain America by one month, dressed in a red, white, and blue costume and was billed as "America's One Man Army." He received his own comic book several months before the United States entered the war.

Master Comics became best known as the home of Captain Marvel, Jr., who began his long-running series after his debut in *Whiz Comics*. The covers by artist Mac Raboy made the title one of the more attractive superhero comics on the newsstands.

METEOR COMICS

Croyden Publishing Company
Published 11/45   **Issue #s** 1
Major Characters
Captain Wizard 1

Captain Wizard was the lead feature in the package put together by Funnies, Incorporated, for *Meteor Comics*. The Captain debuted several months earlier in *Red Band Comics*. The comic also featured the origin of Baldy Bean, Captain Wizard's corpulent sidekick.

MILITARY COMICS

Quality Comics Group
Published 8/41–10/45   **Issue #s** 1–43
Major Characters
Blackhawk 1–43
Miss America 1–7

Military Comics, which promised its readers "stories of the Army and Navy," featured the high-flying adventures of the Blackhawks.

The other costumed character who briefly shared the title with the international group of aviators was Miss America. Joan Dale, a newspaper reporter, visits the Statue of Liberty and has a transformational experience. "Gosh," the awed woman reporter says, "Just think of all the good a person could do if they had the powers of that Statue!" By expressing such a noble thought, Joan is somehow endowed with magical powers by the lady of liberty to help with our country's war effort.

MINUTE MAN

Fawcett Publications
Published Summer/41–Spring/42   **Issue #s** 1–3
Major Characters
Minute-Man 1–3

After his debut in *Master Comics* (February 1941), the patriotic Minute Man received his own comic book months before the United States entered the war. Army private Jack Weston dons a red, white, and blue uniform to fight enemy agents as the Minute Man. Weston's secret identity as an undercover patriot is shared by General Milton, who sends him on his unsanctioned missions. The adventures of "The One-Man Army" were usually written by Otto Binder and drawn by Charles Sultan, Phil Bard, and Clem Weisbecker.

MISS AMERICA

Marvel Comics
Published 1944–11/44   **Issue #s** 1, 2
Major Characters
Miss America 1, 2

Marvel's first successful superheroine, Miss America, premiered in *Marvel Mystery Comics* and got her own magazine before the war was over—a good accomplishment in those paper-rationed days. The first issue was titled *Miss America Comics* and featured Marvel's red-white-and-blue hero in a series of adventures drawn by Pauline Loth. With the second issue, the book was retitled *Miss America Magazine*, and Miss America, the superheroine, began taking a backseat to teenage strips like Patsy Walker and Hedy Wolfe. Movie reviews and teen features also appeared and the front cover of the second issue was a photograph of a girl dressed up in a Miss America uniform. It looked less and less like a comic book and more like a teen magazine for girls. The title was published as a teen comic until 1958 but Miss America no longer appeared as a costumed heroine after the second issue.

MISS FURY
Marvel Comics
Published Winter/42–Winter/45 **Issue #s** 1–8
Major Characters
Miss Fury 1–8

Tarpe Mills, the creator of Miss Fury, began her comic book career at the Funnies, Incorporated, studio by drawing comic strip adaptations of fictitious Hollywood films for *Funny Pages* (October 1939) and *Target Comics* (February 1940).

In April 1941 Mills began drawing a Sunday comic strip called the Black Fury, one of the first female costumed crime fighters to appear in the newspapers. The character soon became known as Miss Fury and she hid her identity as socialite Marla Drake under a black, leopard-skin costume given to her by an African witch doctor. Mills packed her Miss Fury strips with violent action, hair-pulling catfights, spiked heels, kinky fashions, and cruelly sensual villains. The feature lasted until 1952, albeit in only a few newspapers.

The Miss Fury comic books were reprints from the newspaper strips. As the strip went on, Miss Fury gradually discarded her skin-tight, leopard-skin costume for more traditional working attire. By issue #6 of her comic book, Marla Drake wore her black leopard costume only for her cover appearances.

MODERN COMICS
Quality Comics Group
Published 11/45–10/50 **Issue #s** 44–102
Major Characters
Blackhawk 44–102
The Spirit 83, 102

After the war was over, Quality Comics changed the name of *Military Comics* to the more forward-looking and peaceful sounding *Modern Comics*. The Blackhawks, however, still continued without missing a punch as they turned their attention from the Nazis to Cold War dictators and communist insurgents.

MORE FUN COMICS
DC Comics
Published 2/40–1/46 **Issue #s** 52–107
Major Characters
The Spectre 52–101
Doctor Fate 55–98
Johnny Quick 71–107
Aquaman 73–107
Green Arrow 73–107
Superboy 101–107

More Fun Comics was the home of the Spectre and Doctor Fate, two early heroes from 1940 who were also founding members of the Justice Society of America in *All-Star Comics*.

In 1941, Mort Weisinger, an editor of a science fiction pulp magazine called *Thrilling Wonder Stories*, was hired as a writer and story editor for DC Comics. His first assignment was to come up with new heroes for *More Fun Comics*. Taking a cue from the Flash, Weisinger came up with another super-fast character known as Johnny Quick. Johnny Chambers gains the powers of accelerated movement by uttering a magical mathematical formula: "3X2(9YZ)4A." While not as snappy as the other magical superhero word "Shazam," the formula was enough to turn Johnny into one of the "quickest" persons on earth.

Next, Weisinger borrowed from the Robin Hood legend and came up with an archer who fought crime with a quiver full of gimmick arrows. Green Arrow and his ward Speedy were popular enough to star as members of the Seven Soldiers of Victory in *Leading Comics*. George Papp drew most of the emerald archer's adventures.

Weisinger's next creation for *More Fun* was Aquaman, the king of the seven seas and son of Atlantis. An underwater hero in the tradition of the Sub-Mariner, Aquaman was drawn initially by Paul Norris. The sea-going superhero outlasted all his other watery competition and eventually moved to *Adventure Comics*.

Superboy, who made his debut in *More Fun Comics*, also moved over to *Adventure* and, finally, into a comic book of his own.

MYSTERY COMICS
William H. Wise/Better Publications
Published 1944 **Issue #s** 1–4
Major Characters
Brad Spencer, Wonderman 1–4
The Magnet 1–4

When a "sizzling voltage of a secret current" gives Brad Spencer the power to will his body to become as hard as a "block of steel," he turns into a costumed hero known as Wonderman. With his girlfriend Carol, Brad spends his time as Wonderman fighting evil goddesses and interplanetary despots. Brad and Carol also appeared in *Wonder Comics*.

Grant Halford uses his uncanny invention, the Geo-Locater, to track down Nazis and criminals. He captures them in his identity as the Magnet and is assisted by his girlfriend Debby and an African tribesman named Sidi. Wearing a fur loincloth and a tiger-head cowl, Sidi is a formidable ally for the Magnet, although he persisted in speaking in

Miss Fury #4 © 1944 Marvel Entertainment Group, Inc.

More Fun Comics #71 © 1941 DC Comics, Inc.

Mystery Men Comics #3
© 1939 Fox Features
Syndicate. Lou Fine.

Mystic Comics #2 © 1940
Marvel Entertainment
Group, Inc.

Hollywood jungle movie patois: "Car ready, Bwana! Now we chase-um fella!"

MYSTERY MEN COMICS

Fox Features Syndicate
Published 8/39–2/42   Issue #s 1–31
Major Characters
The Blue Beetle 1–31
Green Mask 1–31
The Moth 9–13
The Lynx 14–31
The Wraith 26–31

The "mystery men" in Victor Fox's second comic book came in two colors: The Green Mask and the Blue Beetle. The Green Mask was groomed to be the star of the comic and appeared on the front cover for four of the first five issues. The Blue Beetle, however, soon got a costume, super-powers, and even better art to push the Green Mask into second place. The Blue Beetle received his own magazine within a few months of his debut and the Green Mask got his own comic the following year.

The third most popular hero in *Mystery Men* was the Lynx (August 1940), who ran around in animal-print briefs and red boots. He was assisted by Blackie the Mystery Boy. The Lynx and his boy Blackie (known only as Jim and Phil) were usually drawn by Arturo Cazeneuve. Other men of mystery included the Moth (April 1940) and the Wraith (September 1941), who followed the tradition of the Spirit, Spectre, and other back-from-the-dead heroes.

MYSTIC COMICS (1)

Marvel Comics
Published 3/40–8/42   Issue #s 1–10
Major Characters
Blue Blaze 1–4
Dynamic Man 1–4
Flexo, the Rubber Man 1–4
Black Widow 4, 5, 7
The Thin Man 4
Black Marvel 5–9
Blazing Skull 5–9
The Terror 5–10
Destroyer 6–10
Challenger 6–10
The Witness 7–9
Fathertime 10

The third Marvel comic book spewed out a dozen superheroes, ranging from the Witness ("judge, jury, and avenger of evil") to the Thin Man (who could make himself as flat as a sheet of paper) and the Black Marvel (a boy who becomes a costumed avenger after an initiation by the "Blackfeet" Indian tribe).

Marvel's first costumed heroine also appeared in *Mystic Comics* as well. The Black Widow, originally a

young woman medium named Claire Voyant, is murdered and becomes "Satan's ambassador." Part of her ambassadorial duties include taking the souls of evildoers straight to hell by exercising her touch of death ("And so the Black Widow is going to take your evil, merciless soul to the place it belongs—are you ready?"). The Widow was drawn by Harry Sahle and written by George Kapitan. Stan Drake also worked on this cold-blooded heroine, who later appeared in *All Select* and *USA Comics*.

The Destroyer first appeared in the October 1941 issue in two stories by the Jack Binder studio. While reporting on the war in Germany, journalist Keen Marlow is thrown in jail, even though America and Germany are not yet at war. While imprisoned, Marlow meets a professor who has devised a special formula to turn soldiers into super-men. Drinking the "super liquid," Marlow becomes the Mighty Destroyer and takes a vow "not to rest until he has destroyed the Nazi hordes." The Destroyer was written by Stan Lee, Otto Binder, and Ray Gill. The character, who also appeared in *All-Winners, USA Comics,* and *Kid Komix,* was drawn by Al Avison and John Forte, among others.

MYSTIC COMICS (2)

Marvel Comics
Published 10/44–3/45   Issue #s 1–4
Major Characters
The Angel 1–3
Destroyer 1–4
The Human Torch 1, 2
Young Allies 4

The second go-round for this Marvel title was originally envisioned as a showcase for the Angel, Marvel's fourth most popular costumed hero. After appearing on the front covers and in two stories in both the second and third issues, however, the Angel was bumped from the last issue by the Young Allies.

NAMORA

Marvel Comics
Published 8/48–12/48   Issue #s 1–3
Major Characters
Namora 1–3
Sub-Mariner 1–3
The Blonde Phantom 2

Namora, the female cousin of the Sub-Mariner, made her debut in the May 1947 issue of *Marvel Mystery Comics*. While the Sub-Mariner is "somewhere in Asia on a case," a gang of criminals in a submarine attack the underwater kingdom of Sub-Mariner's people. The spear-carrying gangsters murder most of the underwater dwellers and loot the kingdom. When the Sub-Mariner returns, he discovers that the only survivor is a young woman named Aquaria Nautica Neptunia. Together, they swear revenge for their people's deaths and Aquaria takes the new name of Namora which means "avenging daughter." Besides appearing regularly in *Marvel Mystery Comics*, the "Sea Beauty" also co-starred with the Sub-Mariner in *Sub-Mariner, Human Torch,* and *Captain America Comics.*

NATIONAL COMICS

Quality Comics Group
Published 7/40–11/49   **Issue #s** 1–75
Major Characters
Uncle Sam 1–45
Wonder Boy 1–26
Quicksilver 5–71, 73

Will Eisner's studio put together *National Comics* for Quality Comics and created a memorable superhero along the way. Uncle Sam, an early patriotic hero, was the comic book version of the James Montgomery Flagg World War I recruiting poster character ("I Want You"). The patriotic hero teams up with a boy named Buddy whose father was murdered by Nazi infiltrators. Together, they starred in every issue of *National Comics* until the end of the war (December 1944), as well as appearing in *Uncle Sam Comics.*

Wonder Boy (no relation to an earlier Eisner hero, Wonder Man) was an extraterrestrial teenager who came to Earth to fight crime and injustice. Possessing the "strength of a thousand men," Wonder Boy still acted much like a normal Earth boy, riding his bicycle to the scene of the crime and protecting his girlfriend, Sally Benson, from trouble. One of the earlier "kid" heroes, Wonder Boy was drawn by John Celardo, Nick Cardy, Klaus Nordling, and Al Bryant.

Quicksilver, "the King of Speed," was Quality's version of the Flash. "Swift as the night wind—silent as the shadow of a hawk—ruthless as the killer shark against the cruel minions of crime . . . that's Quicksilver, former circus acrobat turned crime-fighter!" The blue-suited speedster, who operated out of a secret laboratory and read comic books in his spare time, was drawn by Nick Cardy, Jack Cole, Paul Gustavson, Alex Kotzky, and Fred Guardineer.

NEW YORK WORLD'S FAIR COMICS

DC Comics
Published 5/39–5/40   **Issue #s** 1, 2
Major Characters
The Sandman 1, 2
Superman 1, 2
Batman and Robin 2
The Hourman 2

When the World's Fair came to New York in 1939, there was a flurry of commercial activity to take advantage of the enormous publicity and crowds generated by the event. DC Comics decided to

publish a souvenir comic book edition for the World's Fair and it hastily collected stories already written and drawn for other comics. It put the stories in a ninety-six-page comic book which retailed for twenty-five cents. Poor sales resulted in the comic being re-stickered with a fifteen-cent price tag, and subsequent sales were good enough for a 1940 issue.

The 1939 issue came out in such a hurry that no one caught an obvious error: Superman appeared on the cover as a blond. The 1939 issue also marked the first appearance of the Sandman, who would later make his official debut in the July 1939 issue of *Adventure Comics*. The 1940 issue marked the first time Superman and Batman appeared together on a comic book cover. The comic also featured the second appearance of Robin the Boy Wonder (who made his debut in the April 1940 issue of *Detective Comics*).

NICKEL COMICS

Fawcett Publications
Published 5/40–8/40   **Issue #s** 1–8
Major Characters
Bulletman 1–8

As an experiment, Fawcett published this thirty-six-page, biweekly comic book, which sold for five cents. At the time, most comics were twice as long, sold for twice as much, and generally appeared on a monthly or bimonthly basis. Evidently, distributers and retailers didn't care for the lower-priced oddity, and the experiment ended after four months. The comic book did, however, introduce Bulletman. With the cancellation of *Nickel Comics*, Bulletman moved to *Master Comics* and then to his own magazine.

OUR FLAG COMICS

Ace Magazines
Published 8/41–4/42   **Issue #s** 1–5
Major Characters
Captain Victory 1
The Unknown Soldier 1–5
The Flag 2–5

This "red, white, and blue" comic book was the home of such patriots as Captain Victory, The Unknown Soldier, and The Flag. The Unknown Soldier ("Defender of Liberty"), appropriately enough, had no name or identity but represented "the spirit of the boys who died to see that our nation will live forever." He appeared whenever democracy was threatened and blasted away Nazi-rats with his nitroglycerin pistol. Captain Victory, who wore a star-shaped mask, lasted only one issue, but his costume design and patriotic mission was incorporated into another Ace hero, Captain Courageous, who made his debut the following

National Comics #3 © 1940 Comic Magazines, Inc. Will Eisner and Reed Crandall.

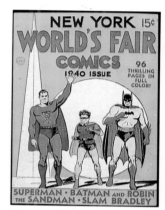

New York World's Fair Comics #2 © 1940 DC Comics, Inc. Jack Burnley.

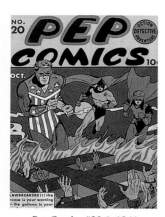

Pep Comics #20 © 1941 Archie Comic Publications, Inc. Irv Novick.

Plastic Man #39 © 1953 Comic Magazines, Inc.

month in *Banner Comics.*

The Flag, however, outdid all the others in sheer patriotic zeal. Flying through the air in his flag-colored costume, he left behind a stream of sparkling stars. The Flag began his life as an abandoned baby on the doorsteps of a crippled World War I veteran and flag-maker, John ("Old Glory") Courtney. Courtney discovers the child on Flag Day and, even more auspiciously, sees that the baby has a flag birthmark on his chest. He names the boy Jim and raises him as his own. On his twenty-first birthday, Jim Courtney has a vision in which he meets George Washington and Abraham Lincoln. Washington tells him that "his life was selected by us to perform hard and dangerous tasks" and he is given the power of a hundred men and immunity from weapons. He becomes The Flag when he touches his birthmark.

PEP COMICS

MLJ/Archie Comics
Published 1/40–1/48   **Issue #s** 1–65
Major Characters
Comet 1–17
The Shield 1–65
Fireball 12–20
The Hangman 17–47
The Black Hood 48–51, 59, 60

Besides being the birthplace of the Shield (MLJ Publication's most successful superhero), *Pep Comics* also featured the first appearances of the Hangman and the Comet.

John Dickering, while working as a chemist in a Manhatten research lab, discovers a gas that is "fifty times lighter than hydrogen." He injects the gas into his bloodstream and discovers that he can "make great leaps through the air." The excitable scientist continues to give himself happy-gas injections until a toxic load builds up behind his eyes. Now when his eyes cross, two powerful beams come out and disintegrate whatever he is looking at. He hides his destructive power behind a pair of protective glasses and becomes a costumed hero known as the Comet. As the Comet, Dickering is a ruthless crime fighter, often blasting and killing his adversaries.

With such a deadly reputation, the Comet is the target of a fatal ambush by gangsters (July 1941). His brother, Robert Dickering, vows vengeance over his dying brother and takes over his crime-fighting duties by dressing up as the Hangman. Jack Cole wrote and drew the early adventures. Cliff Campbell drew later stories, and writing chores were handled by Abner Sundell and Joe Blair.

Ted Tyler, a firefighter, is knocked unconscious by an arsonist inside a blazing laboratory. He is coated and then roasted in a chemical bath which somehow gives him the power to absorb and control flame. The Fireball, originally drawn by Paul Reinman, devoted his life to fighting firebugs with fire.

PHANTOM LADY

Fox Features Syndicate
Published 8/47–4/49   **Issue #s** 13–23 (No 1–12)
Major Characters
Phantom Lady 13–23
The Blue Beetle 13

After a modest series in *Police Comics* (1941–1943), the Phantom Lady was brought back four years later by a different publisher. Pure licentiousness was the *raison d'être* for this new comic from Fox Features Syndicate, where buxom was the byword. Matt Baker, a specialist in drawing knockout-beautiful women, applied himself diligently to this larger-than-life character.

PLASTIC MAN

Vital Publications/Quality Comics
Published Summer/43–2/55   **Issue #s** 1–52
Major Characters
Plastic Man 1–52

After making his debut in *Police Comics,* Plastic Man received his own magazine in 1943. The second issue was published the following year and the series began as a quarterly publication with the third issue in Spring 1946. There were usually three Plastic Man stories in each issue, with a secondary humorous strip which featured Woozy Winks, Plastic Man's polka-dot-wearing sidekick.

Jack Cole wrote and drew many stories until November 1950. Other artists who drew Plastic Man included Alex Kotzky, John Spranger, Andre LeBlanc, and Charles Nicholas. Reprints of earlier Cole stories begin in issue #44 and the last original story appears in #52. Plastic Man continued to be published until November 1956, two years after the Comics Code took effect. The reprinted stories were often revised to conform to new code regulations which downplayed violence and horror.

POCKET COMICS

Harvey Publications
Published 8/41–1/42   **Issue #s** 1–4
Major Characters
The Black Cat 1–4
Phantom Sphinx 1–4
Red Blazer 1–4
The Spirit of '76 1–4
Zebra 1–4

Publisher Alfred Harvey came up with what he thought was a revolutionary idea in comic books: a pocket-sized comic with 100 pages which still cost a dime. Kids could carry them in their pockets and get nearly twice as many pages as a regular-sized comic book. Unfortunately, too many kids "pocketed" the small comic book without paying for it first. The pocket format was dropped after newsstand dealers complained, but not before several superheroes were introduced in the first issue.

Harvey's most popular costumed hero, the Black Cat, made her debut here before receiving a series in *Speed Comics*.

Gary Blakley, a West Point cadet, becomes The Spirit of '76 when he dons a Revolutionary War costume (with bulletproof vest) and a black mask in order to fight crime without jeopardizing his student status. The series continued in *Green Hornet Comics*.

John Doyle, a criminal lawyer, is framed for a crime when he uncovers a crooked political scheme. Escaping from prison, the disbarred lawyer uses his black-and-white jail uniform as the basis for his costume as the Zebra. Doyle operates as "the striped striker for right" to clear his name. The Zebra also appeared in *Green Hornet Comics* and *All-New Comics*.

The Red Blazer, who has the power to control heat and fire, comes into being when a scientist gives a cowboy the power of "Astro-Pyro" Rays. Drawn initially by Al Avison, this Human-Torch-inspired hero also appeared in *All-New Comics* with a young sidekick named Sparky.

POLICE COMICS

Quality Comics Group
Published 8/41–10/50   **Issue #s** 1–102
Major Characters
Firebrand 1–13
Human Bomb 1–58
Phantom Lady 1–23
Plastic Man 1–102
The Spirit 11–88, 90, 92, 94–102
The Raven 20–22
Spider Widow 21, 22

Police Comics was conceived as a comic book about costumed detectives and crime-fighting heroes. The two most popular characters were Jack Cole's stretchable sleuth, Plastic Man, and Will Eisner's masked detective, the Spirit (whose stories were reprinted from the weekly newspaper comic sections). Other popular costumed characters included the Phantom Lady, Firebrand, and the Human Bomb.

Roy Lincoln, a scientific genius, discovers a highly explosive chemical compound. To prevent Nazi agents from getting the formula, the scientist swallows his "bomb" capsule. The chemical transforms Lincoln into a Human Bomb whose hands and touch are truly explosive. He wears special gloves and an asbestoslike costume to contain his bombastic nature. When he wants to bust his way through a wall or take out a criminal, the Human Bomb just takes off his gloves. He was joined by a comic sidekick known as Hustace Throckmorton, who possessed similar "human bomb" powers but which were directed out of his *feet* instead of his hands (which meant he often went barefoot into battle). The Human Bomb was written and drawn by Paul Gustavson.

The Firebrand was originally Naval reserve officer and playboy Rod Reilly. Assisted by his manservant, Slugger Dunn, Reilly dons a crimson-colored costume to become the crime-fighting and Axis-smashing Firebrand. The character was first drawn by Reed Crandall and later by Gil Fox and Alex Blum.

POPULAR COMICS

Dell Comics
Published 12/40–4/43   **Issue #s** 46–86
Major Characters
Martan, the Marvel Man 46–71
Professor Supermind and Son 60–71
The Owl 72–86
Captain Midnight 76–78

After subsisting mostly on newspaper strip reprints for its first four years, *Popular Comics* introduced two original superheroes. Martan the Marvel Man, drawn by Bill Ely, was an alien superman from the planet Antaclea who uses his telepathic powers, super strength, and a ready raygun to battle outer space invaders who wish to conquer Earth. Martan is joined by his wife Vana. Both wear matching green miniskirts with metallic pullovers.

Professor Warren, a white-goateed research scientist known to the world as "Supermind," invents an ultra-frequency device to give his son Dan "superhuman energies" such as super speed, the power to fly, and an electric force field around his body. Guided by his dad's all-seeing invention, the "televisioscope," Dan can spot trouble anywhere in the world. Professor Supermind's son displays his power by smashing warships and tossing around boxcars loaded with thermite bombs. The stories and art were by Maurice Kashuba, an artist/writer who had previously worked for Centaur Publishing and DC's *More Fun Comics*. Professor Supermind was canceled with the February 1942 issue in order to make room for the Owl, a costumed hero refugee from the recently canceled *Crackajack Funnies*.

PRIZE COMICS

Prize Publications
Published 3/40–2/48   **Issue #s** 1–68
Major Characters
The Black Owl (I) 2–33; (II) 34–53, 55–64, 66, 67
Green Lama 7–34
Dr. Frost 7–34
Airmale 34–43
Yank and Doodle 13–68

The major costumed heroes of *Prize* were the Black Owl and the young brother team of Yank and Doodle. In issue #33, the original Black Owl passes on his costume to the father of the two boys who are Yank and Doodle. With Dad as the Black Owl, Yank and Doodle make the family a heroic three-some.

Police Comics #18 © 1943 Comic Magazines, Inc.

Popular Comics #60 © 1941 Dell Publishing Co., Inc.

Red Band Comics #4
© 1945 Enwil Associates

The Green Lama, a Tibetan-trained hero who first appeared in a pulp magazine, made his comic book debut in the December 1940 issue. Written by pulp writer and creator Ken Crossen, the early adventures of the Green Lama were drawn by Mike Suchorsky, Jack Binder, and Dick Briefer.

Dr. Frost, who wears green trunks, blue boots, and a snowflake collar, can shoot blasts of icy air from his fingers and create solid ice barriers around himself and others. Drawn initially by Ben Thompson (December 1940) and later by Maurice Gutwirth, the super-cold superhero owed a debt to Sub-Zero Man from *Blue Bolt Comics*.

Rounding out the *Prize* line of costumed heroes was a patriotic pair known as Airmale and his sidekick Stampy, who joined him in December 1943.

PUNCH COMICS

Harry 'A' Chesler
Published 12/41–1/48   **Issue #s** 1–23 (No 4–7)
Major Characters
Mr. E 1, 2
Captain Glory 2, 12
The Master Key 9–21
Rocketman and Rocketgirl 9–11, 13–20

The third in the series of comics by Harry 'A' Chesler, *Punch Comics* followed *Yankee* and *Scoop Comics* by introducing a new superhero—Mr. E. Mr. E has no other name or alter ego. He does have a magical statue of a god called King Kolah from an extinct civilization. Mr. E keeps King Kolah in a subterranean temple inside his Washington, D.C. home. The ancient idol, which looks like a squatting blue pharaoh in a bathing suit, has the power to show Mr. E scenes of trouble from far away. It can also dispatch magical messengers in various guises to help Mr. E. Dressed in a red jumpsuit open at the chest, Mr. E often ended each adventure bowing his head before his blue statue, bathed in golden light: "All wise and powerful King Kolah, I humbly report that with the aid of your messengers of justice, the menace has been destroyed." George Tuska and Charles Sultan, among others, drew the adventures of this idol-worshipping crime fighter who also appeared in *Dynamic Comics*.

RED BAND COMICS

Enwil Associates
Published 2/45–5/45   **Issue #s** 1–4
Major Characters
Bogeyman 1, 2
Captain Wizard 3, 4

Sam Cooper, who drew the Hangman, Mr. Justice, the Black Hood, and other heroes for MLJ Publications, was also the artist of the haunting avenging hero known as the Bogeyman. Bearing a strong resemblance to Will Eisner's Spirit, the motto of this slouch-hat, domino-masked hero was: "The Bogeyman will get you if you don't watch out!" The Bogeyman also made an appearance in *Merry Comics* (December 1945).

Captain Wizard began his career as a war veteran who is accused of a murder he did not commit. While hiding in a wax museum from the police, the veteran is given a magical cloak and costume by a magician named Theophrastus Bombastus Paracelsus. "Clothe thyself in this armor of righteousness! Fearless thou art . . . so remain secure in the knowledge that as long as thou art clothed in this, thou can dare the slings and arrows of outrageous fortune! Be off, do good, and . . . as thou dost will, so will the cloak do!"

RED CIRCLE COMICS

Rural Home Publishing Company
Published 1/45–4/45   **Issue #s** 1–4
Major Characters
The Prankster 1–3
The Judge 1–2

The Prankster was an unusual hero, even by the offbeat standards of the sprouting small publishers of the mid-1940s. Michael Morgan, a stand-up magician with a twisted sense of humor, becomes the Prankster when he foils a robbery with "a funny mask and a loaded water pistol." Morgan uses his night-club magician stage props, such as a hand joy-buzzer and squirting flower, to foil crooks: "Comedy battles crime—and wins!"

On the other hand, the Judge (as drawn by Chu Hing), was strictly serious business. After his father is killed and the murderer goes free, young Jim pursues a career in law to see that justice is done. When the legal system allows a criminal to escape punishment, he slips on a black mask, grabs a gavel, dons a purple judicial robe and becomes the Judge. "Eventually the law catches up with all of you mugs—meantime, here's my brand of justice!"

RED DRAGON (1)

Street and Smith
Published 1/43–1/44   **Issue #s** 5–9 (No 1–4)
Major Characters
Captain Jack Commando 5–7
Red Dragon 6–9
Black Crusader 6, 8

The Red Dragon was a superhero born from the anti-Japanese sentiment running high during World War II. Bob Reed watches helplessly as Japanese murder his parents. Swearing vengeance, he studies the art of Far Eastern sorcery and discovers the magic words "Po-She-Lo," which transform him into the Red Dragon. As the Red Dragon, Reed can fly or transfer his powers of flight to others, dispel illusions, and transform matter. With his Chinese friend Ching

Foo and his pet Komodo dragon, Reed wages war against the Japanese and villains like the Yellow Dragon. "I, the Red Dragon, conjure up the ancient and forbidden magic of Tibet in my fight against the bestial Jap!" John Meditz was the artist on these stories.

Captain Jack Commando was another patriotic costumed hero. This one was created by the Binder brothers; Otto wrote it and Jack drew it.

The story of the Black Crusader begins when Joe Mills discovers he has a blood clot on the brain and could go at any time. Having nothing to lose, he decides to risk his life by fighting crime as the Black Crusader. (Despite the name, Mills dresses in gray.) John Spranger and Andre LeBlanc, who had previously drawn both Sheena and Captain Marvel, were responsible for bringing the Black Crusader to life.

RED DRAGON (2)

Street and Smith
Published 11/47–7/49   **Issue #s** 1–7
Major Characters
Red Dragon 1–7

When Edd Cartier started drawing the Red Dragon in *Super Magician Comics* (December 1946), Street and Smith knew it was time to bring back the character for a second series in his own book. Cartier, who wrote as well as drew the Red Dragon stories, began his career as a science fiction artist. In 1939, he drew several covers for Street and Smith's fantasy magazine *Unknown,* as well as interior illustrations.

After the first four issues of Red Dragon, Edd Cartier left comics to devote more time to illustrating Street and Smith's best-selling science fiction magazine, *Astounding.* Cartier was followed by artist Joe Maneely.

RED RAVEN COMICS

Marvel Comics
Published 8/40   **Issue #s** 1
Major Characters
Red Raven 1
Human Top 1
Mercury 1

Joe Simon was hired by Marvel publisher Martin Goodman to put together a new comic book. Working with his new partner Jack Kirby, the two came up with the idea for a hero called the Red Raven. A young boy, the only survivor of an airplane crash, is raised on a mysterious flying island by a race of bird people. Learning to fly with artificial wings, the boy dons a red costume on his twentieth birthday and goes off on a mission as the Red Raven to eliminate the "elements that make for unhappiness in the world." Simon assigned the story

to artist Louis Cazeneuve, whom he had worked with at Fox Features Syndicate.

For the second feature, Kirby drew his first character for Marvel Comics, the mythological Mercury. The super-swift hero made his only appearance in *Red Raven* but was recycled by Simon and Kirby into a character called the Hurricane for *Captain America* comics.

RED SEAL COMICS

Harry 'A' Chesler
Published 10/45–12/47   **Issue #s** 14–22 (No 1–13)
Major Characters
Black Dwarf 14–18, 20–22
Veiled Avenger 16
Lady Satan 17, 18, 20, 21

Although *Red Seal Comics* was best known for its lead feature, the Black Dwarf, another equally appealing dark character was the mysterious Lady Satan. Originally appearing in *Dynamic Comics,* Lady Satan is a mistress of the occult. Her magic gives her the strength of twenty men and her serpent-shaped ring, which can emit vapors derived from "dragon scales," helps her to "unveil the shadow world." Lady Satan, seductively attired in a clinging, red satin gown with a black domino mask, was often involved in adventures involving skeletons, ghosts, murders, and bondage. The brimstone-scented lady also appeared in *Bulls-Eye Comics.*

SAMSON

Fox Features Syndicate
Published Fall/40–9/41   **Issue #s** 1–6
Major Characters
Samson 1–6
The Topper 6

After his debut in *Fantastic Comics,* this descendant of the biblical strongman received his own magazine. Many of the stories, which were often written by Robert Kanigher, revolved around the "yellow-haired giant" somehow being trapped into having his hair cut so he would become weak. Fortunately his hair often grows back in only a few minutes. Samson is accompanied, sometimes to his worriment, by a young boy named David who yanks a mean slingshot. No one ever commented that Samson and David walked around in loincloths and sandals in the middle of the city. Artists included Alex Blum, Al Carreno, and Pierce Rice. The long-haired strongman also appeared in *Big 3 Comics.*

Barry Graham made his debut as the Topper in the last issue of *Samson* and then continued his series in *U.S. Jones.*

Red Dragon #7 © 1949 Street & Smith Publications, Inc. Bob Powell.

Samson #5 © 1941 Fox Features Syndicate

Sensation Comics #54
© 1946 DC Comics, Inc.
H.G. Peter.

Shadow Comics Vol. 2 #6 ©
1942 Street & Smith
Publications, Inc.

SCIENCE COMICS

Fox Features Syndicate
Published 2/40–9/40 **Issue #s** 1–8
Major Characters
Dynamo 1–8
The Eagle 1–8

The science was pretty thin in *Science Comics*, although Cosmic Carson and Perisphere Payne followed the tradition of space helmets and rayguns found in Buck Rogers and Flash Gordon. The real stars, however, were the costumed heroes—particularly Dynamo, the master of electricity. In the first issue, Jim Andrews discovers he can shoot electricity from his hands and electrocute anyone by his touch. He devises a red costume with a lightning motif and becomes known as Electro. The same month he was introduced, however, Marvel Comics also featured a character called Electro (The Marvel of the Age) in *Marvel Mystery Comics*. With the second issue, Electro was renamed Dynamo. Dynamo also appeared in *Weird Comics* and *Blue Beetle* and was drawn initially by H. Webber and then by Ramona Patenaude. The Eagle also made his debut here in a story drawn by Louis Cazeneuve.

SCOOP COMICS

Harry 'A' Chesler
Published 11/41–3/42 **Issue #s** 1–3
Major Characters
The Master Key 1–3
Rocketman and Rocketgirl 1–3

Ray Cardell, a "cafe society playboy," is a millionaire. After a laboratory accident involving "ultra-shortwaves" gives him X-ray vision, Cardell decides to use his all-seeing eyeballs to go on a crime-smashing spree as the Master Key. Nattily dressed in white dinner jacket, tux pants, cummerbund, and a snap-lid white fedora, the Master Key spends a good part of his time saving Elaine, his socialite girlfriend.

Cal Martin and his fiancee Doris Dalton are secretly Rocketman and Rocketgirl. They have the power to fly through the air thanks to Cal's invention: a three-cartridge rocket pack. The two wear identical costumes, with a skintight hood and a smoking rocket pack mounted about six inches below their brains. In issue #2, they acquire a sidekick named Rocket Boy (Billy Wood).

SENSATION COMICS

DC Comics
Published 1/42–11/51 **Issue #s** 1–106
Major Characters
Wonder Woman 1–106
Mr. Terrific 1–63
Wildcat 1–90
Little Boy Blue 1–34, 37–82

The Whip 43
The Atom 86

Sensation Comics is best known as the home of Wonder Woman. H. G. Peter drew the Amazon Princess, except for a few issues (#s 17–19, 21) by illustrator Frank Goodwin.

Wildcat, the second-longest-running feature in *Sensation*, was created by writer Bill Finger and artist Irwin Hasen. Ted Grant, world heavyweight champion, becomes a feline-costumed crime fighter known as Wildcat after he is framed in a crooked fight. Accompanied by his manager and sidekick Stretch Skinner, the Wildcat relies on his natural pugilistic talents to take on criminals.

Terry Sloane, a child prodigy and millionaire by the time he is twenty-one, is bored with life to the point of being suicidal. He finds a reason to live, however, when he discovers the thrill of fighting crime. As he beats up a gang of thugs, he is greeted by cries of "Terrific!" from his admirers. Sloane, or "The Amazing Man of a Thousand Talents" as he is known, decides to adopt the name Mr. Terrific and a costume to fight crime undercover. He uses his wealth to establish the "Fair Play Club" to promote justice.

Tommy, the young son of District Attorney Dan Rogers, begins a career as a boy superhero when he overhears the trouble his father is having with criminals. With his friends Tubby and Toughy, Tommy raids the attic and they put together matching blue costumes. They form a kid gang known as Little Boy Blue and the Blue Boys and they come together to battle crime whenever Tommy blows on his bugle.

SHADOW COMICS

Street and Smith
Published 3/40–8/49 **Issue #s** 1–101
Major Characters
The Shadow 1–101
Doc Savage 1–3, 34–52, 54–69, 73–87, 89–93, 95–101
The Hooded Wasp 7–14, 16, 18–21, 23–32
Supersnipe 15, 22
The Shadow, Jr. 69, 74, 77

The *Shadow* comic book, based on the popular radio show and pulp magazine character, fashioned the black-cloaked hero for a young audience. In the comics, the Shadow made good use of his powers of "invisibility" and was even aided for a short time by a young sidekick known as Shadow, Jr. (December 1946).

The Doc Savage feature in *Shadow Comics* began two months before the Man of Bronze received his own comic book. The series was suspended while *Doc Savage Comics* was published and then resumed (January 1944) after Doc's comic was canceled.

The Hooded Wasp (November 1940), decked out in colorful boots, cape, and bodysuit with a little wasp insignia on his chest, was one of Street and Smith's most popular original superheroes. He was later joined by a teenage sidekick ignominiously named the "Wasplet" (July 1943). Jack Binder and his studio usually handled the artwork. Ed Gruskin, who scripted the Supersnipe and Doc Savage features for Street and Smith, also wrote the Wasp's adventures.

SHIELD-WIZARD COMICS

MLJ/Archie Comics
Published Summer/40–Spring/44   **Issue #s** 1–13
Major Characters
The Shield 1–13
Wizard 1–13
Dusty, the Boy Detective 5–12
Roy, the Super Boy 8, 10–13

The Shield and the Wizard were MLJ's two most promising superheroes in early 1940 and this title was a second place to showcase their talents. Although the two heroes were first featured together as a team in *Top Notch Comics,* they appeared solo in this new title. The Wizard was quickly eclipsed by other rising MLJ heroes, like the Black Hood and the Hangman, and the Shield remained the lead feature in *Shield-Wizard Comics.* The Shield was usually drawn by Irv Novick, while Edd Ashe initiated the art chores on the Wizard.

SILVER STREAK COMICS

Lev Gleason Publications
Published 12/39–5/42   **Issue #s** 1–21
Major Characters
The Claw 1, 2, 6–11
Silver Streak 3–19
Daredevil 6–17
Captain Battle 10–21

Silver Streak Comics is best remembered as the home of both the villainous Claw and the spike-belted hero, Daredevil. The two engaged in a battle royal over a half dozen issues until Daredevil finally bested the Oriental henchman and then went on to star in his own comic book.

Silver Streak (March 1940) was the title character. Due to a "secret fluid" in his blood which made him immune to the forces of gravity, this costumed hero could run at super-speed and also fly. He appeared right on the heels, so to speak, of the Flash, another super-fast character. The super-speedster also gives some of his "secret fluid" to a youngster named Mickey O'Toole who also gains the powers of super-speed (June 1941). Mickey first calls himself "Mercury" but then changes his name to "Meteor." The Silver Streak is also assisted by a fast-flying falcon named "Whiz," who got his super-speed from a blood transfusion given to him by his master (more of that "secret fluid" being passed

around). Silver Streak was originally drawn by Jack Cole and later by Don Rico.

Captain Battle (May 1941), a wounded World War I veteran, devotes his life to putting an end to the horrors of war. In his mountaintop laboratory, Battle invents such weapons as a "dissolvo-gun," which melts bone and tissue to a "gelatinous mass," a "luceflyer" jet pack, and a "curvoscope," which allows him to spy anywhere on Earth. He is assisted by his secretary Jane Lorrain and gains a junior sidekick, Hale Battle (July 1941).

SKYMAN, THE

Columbia Comics Group
Published 1941–1948   **Issue #s** 1–4
Major Characters
Skyman 1–4
The Face 1

Allen Turner is raised by his uncle after his parents die in an airplane crash. The boy grows up to be an outstanding athlete and scientist. He makes a vow to use his physical and mental abilities (as well as his inherited fortune) to fight crime from the skies as the Skyman. Turner builds a huge boomerang-shaped airplane called the Wing, which flies by using the power of the north and south magnetic fields. The red-white-and-blue aircraft (based on Northrop's experimental N-1-M plane known as the Flying Wing) can attain speeds of 800 miles per hour and also hover stationary so Skyman can descend to Earth on a cable rope.

Skyman, who made his debut in *Big Shot Comics,* was one of the more dashing costumed aviators. He was often in the company of his beautiful girlfriend, Fawn Carroll. Ogden Whitney, who worked with Columbia Comics editor Vince Sullivan at DC Comics in 1939 on such features as "Carver Carson" and the "Sandman," drew nearly all the Skyman stories (including those in *Big Shot Comics*) until he entered the service in 1943. He resumed drawing Skyman in 1946 after his discharge. Mart Bailey filled in during Whitney's absence, with Collie Stern also handling some stories. Writers included Gardner Fox (who wrote the first twenty-four Skyman stories), Ray Krank, and Whitney himself during his second term on the feature.

SMASH COMICS

Quality Comics Group
Published 8/39–10/49   **Issue #s** 1–85
Major Characters
Invisible Hood 1–32
Magno 13–21
The Ray 14–40
Midnight 18–85
The Jester 22–85
Wildfire 25–37
Lady Luck 42–85

The Skyman #3 © 1948 Columbia Comic Corporation. Ogden Whitney.

Smash Comics #29
© 1941 Comic Magazines,
Inc. Gill Fox.

Sparkler Comics #4 © 1941
United Features Syndicate

Smash Comics, the second title from Quality Comics, featured several minor and well-done superhero series. The first costumed character was the Invisible Hood (secretly Kent Thurston), who dons a chemically treated, brown-hooded robe in order to disappear from evildoers. Paul Gustavson wrote and drew the adventures of both Magno, a living electromagnet, and the Jester, a rookie cop who fights crime in a clown suit. Jim Mooney, who drew superheroes like Lash Lightning and the Flag for Ace Publications, was the artist for Wildfire, a heroine who controls fire and flame. The flaming redhead (secretly Carol Vance Martin) dressed in scarlet hotpants and jogging bra and received her powers from the god of fire.

The most popular hero in *Smash Comics* was Midnight, a masked detective in the tradition of the Spirit. Written and illustrated primarily by Jack Cole, the tongue-in-cheek series also enjoyed the artwork of Reed Crandall and Paul Gustavson.

The best-drawn hero in *Smash Comics,* however, was the Ray, drawn by Lou Fine and ably continued by Reed Crandall. Reporter Happy Terrill is exposed to intense solar radiation when he enters the upper stratosphere in a runaway hot air balloon. Afterwards, radiance of any kind triggers his transformation into a sunburst-colored hero called the Ray, who can fly on light rays, control magnetic rays, and turn into a ray of pure energy. The more light he receives, the stronger he becomes.

The Lady Luck feature from the *Spirit* newspaper comic section was reprinted in *Smash Comics* and the popular female crime fighter took over the title as her own with issue #86.

SPARKLER COMICS

United Features Syndicate
Published 7/41–7/46   **Issue #s** 1–57
Major Characters
Spark Man 1–45, 47, 50–57

"The Spark Man, master of a terrifying electrical power, moves in the shadows of the night in defense of the weak—who is he? Have you guessed? Is he Quill Davis, whose newspaper stories defend the Spark Man? Is he Val Hall, millionaire sportsman, and friend of the oppressed? Is he Omar Kavak, famous violinist, whose music thrills thousands?"

For the first nine issues, writer Fred Methot and artist Reg Greenwood coyly kept the secret identity of their latest superhero, the Spark Man, from the readers. The cleverly plotted stories had all three men as likely possibilities. The character came about when our man of mystery learns how to supercharge his body with static electricity and then discharge a powerful spark through the index finger of a specially designed glove. A regular sort of superhero who foils arsonists and jewel thieves, the Spark Man joins the army in November 1942 and discards his superhero costume for a GI uniform. He also loses his electrical zapping powers. Discharged from the

army in September 1945, the Spark Man again puts on a costume but remains a non-super-powered crime fighter until his end in 1946.

And, by the way, Spark Man was secretly Omar Kavak—the world's first classical violinist superhero.

SPECIAL COMICS

MLJ/Archie Comics
Published Winter/41   **Issue #s** 1
Major Characters
Boy Buddies 1
Comet 1
The Hangman 1

Published as a showcase title for the Hangman, *Special Comics* also featured the last appearance of the Comet. The Boy Buddies also made their first appearance as a team in this issue. The "buddies" were MLJ's two juvenile superhero sidekicks: Dusty the Boy Detective (from the Shield series) and Roy the Super Boy (from the Wizard series). The two teens were MLJ's answer to DC Comics's *Boy Commandos* and Marvel Comics's *Young Allies.* With the second issue, the title officially became *Hangman Comics.*

SPECIAL EDITION COMICS

Fawcett Publications
Published 8/40   **Issue #s** 1
Major Characters
Captain Marvel 1

Appearing before the first issue of *Captain Marvel Adventures,* this issue with four Captain Marvel stories was an experiment to test the drawing power of a Captain Marvel comic book.

SPEED COMICS

Brookwood/Speed/Harvey Publications
Published 10/39–1/47   **Issue #s** 1–44
Major Characters
Shock Gibson 1–44
Captain Freedom 13–44
The Black Cat 17–38, 44

Speed Comics featured one of the earliest superheroes to gain his powers from electricity. Scientist Charles Gibson becomes the supercharged human dynamo Shock Gibson when lightning strikes his laboratory. Shock learns to "humanize" and use electricity to fight "crime in its degenerate forms."

When the comic was taken over by Alfred Harvey (September 1941), Shock underwent a costume and name change (to Robert) and also became a "millionaire research scientist." When war breaks out, Shock enlists as an Army private to electrify the Japanese. Indeed, his name alone causes trouble for his Oriental opponents ("Aha so! *Thock Gibson!* Now you die so horribly!"). Artists included

Al Avison, Al Byrant, Arturo Cazeneuve, Joe Kubert, and Bob Powell.

Don Wright, "famed newspaper publisher," becomes Captain Freedom, a costumed defender of the poor and oppressed. He befriends three young boys—Slim, Lefty, and Whitey—who form a club to help the Captain, called the Young Defenders. Joanie, a tagalong girl, is allowed to join the group and quickly proves her worth with some well-placed kicks and punches. Beanie, a bald-headed urchin with a slingshot, replaced Whitey in later issues. With America's entry into war, Captain Freedom and the Young Defenders became the first line of defense on the home front. The Captain's adventures were usually drawn by Pierce Rice and later by Al Avison.

Note: Issue #s 14–16 are the same small size (5" by 7") as Harvey's Pocket Comics and also contain 100 pages.

SPIRIT, THE (1)

Vital Publications/Quality Comics
Published 1944–8/50   **Issue #s** 1–22
Major Characters
The Spirit 1–22

Will Eisner's *The Spirit,* which made its debut as the lead feature in a 1940 Sunday comic section supplement, was reprinted in *Police Comics* by publisher Everett "Busy" Arnold who helped launch the Spirit as a newspaper feature. The weekly Sunday Spirit stories (which ran seven pages) were also reprinted in a comic book. The first three issues (which were unnumbered) were published by Vital Publications. "Busy" Arnold published the remaining issues. Six Spirit stories appeared in #s 1–3, five stories in #s 4–14, and three stories in the remaining issues.

SPIRIT, THE (2)

Fiction House
Published Spring/52–1954   **Issue #s** 1–5
Major Characters
The Spirit 1–5

After Quality Comics ceased publication of *The Spirit,* Will Eisner negotiated with Fiction House to continue reprinting the stories from the Sunday Spirit newspaper sections in comic book format. Four stories (seven pages long) appeared in each issue.

SPITFIRE COMICS

Harvey Publications
Published 8/41–10/41   **Issue #s** 1, 2
Major Characters
The Fly-Man 1, 2
The Clown 1, 2

Clip Foster, a heavyweight boxer, is shrunk to the size of a fly by his inventor father as an experiment.

Before his father can reverse the shrinking process, gangsters enter the lab and kill the inventor. They also knock over acid, which burns away most of Clip's face and hair. Disfigured and unable to return to normal size, the fly-sized man makes a vow to avenge his father's death and creates a costume to hide his injuries. He devises a pair of orange wings for flight and so becomes the Fly-Man. His rope weapon allows the miniature man to rappel down walls, hurl objects like a slingshot, and strangle king-sized enemies. Sam Glanzman created the Fly-Man, his first published work for the comics. He recalled that it was "written, penciled, inked, lettered, and colored by myself. I used the pen name Sam Glanz. There *seemed* to be a great deal of prejudice against anyone with a Jewish name at the time."

Also appearing in this 100-page, pocket-sized comic book was a whimsical costumed hero called the Clown. Ed Winiarski drew the adventures of this big-top character who hid his secret identity of Nick Nolan behind grease paint and a red rubber nose.

SPOTLIGHT COMICS

Harry 'A' Chesler
Published 11/44–3/45   **Issue #s** 1–3
Major Characters
Black Dwarf 1–3
Veiled Avenger 1–3

Shorty Wilson, a wealthy sportsman and former All-American football player, dresses up in a ground-sweeping black robe and a pulled-down slouch hat to become the Black Dwarf. His secret headquarters, a dingy walk-up apartment, is on the wrong side of the tracks. There he is joined by his squad of ex-crooks: Nitro, a famous safe cracker; Human Fly, an escape artist, and Arsenic, a beautiful but deadly gun moll ("She makes a specialty of *lead poisoning*!"). The Black Dwarf and his questionable cohorts live in a dark and violent world where fist and gun replace rule and reason. Everyone, including Shorty, operates outside the law: "You can't play blind man's bluff when your shoes squeak, chum! Take a bite of knuckle pie!" The Black Dwarf (usually drawn by Paul Gattuso) also appeared in *Red Seal Comics.*

Joining the Black Dwarf in *Spotlight Comics* was another shadowy hero. Ginny Spears disguised her features and became the not-too-ladylike Veiled Avenger. Ginny continued her thinly veiled, man-kicking adventures in *Red Seal Comics.*

SPY SMASHER

Fawcett Publications
Published Fall/41–2/43   **Issue #s** 1–11
Major Characters
Spy Smasher 1–11

After his debut in *Whiz Comics,* Fawcett's fighting aviator received his own comic book with four stories in each issue. Otto Binder wrote many of

*Speed Comics #1 © 1939
Brookwood Publications*

*Spitfire Comics #2 © 1941
Harvey Features Syndicate.*

*Star Spangled Comics #35
© 1944 DC Comics, Inc.
Joe Simon and Jack Kirby.*

*Startling Comics #10
© 1941 Better Publications,
Inc. Ed Wexler.*

the stories in this series, which ended before the war.

STAR SPANGLED COMICS

DC Comics
Published 10/41–7/52 **Issue #s** 1–130
Major Characters
The Star Spangled Kid and Stripesy 1–86
Tarantula 1–19
The Guardian and the Newsboy Legion 7–64
  (No Guardian #58, 64)
Robotman 7–82
TNT 7–23
Liberty Belle 20–68
Robin, the Boy Wonder 65–130
Merry The Gimmick Girl 81–90

The Star Spangled Kid reversed a comic book tradition by becoming the first young hero to have an *adult* sidekick. Sylvester Pemberton, boy millionaire, breaks up a Nazi demonstration with the help of ex-boxer Pat Dugan. The boy and boxer become a costumed duo to continue fighting Nazi covert activity. Sylvester dresses up as the Star Spangled Kid and Dugan (who also serves as the kid's chauffeur) dons a red-and-white-striped shirt to become Stripesy. Artist Hal Sherman recalled that "Jerry Siegel had written the Star Spangled Kid and they wanted me to illustrate it. So I went back and created the logo and the characters. And I suggested things to Siegel. About the car, for instance, to make it also a submarine, airplane, and so on. Actually, the car was years ahead of the James Bond series." In the June 1948 issue, writer Otto Binder introduced Mary Pemberton, the sister of the Star Spangled Kid, as a costumed heroine known as "Merry, Girl of 1000 Gimmicks."

Joe Simon and Jack Kirby continued their "boy gang" theme with the Newsboy Legion, a group of crime-fighting kids (Tommy, Scraper, Gabby, and Bigwords) who were assisted by police officer Jim Harper disguised as the costumed Guardian.

Robotman, a mechanical man with a human brain who disguises his features with a sheath of human skin, was originally developed by Jerry Siegel and Joe Shuster. Artist Jimmy Thompson drew the majority of the stories of this unusual hero and his mechanical dog sidekick, Robbie.

Mort Weisinger wrote two features for *Star Spangled*: The Tarantula (loosely based on the Spider hero pulps) and TNT ("the human hand grenade") and his sidekick, Dan the Dyna-Mite.

STARS AND STRIPES COMICS

Centaur Publications
Published 5/41–12/41 **Issue #s** 2–6 (No #1)
Major Characters
Amazing Man 2–6
The Iron Skull 2–6

Mighty Man 2–6
Minimidget 2–6
Shark 2–6
The Stars and Stripes 4–6

Centaur decided to send its superheroes from *Amazing Man Comics* to war with this new title. To further hype the comic's patriotic appeal, a trio of American servicemen (Pepper, Van, and Whitey) appear as the "Stars and Stripes." This gung-ho, Axis-fighting team, dressed in complementary flag-colored tops and matching brown prison trousers, got its start when all three escaped from a German concentration camp. Pepper, Van, and Whitey sign an oath in blood to protect America from her enemies.

STARTLING COMICS

Better/Standard Publications
Published 6/40–9/48 **Issue #s** 1–53
Major Characters
Captain Future 1–40
The Fighting Yank 10–49
The Four Comrades 16–31, 33, 34, 36
Pyroman 18–26, 28–43
The Scarab 34

Publisher Ned Pines named this comic after his science fiction magazine *Startling Stories*. He even named the hero of the first issue, Captain Future, after the successful pulp magazine hero created by Edmond Hamilton and Mort Weisinger. Dr. Andrew Bryant, an engineer, places himself in the crisscross path of a gamma ray and an infra-red ray. The meek engineer gets a shot of machismo from the rays, gains the ability to fly and hurl energy bolts, and assumes a new identity—Captain Future.

Another scientist-engineer in *Startling Comics* who turned superhero was Dick Martin—better known as Pyroman. Dick, an electrical engineering student at Central Technical School, becomes innocently mixed up in an arson fire. Dick is arrested instead of the arsonist and sentenced to die in the electric chair. When the electrical charge surges through his body, he becomes a super-charged dynamo instead of fried meat. He bursts through the walls of prison and hides his identity with an old masquerade costume. With his electrically charged body, he can surround himself with a force field and shoot bolts of fiery energy from his hands.

During the early war years, Better Publications introduced a kid gang called The Four Comrades (August 1942) drawn by Maurice Gutwirth. The four costumed adolescents (Pudge, Buzz, Tip, and Tommy) wore identical uniforms of red shorts, red gloves, high-top boots, and blue polo shirts with star-spangled lapels.

STUNTMAN COMICS

Harvey Publications
Published 4/46–6/46   **Issue #s** 1–2
Major Characters
Stuntman 1, 2

The three Flying Apollos, a circus acrobat team, are reduced to one member when two partners are killed in a trapeze accident. Fred Drake, the last of the Flying Apollos, suspects foul play and decides to use his acrobat costume as an undercover disguise to find the murderer. While tracking the killer, Drake runs into movie star Don Daring and the two men are amazed to see they look almost exactly alike. Daring offers Drake a job as his movie double and stuntman—someone who can substitute for him in the action scenes. Drake becomes the Stuntman and, after capturing his partners' murderer, decides to continue his crime-fighting career. As the Stuntman, he is assisted by Daring and actress Sandra Sylvan.

Joe Simon and Jack Kirby, fresh out of the service after the end of the war, created Stuntman, along with the *Boy Explorers,* for Harvey Comics. The first five issues of the book were planned so that Stuntboy and Stuntgirl could be introduced in the third issue. The title, however, was canceled after two issues. Simon, who was responsible for starting up a line of new characters and titles for Harvey Comics, recalled he and Kirby often felt that this was some of their best work. Stuntman also appeared in *All-New Comics, Black Cat Comics,* and *Green Hornet Comics.*

SUB-MARINER

Marvel Comics
Published Spring/41–6/49   **Issue #s** 1–32
Major Characters
Sub-Mariner 1–32
The Angel 1–21
Young Allies 22
The Human Torch 23, 29
The Blonde Phantom 25–28, 30
Namora 23–30
Captain America 31

After a series in *Marvel Mystery Comics* and the *Human Torch,* the Sub-Mariner received his own magazine at about the same time that Captain America first appeared in his title.

The Angel, who shared *Marvel Mystery Comics* with the Human Torch and the Sub-Mariner, got second billing in this title until he was dropped in late 1946 from all the Marvel comics. The Blonde Phantom replaced the Angel as the primary backup feature. Sub-Mariner's aquatic cousin, Namora the Sea Beauty, became a major supporting character beginning in 1948.

The origin of the Sub-Mariner was retold in issue #32, which marked his last 1940s appearance. With

issue #33, the comic book was retitled *Best Love.*

SUN GIRL

Marvel Comics
Published 8/48–12/48   **Issue #s** 1–3
Major Characters
Sun Girl 1–3
Miss America 1
The Blonde Phantom 2, 3

A tide of femininity was sweeping through Marvel Comics in 1948. In August alone three "beautiful" heroines received their own comic books: Venus (The Most Beautiful Girl in the World), Namora (The Sea Beauty), and Sun Girl (The Mysterious Beauty).

Sun Girl made her debut the same month that the Human Torch's sidekick, Toro, made his last 1940s appearance in *All Winners Comics.* By the next month, the blue-eyed blonde was fighting side by side with the Man of Flame. Sun Girl, a judo expert and accomplished acrobat, used a sunbeam ray to confuse and blind crooks. More often, Sun Girl used her sunbeam weapon for dramatic lighting effects than mayhem. The Mysterious Beauty (her identity was never revealed) also appeared with the Human Torch (and occasionally went solo) in *Captain America, Human Torch, Marvel Mystery Comics,* and finally, in a two-page story in *Marvel Tales* (September 1950).

SUPER MAGICIAN COMICS

Street and Smith
Published 9/41–2/47   **Issue #s** 2–56
Major Characters
Supersnipe 11
The Shadow 13
Tigerman 17–21
Red Dragon 20–56
Mr. Twilight 29

Blackstone the Magician headed up this anthology of magic, adventure, and costumed hero stories. The Red Dragon, who made his debut in his own comic book, had a three-year series, with art by Charles Coll, Louis Gulick, John Meditz, and Edd Cartier. A short series starring Professor Greg Lee as Tigerman, was drawn primarily by John Meditz.

SUPER-MYSTERY COMICS

Ace Magazines
Published 7/40–4/46   **Issue #s** 1–33
Major Characters
Magno and Davey 1–33
Vulcan 1–14
Black Spider 3–12
Dr. Nemesis 15, 16, 18, 19
The Sword 15–27

Sub-Mariner #3 © 1941 Marvel Entertainment Group, Inc. Alex Schomburg.

Super Mystery Comics Vol. VI #2 © 1946 Ace Magazines, Inc. Rudy Palais.

Superman #13 © 1941 DC Comics, Inc. Joe Shuster.

Supersnipe Comics Vol. 4 #7 © 1948 Street & Smith Publications, Inc.

Ace Magazines's most enduring superhero, Magno the Magnetic Man, was the star of *Super-Mystery Comics.* He was joined by his sidekick Davy in the fourth issue and they shared the title with several other costumed heroes.

Vulcan, a descendant of the Roman god of fire, was born in the warm South Seas Islands. He has control over fire and flame and can fly through the air—somewhat similar to the Human Torch. The art was usually by Maurice Gutwirth or Jack Alderman. Otto Binder contributed several scripts as well.

The Black Spider was District Attorney Ralph Nelson. When criminals go free because of insufficient evidence, Nelson puts on his disguise of terror and hits the streets. Only his loyal secretary Peggy Dodge knows that her boss is a masked vigilante who takes the law into his own hands.

The Sword first appeared in *Captain Courageous Comics* and then in *Lightning Comics* before settling down for a two-year run in this title. Arthur Lake is a weak and frail lad whose father is an airplane manufacturer. On a trip to England, the young man discovers the Lost Tomb of King Arthur and the legendary sword, Excalibur. Whenever he draws Excalibur from the stone, he gains the "strength of many times ten" men. As the Sword, he prevents foreign spies from stealing his dad's aircraft plans. In issue #15, he gains a sidekick, Lance Larter, who becomes the Lance whenever Lake pulls out Excalibur and turns into the Sword.

SUPERBOY

DC Comics
Published 3/49–1/55   **Issue #s** 1–38
Major Characters
Superboy 1–38

After his debut in *More Fun Comics,* Superboy became the last major superhero of the Golden Age to receive his own magazine. In addition to three or more stories in each issue, Superboy appeared regularly in *Adventure Comics.*

SUPERMAN

DC Comics
Published Summer/39–2/55   **Issue #s** 1–95
Major Characters
Superman 1–95
Batman 76

After his debut in *Action Comics,* Superman became the first superhero to receive his own magazine. Originally a quarterly publication (the first three issues featured reprints from *Action Comics* and the daily newspaper strip), the comic book became a successful bimonthly by its sixth issue. Averaging sales of more than a million copies each issue during the war years, *Superman Comics* became the best known comic book of the 1940s.

Collectors take note of the May 1952 issue, in which Superman and Batman learn each other's secret identities and experience that special superhero bonding.

SUPERSNIPE COMICS

Street and Smith
Published 10/42–8/49   **Issue #s** 6–49 (No 1–5)
Major Characters
Supersnipe 6–49

After his debut in *Shadow Comics,* ten-year-old Koppy McFad ("the boy with the most comic books in America") received his own comic book as the costumed hero, Supersnipe. Writer Ed Gruskin recalled that the "original concept of Supersnipe was that of artist George Marcoux." While watching a parade, Marcoux dodged a young boy on a speeding bicycle who wore a homemade superhero cape. Instead of a guttersnipe, Marcoux called the rude-costumed urchin a "Supersnipe," and the idea for a young boy superhero was born. Gruskin remembered that editor Bill deGrouchy "saw great potentialities" for the character and discussed just what kind of boy Supersnipe was with Marcoux.

Gruskin, who was called in to write the scripts after Supersnipe was created, summarized the boy hero: "He was highly imaginative, an average student in school when he applied himself, a leader among kids his own age, a fair athlete able to absorb terrfic punishment, a faddist (a follower of the kid fads of the day), and finally he was an avid reader of comic books and student of the super-qualities and super-techniques of the comic book heroes."

Koppy dresses up as a comic book hero by borrowing his father's lodge uniform and his grandfather's flannel underwear. Although the only super-power he possesses as Supersnipe is the ability to fly when he fills his uniform with helium, the boy uses his ingenuity, bravery, and knowledge of comic books to overcome adversity. While Supersnipe was a gentle parody of the superheroes, his alter ego Koppy McFad was a highly likable and credible character. After all, when it came to comic books, he was the hero who "reads 'em, breathes 'em, and sleeps 'em!"

SURE-FIRE COMICS

Ace Magazines
Published 6/40–10/40   **Issue #s** 1–4 (Two #3s)
Major Characters
Flash Lightning 1–4
Raven 1–4

Ace Magazines, a publisher of popular fiction magazines, entered the comic book field with this anthology title of superheroes, magicians, and aviators. Its first costumed hero, Flash Lightning, received his powers of lightning speed, flight, and the ability to hurl lightning bolts from "an Egyptian mystic known only as the Old Man of the Pyramids." Flash was drawn by Herbert "Red" Holmdale of the Jack Binder shop, who also had a hand in drawing the adventures of *Sure-Fire*'s other costumed character, the Raven.

The Raven was Detective Sergeant Danny Dartkin, who sported a dark-purple costume in order to fight crime outside the law: "The mysterious Raven goes forth to rob denizens of the underworld and turns his loot over to the unfortunates of the city." The Raven, who often ran afoul of the law in his "Robin Hood" mission, was often helped out of a jam by the police chief's daughter Lola Lash, who knew his secret identity.

TARGET COMICS

Novelty Publications
Published 2/40–8/49   Issue #s 1–105
Major Characters
White Streak 1–22
Target 10–84, 86–95, 98, 103

When the publishers of the *Saturday Evening Post* and *Ladies Home Journal* decided to get into the comic book business, they used the services of the Funnies, Incorporated, comic book studio to put together their first title—*Target Comics*. Carl Burgos, who created the Human Torch for Marvel Comics a few months earlier, drew *Target*'s first superhero feature, the White Streak. Like the Human Torch, the White Streak was an android who was programmed to help mankind in desperate times of war. Invented by an ancient South American civilization, the android (dubbed "Manowar") lays inactive for hundreds of years until awakened by World War II German bombers. The White Streak can shoot "knife–like electrons" from its eye slits. The antiwar android assumes a human identity—Dan Sanders—and joins the FBI to fight America's enemies.

The second superhero in *Target* borrowed the title for his namesake. Niles Reed, a military spy, is also a metallurgist. After his brother is slain by gangsters, Reed makes an indestructable metallic fiber suit. Dressed in a bullet-proof costume, he exhibits a wry sense of humor by sporting a red, white, and blue bull's-eye target on his chest. Calling himself the Target, Reed avenges his brother's death and then assists the military on the home front. In his second adventure, he is blessed with not one but *two* young sidekicks: Dave and Tommy Reed, dubbed the Targeteers, who provided enough horseplay and wisecracks to stretch the feature until the end of the decade. Early artists included Sid Greene, Bob Wood, and John Jordon.

TERRIFIC COMICS

Continental/Holyoke
Published 1/44–11/44   Issue #s 1–6

Major Characters
The Boomerang 2–5
The Reckoner 5, 6

Lloyd Raleigh decides to fight crime undercover in the disguise of the Boomerang. By his second adventure, Lloyd is joined by his girlfriend Diana, who gets her own costume. The feature was originally drawn by L.B. Cole and later by Manny Stallman. The Reckoner, who made his debut in *Cat-Man Comics,* was secretly Matty Martin. After dressing in evening clothes, top hat, cloak, and black mask, Matty dispenses his own brand of justice. Artists on the feature included Don Rico and Bob Fujitani.

THRILLING COMICS

Better/Standard Publications
Published 2/40–4/51   Issue #s 1–80
Major Characters
Doc Strange 1–64
Woman in Red 2–18, 20–22, 24–30, 34, 35, 38, 46
American Crusader 19–35, 37–39, 41

The first successful comic book ("A Thrill on Every Page!") published by Ned Pines was named after his popular science fiction magazine *Thrilling Wonder Stories.* Dr. Hugo Strange performs an experiment that distills the atoms of the sun into a potent elixir he dubs "Alosun." When he takes a swig of Alosun, he temporarily gains super-strength and can leap through the air. Doc Strange wears a red muscle shirt, blue riding pants, and brown boots. His boy assistant, named simply Mike (beginning in #24), was too young to drink Alosun but still wore a tasteful green cape. The solar-powered hero also appeared in *America's Best Comics.* Early stories were written by Richard Hughes and drawn by Alex Koster. Otto Binder also wrote early scripts; other artists included Ken Platt, George Mandel, and Jack Binder.

The Woman in Red was one of the first female costumed crime fighters. Although possessing no super-powers, police investigator Peggy Allen fought criminals in a scalp-to-toe, red cowl and dress. In issue #34, the Woman in Red shortened her skirt, abbreviated her mask, and added a flashy cape.

The American Crusader, drawn by Max Plaisted, was originally physics professor Archibald Masters. Masters's experiment on an atom smasher backfires and alters his atomic structure so that he has unlimited powers. This early atomic-powered superhero gained a young partner in issue #21 named Mike. Making his debut in the August 1941 issue (four years before the atomic bomb), the American Crusader may be the first radioactivity-created superhero.

Target Comics #4 © 1940 Novelty Publications

Thrilling Comics #46 © 1945 Better Publications, Inc. Alex Schomburg.

*Top-Notch Comics #8
© 1940 Archie Comic
Publications, Inc.*

TIP TOP COMICS

United Feature Syndicate
Published 10/40–6/46 **Issue #s** 54–119
Major Characters
Mirror Man 54–99
Triple Terror 54–119

Beginning in April 1936 as a reprint anthology of the most popular Sunday strips distributed by the United Feature Syndicate, *Tip Top Comics*'s major stars were Tarzan, Li'l Abner, Captain and the Kids, and Fritzi Ritz. By 1940, however, it was obvious that superheroes were the most popular characters in the comic book marketplace. *Tip Top* added two original features drawn especially for the comic book: Mirror Man and Triple Terror.

Dean Alder, the headmaster of a prep school, discovers a magical garment which gives him the powers to dematerialize whenever he "walks" through a mirror. In his mirror-shadow state, Dean has super strength and cannot be harmed. To return to his normal state, he has to walk through the same mirror *backwards*. Mirror Man was created by writer Fred Methot and artist Reginald Greenwood.

Greenwood and Methot also related the adventures of Triple Terror, a team of three brothers who wear identical costumes. Richard, a master of electronics, takes the name of Lectra; Barton, an expert in chemicals, calls himself Chemix; while brother Bruce, who is modestly described as the "mental master of men," becomes known as Menta.

After Mirror Man and Triple Terror vanished, the comic book again subsisted on Sunday strip reprints.

TNT COMICS

Charles Publishing Company
Published 2/46 **Issue #s** 1
Major Characters
Yellowjacket 1

The Yellowjacket, who made his debut in his own title, made an appearance in this one-shot comic book, which also featured such likely characters as Beau Brummel and the Schnook.

TOP-NOTCH COMICS

MLJ/Archie Comics
Published 12/39–4/44 **Issue #s** 1–44
Major Characters
The Wizard 1–27
Bob Phantom 3–25
The Shield 7
The Firefly 8–27
The Black Hood 9–44

Blaine Whitney is the Wizard—"The Man with the Super Brain." Trained from youth to be a mental wizard, Blaine possesses a photographic memory and "supersensory perception," which allow him to tune in to criminal activities. Originally a dapper dresser, appearing in tux, top hat, evening cape, with a red-domino mask, the Wizard didn't get around to wearing a full-fledged costume until August 1940—a costume which also gave him the added advantage of invulnerability. With the September 1940 issue, the Wizard met an orphan shoeshine boy who became his crime-fighting partner, Roy the Super Boy. The other supporting characters included their friend Jane Barlow and an overly helpful cab driver named Moe. Edd Ashe drew the Wizard's first adventures and Harry Shorten wrote the origin story. William Woolfolk also wrote scripts, while later artists included Al Camereta and Paul Reinman. The Wizard also appeared in *Shield-Wizard Comics*.

The Firefly, created by artist/writer Bob Wood, was originally biochemist Harley Hudson. Hudson discovers the secret which lets him simulate the "tremendous strength of insects." Most of his supernatural adventures were drawn by MLJ workhorse Warren "Bob" King.

The hero with the greatest staying power was the Black Hood, written by Harry Shorten and drawn by Al "Camy" Camerata. The Hood was the only superhero to survive the format change in issue #28 when the comic was retitled *Top-Notch Laugh Comics* and new features like "The 3 Monketeers" and "Señor Siesta" began.

TOUGH KID SQUAD

Marvel Comics
Published 3/42 **Issue #s** 1
Major Characters
Tough Kid Squad 1
The Human Top 1

The Tough Kid Squad was Marvel's homage to its successful *Young Allies* and DC Comics's *Boy Commandos*. Wally and Tom Danger are twins separated at birth; one is raised like a prince, the other like a pauper. Years later, the two boys meet and team up as the masked Danger Twins. Together with their friends Butch, Derrick, and Eagle, they form the Tough Kid Squad to take care of bad guys like the evil Dr. Klutch.

The Human Top first appeared in *Red Raven Comics* but didn't get around to having an origin story until nearly two years later in this—his last—appearance. Bruce Bravelle was the fastest human alive as a result of an electro-magnetic experiment. When he crosses his arms over his chest, magnetic currents cause him to spin wildly like a human top. He can whirl around so fast that nearby criminals are spun unconscious.

U.S. JONES

Fox Features Syndicate
Published 11/41–1/42 **Issue #s** 1, 2
Major Characters
U.S. Jones 1, 2
The Topper 1, 2

U.S. Jones wears a stars-and-stripes costume with the big letters "US" across his chest. He had no secret identity; people called him Jones in or out of his patriotic garb. The character originally appeared in *Wonderworld Comics* (with a different costume design) and was often drawn by the brothers Louis and Arturo Cazeneuve.

The Topper (aka Barry Graham) made his debut in *Samson Comics* and finished out his short life here.

UNCLE SAM QUARTERLY

Quality Comics Group
Published Fall/41–Fall/43 **Issue #s** 1–8
Major Characters
Uncle Sam 1–8
Black Condor 2
Neon, the Unknown 2
Quicksilver 2
Red Bee 2
The Ray 2
The Spider 2

After his debut in *National Comics,* Uncle Sam received his own magazine at about the same time all the other patriotic superheroes were coming into their own. The origin of the character was retold in the first issue. In the second issue, a half dozen other Quality Comics characters made their guest appearance in a story drawn by Lou Fine.

USA COMICS

Marvel Comics
Published 8/41–Fall/45 **Issue #s** 1–17
Major Characters
Defender 1–4
Whizzer 1, 2, 4, 6, 8–12, 14–17
Jack Frost 1–4
Mr./Major Liberty 1–4
The Vagabond 2–4
Black Widow 5
Captain America 6–17
Destroyer 6, 8–14, 16, 17

Marvel publisher Martin Goodman made this a popular stronghold for Marvel's growing line of patriotic heroes like Captain America, Major Liberty, the Defender, and the Destroyer.

The most successful character introduced in the comic was a super-speedster, the Whizzer. Al Avison and Al Gabriele drew the first adventure, which begins in an African jungle. Dr. Emil Frank's son, Bob, is dying from fever. A snake tries to attack the boy as he lies in bed, but suddenly a mongoose darts forward and kills the viper. The doctor figures that since the mongoose has such a will to fight, he will inject some of its blood into Bob to give him similar strength. It works. Bob lives, and as an extra benefit, has the super-speed of a mongoose, which makes "him faster than any human in the world!" After his dad dies, Bob makes a costume and comes to America. The character appeared thirty-eight times in the comics (drawn by Howard James, Mike Sekowsky, and George Klein) and had a series in *All Winners* and *All Select Comics.*

Jack Frost, an early Stan Lee creation drawn by Mike Sekowsky, had frigid-blue skin and wore blue bathing trunks. The super-cold hero hailed from the Arctic Circle. Frost has the powers to radiate cold, create icicle weapons, and ride on north winds. The character is slightly similar to Dr. Frost, who appeared the previous year in *Prize Comics.*

Major Liberty, drawn by Syd Shores, was American history teacher John Liberty. Visited by the ghost of Paul Revere, Liberty is empowered with the strength of the heroes of the Revolutionary War so he may defeat World War II enemy agents.

V • • • — COMICS

Fox Features Syndicate
Published 1/42–3/42 **Issue #s** 1, 2
Major Characters
V-Man 1, 2
Black Fury 1, 2
Banshee 1, 2

This unusally named comic (containing three dots and a dash for the Morse code equivalent of "V") stood for Victory (as in USA over the Axis) and was Victor Fox's calculated attempt to take advantage of the patriotic fervor that was sweeping through superhero comic books in late 1941.

The lead feature was a star-and-striped hero named V-Man. Although not possessing any super-powers, Jerry Steele dressed up in a red, white, and blue uniform to battle Nazi agents and also relied on his special "V-Radio Ring." A group of self-appointed partriots known as the V-Agents also appeared in both issues.

Inside the comic book, V-Man and his V-Agents exhorted readers to join the "V-Boys Defense Corps" for ten cents: "Come on boys and girls! You don't want to miss this chance to display real American-ism . . . Here's our oath: I swear by the sign of the 'V' that I will be clean, honest, truthful, ever ready to defend my country and its ideals—to work for victory—for defense—for the fullest devotion to our flag and country!"

V-Man was drawn by Ramona Patenaude in his early appearances and then by Sol Brodsky, among others, in the *Blue Beetle* comic book.

USA Comics #8 © 1943 Marvel Entertainment Group, Inc.

V • • • — Comics #1 © 1942 Fox Features Syndicate

SUPERHERO COMICS OF THE GOLDEN AGE

Weird Comics #12 © 1941
Fox Features Syndicate

Both the Black Fury and the Banshee joined V-Man in this title after making their debuts several months earlier in *Fantastic Comics*.

VARIETY COMICS

Croydan Publishing Company
Published 1944–1946   **Issue #s** 1–3
Major Characters
Captain Valiant 1–3

"Variety is the spice of comics! Each issue contains a variety of new and original features!" This anthology comic book, with a mix of sports, jungle, mystery, and teenage humor stories, had a costumed hero as its lead feature. Bruce Barton, an actor by trade, pulls on a blue hood and red jumpsuit to fight crime both around and outside the theater as Captain Valiant. Marvin Stein drew the Captain Valiant stories.

VICTORY COMICS

Hillman Periodicals
Published 8/41–12/41   **Issue #s** 1–4
Major Characters
The Conqueror 1–4
The Crusader 1–4

Victory Comics was one of the patriotic comics rushed out months before the U.S. entry into World War II. Each issue promised "10 Smashing War-Action Features," and two of these were costumed heroes.

The Conqueror, created by artist Bill Everett and written by Gilbert James, wore a mostly white costume, accented with red-and-blue stripes, and had a big gold star on his forehead (so you know he was a good guy!). He didn't have any super-powers—just a regulation army revolver strapped conspicuously on his thigh.

The comic's other costumed patriot, the Crusader (drawn by George Mandel), also knocked out Nazi teeth with religious ferocity.

WEIRD COMICS

Fox Features Syndicate
Published 4/40–1/4   **Issue #s** 21–20
Major Characters
Birdman 1–4
Sorceress of Zoom 1–20
The Dart 5–20
Dynamite Thor 6
The Eagle 7–20
Dynamo 7–19
The Black Rider 17–20

Weird Comics lived up to its name, with heroes like Sorceress of Zoom, Birdman, and Dynamite Thor, "the explosion man," who propelled himself through the air with sticks of dynamite.

The most popular hero in the magazine, however, was the Dart, who appeared on a majority of the covers. The Dart's origin (August 1940) begins two thousand years ago in Rome. Caius Martius, a gladiator who champions the cause of the oppressed, is given the ability to fly by the Roman gods. A sorcerer, however, imprisons the flying gladiator inside a block of stone and he remains there until the twentieth century. Caius awakens inside a modern museum and assumes the guise of an ordinary American with the surname of Wheeler. Caius Martius Wheeler soon discovers that corruption and evil exist in modern America just as in ancient Rome. He devises a bright yellow costume with a red arrow-dart on the chest and, armed with his gladiator sword, becomes the crime-fighting Dart. He befriends a young boy (Andy Marlow) who becomes his similarly costumed sidekick, Ace the Amazing Boy.

The Eagle, Fox's contibution to the patriotic superhero subgenre, continues his adventures here after making his debut in *Science Comics*.

WHAM COMICS

Centaur Publications
Published 11/40–12/40   **Issue #s** 1, 2
Major Characters
The Sparkler 1, 2
Speed Centaur 1
Blue Fire 2
Solarman 2

The Sparkler, secretly Red Morgan, discovers a disappearing suit which he puts to good use in an origin story written and drawn by John Kolb.

Blue Fire, originally Jack Knapp, gains the power to walk through walls, melt objects, and project heat. In his only appearance (drawn by Louis Glanzman), he uses his powers to defeat a cool character known as the Frost, who can turn men into icicles.

Frank Thomas drew the only appearance of Solarman for the last issue of *Wham Comics*. Speed Centaur, who had a series in *Amazing Mystery Funnies*, made his last appearance in *Wham Comics*.

WHIRLWIND COMICS

Nita Publications
Published 6/40–9/40   **Issue #s** 1–3
Major Characters
Cyclone 1–3

The Cyclone (aka Peter Blake) was the token costumed hero in a comic which seemed to star only double-name adventurers, like Smash Dawson, Wings Bordon, Dick Blaze, Scoop Hanlon, and Snapper Smith. The stories and art for *Whirlwind* (the only comic book from Nita Publications) was packaged by the Bert Whitman shop, which also put together *Crash Comics* and the early *Green Hornet Comics*.

WHIZ COMICS

Fawcett Publications
Published 2/40–6/53   **Issue #s** 2–155 (No 1)
Major Characters
Captain Marvel 2–155
Ibis the Invincible 2–106, 108–155
Spy Smasher 2–75
Captain Marvel, Jr. 25
Commando Yank 102
Bulletman 106

The first Fawcett comic book featured the origins of three popular heroes who eventually earned their own comic books: Captain Marvel, Spy Smasher, and Ibis the Invincible. The monthly comic book was so popular, it was published fourteen times a year in 1941 and thirteen times in 1942. For a brief time in 1946, *Whiz Comics* featured two Captain Marvel stories in each issue.

WONDER COMICS

Better/Standard Publications
Published 5/44–10/48   **Issue #s** 1–20
Major Characters
The Grim Reaper 1–17
Spectro, The Mind Reader 1–5, 7–8, 16
Brad Spencer, Wonder Man 9–20

The title for this comic came from the popular science fiction pulp magazine *Thrilling Wonder Magazine,* which was also published by Ned Pines of Better/Standard Publications. The comic began with two costumed heroes but evolved into a science fiction title.

The Grim Reaper made his debut in *Fighting Yank #7,* and his origin was revealed in *Wonder Comics #2.* Bill Norris, a master of disguise, wears a purple hood and cape with a large skull-and-crossbones. He uses his fists and an occasional pistol to whip criminals into line. When a terrified crook yells, "It's the Grim Reaper!", Norris calmly replies, "That's right! It's harvest time—and rats get ploughed under!" "POW! POW! OOOFF!" Al Camerata drew the feature.

The other costumed hero was Spectro the Mind Reader, a superhero detective who could look into the minds and souls of criminals.

Brad Spencer, Wonder Man, made his debut in a 1944 one-shot comic called the *Complete Book of Comics and Funnies* and then appeared in all four issues of *Mystery Comics* in 1944. In December 1946, Brad moved over to *Wonder Comics,* where he had science fiction adventures fighting Dr. Voodoo and Lilith, the Goddess of Evil. The early stories were drawn by Bob Oksner, whose predilection for sketching beautiful women fit in well with the girl-grabbing villains.

WONDER COMICS

Fox Features Syndicate
Published 5/39–6/39   **Issue #s** 1, 2
Major Characters
Wonder Man 1

Victor Fox, an accountant for the publishers of *Action Comics,* decided to go into the comic book business himself when he saw the profits that Superman was making. He engaged the services of the Will Eisner and Jerry Iger studio and ordered a hero with a red costume and similar powers to Superman to be called Wonder Man. Eisner wrote and drew the fourteen-page story for *Wonder Comics,* which introduced Fred Carson, a meek radio engineer for International Broadcasting, as Wonder Man—"the mightiest human on Earth." Fred obtains his "Herculean powers" from a magic ring given to him by a Tibetan yogi. As Wonder Man, he can leap over buildings, deflect bullets with his hands, and outrun a train if need be.

Wonder Man was the first character to imitate Superman and he drew the immediate attention and ire of the publishers of *Action Comics.* Fox, who was publishing *Wonder Comics* out of the same office building as the publishers of *Action Comics,* was slapped with a lawsuit which claimed Wonder Man infringed on Superman's copyright. Fox dropped the character and replaced him in the second issue with Yarko the Great ("Master of Magic"). With the third issue, Fox retitled his magazine *Wonderworld Comics* and began over again with another superhero.

WONDER WOMAN

DC Comics
Published Summer/42–2/55   **Issue #s** 1–72
Major Characters
Wonder Woman 1–72

After her debut in *All-Star Comics #8* and a successful six-month run as the lead feature in *Sensation Comics,* Wonder Woman received her own comic book. Although Sheldon Mayer was the official editor, it was William Marston, the heroine's creator, who wrote the scripts and closely supervised the artwork. Mayer's main job was keeping Marston's feminist salvos and bondage fantasies in line with what was acceptable for a children's comic book at the time.

Almost every issue had three Wonder Woman stories and a nonfiction feature called "Wonder Women of History." Written initially by Alice Marble, a world-famous tennis player and the comic's designated associate editor, the series's first installment was on Florence Nightingale. Other real-life heroines profiled in the comic book included Juliette Low, founder of the girl scouts, and Hannah Adams, America's first woman author.

After the February 1955 issue (the last issue

Wonder Comics #11
© 1947 Better Publications, Inc. Graham Ingels.

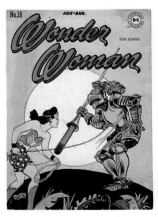

Wonder Woman #18
© 1946 DC Comics, Inc. H.G. Peter.

Wonderworld Comics #7 © 1939 Fox Features Syndicate. Lou Fine.

Wow Comics #37 © 1945 Fawcett Publications, Inc.

before the Comics Code took effect and hence the arbitrary end of the "Golden Age"), the Wonder Woman comic book was published without interruption for more than thirty more years.

WONDERWORLD COMICS

Fox Features Syndicate
Published 7/39–1/42   **Issue #s** 3–33
Major Characters
The Flame 3–33
The Black Lion 21–27
U.S. Jones 28–33

After Victor Fox's first superhero (Wonder Man) resulted in a copyright lawsuit by the publishers of Superman, he came out with a costumed hero who initially had no super-powers, called the Flame. The yellow-costumed masked man, created by the Eisner and Iger studio for *Wonderworld Comics,* was originally drawn by Lou Fine.

The Flame slowly acquired a set of super-powers as Fox's fear of another lawsuit subsided. He could first appear and disappear inside a flame and later (after the debut of Marvel's Human Torch) had the power to cover his body with flames of fire. He also got a "Flame Gun," a handy flamethrower which he used to create bridges of fire, and a fancy flame-shaped aircraft for his superhero errand-running.

Like Fox's first hero, Wonder Man, the Flame also obtained his powers from the mysterious East, when a group of lamas teach him the "greatest mystic secret . . . the power over flame." His origin was not revealed until the March 1940 issue and until late 1941, he had no secret identity. With the arrival of editor Abner Sundall from MLJ Comics, however, the Flame got an alter ego (Gary Preston) and a girlfriend, Linda Dale, who became the Flame Girl (October 1941). The Flame also appeared in his own magazine and in *Big 3 Comics.*

Another hero introduced in *Wonderworld Comics* who later received his own comic book was the patriotic U.S. Jones. The other superhero introduced in *Wonderworld Comics* was the Black Lion (secretly George Davis), whose nephew Larry serves as his costumed sidekick, Cub.

WORLD'S FINEST COMICS

DC Comics
Published Spring/41–1/55   **Issue #s** 1–74
Major Characters
Superman 1–74
Batman and Robin 1–74
Crimson Avenger 1–5
The Sandman 3–7
TNT 5
The Star Spangled Kid 6–18
Aquaman 6
Green Arrow 7–74
Boy Commandos 8–41

With the success enjoyed by the 1939 and 1940 *New York World's Fair Comics,* DC Comics decided to bring back the ninety-six-page, fifteen-cent comic book format in Spring 1941 for an anthology called *World's Best Comics.* The comic featured Superman and Batman, DC's two biggest stars, as well as a variety of adventure and humor strips. With its second issue, the comic was retitled *World's Finest Comics* and every cover featured Superman, Batman, and Robin—usually in a whimsical group pose such as playing tennis, planting a Victory Garden, ice skating, or even changing a flat tire for a group of teenagers.

Green Arrow began as a regular feature in the Fall 1942 issue; other features included Zatara the Magician, Tomahawk, and the Boy Commandos. The early issues were bound in a cardboard cover and had a square binding to accommodate the large number of pages.

During the paper shortage of World War II, the page count fell from ninety-six pages to seventy-six pages and then shrank to sixty-eight pages in 1952. By the May 1954 issue, readers were not eager to spend fifteen cents for a comic book, so the page count was dropped to thirty-six and the price lowered to ten cents. With the reduced page count, editor Jack Schiff had to save space, so he combined his two biggest stars—Superman and Batman—into one feature beginning in issue #71. The Superman-Batman combination was a hit with the readers and the team-up format was carried on for another thirty years.

WOW COMICS

Fawcett Publications
Published Winter/40–Fall/48   **Issue #s** 1–69
Major Characters
Mr. Scarlet 1–69
Commando Yank 6–64
Phantom Eagle 6–69
Mary Marvel 9–58
Captain Marvel 9
Captain Marvel, Jr. 9

After her debut in *Captain Marvel Adventures,* Mary Marvel made her home in *Wow Comics* before receiving her own comic book. Although Mary was the star of *Wow,* three other costumed heroes shared the spotlight for a longer time.

Mr. Scarlet made his debut in the first issue and was created by writer/editor Ed Herron and artist Joe Simon. Brian Butler was originally a successful attorney until he put himself out of a job by his actions as the costumed crime frighter, Mr. Scarlet. Out of work, the "struggling lawyer" is "forced to seek menial means of livelihood" by performing a variety of odd jobs. Each issue found Butler trying to make a buck while also plying his trade as Mr. Scarlet, "a red-robed battler for justice." Mr. Scarlet was joined by a young boy sidekick named Pinky (Winter 1941), who wore a similar costume. Mr.

Scarlet and Pinky, billed as the "crimson crusaders of justice," made an interesting pair of heroes as they drifted from one low-paying job to the next.

The Phantom Eagle was originally a young airplane mechanic named Mickey Malone. Too young to enlist in the war effort, Mickey becomes a costumed aviator known as the Phantom Eagle. Along with his "girl companion" Jerry Sloane, he fights battles in his cometplane. He is also the leader of the Phoenix squadron, "a group of six European boys each from a conquered country" who fly phosphorescent-coated planes against the Axis.

Commando Yank, billed as "America's one man regiment with the punch of a mule," was originally Chase Yale, a "complacent war correspondent," who dons a costume to wage his own war.

YANKEE COMICS

Harry 'A' Chesler
Published 9/41–3/42 **Issue #s** 1–4
Major Characters
Yankee Doodle Jones 1–4
The Echo 1–4
Yankee Boy 2–4

Yankee Doodle Jones, wearing barber-pole-striped pants, star-spangled blouse, and GI hat was Harry 'A' Chesler's shot at a patriotic superhero. Appearing with a more subdued star-speckled kid sidekick named Dandy, Yankee Doodle Jones also appeared in *Dynamic Comics* and *Bulls-Eye Comics*.

Yankee Boy, who in everyday life is school boy Victor Martin, was another star-spotted hero. He assisted Inspector Foley off the record in solving hometown crimes that ranged from sabotage to land grabbing. Yankee Boy was one of the first teenage costumed crime fighters who operated without the benefit of an adult mentor. He also appeared in *Dynamic Comics*.

The other major Chesler hero who made his debut in *Yankee Comics* was the Echo. Jim Carson is the world's best ventriloquist and nosiest amateur sleuth. He works as the Echo with his brother (a research chemist with the unlikely name of Dr. Doom) and possesses a belt buckle which can turn him invisible. Artists on the Echo, who also appeared in *Dynamic Comics*, included Rafael Astarita, Paul Gattuso, and Ruben Moreira.

YELLOWJACKET COMICS

Frank Communale Publishing Company
Published 9/44–6/46 **Issue #s** 1–10
Major Characters
Yellowjacket 1–10
Diana, the Huntress 1–10

When Vince Harley, a crime-fiction writer for *Dark Detective Magazine*, searches for the perfect crime plot, he becomes involved in a jewel robbery. The

would-be thieves knock Harley unconscious and then use a convenient carton of angry "yellow jacket bees" to finish off the meddling writer. Although hundreds of yellow jackets swarm over his prostrate body, Harley is unharmed since he is "one of those rare people that bees don't sting." The harrowing experience causes Harley to seek revenge disguised in the black-and-yellow costume of the Yellowjacket. He also acquires the powers to direct bees to help him in his crime-fighting chores. In fact, he is often accompanied by a swarm of willing bees who attack on his command ("Bees—stop him!"). Many of the Yellowjacket stories were written and drawn by Marvin Levy with artist Ken Battlefield also contributing. The character also appeared in *Jack in the Box Comics* (October 1946) and *TNT Comics* (February 1946).

YOUNG ALLIES

Marvel Comics
Published Summer/41–10/46 **Issue #s** 1–20
Major Characters
Young Allies 1–20
Fathertime 3
The Vagabound 4
Captain America 5

The Young Allies was the first of several popular "kid gang" comic books. Marvel's two junior heroes, Bucky from Captain America and Toro from the Human Torch, team up with four kids from Captain America's new youth brigand, the Sentinels of Liberty, to form the Young Allies. Following the tradition of the Dead End Kids from the Warner Bros. movies, the four boys who made up the Young Allies were a cast of caricatures: a tough guy (Knuckles, aka Percival O'Toole), a fat kid (Tubby Tinkle), a bespectacled bookworm (Jeff Sandervilt), and a black boy for "comic" relief named Whitewash Jones ("Oh, Lawdy! Ah's scared! Do yo' suppose we is *really* daid?").

Banding together, the four boys and the two superhero sidekicks spend a lot of time fighting Axis agents and villains like the Red Skull while "uttering their famed war cry—YAHOO!"

Joe Simon and Jack Kirby came up with the concept for the Young Allies. Simon recalled that the comic was inspired by one of his favorite boyhood novels, *The Boy Allies*, which was set in World War I. Simon and Kirby drew the cover and first page before turning the comic over to writer Otto Binder and artist Charles Nicholas. With issue #2, Stan Lee became the editorial and art director. Lee wrote several scripts, as did Binder; other artists on the feature included Syd Shores, Al Avison, Al Gabriele, Mike Sekowsky, and Don Rico.

The Young Allies became one of Marvel's best-selling comics and appeared in several other titles, including *Kid Komix, Marvel Mystery, Mystic, Amazing,* and *Complete Comics.*

Yellowjacket Comics #8 © 1946 Frank Communale Publishing Company

Young Allies #13 © 1944 Marvel Entertainment Group, Inc. Alex Schomburg.

*Zip Comics #9 © 1940
Archie Comic Publications,
Inc. Charles Biro.*

ZIP COMICS
MLJ/Archie Comics
Published 2/40–Summer/44 **Issue #s** 1–47
Major Characters
Steel Sterling 1–47
Scarlet Avenger 1–17
Inferno, the Flame Breather 10–13
Black Jack 20–35
The Web 27–38
Red Rube 39–47

Steel Sterling was the undisputed star of *Zip Comics,*
but other MLJ superheroes also made their debut
here. One such hero was Steel's helper, Inferno, the
Flame Breather. After originally appearing in Steel
Sterling, Inferno got a series in *Blue Ribbon Comics*
written by Joe Blair and drawn by Paul Reinman.

Jim Kendell becomes the Scarlet Avenger when
he dons a scarlet cloak with attached mask over his
green business suit. The Scarlet Avenger (whose
calling card depicts a flaming skull with an arrow
through the eye socket) was written by Harry
Shorten and originally drawn by Irving Novick.

Jack Jones, a detective who likes to play
blackjack at the police station, is captured and
thought to be murdered by criminals. He escapes,
however, and goes undercover as the Black Jack
(with an Ace of Spades costume). Drawn by Irving
Novick, Al Camerata, Red Holmdale, Sam Cooper,
and Bob King, Black Jack fought villains like Poker
Face and Black Seven.

John Raymond, a professor of criminology, tries
to understand why his brother became a hardened
criminal. To get the inside story on crime, Raymond
becomes a costumed hero known as the Web in
hopes of ensnaring crooks in their own web of
crime. Drawn by John Cassone and Irving Novick,
the Web was more often a violent vigilante than a
bookish academic.

Reuben Reuben, a cub reporter for the *Daily Sun,*
can call upon the powers of his ancestors by simply
shouting "Hey Rube," which causes the all-powerful
Red Rube to appear in a puff of smoke. This thinly
inspired imitation of Captain Marvel was drawn by
Bill Vigoda and Harry Sahle.

BIBLIOGRAPHY

Andrae, Thomas. "Origins of the Dark Knight: A Conversation with Batman Artists Bob Kane and Jerry Robinson." *Overstreet Comic Book Price Guide.* Vol. 19. Cleveland, Tennessee: Overstreet Publications, 1989.

Bails, Jerry G. *The Collector's Guide: The First Heroic Age.* St. Claire Shores, Michigan: Jerry Bails, 1969.

Bails, Jerry. "All Star Comics: The Justice Society of America." *Golden Age of Comics* #8 February (1984).

Bails, Jerry and Hames Ware, eds. *Who's Who of American Comic Books.* St. Claire Shores, Michigan: Jerry Bails, 1974.

Barry, Dan. Interview. *Comics Interview* #82, 1990.

Barry, Dan. Interview. *Amazing Heroes* March, 1988.

Beck, C.C. Interview. *Comics Journal* #95 February, 1985.

Beck, C.C. "Otto Binder As I Remember Him." *Rocket's Blast-Comic Collector* #115 (1973).

Benton, Mike. *Comic Book Collecting For Fun and Profit.* New York: Crown Publishers, 1985.

——— *The Comic Book In America: An Illustrated History.* Dallas, Texas: Taylor Publishing Company, 1989.

——— *Horror Comics: The Illustrated History.* Dallas, Texas: Taylor Publishing Company, 1991.

——— *Superhero Comics of the Silver Age: The Illustrated History.* Dallas, Texas: Taylor Publishing Company, 1991.

——— *Science Fiction Comics: The Illustrated History.* Dallas, Texas: Taylor Publishing Company, 1992.

Bester, Alfred. Interview. *Comics Interview* #32, 1986.

Binder, Otto. "Letter to Roy Thomas." *Amazing World of DC Comics* #17 April, 1978.

Business Week. "Superman Scores." April 18, 1942.

Daniels, Les. *Marvel: Five Fabulous Decades of the World's Greatest Comics.* New York: Harry N. Abrams, Inc., 1991.

DC Comics. *Fifty Who Made DC Great.* New York: DC Comics, Inc., 1985.

DeFuccio, Jerry. "Charles Clarence Beck: The World's Second Mightest Mortal." *Overstreet Comic Book Price Guide.* Vol. 15. Cleveland, Tennessee: Overstreet Publications, 1985.

Dooley, Dennis and Gary Engle, eds. *Superman at Fifty.* Cleveland, Ohio: Octavia Press, 1987.

Eisner, Will. Interview. *Overstreet Comic Book Price Guide.* Vol. 6. Cleveland, Tennessee: Overstreet Publications, 1976.

——— Interview. *Comics Journal* #46 May, 1979.

——— Interview. *Comics Journal* #89 March, 1984.

Everett, Bill. "Everett on Everett." *Alter Ego* #11, 1978.

Everett, Bill. "Letter to Jerry DeFuccio." *Robin Snyder's History of the Comics* Vol. 2 #7 July, 1991.

Feiffer, Jules. *The Great Comic Book Heroes.* New York: Dial Press, 1965.

Flessel, Creig. "Apples and Comic Books." *Robin Snyder's History of the Comics* Vol. 1 #12 November, 1990.

Fox, Gardner. Interview. *Comics Interview* #9 March, 1984.

Fox, Gardner. Interview. *Amazing Heroes* #113 March 15, 1987.

Fox, Gill. Interview. *Comics: The Golden Age* #2 May, 1984.

Gold, Mike, ed. *The Greatest Golden Age Stories Ever Told.* New York: DC Comics, Inc., 1990.

Goulart, Ron. *Focus on Jack Cole.* Seattle, Washington: Fantagraphics Books, 1986.

Goulart, Ron. *Great History of Comic Books.* Chicago: Contemporary Books, 1986.

Goulart, Ron, ed. *The Encyclopedia of American Comics.* New York: Facts on File Publications, 1990.

Horn, Maurice, ed. *World Encyclopedia of Comics.* New York: Chelsea House Publishers, 1976.

Kane, Bob with Tom Andrae. *Batman and Me.* Forestville, California: Eclipse Books, 1989.

Kanigher, Robert. Interview. *Comics Journal* #s 85 and 86, October/November, 1983.

Keltner, Howard. *Howard Keltner's Index to Golden Age Comic Books.* St. Claire Shores, Michigan: Jerry Bails, 1976.

Kirby, Jack. Interview. Golden Age of Comics #6 November, 1983.

——— Interview. *Comics Feature* #44 May, 1986.

——— Interview. *Comics Interview* #41, 1986.

——— Interview. *Amazing Heroes* #100 August, 1986.

——— Interview. *Comics Journal* #134 February, 1990.

Korkis, Jim. "Wild Bill: That Man from Atlantis." *Golden Age of Comics* #8 February, 1984.

Kotzky, Alex. Interview. *Comics Interview* #100, 1991.

Lee, Stan. Interview. *FOOM* #17 March, 1977.

Mayer, Sheldon. Interview. *Amazing World of DC Comics* #5 March, 1975.

Murray, Will. "Project: Captain America." *Comics Scene* #14 August, 1990.

O'Brien, Richard. *The Golden Age of Comic Books*. New York: Ballantine Books, 1977.

O'Neil, Dennis, ed. *Secret Origins of the Super DC Heroes*. New York: Crown Publishers, 1976.

Overstreet, Robert M. *Overstreet Comic Book Price Guide*. Vol. 21. Cleveland, Tennessee: Overstreet Publications, 1991.

Reed, Rod. Interview. *Comics Interview* #18 December, 1984.

Robinson, Jerry. Interview. *Comics Interview* #s 56–58, 1988.

Rovin, Jeff. *The Encyclopedia of Superheroes*. New York: Facts on File Publications, 1985.

Schiff, Jack. "Reminiscences of A Comic Book Editor." *Overstreet Comic Book Price Guide*. Vol. 13. Cleveland, Tennessee: Overstreet Publications, 1983.

Siegel, Jerry and Joe Shuster. Interview. *Nemo: The Classics Comic Library* #2 August, 1983.

Siegel, Jerry and Joe Shuster. Interview. Siegel and Shuster: Date Line 1930s. Eclipse Comics. November, 1984.

Simon, Joe with Jim Simon. *The Comic Book Makers*. New York: Crestwood/II Publications, 1990.

Steranko, Jim. *The Steranko History of Comics, Volumes I & II*. Reading, Pennsylvania: Supergraphics, 1970–1972.

Ward, Bill. "The Man Behind Torchy." *Overstreet Comic Book Price Guide*. Vol. 8. Cleveland, Tennessee: Overstreet Publications, 1978.

Wertham, Fredric. *Seduction of the Innocent*. New York: Rinehart & Company, 1954.

Woolfolk, William. Interview. *Comics Interview* #s 28–29, 1985.

INDEX